The Wars
of
Napoleon

The Wars
of
Napoleon

Albert Sidney Britt III

Thomas E. Griess
Series Editor

DEPARTMENT OF HISTORY
UNITED STATES MILITARY ACADEMY
WEST POINT, NEW YORK

SQUAREONE
PUBLISHERS

Series Editor: Thomas E. Griess
Cover Designer: Phaedra Mastrocola
In-House Editor: Joanne Abrams

Square One Publishers
Garden City Park, NY 11040
(516) 535-2010
www.squareonepublishers.com

Illustration Credits
The publisher would like to thank Dr. George Lankevich
for the use of his historical library collection, which was
the source of much illustrative material.

All original artwork was produced by Edward J. Krasnoborski.

Library of Congress Cataloging-in-Publication Data
Britt, Albert Sidney, 1936-
The wars of Napoleon / Albert Sidney Britt, III.
    p. cm.
  Reprint. Originally published: West Point, N.Y. : United States
Military Academy, 1972.
  Includes bibliographical references and index.
  ISBN 0-7570-0154-8
    1. Napoleon I, Emperor of the French, 1769-1821. 2. First Coalition,
War of the, 1792-1797. 3. Second Coalition, War of the, 1798-1801. 4.
Napoleonic Wars, 1800-1815. 5. France—History, Military—1789-1815.
I. Title.

DC203 .B875 2003
940.2'7—dc21
                                                    2003011776

Contents

To those genuine professionals from many countries whose understanding of war has helped improve mankind.

Illustrations

Acknowledgements

This work is the product of many dedicated people here at West Point, in the Army, and in countries abroad. The contributions of the following have been most important: Colonel Thomas E. Griess, who issued the task of producing the book and provided editorial assistance from start to finish; Lieutenant Colonel James E. Torrence, whose appreciation for historical personalities encouraged a deeper study of Napoleon's philosophy of war; Mr. Edward Krasnoborski, whose thorough, professional touch and many years of cartographic experience made the maps such a superior product; Lieutenant Colonel Grayson Woodbury, who organized and helped in the translation of Camon's *La Bataille Napoleonienne* and Davout's *Memoirs;* Colonel John R. Elting, a leading authority on the subject, who made valuable comments and criticisms; the staff of the Kriegsgeschichtliche Museum in Vienna, who offered every assistance in the quest for information about the Austrian Army; Lieutenant General P.A. Zhilin, Director of the Institute of Military History, Ministry of Defense of the Soviet Union, for a valuable interview concerning the 1812 campaign; Lieutenant Colonel and Mrs. Berthold von Stauffenberg, who gave me a guided tour of the Danube between Ulm and Donauworth; and especially Lieutenant Colonel Robert L. Ackerson, Lieutenant Colonel Douglas M. Craver, and Major John F. Votaw, who helped deal with all the administrative details that threatened to overwhelm the project. Also deserving of credit are Professor Peter Paret for scholarly guidance, Professor David G. Chandler for expert advice, and the following officers for their active interest and critical comments: Lieutenant Colonels James L. Morrison, Elmer C. May, Bruce D. Smith, James R. Ransone, Dave R. Palmer, James B. Agnew, John H. Bradley, and Walter S. Barge; Majors Gerald P. Stadler, Glenn H. Lehrer, and William A. Stofft; and Captain Michael D. Krause. Major Harold W. Nelson translated parts of General Zhilin's book *The Great Fatherland War* in 1812, and Major Josiah Bunting, III offered useful advice on sources concerning the British Army. The entire staff of the United States Military Academy Library supported the research effort; without their energetic assistance, the project could not have been completed.

With customary thoroughness, Mrs. Dorothy Waterfield supervised the preparation of the manuscript. Mrs. Sharen Pacenza and Mrs. Judy Pacenza typed the text.

Three others have contributed—Jerre, William, and Sidney, all of whom have lived on the edge of the nineteenth century, and on several occasions have rescued the author from it when absorption tended toward delusion.

Albert Sidney Britt III
West Point, New York

Foreword

Cadets at the United States Military Academy have studied Napoleon Bonaparte's battles and military theories since the 1820s. In terms of classroom hours, this early instruction was very brief, but by 1902 military history was being taught in a course that was a year in length and included a fairly extensive treatment of Napoleonic warfare. Nine years later, Gustave J. Fiebeger, head of the Department of Military Art and Engineering, prepared the first departmentally sponsored text on Napoleon's campaigns (*Campaigns of Napoleon Bonaparte, 1796—97*) and used it in the course of instruction. In 1939, T. Dodson Stamps, the new departmental head, introduced a specially designed atlas to support the text then being used to study Napoleon's campaigns. This concept of a closely integrated narrative and graphical portrayal has been a feature of the course entitled History of the Military Art since that time.

In 1963, Vincent J. Esposito, Stamps' successor as head of the Department of Military Art and Engineering, adopted for departmental use the unique *A Military History and Atlas of the Napoleonic Wars,* which he had coauthored with John R. Elting. In 1967, however, changes in the scope of the course in the History of the Military Art required the development of a new text. Course-long themes, broader treatment of military history, and less emphasis on operational detail were among the changes that dictated new textual and teaching approaches.

The Wars of Napoleon was conceived as a text that would present developments in the military art during the Napoleonic era, using Bonaparte's campaigns as the primary instructional vehicle, but encompassing broader themes in military history than the purely operational ones. To support this text and its broader approach, new maps had to be designed, crafted, and integrated in a campaign atlas. Both the new text and its supporting atlas were prepared by Albert Sidney Britt III during the period when he served as a faculty member of the Department of History.

The Department of History and a large number of students are indebted to Colonel Britt for his careful work, unstinting attention to detail, and selfless efforts, all performed under the pressure of time and with minimal resources. Relying upon some primary source material and many secondary sources, he has written a thoughtful and stimulating narrative that combines operational and institutional treatments of military history. Generalship, professionalism, strategy, logistics, and sociopolitical factors are key themes that run throughout Britt's text and are developed clearly and effectively. His work in the designing of supporting maps is equally sound and provides an indispensable aid to the study of the narrative. The Department of History is also indebted to Mr. Edward J. Krasnoborski, who supervised the entire map-drafting effort and brilliantly performed most of the cartographic work.

The present edition of *The Wars of Napoleon* is essentially the text that was published at the Military Academy in 1972. As editor, I have attempted to clarify certain passages for the general reader, amplify purely military terminology, and improve the evenness of the narrative. The editor is grateful for the advice and suggestions rendered by Rudy Shur and Joanne Abrams of Square One Publishers. Their assistance was timely and helpful. Ms. Abrams immeasurably improved the narrative through her painstaking editing, corrections of lapses in syntax, and penetrating questions related to clarity of expression.

Thomas E. Griess
Series Editor

Introduction

Of all the conquerors from Charlemagne to Hitler who tried to unite Europe under their rule, Napoleon Bonaparte most nearly succeeded. At its zenith, the Empire he created stretched from the Atlantic coast to the Russian steppe, from the North Sea to the Mediterranean. Nearly a million men died in less than a quarter of a century trying to prove that Napoleon's brand of equality could be won at cannon point. Meanwhile, proud dynasties learned slowly that traditional military practices could not contain the revolutionary ideas and armies that rapidly transformed the old Europe known to Louis XIV and Frederick the Great. It hardly needs saying that these spectacular wars will remain a source of instruction and inspiration as long as men strive for change and hunger for power.

The rise and fall of the French Empire was a complex mosaic of events. Bonaparte's sweep to power dominates the story; inevitably, his worshipers have elevated his deeds to legend. However, one must also account for the poor performance of his opponents before discovering how Europe learned from its tormentor and briefly unified itself to overthrow him. This reversal cannot be explained simply by tracing the path of Napoleon's battles. To fully understand the dramatic growth of the military art, one must consider war in context, recognizing the importance of the contemporary shifting human currents. Changes in warfare in Napoleon's time accompanied an abrupt transformation of European society. Napoleon earned his fame because he observed, understood, and exploited those changing forces. He ultimately fell from power, however, because he disregarded the potential of revolutionary change in other countries and in their armies.

France's major antagonists—England, Austria, Russia, and Prussia—provided a supporting cast of millions on the European stage, and Napoleon was the artist who played only to a crowd. He took his cue from Revolutionary Paris, where the favor of beautiful women helped determine a man's status and bravery became acknowledged as a symbol of equality. Napoleon adapted his own flair for the romantic to this atmos-phere to attract enormous popular support. The Revolution had already freed warfare from past constraints by liberating individual talents and making combat more personal. Generalship—the art of command—now rose to overriding importance in European warfare.

Napoleon's generalship is sometimes difficult to analyze. The Emperor himself caused much of the difficulty by his unseemly practice of altering certain facts in his written reports. Half a century later, French archivists followed suit by hunting down and eliminating some of the documents that might have tarnished their hero's reputation. These problems of historiography should not deter the serious student of war. The best way of studying Napoleon is to accept nothing completely without supporting evidence. This should enhance rather than diminish his stature as a commander. One need only be aware of the practical problems in military planning and operations to wonder at the sureness with which Napoleon flung the *Grande Armée* into every corner of Europe. The brilliant intellect tirelessly at work, estimating time and place for the decisive stroke, dazzles students today just as it bewildered his enemies—and some of his subordinates—over a century and a half ago. Anyone who knows just a little about morale will never cease to marvel at the magnetic power of the personality that lifted armies out of misfortune and despair, from the early days in Italy to the last desperate hours at Waterloo.

If generalship is the central theme running all through the Napoleonic epoch, strategy is surely the primary means by which the master worked his art. In contrast to Frederick—the master of battles who learned strategy—Napoleon was a natural strategist. He made strategy flexible, adjusting it to the needs of policy, avoiding enemy strength, and capitalizing on the errors of opposing generals. There was a fluid transition between Napoleonic strategy and tactics; the one blended into and directed the other. Battles were anticipated, not feared, and the French Army fought them where it found them. When a major engagement began, usually it was undertaken with the intention that it would prove decisive. Thus, Napoleonic strategy accepted higher risks for the promise of greater gains. Napoleon was like a shrewd speculator who continually reassesses his vulnerabilities in the light of necessities. Later in his career, however, ambition and overconfidence obscured his view of reality; the recurring urge to strike overcame his better instincts and made him into a reckless gambler.

In that age of upheaval, when kings became fugitives, the structure of the military profession shifted uneasily on its aristocratic foundation. For the first time in centuries, the entire tradition of warfare came into question. Before the French Revolution, the Crown had first claim on the loyalty of soldier and officer. After the deluge in France, nobility counted for little, talent for a great deal. To Napoleon, talent consisted mostly of bravery and initiative. Both were imperative in the conduct of officers and soldiers. The daredevil capture of the bridge at Vienna in 1805, when Marshals Murat and Lannes convinced the Austrian Prince that there was an armistice, is an example of the sort of inspirational leadership that Napoleon expected of his lieutenants.*

In spite of France's military victories, professionalism failed to mature in the French Army. Napoleon made all the key decisions; he also developed his own estimates and usually dictated to his subordinates. His staff grew in numbers, but he never used it for anything but collecting the information he demanded and communicating his instructions. There was no effective school system designed to train promising young officers for high level command and staff positions. Expertise was sacrificed to improvisation. As long as the Army continued to win, why reform it? (On the other hand, the Emperor continued to pour money into rebuilding the French Navy, which rarely won a battle, and lay rotting in port during most of his wars.) Those armies that were not as fortunate in battle saw cogent reasons for improving on existing systems. In fact, Prussia decided on the bold course of reforming its entire command, staff, and school system—as well as the Government. In the last years of the war, Prussia instituted a new device for control and coordination at brigade, division, corps, and army levels: the General Staff. No other nation attained such efficiency in the employment of military power, although England and Austria could claim that two decades of fighting against French armies substantially improved the professional abilities of their fighting forces.

The evidence is inconclusive on the subject of logistics. Bonaparte fed his ragged Army of Italy off the plains of Lombardy, and his *Grande Armée* in the Danube Valley. But he encountered barren and hostile steppes in eastern Europe,

and he never devised a way to forage for ammunition. Although Napoleon appreciated the importance of logistics and worked hard to support his armies, he failed to build an effective logistical system, as Wellington did in Spain. As the makeup of his army changed later in his career, Napoleon relied more on firepower, and consequently more on logistics. The classic interaction of technology, tactics, logistics, and strategy thus worked to his disadvantage. At the time when he needed strategic freedom most, logistics came home to haunt him. The *Grande Armée* did not freeze in Russia; it starved.

No commander has unlimited freedom in the exercise of his art. If logistics, doctrine, or technology do not limit his courses of action, the chances are that policy will. In contrast to Caesar, who shrewdly gauged the nature of his wars, Napoleon ultimately found the political component of war most difficult to manage. In his early campaigns in northern Italy and southern Germany, he accurately appreciated the relationships between European powers and cleverly foresaw the capabilities and possible reactions of each. But as the Empire expanded, and people—as well as governments—became inflamed against him, all of Europe simmered. Napoleon was fortunate to preserve his imperial rule beyond 1809. In that critical year, insurgency smoldered in the Austrian Tyrol and burned in Spain; Prussia stirred and England threatened. While Frenchmen garrisoned opposite ends of an uneasy Europe, Austria chose to move. Only Napoleon's quick reactions—and the Archduke Charles' slow pace—saved the Empire from a setback at perhaps its weakest moment. But it was only saved to meet a worse fate in 1812 and 1813, and it was the political overreach of the Emperor, as much as his military mistakes, that hastened its end. The Emperor Napoleon finally gave General Bonaparte a mission beyond the capability of his army.

These are the main themes of *The Wars of Napoleon*. Napoleon is the central character, but by no means the villain, in this chronicle of human conflict. More than most professional soldiers would care to admit, the "Ghost of Napoleon," to quote Sir Basil H. Liddell Hart, has lingered about many a general's campfire and intruded on nearly every twentieth century battlefield. More than a few of the Western World's most celebrated Great Captains have been captivated by Napoleon's brilliance and have emulated his unceasing quest for the great battle designed to bring the enemy to terms. Battle is only one component of war, however, and armies only the more visible performers. In the age of the Democratic Revolution, the people have gradually taken on a more decisive role in national wars. The growing strength of public opinion had already forecast its power in the French Revolution; ultimately, it became the overriding cause of Napoleon's downfall.

*Compare this feat with the attitude in vogue less than 50 years earlier, when a French nobleman claimed credit for sparing the life of Frederick while the Prussian King reconnoitered a crossing site near Rossbach. To deliberately open fire on a monarch ran counter to the professional code.

The Conquest of Europe

PART I
THE GROWTH
OF NAPOLEON

All great events hang by a single thread.
The clever man takes advantage of
everything, neglects nothing that
may give him some added opportunity.
                    Bonaparte to Talleyrand
                            September 1797

The Italian and Egyptian Campaigns

Rioters surged through the streets, protesting against their Government. Hunger and unemployment reinforced the ugly mood of the crowd. It was October 1795, six years after the outbreak of the French Revolution, and Paris was torn by violence again. Members of the French Government cast about for someone experienced and ruthless enough to use guns to control the mob. They found Napoleon Buonaparte, an artillery officer who had recently been promoted to the rank of General of Brigade. The political commander of French troops in the metropolitan area offered Buonaparte the job of quashing the insurrection, giving the young artilleryman three minutes to consider. "General," the young man replied, "I accept. But I warn you that once the sword is out of the

La Marseillaise (Arc de Triomphe de L'Etoile)

scabbard I shall not sheathe it again until order is restored."[1] The wildest imagination could not have foreseen that it would take all of Europe 20 years to sheathe the sword of Napoleon and finally restore order on the Continent.

Napoleon Buonaparte (as his family then spelled the name) was born in Corsica in August 1769 into a large family of the lower nobility. Since Corsica had just become a French possession, he qualified for an appointment to a semi-military French school. Entering the school at Brienne at the age of 9, he could barely read or speak the French language, and, at first, he was not accepted by his classmates because of his accent and his awkward appearance. He turned to reading, both to learn French and to develop his mind. After five years of hard work, his main reward was the habit of study. It was a habit that never failed him.

The young Corsican then attended the *École Militaire* in Paris, completing the two-year course in less than a year. At this time he began to discover those extraordinary mental powers which already separated him from his contemporaries. He read widely, favoring works of great depth— Rousseau's *Confessions* and Plato's *Republic*—and he excelled in geography, history, and mathematics. Buonaparte's personality developed more slowly, but the raw material was there. He was an intense, abrasive sort of person whom people easily remembered. One of his superiors at the military school in Paris described him this way:

> Retiring and diligent, he prefers study to amusements of any kind, and delights in the reading of good authors; loves solitude, is obstinate, proud, and exceptionally inclined to egotism; speaks little, is energetic in his answers; ready and severe in his refutations; possesses much love of self, is ambitious and hard-working. This young man deserves to be pushed on.[2]

There was no need to push the young lieutenant. Highly motivated and ambitious by nature, he had already determined to drive himself.

Napoleon Buonaparte, 1784

The Rise of Buonaparte

For the next several years, Buonaparte served in garrison regiments in France. During this apprenticeship, he applied himself as he had in school, devouring information and mastering every detail of service within a small military unit. Later, on duty at the Artillery School at Auxonne, he was selected to conduct experiments on explosive shells. At the same time, the young officer continued to develop intellectually. At 19, he began writing an essay, "On Royal Authority," in which he observed that few monarchs deserved the throne on which they sat.* He spent his furloughs on his native Corsica, trying to stir the islanders to revolt against French rule.

In 1792, Lieutenant Buonaparte returned to France, shortly after the French Government declared war on Austria. Noting that "Paris is in ferment," he now saw the Revolution at firsthand and watched the monarchy he had criticized dissolve in mob rule. Although in sympathy with the Revolutionary cause, he found the experience distasteful, and reflected on the incompatibility of rebellious patriotism with discipline and authority. The lieutenant was not a revolutionary, but an army officer who pragmatically concluded that armies do not thrive on dissent.

Buonaparte must have been astonished at the vigor with which France threw itself into war in the following year. The other powers of Europe—Prussia, Austria, and Holland—announced their intention to stamp out this French Revolutionary threat to dynasties everywhere, and coalition armies soon hovered on France's northeastern borders. To stave off disaster, the embattled French Government resorted to conscription, calling three-quarters of a million Frenchmen into the service. Young men trained to fight while married men worked in the factories; women staffed the hospitals; even the very old and very young served some useful function.† Like the downpour following a thunderclap, war quickly outgrew the limitations previously imposed upon it. The age of dynastic encounters began to die; the war of peoples was born.

Revolution proved to be a mixed blessing for the French Army. The experienced cadre was carried off in the torrent; those nobles who still retained their heads fled to the safety of neighboring countries, where kings still preserved order. Non commissioned officers rose to the ranks of colonel and general. To make up for the missing expertise and training, French commanders were directed "to act offensively and in masses. Use the bayonet at every opportunity. Fight great battles and pursue the enemy until he is utterly destroyed."[3] The standing armies of the eighteenth century could not cope with Revolutionary fervor and the nation in arms. Nor could soldiers drilled in the linear doctrine of Frederick the Great stand against swarms of skirmishers, who moved through woods and in open order over broken ground, fired from concealed positions, and took cover without command. By 1794, the new style of warfare had proved superior to the old. French armies pressed their opponents on every front. The war for survival against the First Coalition now became a full-fledged "Crusade Against Kings."

Young Buonaparte did not miss his cue. He saw that in the midst of turmoil, power belonged to the man who was bold enough to seize it, not to the dutiful soldier quietly awaiting his turn. He was an opportunist, ready to make good every occasion that fortune offered. His first chance came in September 1793 on the Mediterranean shore. En route to an assignment with the French Army of Italy, Buonaparte stopped to observe the siege of Toulon. A sizable French force was trying to recapture the town from Royalists and drive away the supporting British fleet. The French artillery commander was wounded, and Captain Buonaparte took over the direction of the guns. He quickly discerned that a key peninsula controlled both inner and outer harbors, and after several months of preparation, concentrated the offensive efforts on

---

*It would be interesting to speculate on how fast and how far this temperamental youth would have risen if he had grown up a subject of the authoritarian Frederick the Great, instead of in pre-Revolutionary France.

†The "Organizer of Victory" during France's Revolutionary wars was an engineer officer of middle-class origins, Lazare Carnot, whose businesslike methods were inspired by creative ideas and a firm belief in patriotism. It is a reasonable generalization to say that Carnot built the military system that Buonaparte later employed.

that point. This dogged application of common sense produced success with Buonaparte also managing to participate in the final assault, in which he was lightly wounded. Three days later, he was promoted to General of Brigade. The commander of forces engaged in the siege praised the new general's performance. Another officer wrote to the War Minister: "Words fail me to describe Buonaparte's merits. He has plenty of knowledge, and as much intelligence and courage; and that is no more than a first sketch of the virtues of a most rare officer."[4] He did not mention that Antonio Cristaforo Saliceti, the senior French political representative on hand for the siege, was an old friend of the Buonaparte family. It was through his influence that Buonaparte had been given his first opportunity to excel and gain attention.

In March 1794, the 24-year-old general was appointed artillery commander for the Army of Italy and participated in a successful offensive along the Mediterranean coast. In this operation, which encountered little resistance, he earned a reputation as a planner. His searching mind also began to envision greater things in Italy. This memorandum, written after the operation, reveals his sure grasp of strategy *(See Atlas Map No. 2)**:

> In order to deal with Austria, we must crush Piedmont. . . . Once in the plain of Piedmont we can brush away the King of Sardinia and drive the Austrians from Lombardy. Austria must then bring troops from the Rhine to defend herself in Italy and our army of the Rhine will be able to take advantage of the Austrian Army that confronts it.[5]

Thus Buonaparte revealed the genesis of his Italian strategy, the program he would put into dazzling execution just two years later.

The young Corsican's talent for planning had not gone unnoticed by his political friend, Saliceti, who recommended him for an assignment as a plans officer in the War Ministry. While serving in this post in the fall of 1795, he realized that another governmental crisis was brewing. In October, angry crowds besieged the legislature. It was anarchy again, and in all of Paris only one man—Napoleon Buonaparte—seemed to know the cure: "a whiff of grapeshot." The guns were brought by a cavalry officer named Joachim Murat, but they were positioned at Buonaparte's personal command. Two hundred insurgents died on that bloody day, and order was restored in Paris. Buonaparte never forgot the savage lesson: for one short afternoon the legitimacy of the Government rode on the carriages of its cannon.

Buonaparte's fortunes were now tightly linked to France's future. In the winter of 1795, the hero of Paris divided his at-

Bonaparte, Commander-in-Chief of the French Army of Italy

tention between two absorbing problems: marriage and command. The first he solved in March 1796 by marrying the restless Josephine de Beauharnais, a seductive widow six years his elder, who had barely escaped the guillotine during the Revolution.† Two days later, Bonaparte—he now changed the spelling to the French version—left Paris to achieve his second goal: command of the Army of Italy.

Army Commander

The new commander of any military organization is on the spot. Until he earns respect, subordinates and superiors are quick to note mistakes. Men respond grudgingly to the first unaccustomed orders, and a sense of transience and uncertainty tends to hinder the effectiveness of the entire unit. Bonaparte's assumption of command in March 1796 took place amidst especially unsettling circumstances. *(See Atlas Map No. 1.)* The Army of Italy was in difficult straits. Its positions lay along the crest of the Maritime Alps, a rugged

---

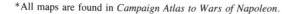

*All maps are found in *Campaign Atlas to Wars of Napoleon.*

†Some historians have made an interesting issue out of the fact that Josephine had recently been the mistress of one of the members of the Directory (the executive branch of the Government), the same man (Paul Barras) who had given Bonaparte his role in the streets of Paris. Rose Beauharnais' husband had been executed during the Terror in 1794, and Rose only escaped death because of the overthrow of Robespierre. Bonaparte disliked the name Rose and used Rose's middle name, Josèphe (Josephine), instead.

Marshal André Massena

wasteland that barely supported the needs of the local inhabitants. A tenuous line of communication ran from Nice to Savona, and British naval squadrons easily interdicted the exposed coastal road. The men had not been paid in months; they needed food and clothing, and some lacked muskets. Units were dispersed for foraging; there was little thought about closing with the enemy that occupied the passes to the north. With an opponent in front and a hostile sea behind, the Army of Italy squatted in its miserable, rockbound quarters and talked of mutiny. *(See Atlas Map No. 2.)*

Bonaparte had to energize his dispirited command. He first turned to his immediate subordinates: Louis-Alexandre Berthier, his chosen chief of staff, a small man with a large memory; thin, dark, and energetic André Massena, a veteran of seven years of smuggling and fighting in Italy; Pierre François Augereau, flamboyant product of Paris slums and foreign armies—a daring, swaggering *sabreur*; and old, modest Jean Mathieu Serurier, whose most outstanding feature was a pronounced scar across his face, a memorial of faithful service in the Seven Years' War. This group averaged 16 years older than their thin, sallow chief. When they first assembled to meet him, he hardly seemed tall enough to wear a sword. Massena, in particular, was affronted. He was the senior division commander, under whose leadership several minor successes had been won. Augereau—a chronic grumbler—agreed that Massena should have succeeded to command of the army.

Within a few minutes, these veterans revised their opinion of the callow youth sent down to lead them. After sharply questioning his commanders on the strength and location of their forces, Bonaparte announced that he intended to inspect the army and, shortly, to commence an offensive against the enemy. After that brief meeting, no one doubted who was in command.

The new commander also spoke to his troops:

Soldiers! You are hungry and naked; the government owes you much, but can give you nothing. Your patience and courage, displayed among these rocks, are admirable, but that brings you no glory. . . . I will lead you into the most fertile plains on earth. Rich provinces, wealthy cities, all will be at your disposal; there you will find honor, glory and riches. . . [6]

Testing Ground for Generalship

"Italy is surrounded by the Alps and the sea." This geographical fact, succinctly stated in Bonaparte's memoirs, governed his plans as much as problems of supply. On the south side of the Maritime Alps, terraced slopes plunge into brilliant Mediterranean waters; to the north, jagged ridge lines reach toward the Po River, which winds lazily around the prominent hill mass south of Turin. White-topped Alpine ranges frame the entire Po basin, forming a natural amphitheater for war. *(See Atlas Map No. 2.)*

There are many ways for a modern gladiator to enter this arena—from several points along the Mediterranean coast between Genoa and Nice, or from the mountain passes separating France and Italy. However, only one route—that from Savona through the Cadibona Pass to Ceva—offered Bonaparte quick access to a central position between the Austrian and Sardinian armies. Also, this was the only route that could accommodate the passage of artillery. Bonaparte remembered this fact from personal observations made a year

Bonaparte's Proclamation to the Army of Italy, 1796

and a half earlier. It was the salient feature of his plan to separate the enemy armies, drive rapidly into the Po Valley, and acquire "for the brave army the clothing and foodstuffs which can be seized in the Piedmontese and Milanese plains."[7]

Before leaving the comforts of Paris for the vicissitudes of the field, Bonaparte persuaded the Directory to phrase his mission in such a way as to give him a measure of latitude in executing his plans. He was to aim his main effort against the Austrians, the directive said, "to drive the enemy beyond the Po" and seize Milan. The Directory pointed out, however, that this task could only be achieved after overthrowing the Sardinian Army and concluding peace with the Kingdom of Sardinia.* In fine print, the order further stated that the Army of Italy must accomplish this initial objective by taking Ceva, thus outflanking the Piedmontese garrison at Cuni and threatening Turin. How else could France's will be imposed on the government at Turin than by the capture of key outposts on the frontier? To Vauban or Turenne, the scheme would have been entirely in keeping with accepted ideas on strategy. To the ambitious Bonaparte, however, only the conquest of all Italy was a fit project for his undertaking.

After evaluating his men and their commanders, Bonaparte began to implement his plans. Administration and logistics constituted the greater part of his immediate concern. Threatening letters went out to civilian contractors who had stolen supplies. The Directory was informed of major deficiencies. One battalion mutinied, having received neither boots nor pay; it was marched to the rear, and its leaders were placed under arrest. Division commanders were ordered to replace unserviceable muskets, check on the issue of rations, and hasten the reorganization of their units. The smallest detail did not escape the commander's eye: "Fresh meat will be issued five times per decade [10 days]; battalions which have drawn salt meat today will have fresh meat tomorrow, and those which have had fresh meat will have salt . . . "[8]

As long as anyone could remember, Army headquarters had reposed at Nice, nearly 100 miles from the fighting front. "We will move the headquarters forward to Albenga," snapped Bonaparte to his chief of staff. To Josephine he found time to write, "you are the one thought of my life." Bonaparte's other thoughts are not hard to reconstruct: as soon as possible to set the army in motion across the ridges dividing the opposing forces. He planned to attack on April 15, 1796, just two weeks after assuming command. In the interim, as so often happens in war, the other side moved first. *(See Atlas Map No. 2.)*

General Baron Johann P. Beaulieu, a veteran of campaigning in Flanders, was not especially happy with his new command in Italy. The Austrian general planned a major offensive to drive the French back on Nice, but his forces were

*The Kingdom of Sardinia comprised the state of Piedmont and the island of Sardinia. Its capital was Turin.

spread all along the western Po Valley, and he was under instructions not to allow Austrian units west of the Tanaro River. The city of Genoa occupied his immediate attention. Although the Republic of Genoa was neutral, under French pressure it might take sides. A British squadron under the command of Horatio Nelson lay off the coast near Voltri to support Austrian operations in that direction. The Sardinian Army, commanded by an Austrian general, covered the western passes. Although Sardinia was nominally allied to Austria, it was no secret that the Sardinian King and his advisers only waited to determine which power in Italy was strongest before deciding whether to remain loyal to the Hapsburg Crown. It was an uneasy alliance; neither Austrians nor Sardinians placed full trust in each other. Beaulieu resolved to make the best of it by attacking the French units east of Savona with a limited offensive.

Bonaparte's Penetration Between the Austrians and Sardinians

The Austrian attack began on April 10. Alerted by reports from his mountain outposts, Bonaparte reacted promptly and vigorously. While the army's advance elements withdrew under pressure from Voltri, Bonaparte regrouped the demi-brigades in Massena's and Augereau's divisions for an advance inland to Carcare and Dego. Laharpe was to attack Argenteau head-on at dawn on April 12; Massena to "press the enemy . . . by outflanking him at Montenotte"; Serurier to "make demonstrations that will alarm the enemy, but without exposing your troops."[9] Division commanders received march objectives and subsequent orders to reconnoiter in search of major enemy formations.

Shortly before midnight on April 11, Massena's men began to move. At daybreak, Laharpe's lead unit made contact with Argenteau's main force. Hit in front by Laharpe and in rear by Massena, Argenteau vainly strove to hold his formation together, but 11,000 scrambling Frenchmen broke the Austrian's nerve. After this sharp fight at Montenotte, Argenteau no longer commanded an organized unit. Moreover, Beaulieu had placed his eastern wing out of the fight two days before by advancing on Voltri. Bonaparte now turned to deal with the Sardinians.

Unlike the Austrians, the Sardinians were determined to hold out. For nearly two days they defended the heights of Millesimo against repeated assaults by Augereau's men. The colonel commanding the final assault recalled, "My carabiniers held me up in the air; with one hand I grasped the walls. I parried the stones with my saber, and my whole body was the target for two entrenchments dominating the position ten paces off."[10] The Sardinians did not surrender until April

14, when their supplies ran out. Meanwhile, Massena's force cleared Dego, allowing Bonaparte to reposition Laharpe's division in reserve. However, Massena's famished men, who had scattered to plunder Dego, were thoroughly surprised by the chance arrival the next morning of disoriented Austrian reinforcements. The French soldiers panicked and poured south toward a small village, where Massena had spent the night enjoying his own special share of the spoils. Bonaparte furiously called Laharpe's division back to restore the situation. After recapturing Dego, the Army of Italy still held a solid position between the enemy armies; but time was running out on Bonaparte. If his men did not soon break out of the hills onto the Piedmont plains, the hungry army would cease to exist as an army. *(See Atlas Map No. 3.)*

The Defeat of the Sardinians

The Army of Italy spent the sixteenth reconnoitering in force. No major contact developed except at Ceva, where Sardinian General Baron Michael von Colli's delaying troops had assumed a new entrenched position. Augereau failed to overrun it in a brisk attack from march column; however, the steady advance of Serurier's force, descending the Tanaro Valley, convinced the Sardinian commander to withdraw that night to a stronger position farther to the west. Three more days passed while French commanders fought to keep their mutinous soldiers in ranks and tried to find a way across the swollen Tanaro and its raging tributaries. One regimental commander swam across under fire in an attempt to inspire his men to cross, but no one would follow. The green fields north of Mondovi were clearly visible from the heights above Ceva; however, in the face of determined resistance and roaring rivers, it appeared that the Army of Italy would starve before it could fight its way through. At this crucial point, Sardinian determination collapsed. On April 22, Serurier reported that Colli was in full retreat near Mondovi. Bonaparte promptly committed Serurier's division and the unused French cavalry to the pursuit. Captain August Frédéric Marmont, one of Bonaparte's aides-de-camp, recorded this account of Serurier's action:

> To form his men in three columns, put himself at the head of the central one, throw out a cloud of skirmishers, and march at the double, sword in hand, ten paces in front of his column: that is what he did. A fine spectacle, that of an old General, resolute and decided, whose vigour was revived by the presence of the enemy. . . . Placed near him in this perilous moment, my only occupation was to admire him.[11]

The battle at Mondovi may have been the most important of Bonaparte's career. Colli's rearguard still fought, and the French cavalry commander died crossing a ford. The pursuit began to stall. At the knife edge of decision, Colonel Murat rode forward to maintain the impetus of the attack. On the following day, the King of Sardinia requested an armistice, even though his troops successfully withdrew to the north. In less than two weeks, the vigor of French troops and the imaginative and ruthless methods of their young commander had broken through a barrier that had kept the Army of Italy away from its goal for years. However, one more day's delay might have been too much for the ragged men who fought, not for liberty and equality, but for sheer survival.

The actions just described emphasize the difference between the structure of Napoleon's forces and the rigid, linear formations of Prussia and Austria. French formations and task organization were flexible enough to accommodate different types of terrain and changing enemy situations. In order to disperse for foraging and marching, the army was organized into divisions, each made up of one or more demibrigades. Bonaparte altered the structure of divisions before and during battle, often shifting demi-brigades from one division to another, as was required by changing situations. The division was neither a heavy nor a standard organization. Its streamlined features and adaptability reflected the revolutionary style of fighting. The French infantry division was built for speed, not comfort.

The French Pursuit of the Austrians

Even before the armistice with Sardinia was signed, Bonaparte began reposturing his army to carry out the second phase of his mission: driving the enemy beyond the Po. Detaching demi-brigades and battalions from parent divisions to form temporary combat teams, he assembled a combined-arms advance guard to lead the way. On May 5, this mobile force, consisting of six light infantry and grenadier battalions and 1,500 cavalry, moved to seize a crossing over the Po. Meanwhile, Beaulieu's army stumbled eastward across the river and began to occupy defensive positions along the north bank from Casale to Piacenza. The Austrian commander left no covering force south of the river and burned the bridges behind him. *(See Atlas Map No. 4.)*

The French crossing of the Po was a classic action. Moving his units at a steady pace, Bonaparte advanced Serurier's division on Valenza and Massena's on Sale to fix the Austrian defenses. The remainder of the army swung through Alessandria along the excellent network of roads on the south bank of the Po. Beaulieu was presented with the difficult task of choosing where to concentrate to meet the French advance. Whether he decided to contest the crossing at Valenza or Piacenza, superior lateral communications on the other side and built-in French mobility allowed Bonaparte the flexibility to change his plans and to cross at either point. At mid-afternoon on May 7, the French advance guard crossed the river at Piacenza in captured boats and rafts. A young colonel named Jean Lannes leaped from the lead boat and proceeded to establish a bridgehead. Beaulieu's tired army could not react with sufficient combat power to match the French buildup. In confused skirmishes on the following day, the advance guard and Laharpe's division covered the movement of the rest of the French army toward the crossing site. That night, Beaulieu's main force lurched into Laharpe's bivouac. French sentries were not alert and firing was indiscriminate. A stray round mortally wounded Laharpe. Impressed by what he could see of French strength in and around Piacenza, Beaulieu beat a hasty path to Lodi and the supposed safety of another river line.

Shortly after the armistice with Sardinia, Bonaparte commented, "I may lose a battle but I shall never lose a minute."[12] The remark was in keeping with his concept of strategy, his method of command, and, indeed, with his entire personal philosophy. He was a man of action. Impatience drove him to unbelievable exertions. He could spend all day riding from one division command post to another, and still have energy to spare after returning to headquarters for the dictation of orders, memoranda, notes, and letters. He could fall asleep at will, and on waking, instantly put his active, searching mind to work, absorbing information, weighing alternatives, and framing orders for transmission to each and every part of the army. No member of his command was for one day untouched by the energy generated by that high voltage temperament. Bonaparte did not simply lead the Army of Italy; he energized it.

The Battle of Lodi

With all of Piedmont behind him and the rest of the Po Valley before him, Bonaparte now hounded his marching soldiers onward. The advance guard reached the Adda River at Lodi on May 10, hit the Austrian rearguard defending the bridge, and halted, stunned by 14 guns positioned on the opposite shore. Riding close behind, Bonaparte saw the telltale milling and disorder of the stalled column, and moved forward to restore the lost momentum. Under fire from the opposite bank only 200 yards away, he personally placed the cannon to sweep the bridge and counter Austrian artillery. He directed the cavalry to search for a ford and, with a fiery speech, inspired the grenadiers to charge across the bridge. The defenders momentarily checked the assault, but more officers (Berthier, Massena, and Lannes) moved up to lead the charge. Dying men fell into the river. The battle swayed from one side to the other. Then, late in the day, French cavalry crossed and threatened both flanks. The Austrian commander conceded the crossing and withdrew under heavy pressure. In later years, Bonaparte reflected, "It was only on the evening of Lodi that I believed myself a superior man, and that the ambition came to me of executing the great things which so far had been occupying my thoughts only as a fantastic dream."[13] It was probably more significant that at Lodi his troops personally observed their commander in action. It was there that the men of the Army of Italy acquired full confidence in their youthful chief. Subsequent events would indicate that this reservoir of faith was almost inexhaustible.

The Conquest of Northern Italy

The action at Lodi, although strategically inconclusive, served to insure that the small, hard marching French army kept the initiative. Since Beaulieu's rearguard had lost its best defensive position, the reeling Austrian army had no choice but to withdraw behind the Mincio River.

Upon entering Milan, Bonaparte received acclaim as a liberator, but less than a week later he was drawn back to the town by news of revolts there and in Pavia. This was no way for a conquered territory to react. To express his displeasure, Bonaparte allowed his troops to plunder the town of Pavia, while Lannes burned the nearby village of Binasco after shooting all its men.* At the same time, agents from Paris imposed levies on the major towns and seized the most valuable works of art for shipment back to France. Thus, Bonaparte's conquests subsidized the other French armies, but he first insured that his own army was paid—in silver. This was a new experience for soldiers who had rarely been paid at all, even in worthless *assignats*. A keen observer of the period, Madame Germaine de Staël, commented that "the Army of the Rhine belonged to the French Republic; the Army of Italy belonged to Bonaparte."[14] In Italy, war paid its own way.

While Bonaparte ransacked northern Italy, the French Government considered its next move. Shortly after his victory over the Sardinian Army, Bonaparte had written to the Directory of his intention to pursue Beaulieu across the Po and seize the whole of Lombardy. "In less than a month I hope to be on the mountains of Tyrol, there to meet the Army of the Rhine . . . to carry the war into Bavaria."[15] The Direc-

---

*This incident provides an interesting sidelight on the personality of Bonaparte. It is apparent that the example of Binasco was precisely what he wanted, whether he ordered the butchery or not. However, when he arrived at the burning village, he wept at the sight and helped to extinguish the flames. He could easily put himself in any emotional state required by the situation.

tory's reply sought to alter his plans. It proposed to divide his army, conferring the command of the northern half on General François Etienne C. Kellermann, while Bonaparte retained only the southern half. With his reduced command, the champion of the Po was to "advance on Leghorn and afterwards menace Rome and Naples." This letter crossed another written by Bonaparte shortly after the Battle at Lodi: "It is possible that I shall soon attack Mantua. . . . If I take that town, there will be no further obstacle to my entering Bavaria; in twenty days I want to be in the heart of Germany."[16] Imagine the scene at his headquarters when Bonaparte learned that his political chiefs intended to shunt him south, in the opposite direction from the target of his ambition!

This long-distance debate on roles and missions came to a sudden end with Bonaparte's stinging rebuttal:

> Kellermann will command the army as well as I can, for no one is more convinced than I that victories are due to the courage and boldness of the troops. But I believe that to combine Kellermann and myself in Italy would be to run the risk of losing all. . . . I think it would be better to have one bad general than two good ones.[17]

The Government could hardly ignore the military logic of this terse critique,* even though it came from a subordinate. The Directory yielded and ordered Kellermann to reinforce the Army of Italy with two of his divisions. Bonaparte remained in sole command in northern Italy, but he dutifully proceeded with his mission in the south (after forcing Beaulieu's army away from Verona and up the Adige Valley). *(See Atlas Map No. 4.)*

By the end of June 1796, Bonaparte had conquered all of northern Italy [†] and cowed the Papacy and Kingdom of Two Sicilies (Naples) into paying for an armistice. With his southern flank secure, he could now think again of his offensive to the north, although the Army of Italy, with only 40,000 men, could not conquer the Austrian Empire by itself. For Bonaparte to fulfill his ambition to invade Bavaria through the Tyrol, the armies of Generals Jean-Baptiste Jourdan and Jean-Victor Moreau would have to carry out a coordinated drive, which never materialized. In fact, it is doubtful that the Directory ever intended to pursue such a decisive program. To the cautious men in Paris, it was important not to go too far. It was enough to milk the Italian principalities of their

wealth, drive the British out of their base at Leghorn, and negotiate a peace with Austria. By trading Lombardy back to Austria in exchange for territory along the Rhine, France could once again secure the natural frontiers of Louis XIV without upsetting the European balance of power. That was playing war by rules that everyone understood.

Bonaparte understood the rules, but had no intention of abiding by them. Nevertheless, he was forced to consider the realities of his situation. He had to invest the sizable Austrian garrison that had stayed behind in Mantua and watch the population of all northern Italy, lest revolt break out again. Also, after two months of continuous marching and fighting, the army needed a rest. Bonaparte needed no exhaustive estimate to conclude that a temporary defensive was in order. As it turned out, the Army of Italy remained on the strategic defensive for over half a year.

The Defense of Northern Italy

Four times in the next six months the Hapsburg Government sent its armies down from the Alps to recapture Austrian possessions in Italy, and four times the outnumbered French fought them off. This constant pressure put Bonaparte's endurance and strategic ability on extended trial. Without its talented chief, it is inconceivable that the weary French army could have outmaneuvered and outlasted its attackers, dumbfounded its critics, and, in the end, achieved its satisfying victory over Austria's professionals. If he had never fought again, these campaigns alone would entitle Bonaparte to history's acclaim.

Bonaparte's defensive task was complicated by several implied missions: maintaining the siege of Mantua, continuing the pacification of Lombardy, insuring the security of his own lines of communication, and supplying his army in the neutral Republic of Venice.* Out of a total complement of over 50,000 men, only a little over 30,000 were available to defend the Alpine passes to the north.[†] In June, the French intelligence service predicted that an Austrian offensive could be expected in about six weeks. Spies later reported that the Austrian war council had appointed an aggressive cavalryman, General Count Dagobert S. Würmser, to command a field army of 50,000 men. The council expected this accomplished soldier to relieve Mantua and recapture northern Italy from the upstart adventurer who had confiscated Austrian property and taken unreasonable liberties with the art of war. *(See Atlas Map No. 5.)*

---

* Bonaparte's personal secretary, Louis-Antoine Bourrienne, put his finger on a singular talent of his chief when he noted: "Bonaparte, like Xenophon and Caesar, excelled in the art of expressing thought."

† Conquered territories included the Republic of Genoa, Piedmont, Lombardy (Duchy of Milan), part of the Duchy of Parma, part of the Republic of Venice, and the Duchy of Mantua.

*Venice governed most of the territory east of the Mincio River and north of the Po.

†The Army of Italy received an extra division from Kellermann's army in May.

Würmser's Two Advances

On the evening of July 28, 1796, the storm struck the Army of Italy. General Bonaparte, enjoying a rare visit from Josephine near Brescia, was awakened by the unpleasant news that General Barthelemy C. Joubert's brigade (of Massena's division) had been attacked and driven out of its positions on the slopes of Monte Baldo. Massena promptly reinforced his faltering frontline troops, but by nightfall of the next day his whole division had been forced back to Peschiera. Fragments of information reached the army commander while he was on the gallop toward Peschiera: another Austrian column had advanced on Verona from the east, and a third had engaged General Baron Philip F. Sauret's division and forced it out of Salo. Where was the Austrian main attack?

It took two hard days of retrograde fighting to find out, although Bonaparte was never entirely sure of Austrian intentions. His running estimate accounted for every factor that could be calculated or surmised: availability and vulnerabilities of friendly forces; strength, location, and movements of the enemy; and terrain that could be used to advantage. The only factor that remained unchanged and predominant in the turmoil of that confused week of hot summer fighting was the objective—to destroy Würmser's army so it could never fight again. To carry out his plan, Bonaparte counted on the tough feet of French soldiers and his own fast thinking.

Marshal Pierre François Augereau

The general had much to do and little time to spare. First, he had to concentrate the army on the open plains south of Lake Garda and prepare to drive General Peter Quasdanovich's force out of Brescia to clear the army's line of communication with Milan. Then he had to make the hard decision to lift the siege of Mantua, surrendering the city to Würmser in order to reinforce the Army of Italy with Serurier's 5,000-man division. Finally, he had to turn on Würmser with all available combat power and drive him out of Italy. The alternative was to withdraw to the west, back behind the Chiese, the Oglio, and perhaps as far as the Adda—rivers that brave men had already dared, and died, to cross. Bonaparte seriously considered that course of action in a moment of hesitation, but after mentioning it to Augereau, he was reassured by his boastful subordinate: "attack first, and then if we are beaten it will be time to think of retreating."[18]

With his spine stiffened by this moral support, Bonaparte resolved to carry out his finely calculated plan. He was aided by the piecemeal efforts of Quasdanovich and Würmser. The two Austrian forces came within a few miles of engaging the Army of Italy simultaneously and crushing it between them. But Quasdanovich withdrew in confusion, partly because of Massena's slashing counterattack at Lonato, and partly because of a lack of information and direction from Würmser. Also, Würmser hesitated while recapturing and resupplying the city of Mantua, which had been gratuitously offered up by the French commander.

Bonaparte filled this two-day respite with a frenzy of activity. He gathered the divisions of Augereau, Massena, and General Count H.F. Despinoy, reinforced by cavalry and Marmont's horse artillery, and directed Serurier to be prepared to attack from the east. His maturing plan was to fix Würmser's main force from the west and envelop it from the rear. The decisive action took place as planned on August 5 near Castiglione. Würmser's army was beaten, but Serurier's enveloping force was too weak to cut the Austrian escape routes and completely destroy the enemy army. The aggressive Austrian commander, who had very nearly accomplished both of his goals, slipped across the Mincio and led his army back into the Tyrol, still full of fight for another try.

Würmser's second offensive attempt, which began on September 2, caught Bonaparte's army in a somewhat weakened posture. The French had had to start all over against the re-provisioned garrison in Mantua. What was worse, the heavy siege guns had been lost when Serurier lifted the siege. Bonaparte realized that his margin of space and time had been cut thin at Castiglione. This time he decided to take the initiative and advance against his opponent. Encouraged by the news of his victory, the Directory now urged Bonaparte to drive through the Brenner Pass and link up with Moreau's Army of the Rhine.* Without the active cooperation of Moreau's army, however, Bonaparte's advance through the Tyrol late in the summer could not be effective. Accepting this unfortunate fact, he decided to advance as far as Trent and then reassess the situation before moving farther.

It was a wise move. Moreau's army reached the limit of its advance on September 3, but Jourdan's Army of the Sambre-et-Meuse lost Würzburg and began to fall back before the attack of the Archduke Charles, thereby uncovering Moreau's north flank. Fearing for his communications along the Danube, Moreau lost his nerve and wrote to Bonaparte that Jourdan's retreat compelled him to do the same. *(See Atlas Map No. 6.)*

Bonaparte had already made up his mind to turn east, not north, from Trent. Learning that Würmser had departed from Trent with a four-day lead, he pushed Augereau forward in pursuit. Massena fell in behind, while General Charles H. Vaubois was left in a blocking position to secure the French north flank. Only 3,000 men remained south of Verona to guard the crossings over the Adige River; and Sahuget—having replaced Serurier, who was ill with malaria—kept a stranglehold on the 15,000 Austrians in Mantua.

Surprised that Bonaparte had followed him down the Brenta Valley, Würmser turned to fight at Bassano. On September 8, after a week of hard marching and little sleep, Bonaparte flung his veteran divisions against Würmser's hastily prepared positions at the mouth of the dominating Brenta gorge. The attack of French skirmishers was irresistible. Lannes' regiment led Massena's attack and Murat led the pursuit. Austrian troops and trains intermingled in retreat, only halting at Mantua, where Würmser attempted to expand his perimeter in order to facilitate subsisting his troops. His forces were almost as strong as Bonaparte's, but his army was finally shut in, along with the remnants of Beaulieu's army, whose soldiers had become permanent residents in the malaria-infested fortress.

The Army of Italy had vanquished another challenger. Indeed, it had locked him up in the swampy cage on the Mincio. But again, the army had not escaped unharmed, especially in the ranks of its leaders. Lannes and Murat were wounded, and Augereau, who suffered from piles, was temporarily disabled by the arduous pursuit. Fortunately, Bonaparte was granted a month and a half to prepare for the next trial at arms. In many ways it was to be his toughest test as a commander. *(See Atlas Map No. 7.)*

Alvintzi's Two Advances to Relieve Mantua

On November 1, 1796, General Baron Josef Alvintzi led the next Austrian army down from the north against the French

defenses. Bonaparte had already positioned his troops well forward. Now, as Alvintzi's offensive gained momentum, Bonaparte drew his covering forces back past the Brenta Valley, surrendering interior lines temporarily to the Austrians. Only by withdrawing to Verona could Bonaparte retrieve a relative advantage. In the north, General Paul von Davidovich gained a series of successes against Vaubois, and by November 10 had advanced to Ala. Meanwhile, Alvintzi marched through Vicenza, after pushing two outnumbered French divisions before his advancing troops. Bonaparte's forces were rapidly losing space in which to maneuver. It was time to fight a battle.

The French attack at Caldiero misfired due to winter weather, inspired Austrian fighting, and failing French morale. Beaten in the open field for the first time in his career, Bonaparte pulled his shaken troops back into the protection of the walled city of Verona. In despair, he wrote to the Directory:

> All our superior officers, all our best generals, are *hors de combat*. . . . The Army of Italy, reduced to a handful of men, is exhausted. . . . Nothing remains to the different corps but their reputation and their pride. . . . Perhaps the hour of the brave Augereau, of the intrepid Massena, of Berthier, or my own, is ready to strike . . . [19]

To Josephine he wrote in a similar vein, advising her to flee from Milan, and telling her that he would join her in Genoa, if he survived. Like Frederick in the Seven Years' War, Napoleon rebounded from defeat. Waiting in Verona would surrender the decision to the Austrians; attacking toward Vicenza would only repeat his error of the day before; and retreating would lead to the loss of all his gains. Rather than electing any of these options, he chose to impose his will on his enemy *by marching down the west bank of the Adige*, crossing into the swamps of Arcola, and stunning the very soul of Alvintzi with an attack on his trains in Villanuova. It was a daring but well-thought-out maneuver. *(See Atlas Map No. 8.)*

Although the French failed to make the crossing unopposed, the threat to Alvintzi's rear drew the Austrian commander away from Verona and the planned linkup with Davidovich. As long as Alvintzi hung back, Davidovich could not find the courage to press on. This fine balance of opposing wills lasted for three days, while Bonaparte struggled to expand his bridgehead and break out into the area north of Arcola. Finally, after bitter fighting, the bravery and open-order tactics of the French captured the enemy position at Arcola. Perhaps the deciding factor was the persistence (or obstinacy) of Bonaparte, who hung on to his enemy's flank,

---

*Moreau was now advancing through Bavaria, against forces weakened by Austrian detachments sent to counter Bonaparte in Italy.

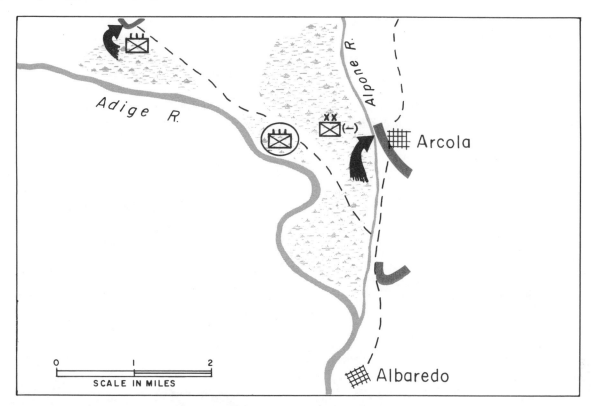

Massena's Division at Arcola, November 17, 1796

with his army divided in the face of peril on three sides. Alvintzi was not beaten at Arcola; he was persuaded to leave. On the same day, Davidovich finally began to push—too late—toward Verona.

The news of this success resounded through every capital in Europe. However, armies cannot campaign forever. Brave men should be conserved, but it is usually the bravest who are the first to fall. Within Massena's and Augereau's divisions, only three general officers came through Arcola unwounded. The effect on morale was noticeable. "I ought not to conceal from *you*," wrote Bonaparte to the Directory, "that I have not found in the troops my phalanxes of Lodi, Millesimo and Castiglione: fatigue and the absence of valiant men have taken from them that impetuosity with which I had the right to hope to capture Alvintzi and the greater part of his army."[20]

The Battle of Arcola was a radical departure from the type of battle that had been fought before the Revolution by generals like Marlborough and Frederick the Great. For one thing, Arcola lasted three days, while Blenheim, Prague, and Leuthen were one-day fights. Second, tactics at Arcola were largely a matter for division commanders, while in the old style of warfare, in which an army fought in one solid mass, the army commander specified formations, routes of advance, time of attack, etc., for every battalion of the army. At Arcola, even small unit commanders and individual soldiers had to exercise initiative. On the third day of the fight, for example, Massena's division was dispersed in three fragments over several square miles of ground. The division commander could not personally lead all these scattered units; demi-brigade commanders had to show initiative and make their own decisions. Also, individual soldiers had to fight on their own in the swampy, dyke country between the Alpone and Adige Rivers. Parade formations had no place on this kind of terrain, where the best techniques were patrols, sniping, bushwhackings, and aggressive small-unit skirmishes. In only one respect did Napoleonic battle retain the trademark of linear warfare: close combat remained more a test of collective willpower than one of firepower, as is suggested by the fact that the French lost twice as many men as the Austrians. The outcome at Arcola was even closer than at Castiglione. In Bonaparte's words, "it was indeed a fight to the death."

With the failure of operations in Germany, it was now essential to French grand strategy that the war in Italy be brought to a successful conclusion. The reduction of Mantua was the Directory's foremost objective. Austria would not negotiate until it fell. With this in mind, Bonaparte faced Alvintzi's second attempt to relieve the embattled city. He had received one encouraging piece of news from intercepted messages: the overpopulated garrison was reduced to eating its horses. (*See Atlas Map No. 9.*)

Believing that Bonaparte had sent sizable forces south to deal again with the reviving Papal States, Alvintzi chose to strike with his main attack down the Adige Valley. Secondary efforts from the east were aimed at fixing French defenses and deceiving Bonaparte as to Alvintzi's true intentions. The first reports from French outposts along the Adige showed substantial pressure all along the eastern front, but failed to identify the Austrian main attack. Reports of light contact by Joubert on January 9 seemed to validate Bonaparte's belief that Alvintzi's main blow would fall between Verona and Legnago. He issued warning orders to Massena, Augereau, and his cavalry reserve for commitment in that threatened sector.

On January 11 Bonaparte was in Bologna, conferring with the Duke of Tuscany. The next day, spurred by reports of sharp fighting, he rode first to headquarters at Roverbella and later to Verona, his purpose being to consult with Massena and gain a better grasp of the situation. It was a tense night. Massena had been under attack all day, and Augereau claimed to be hard hit. Under pressure, tired subordinates began to exaggerate, each magnifying the danger in his sector. How to filter out the truth from the stream of rumor, uncertainty, and error was an exercise at which Bonaparte's mind excelled.

The next morning, Bonaparte wrote to Joubert, asking if he had more than 9,000 enemy before him at La Corona. "It is vitally important that I should know whether the attack being made upon you is serious . . . or merely a secondary affair designed to put us off."[21] Joubert's afternoon report resolved the issue. His division had lost its forward positions on the slopes of Monte Baldo and was moving to occupy its main defenses on the plateau of Rivoli. Reacting with characteristic vigor, Bonaparte issued orders: Augereau was to cover the entire eastern sector; Massena was to move at once to reinforce Joubert; General Baron G.V. Rey was to march on Rivoli; and the cavalry reserve was to follow Massena. With Berthier at his side, the only man in Italy who knew how to capitalize on the smallest margin rode north to supervise the battle personally.

Alvintzi provided the opening by advancing in multiple columns, one far beyond supporting distance on the west, and two separated from the main body by the Adige gorge on the

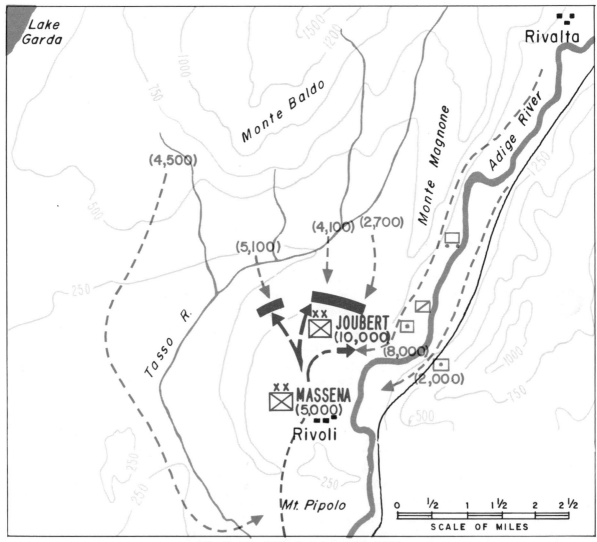

The Battle of Rivoli, January 14, 1797

east. The Austrian artillery rode with these two eastern columns, while Bonaparte's infantry, artillery, and cavalry operated together on the high plateau overlooking the Adige Valley. Joubert's choice of this key position determined the shape of the battle Bonaparte must fight: it would be interior lines* again, in both strategy and tactics.

Bonaparte, too, recognized the importance of the heights at Rivoli, and signaled ahead, ordering Joubert to maintain his position. Arriving at Rivoli shortly after midnight, he peered into the cold, clear night and counted the clusters of Austrian campfires. Alvintzi's capabilities and intentions were etched against the looming massif of Monte Baldo. Bonaparte ordered Joubert to attack.

Massena, arriving ahead of his men and riding forward to coordinate his movements with those of Joubert, narrowly avoided capture. His troops deployed immediately and swept the ground on Joubert's left, allowing Joubert to shift his attention eastward to the Austrians climbing out of the river bed. After these uncoordinated enemy forces had been hammered back to the water line, Bonaparte looked to the south for the last Austrian column, which had serenely taken Mt. Pipolo in splendid isolation. The last of Massena's units now arrived, cheered on by Bonaparte in person: "Brave 18th, I know you; the enemy will not stand before you."[22] "En avant," the soldiers roared in consent, and fell upon the unfortunate Austrians.

In strategy and tactics, central position offered the advantage. Even as Joubert launched a driving pursuit to the north, Bonaparte turned Massena's panting battalions to the south. In desperation, Würmser had striven to break out of Mantua while Augereau gamely held off renewed attacks from the east. Massena's men arrived in time to extinguish Würmser's last hope. After three solid days of marching and fighting, Massena had more than earned his future title: the Duke of Rivoli. Two weeks later, on February 2, 1797, Mantua surrendered. Bonaparte had completed the conquest of Italy.

The Battle of Rivoli offers a point of departure for interjecting a brief analysis of Bonaparte's strategic ability. More than a few military theorists have proposed that Bonaparte developed a campaign formula in Italy and worked all his life refining it in practice.[23] True, his best known actions fit roughly into one of two patterns of maneuver—the envelopment (such as the battle fought at Castiglione) and the operation from interior lines (such as the Battle of Rivoli). But a general's repertoire consists of more than just a stock of game plans, preset for certain contingencies. Decisive results require the entire range of the commander's creative skills. For

*Interior lines describes the condition of a force that can reinforce its separated units faster than separated opposing units can reinforce each other—either because of its central position or its superior lateral communications relative to the enemy.

Rivoli

example, at Rivoli, Bonaparte accepted a fluid situation, fraught with danger and uncertainty, and shaped it to his own advantage. It was necessary to do more than calculate the location of Alvintzi's main attack by comparing those enemy strengths opposing Joubert, Massena, and Augereau. Bonaparte had to *perceive* the culmination of his opponent's effort and *judge* the physical and moral readiness of his own battalions. Computations made from the map could not produce a total assessment; Bonaparte had to *sense* relative combat power. To gain the information he needed, he first had to go where he could see, hear, and feel the fighting. He then had to be ready to react. Marmont recorded that the army commander kept his carriage standing by the door all that night in Verona. To Bonaparte, interior lines was not merely a function of space and time. It was also a state of mind.

Bonaparte's style of command gave life to his strategy and his tactics. The personal aspect of command, although difficult to visualize, must not be minimized. That penetrating glance that exposed men's inner fears, the relentless urge to press his divisions on the march, his flair for appearing in battle at critical moments, the way he spoke to soldiers under fire—all contributed to his getting the most out of every soldier in his army. He was not a man who commanded by remote control, but a general of unequalled sensitivity who lived and suffered, yet also enjoyed the pangs of war.

He understood the effect of motivation and loyalty on performance, and used them to accelerate the velocity of campaigning. Speed of movement and the quest for battle contrasted sharply with old concepts of strategy, in which armies often maneuvered for months before finally engaging in combat. In the warfare waged by Bonaparte, violent combat occurred literally at the opening moves of the campaign.

Speed and violence thus tended to erase any artificial distinction between strategy and tactics. Decisive battle was at once the purpose and the termination of his campaign.

Bonaparte's innate strategic ability was not a pattern of maneuver, but a dynamic, flexible, unstereotyped system of thinking—if it can even be called a system. His strategy was, in large part, a product of his personality. By personally setting the example, he encouraged each individual—from private to general—to exploit his own potential. His far-ranging intellect conceived strategic projects that only a man with his consuming passion for action could oversee, and his physical toughness kept him going night and day until his enemy was forced to capitulate.

Shortly after the action at Lodi, Bonaparte remarked to Marmont: "They have seen nothing yet. . . . In our days no one has conceived anything great; it is for me to set the example."[24] The final conquest of northern Italy confirmed this prophecy, and afterwards the astonishing rise of Bonaparte continued to accelerate. In February 1797, Mantua surrendered. In March, the Army of Italy crossed the Piave River, forcing an army commanded by Austria's Archduke Charles to retreat. Although revolts erupted to his rear, the young conqueror pushed his exposed legions to within 100 miles of Vienna. Austria agreed to negotiate. Now Bonaparte impatiently wrested from the Directory full diplomatic powers and, with the Treaty of Campo Formio (October 17, 1797), dictated a peace. France gained Belgium and other territory along the Rhine to round out her natural frontier, and received Lombardy in exchange for part of Venetia. Part of the Papal States, Milan, Mantua, and Modena became the new Cisalpine Republic, and Genoa was remodelled in the French style and renamed the Ligurian Republic. In one stroke, Bonaparte had recast feudal Italy in the modern image. No wonder he was hailed in Paris as "the young Republican hero, the immortal Bonaparte."

The Egyptian Adventure

Under the existing scheme of government there were two things that France's Alexander could not rectify. He could not cure the domestic problems of the nation, and he could not conquer implacable England. How to strike at England? Bonaparte would wrestle with that vexatious problem for the rest of his career.

With a second-class navy, it was useless to dream of a cross-Channel invasion. Instead, why not strike at England in the East? The wily foreign minister, Charles Maurice Talleyrand, approved of Bonaparte's lofty project. By interdicting British commerce with India, French wealth might increase at British expense. Perhaps a channel might be dug to uncork the east-

ern Mediterranean and give France commercial "interior lines." There were other reasons, too, for the plan—not the least of which was Bonaparte's irrepressible imagination and restlessness. High adventure could not yet be found at home. (*See Atlas Map No. 10.*)

The French expedition destined for Egypt sailed in May of 1798, stopping off to capture Malta on the way, while Admiral Nelson's frigates vainly sought to determine its course. British and French fleets almost sailed through each other the night of June 22–23, and then diverged again. Nelson's faster cruisers arrived off Alexandria to find Aboukir Bay empty, and then sailed north to continue the hunt. On the same day, Bonaparte's lead vessel reached land. The uneasy commander-in-chief precipitately unloaded his seasick troops over unreconnoitered beaches and pushed, that night, for Alexandria. One day later Alexandria was in French hands and, within a month, exhausted, parched French troops fought another battle and captured Cairo. But one cannot rely on fortune indefinitely. On August 2, Nelson returned, found the French fleet anchored in Aboukir Bay, and sailed with a vengeance into its midst. All but three French vessels were sunk, and the flagship was blown up. The setback was irrevocable.

Gone were dreams of dominating the Mediterranean basin. Gone was any hope that the army might return intact to France. Gone was even the barest support from home.* Bonaparte's solution to this crisis was activity—an offensive in the footsteps of Alexander across the burning sands of Sinai to strike at Syria and pre-empt a gathering Turkish counterblow. The expedition failed—partly because of the unexpected fortification encountered at El Arish; partly because of an outbreak of bubonic plague; to a large degree because of a shortage of artillery; but perhaps most of all because of the French commander's overestimate of what his army could accomplish. However, Bonaparte's resourceful spirit never admitted defeat. Although he had failed, he proclaimed a victory to his troops and triumphantly marched the army back to Egypt.

Such a man is more than rare. A general who could rally a beaten army and march it to a winning tune, a commander who could breathe fire into soldiers by exclaiming before a battle that from the pyramids before them "forty centuries look down upon you"—such a man could hardly remain in Egypt.[25] To the Government, faced by a fresh coalition assault in Germany and Italy, he became indispensable. As Bonaparte had hoped, the Directory ordered his return to France. However, the irrepressible Bonaparte needed no invitation to leave Egypt.† Fragments of information had reached

*As the year wore on, Bonaparte sensed the Directory's lack of interest in Egypt because of its concern with the deteriorating situation in Europe. He also learned the personally shattering news of Josephine's infidelity.

†He left Egypt before the arrival of the Directory's summons that ordered him to return *with his army*. That army finally surrendered to the British at Alexandria in 1801.

him by newspaper, courier, and word of mouth: a second coalition had formed against France; a Russo-Austrian army had run the Army of Italy out of its Cisalpine bases, killing Joubert in the hill country north of Genoa; Jourdan had lost a battle on the Rhine; England had clamped a firm blockade on the Atlantic coast; there was fighting in the Netherlands. To Bonaparte, his course of action was clearly dictated by duty—France was in peril, and his services were needed at home. To many of his subordinates who were left behind, however, it was an issue of honor—their commander had deserted them.

The Battle of Marengo: Victory Through Teamwork

Back in France, clever publicity work concealed the failures of the Egyptian Campaign. Bonaparte received a hero's welcome. In November of 1799, he took on the unaccustomed role of activist and led a conspiracy to overthrow the ineffective Directory. For once, his oratory was clumsy, but French troops coerced the legislative body into approval. From this coup d'état, the impatient Bonaparte emerged as First Consul with sweeping powers, both domestic and foreign. He could decide for war or peace. The French Republic was effectively terminated; dictatorship began.

To consolidate his grip on the Government, Bonaparte needed a spectacular success. Political and economic problems could only be solved by political and economic reform. These were undertaken, but results would only show with time. Foreign affairs invited quick action. The Second Coalition, having driven French forces back to the country's natural boundary along the Rhine and Alps, was now starting to crumble. Russia withdrew in December, but Austria continued to hold the line in Germany and Italy. By artful maneuvers and hard fighting, Massena's troops retained control of France's key position in Switzerland. This jutting strategic bastion offered Bonaparte an opportunity for action in Italy or Germany. In the spring of 1800, peace could probably have been negotiated, but Bonaparte wanted to conquer peace rather than negotiate it.

Bonaparte's military scheme was fraught with risk. He selected the tough, resourceful Massena to take over the remnants of the Army of Italy along the Riviera and fix the Austrian Army near Genoa. The 100,000-man Army of the Rhine (now commanded by the spiteful General Moreau)*

---

*Moreau, a competent military leader, but a person naive in political matters, had supported Bonaparte's seizure of power from the Directory, but shortly thereafter became disenchanted with the First Consul. He retained his position for a time, but ultimately was forced into exile in America.

could not be counted on for more than a diversion. The rest was up to Bonaparte and a Reserve Army of roughly 50,000 men, secretly assembled just west of Switzerland. As soon as the army was ready, he planned to move it through the mountain passes of Switzerland and onto the rear of the unsuspecting Austrians in northern Italy. *(See Atlas Map No. 11.)*

Like the spring campaign four years earlier, the Marengo Campaign commenced with the Austrians moving first. On May 1, Bonaparte learned that Massena's army, dispersed to forage, had been split in two. Massena and 10,000 men were forced back to Genoa and invested there by a force roughly twice their number. The remainder of the Army of Italy withdrew to Nice where it confronted the bulk of the Austrian Army, commanded by General Michael von Melas.

Daring couriers carried Bonaparte's orders to Massena: "I count on your holding out as long as possible, at least until May 30."[26] Meanwhile, Bonaparte's energy activated commanders, troops, and supply services. Numbers of guns with the advance guard (commanded by General Lannes), numbers of rations in the depots, numbers of boats to ship supplies forward on Lake Geneva, data on limbers, munitions wagons, horses, oats—Bonaparte had to know every key fact personally, had to insure that his army was moving. No other commander in Europe could expedite the movement of all the interlocking pieces of an army as could this impatient genius.

Especially not Melas in Italy. This competent but conventional commander saw only the army before him, and pursued his single-minded purpose of driving French troops back along the coast into France. He guarded the passes at his rear with forces scattered over a 150-mile mountain front. He established bases at key communications centers in the Po Valley and imposed a tight siege on Genoa. He was ready for anything—except for the thunderbolt that was about to fall upon him from the north.

To Massena, Bonaparte wrote on May 14:

> "The army is on the way. . . . You are in a tight corner; but what reassures me is that it is *you* who are in Genoa; it is at times like these that one man can be worth 20,000."[27]

Bonaparte's Reserve Army advanced through five widely separated passes, thus concealing the location and strength of the main advance. Melas, refusing to believe that an entire army was approaching toward his rear, thought these were only diversionary forces. On May 19 he learned the terrible truth that the French were descending on Italy in strength. He immediately drew off part of his forces on the Mediterranean and turned north to meet the Alpine threat. This first challenge was only the beginning of Melas' problems. Which one of the five approaching columns was the French main effort?

The Great St. Bernard Pass

While the Austrian commander wrestled with this dilemma, the French main force proceeded across the Great St. Bernard Pass. Bonaparte's letter of May 18 to the other consuls pictured a herculean task: "We are fighting against ice, snow, gales and avalanches. Astonished at being so rudely attacked, the Saint Bernard is putting certain obstacles in our way."[28] Faced with natural obstacles, the French army did what it could do best—improvise. Gunners hollowed out tree trunks to transport the artillery; infantrymen built trails and bridges. The First Consul rode a mule.

The crossing of the St. Bernard, rightly celebrated as an extraordinary feat, was nothing compared with the experience that awaited Lannes' advance guard near the exit from the pass. At the narrowest part of the Dora Baltea defile sits Fort Bard. Perched on a commanding rock formation, it completely dominates the narrow valley. Berthier reconnoitered and reported that infantry could bypass the fort, but artillery would have to halt until its capture. This posed new problems. The cavalry could not wait long in the pass for need of forage. Worse, Massena would soon succumb, turning loose 20,000 more Austrians to contest the Alpine crossing. In this crisis, individual initiative and valor came to the fore. The advance guard picked its way around the heights without the all important guns. While the artillery commenced a lively bombardment of the fort, succeeding divisions bypassed the defile. By May 22, Frenchmen were in Ivrea, the gateway to the Po Valley. Also, by this time Melas had figured out the French maneuver and was assembling his strength in Turin.

Poised at the top of the Po Valley, Bonaparte could now choose from several alternatives. Ignoring for the time being Massena's anguished cries for help, he turned his columns east. Melas continued concentrating for a battle near Turin,

while Bonaparte hustled his lightly-armed, fast-moving divisions toward Milan, using Lannes' southward swing to screen his move.

On June 2, French troops entered Milan (the main Austrian supply base) and then plunged south across the Po, while the bewildered Melas wheeled his army to go north or east. Two days later, Massena surrendered Genoa, and on June 9 Lannes' advance guard collided with the Austrian force released from that investment and sent it pounding back to the west. The main Austrian escape routes to the east were now firmly blocked, but Bonaparte dispersed his army to cut off every conceivable avenue of retreat. Meanwhile, unknown to the French commander, Melas had decided to fight his way out, and had ordered a concentration at Alessandria of roughly half his army. Over 20,000 Frenchmen were north of the Po, holding blocking positions. Bonaparte was unaware that just across the Bormida River lay the Austrian army, superior in strength to his own.

Convinced that Melas was still trying to elude him, Bonaparte further fragmented his forces early on June 14, sending one division north of the Po River and another division east to the Scrivia River to search for the Austrian main force. Accompanying this latter division was one of Bonaparte's ablest generals, Louis Charles Desaix, who had just returned from Egypt. At 6:00 a.m., Melas' formation crossed the Bormida River and began to deploy. By 9:00 a.m., his attack was in full stride. General Claude Perrin Victor's battered troops began to withdraw at noon. At first, Bonaparte refused to believe that Melas' attack was more than a feint, and sent out a message urging Desaix to hasten his search to the southeast, *away from the battle already in progress.*

Fort Bard

Desaix had made no contact with Austrian formations along the Scrivia River line, and sent a message to Bonaparte to that effect. Hearing the roar of guns to the northwest, he decided to pause at the swollen river and debate the choices before him. On receipt of Bonaparte's confirming order, he uneasily resumed his march and had just set his troops in motion when a breathless aide galloped up with Bonaparte's frantic message: "I had thought to attack Melas. He has attacked me first. For God's sake come up if you still can."[29]

Desaix at once countermarched his division, moving cross-country toward the smoke and the sound of battle. Arriving at around 3:00 p.m., shortly before his troops, Desaix hastily conferred with his commander. Bonaparte had committed his last reserves, and the Austrians, greatly superior in infantry and guns, were regrouping before launching the pursuit. When asked for his opinion, Desaix is said to have replied, "This battle is completely lost, but there is time to win another."[30]

The second battle, a precision demonstration of a combined-arms attack, began later that day. Infantry led by Desaix met the Austrian advance guard head-on, cavalry struck from a flank, and Marmont's guns tore the heart out of Melas' pursuing column. Within a period of several hours, defeat had been converted into victory; Bonaparte had his brilliant success, and the man who had hastened to arrive in time lay dead among the torn grainfields and broken bodies on the plain of Marengo.

Should not Bonaparte have given Desaix full credit for the successful outcome of this perilous endeavor? Indeed, one can point to several errors committed by the army commander in his estimates of enemy and friendly capabilities during the last week of the campaign—errors that dangerously exposed his vulnerabilities. There is no question that he placed the Reserve Army in grave jeopardy by dividing his strength in the face of the enemy, and that Desaix covered the deficit by his spirited dash to the rescue.

This was entirely characteristic of the French commander's strategic and tactical style. He did not shrink from risk. He accepted it and pushed his army to the threshold of danger, knowing he could count on inspired commanders to elevate their men beyond the superhuman and help him dominate the battle. In Bonaparte's calculations, supporting distance was no arbitrary measurement but an elastic limit, dependent on alertness, initiative, and desire.

When the tired Bonaparte received news of Desaix's death, he simply replied, "Why is it that I am not allowed to weep?" Two days later the First Consul shrewdly reported his success: "I hope the French people will be pleased with their army."[31]

The echoes of Marengo rang through the rest of Bonaparte's career. History has accorded to him the glory for the victory that recovered Italy for France. But there can be no mistaking that it was a team win. Berthier, Massena, Lannes, Marmont, and Desaix made possible the great events that led to the conquest. They also helped confirm their commanding general's dangerous belief that he was a great man who was invincible.

Notes

[1]Octave Aubry, *Napoleon* (New York, 1964), p. 20.

[2]Vincent J. Esposito and John R. Elting, *A Military History and Atlas of the Napoleonic Wars* (New York, 1964), Introduction.

[3]Theodore Ropp, *War in the Modern World* (Durham, 1959), p. 92.

[4]Felix Markham, *Napoleon* (New York, 1963), p. 26.

[5]Spenser Wilkinson, *The Rise of General Bonaparte* (Oxford, 1930), p. 56.

[6]*Correspondance de Napoleon I* (32 vols.; Paris, 1858–1870), I, No. 91, p. 107.

[7]*Correspondance*, I, No. 83, p. 104.

[8]John E. Howard (ed.), *Letters and Documents of Napoleon* (1 vol. to date; New York, 1961–), I, 88.

[9]Howard, *Letters and Documents of Napoleon*, I, 96.

[10]Ramsay W. Phipps, *The Armies of the First French Republic* (5 vols.; Oxford, 1935–1939), IV, 17.

[11]Phipps, *The Armies of the First French Republic*, IV, 25–26.

[12]Wilkinson, *The Rise of General Bonaparte*, p. 132.

[13]Phipps, *The Armies of the First French Republic*, IV, 37.

[14]James Marshall-Cornwall, *Napoleon as Military Commander* (London,1967), pp. 74–75.

[15]*Correspondance*, I, No. 257, p. 201.

[16]Guglielmo Ferrero, *The Gamble: Bonaparte in Italy, 1796–1797* (London, 1961), p. 49.

[17]Howard, *Letters and Documents of Napoleon*, I, 117.

[18]Archibald G. MacDonell, *Napoleon and His Marshals* (New York, 1934), p. 14.

[19]Phipps, *The Armies of the First French Republic*, IV, 109–110.

[20]*Ibid.*, IV, 119.

[21]*Correspondance*, II, No. 1377, p. 238.

[22]David G. Chandler, *The Campaigns of Napoleon* (New York, 1966), p. 118.

[23]See especially H. Camon, *La Bataille Napoleonienne* (Paris, 1899); and George Lefebvre, *Napoleon: From 18 Brumaire to Tilsit, 1799–1807*, trans. by H.F. Stockhold (New York, 1969), pp. 228–231.

[24]Chandler, *The Campaigns of Napoleon*, p. 84.

[25]*Correspondance*, XXIX, p. 450.

[26]*Ibid.*, VI, No. 4760, p. 258.

[27]*Ibid.*, No. 4795, p. 281.

[28]Howard, *Letters and Documents of Napoleon*, I, 424.

[29]Chandler, *The Campaigns of Napoleon*, p. 291.

[30]*Ibid.*, p. 293.

[31]Howard, *Letters and Documents of Napoleon*, I, 466.

The Empire and the *Grande Armée*

2

On Christmas Eve, 1800, a coach carrying the First Consul hastened along a narrow Paris street to the opera. Another carriage followed with his wife and stepdaughter. Suddenly, the coachman of Bonaparte's carriage reined in his impatient team before a cart that blocked the way. In a minute or so the obstacle was removed, and the two carriages resumed their jolting passage. At that moment, there was a blinding flash and a thunderous report. A bomb! It took the lives of 20 bystanders, but was intended solely for the passenger whose headlong ambitions now steered the destiny of France. Although five years of relative peace were to pass before Bonaparte's military engagement at Ulm, nothing more precisely signified the meaning of Bonaparte's life than that destructive explosion. From beginning to end, the career of Napoleon Bonaparte was an expression of the conflict between violence and order.

It took centuries to build the absolute monarchy that ruled France and intimidated Europe, but it took less than four years for revolution to destroy it. When the monarchy fell, the royal army collapsed also. A new army quickly took the old one's place, but, apparently, kings and professional soldiers throughout Europe failed to appreciate the special properties of the revolutionary French Army. This lack of appreciation had its roots in one of the most instructive and often overlooked aspects of Bonaparte's era: the role of popular opinion in war. As the Revolutionary Government incorporated ideological weaponry into the public arsenal, national feeling expanded the war-making potential of the state. On the other hand, nationalism placed certain demands on the Government.

The great wars of the twentieth century have demonstrated convincingly that it is wrong to think of modern armies as independent organisms, obeying their own laws, operating by their own logic, and pursuing their own ends. Changes in military institutions accompany—and cause—changes in society.* There is ample evidence to show that this relationship had its origins in the Age of the Democratic Revolution.[1] Just as the American militia was largely a product of the colonial experience, the *Grande Armée* had its immediate origins in

the French Revolution. To understand Bonaparte's army it is therefore necessary to understand France.

In 1800, France was governed by a virtual dictatorship. In theory, the Constitution divided governmental power between an executive and a legislature; in practice, Bonaparte acted without legislative approval. However, even the most tyrannical despot must consider his subjects' feelings. An overriding tenet of Bonaparte's policy was not only to consider, but to exploit the positive impulses of French attitudes. This premise is fundamental to an understanding of the peculiar relation between the French Army, Government, and people.

From Consulate to Empire

In both a military and political sense, 1800 was a pivotal year in Bonaparte's rise to power. The year of Marengo could have been a year of disaster, in which case Bonaparte would rate only a brief mention in history alongside the names of other distinguished French warriors like Enghien, Turenne, Villars, and Saxe. One reason for his success in the gamble for power was the extraordinary coincidence of his temperament with the collective will of the French people. Bonaparte s passion for achievement appealed to the spontaneous longing of all Frenchmen for *gloire*. At the same time, his almost reactionary instinct to restore authority and order fulfilled the natural desire of a nation tired of strife and war. In the midst of the

---

*A sharp-eyed critic may rightly point out that this theorem—that an army reflects the society from which it is derived—does not always apply. None of the mercenary units of the fifteenth through the eighteenth centuries (the *condottiere* cavalry, the Swiss pike companies, the shanghaied musketeers in Frederick's military machine) necessarily mirrored the attitudes of the states for which they fought. On the other hand, the mercenary army was a product of the organization and outlook of the government that paid for its services. Remembering the miseries of the Thirty Years' War, ministries seem to have made every effort to separate populace and soldiery, in order to minimize the undesirable effects of each on the other. It was the French Revolution that conclusively drew military and public interests together.

Marengo Campaign, he responded to criticism of his growing power by remarking, "I merely act upon the imagination of the nation; when that fails me, I shall be nothing, and another will succeed me."[2] How else does one explain the overwhelming majority by which the French people confirmed his selection as First Consul?* France wanted peace.

Bonaparte also wanted peace and order so that he could proceed with his monumental reconstruction and reform of the nation. The desires of people and Consul thus coincided on the issue of peace, especially since neither would have it on any other than French terms. When Bonaparte replied to the entreaties of the exiled Louis XVIII, he undoubtedly expressed the sentiments of the nation when he said: "You ought not to wish to return to France—you would have to trample across a hundred thousand bodies."[3] His letter to a subordinate, written one month earlier, also is clearly indicative of the national mood: "If we have war, I hope that we shall come out of it brilliantly; if we have peace, the foreign powers will be convinced that we were in a position to force it on them."[4] For all of its strategic brilliance, the victory at Marengo failed to convince "the foreign powers"; that role was reserved for Moreau, whose triumph at Hohenlinden six months later forced Austria to negotiate. However, Marengo did impress the French people, Bonaparte's prime audience. The thought of war at low cost has always been appealing, and this campaign had been quick and cheap. The increased popular support bought by this dazzling victory now encouraged him to bid for even greater power, this time in the form of personal rule.

Negotiations and Peace Treaties

It seems doubtful that many Frenchmen fully appreciated the extent of Bonaparte's thirst for power. Aside from Josephine, only a few close attendants, such as Marmont and Bourrienne, glimpsed the demon that drove their master. After Bonaparte's death, Sir Walter Scott wrote that while "he might have played the part of Washington, he preferred that of Cromwell."[5] This seems highly unlikely. For one thing, Bonaparte could hardly have restrained his dynamic will and put aside his personal ambitions, as Washington had done. For another, the young ruler had to satisfy the paradoxical desires of the French people. In the First Consul's own words, "between old monarchies and a young republic the spirit of hostility must always exist . . . my destiny is to be fighting almost continually."[6] Thus, the years of peace were only an interlude between general wars during which Bonaparte channeled his amazing capacity for work into negotiating for a stronger position in Europe and into the reconstruction of France.

Three years later he could point to impressive achievements: the Treaty of Lunéville with Austria (1801), the Peace of Amiens with England (1802), the Concordat with the Pope (1802), and the French-supervised restructuring of Germany (1803).

The Treaty of Lunéville (February 9, 1801) was a logical outcome of the military victories gained by France over the Hapsburg armies from 1793 to 1800. By this treaty, France regained those acquisitions Bonaparte had purchased with his triumphant campaigns and negotiations in 1796, 1797, and 1800. The most important of these possessions were the west bank of the Rhine, the Belgian provinces, and the Cisalpine Republic. *(See Atlas Map No. 12.)* "If faith is again broken with us," Bonaparte haughtily declared, "we shall immediately enter Prague, Vienna, and Venice." This was how France liked to win her peace, and the French people acclaimed their First Consul as "the savior and the father of his country."[7]

The Peace of Amiens, concluded between France and England the following year on March 27, 1802, occasioned little rejoicing in England, although that country had the most to gain from a treaty after Austria's withdrawal from the war in 1801 had left her to fight France alone. England had opposed France for compelling reasons. Many British leaders saw their role as maintaining the balance of power, which required preventing any one power from gaining hegemony on the Continent; others believed that Great Britain must deliver Europe from tyranny. The merchants viewed the war as a worldwide battle for markets. William Pitt, who resigned in 1801 after 18 years of service as Prime Minister, considered

Josephine

*The vote was 3,011,007 to 1,562 in favor of Bonaparte.

the fighting as "indemnity for the past, security for the future." Lord William Grenville, who became Prime Minister in 1806, stated the issue in very pragmatic terms: "whether the French should possess the whole of the maritime coast of the continent opposite to this country." England fought for all these reasons; no less did she fight because, for the better part of eight centuries, England and France had been at war. Small wonder that both sides viewed the treaty only as a truce. When questioned on the outcome of the negotiations, one British official dourly replied, "Peace, Sir, in a week, and war in a month."[8]

For Bonaparte, the treaty was a crowning success, in both foreign and domestic terms. Whereas England agreed to surrender her conquests in the Mediterranean (especially recently captured Egypt and Malta), Bonaparte refused to relinquish any of the French-occupied territories along the Rhine and in Italy. Already he had secretly annexed Piedmont, become the head of the Italian Republic (which had been the Cisalpine Republic), and begun to convert the Ligurian Republic (the old Republic of Genoa) into a French province. The Batavian Republic (Holland) and the Helvetic Republic (Switzerland) had long since fallen under French control, although not without diplomatic opposition from England. The Peace of Amiens, therefore, represented a stunning fulfillment of the spread of French power in Western Europe. *(See Atlas Map No. 12.)* England consoled herself by confirming her supremacy on the seas.

The Concordat with the Pope, signed by papal authorities in December 1801 and ratified by France in March 1802, was a masterpiece of statesmanship. This religious treaty authorized the Government to appoint bishops and archbishops, subject to confirmation by the Papacy. The Pope consented to the sale of church property confiscated during the Revolution. By this stroke, Bonaparte placated that substantial portion of France's population (the Roman Catholics) who had been hostile to the Revolution, while safeguarding the religious freedom of non-Catholic citizens. Lunéville and Amiens gave France a respite from military conflict; the Concordat stilled religious conflict. All three measures combined to gain even wider support from the French people for their leader's ambitious projects.

The problem of Germany still confronted Bonaparte. Enlightened despotism in the eighteenth century had made little progress toward modernizing the feudal mosaic of principalities, imperial cities, duchies, and church estates of the moribund Holy Roman Empire. With an eye on this disposable land, Bonaparte had promised in the Treaty of Lunéville to compensate Prussia and Austria for the territories France had seized west of the Rhine. He cleverly turned this promise into an opportunity to intervene in German affairs. Talleyrand arranged the complicated negotiations for property with two

Prince Charles Maurice Talleyrand

aims in mind: to pocket a small fortune in bribes from anxious title holders, and to pull the major German states of Prussia—Baden, Württemberg, and Bavaria—away from Austrian influence. This divide-and-rule policy increased the power of the larger German states at the expense of the smaller provinces and ecclesiastical estates. It also created some order in the political map of Germany and further diminished Austrian and Church influence in this key part of Europe. Negotiations ended in February 1803, at which time the Holy Roman Empire remained only in name. Having played the key role in restructuring Germany, Bonaparte now had ample precedent for future incursions across the Rhine. *(See Atlas Map No. 13.)*

This brief review of French political history necessarily slights domestic affairs. It should be noted that Bonaparte's domestic policy was essentially the same as his foreign policy. He sought to act in whatever way afforded the maximum support from the various elements of French society. In May 1802, he created the Legion of Honor to reward public service and distinguished military achievement. This distinction markedly resembled the old royal orders, and was stoutly opposed by the Council of State and the Legislature. But men will die for a bit of ribbon, as Bonaparte once cynically remarked, and the idea soon caught the imagination of soldier and civilian alike. In August, the First Consul extended his hold on the Government by obtaining popular consent to his Consulate for life, including the right to choose his own successor. Henceforth, Bonaparte dominated both executive and legislative functions. The dictatorship was edging ever closer to absolute monarchy.

Bonaparte's Tightening Control Over France

In addition to strengthening his grip on the operation of the Government and accelerating French expansion into neighboring territories, Bonaparte undertook a substantial program of reform in nearly every area of French public life. Education, commerce, public works, and law came under the close scrutiny of some of the brightest minds in France. Bonaparte himself participated in the discussions leading to reform. If an institution proved to be inefficient, he reorganized it; if an individual was incompetent, he replaced him; when he found unnecessary agencies, he abolished them. To this day, French Government, education, and law bear the stamp of Bonaparte's lasting reforms.

Even the First Consul's driving will could not have accomplished these feats of statesmanship without almost unconditional authority. By 1803, his mastery of France was almost as complete as Frederick's total control of the Prussian state had been half a century earlier, except that Frederick had ruled only 2.5 million obedient Prussians, whereas Bonaparte governed nearly 30 million loyal Frenchmen.* There was also an obvious difference in the nature of their regimes. Frederick, as "the First Servant of the State," chose to identify with the aristocracy and Government rather than the Prussian people. Bonaparte consciously adopted a pose that appealed to all social classes. Frederick served the Prussian state; Bonaparte personified the French nation. The implications of this difference are enormous, in terms of both political and military leadership.

Not all French citizens, civil or military, accepted Bonaparte's brand of dictatorship. A rebellious and renegade element still roamed the countryside, robbing travelers, kidnapping officials, and encouraging dissent. Royalists and extreme revolutionaries plotted conspiracies against Bonaparte's regime. Two of Bonaparte's army chiefs, Bernadotte and Moreau, also intrigued against the First Consul. In the legislative body there was a criticism of his arbitrary methods. Bonaparte reacted angrily to this opposition. He believed, like Frederick, that a system of government must be responsive to the decisions of a single executive, not bound to agreement of a corporate body. In political as well as military matters, the director must have full freedom to execute his designs. Even a constitution must not interfere with the governmental process. The Tribunate earned a characteristic rebuke for its debates on his policies: "In the Tribunate are a dozen or so metaphysicians only fit for the garbage heap. They are vermin on my clothes. I am a soldier, a son of the Revolution, and I will not tolerate being insulted like a king."[9]

*This was one-sixth of the population of Europe.

Marshal Jean Baptiste Bernadotte

Nor would Bonaparte tolerate criticism in the press or in literature. The Revolutionary Government had inaugurated censorship of the press. In 1799, Bonaparte sharply reduced the number of Parisian daily newspapers in an effort to control them. One, the *Moniteur*, became virtually an official organ. During the Marengo Campaign, he directed the Minister of Police to prohibit journalists from printing any information pertaining to movements of the Army. This man, who rode the currents of public opinion, understood too well that the printed word could be a dangerous weapon. "Three hostile newspapers are more to be feared than a thousand bayonets," he shrewdly observed. In 1803, he struck at his intellectual detractors, sending into exile the lively and outspoken Germaine de Staël, whose salon had become a center of political intrigue. Her books favored the ideal of freedom in speech and thought, but that kind of civil liberty had long since been sacrificed to the strengthening of central authority.[10]

Napoleon I

The circumstances leading to the establishment of the hereditary empire are well established. In Bonaparte's mind, the Consulate was only an interim step between the Republic and the Empire. The vote on the Consulate for life provided a favorable sounding of French opinion, but it took another threat of assassination to drive the First Consul to the final decision on imperial rule. French police, headed by arch intriguer Joseph Fouché,* discovered the conspiracy and quickly rounded up its leaders, including Moreau, a Royalist sympathizer. Interrogation of the conspirators revealed that they had planned to meet a Bourbon prince on French soil. Bonaparte promptly ordered a reprisal against the Duke of

Enghien, a descendant of the famous Prince of Condé. Enghien was kidnapped from Baden on March 15, 1804; one week later, he was tried and shot, both in the same night. Although the Duke of Enghien was not connected with the plot, this brutal repression effectively ended the conspiracy.

Following the Enghien incident, Fouché had no difficulty convincing the First Consul that the establishment of a hereditary dynasty would prevent further attempts on his life. Not surprisingly, the Senate and Tribunate promptly proclaimed Bonaparte emperor on May 18, and Pope Pius VII

*Of this clever and ambitious man, Napoleon said, "He needs intrigue like food . . . he is always in everybody's shoes."

The Coronation, December 2, 1804

Joseph Fouché

presided at the coronation on December 2, 1804. Placing the crown on his own head, Napoleon I completed the transformation of France into an instrument of aggression. The Constitution was amended to read that "the government is entrusted to an hereditary emperor," and the elevation of Napoleon to that office was ratified by a plebiscite (3,572,329 in favor, 2,569 opposed).[11]

At the time of the coronation, France and England nominally had been at war for 18 months. England declared war on May 16, 1803, after breaking off discussions regarding her refusal to surrender Malta. France retaliated by occupying Hanover and threatening England from the large army encampment at Boulogne. Now, with Napoleon crowned Emperor of France, that country seemed ready to dominate the Continent; it was equally clear that England seemed determined to fight to prevent such a French ascendancy. From 1804 on, it would have been extremely difficult for Napoleon to realign French foreign policies. The English declaration of war alone made the conflict a matter of national honor. Besides, Napoleon's irresistible impulse to play for higher stakes was bound to lead the armies of the Empire across the Rhine, and perhaps across the English Channel.

The Problem With England

If there was a definite tendency in the last half of the eighteenth century for European statesmen to view deliberate acts of war with supreme distaste, the new Emperor of the

French had no such reluctance to resort to the sword. In a private conversation prior to the coronation, he revealed his philosophy on the use of war as an instrument of policy: "A First Consul cannot be likened to these kings-by-the-grace-of-God, who look upon their states as a heritage. . . . His actions must be dramatic, and for this, war is indispensable."[12] No matter that he was about to make the French state itself into an inheritance; the important thing was that the British had, for once, surprised him by abruptly breaking off negotiations over their retention of Malta and then declaring war. The experiment with peace had ended.

No amount of flaming verbiage could hide the fact that France was poorly prepared to strike directly at England. French engineers worked overtime to renovate the harbors near Boulogne, but shipbuilders could hardly match the British numbers in sail. In fact, both antagonists were ill-prepared to enter into the sort of death struggle required to achieve a clear-cut victory. Aside from a cross-Channel invasion, infeasible in 1803, how could France have forced the decision? On the other hand, how could the mistress of the seas strike at France, whose repository of power lay in her land forces?

The key to this dilemma seemed to lie in economic warfare. Commerce was the lifeblood of England, and overseas trade her Achilles' heel. At the same time, France's major weakness was a shortage of capital. Napoleon resolved to interdict Britain's trade by threatening the choke points of the Mediterranean, closing the Dutch ports to British commerce, and occupying Hanover. *(See Atlas Map No. 13.)* In the process, however, he injured his own commerce and nearly plunged the country into fiscal ruin. Mercantilism was the wrong game to play with "the nation of shopkeepers," as Frenchmen derisively termed their adversary.

It would take an invasion, or the threat of invasion, to overcome British intransigence. But no amount of revolutionary fervor could improvise a fleet—the *sine qua non* for any successful amphibious operation. Admiral Sir William Cornwallis' squadrons persistently hugged the coast and blockaded French warships in Brest, offering daily, visible evidence of the combat superiority that no French admiral dared to challenge.[13] Not only did British naval forces outnumber the French, but constant sea service had maintained their edge over the French in all aspects of seamanship, gunnery, and signaling. French naval strategy reverted to the theory of the "fleet in being" and to commerce raiding. By mobilizing the shipbuilding resources of the Continent, Napoleon hoped to augment his fleet sufficiently to wear down the British Navy, which was forced to disperse for patrol and blockade. He thus hoped to nullify the British naval advantage without ever fighting the British fleet.

In land operations, Napoleon's strategy rarely conformed

to set plans. He usually projected his deployment in order to develop the situation—to draw enemy forces out of their chosen positions and create an opening that his fast-moving army could exploit. He could calculate rates of movement for his corps and divisions with fair precision, and a delay encountered because of weather or mischance could always be made up by one of those electrifying forced marches that was the hallmark of French infantry. In other words, land operations were largely a function of the skill of soldier and commander. In naval operations, however, there was a third element in the strategic equation—weather. A fickle wind might becalm a fleet for days; a storm could do as much damage to a flotilla as a squadron of British ships of the line.

For some reason, Napoleon never completely excused his admirals for failing to conquer the elements. In his mind, the conquest of the Alps and the desert had proved that there was no such word as impossible in the French language. Perhaps his understanding of maritime policy was limited by his experience in the relatively placid Mediterranean. Whatever the cause, on naval issues there was definitely a blind spot in Napoleon's thinking. Although he studied naval affairs avidly, he often overcommitted his naval forces, and never learned to coordinate land and sea strategy properly. His inability to invade England from 1803 to 1805 should have alerted him to the gravity of this shortcoming. In any other year except victorious 1805, the defeat at Trafalgar might have tempered his overconfidence.

Trafalgar

When England declared war, France had only 14 ships of the line capable of getting underway. The Dutch Navy had 17, but most of these were committed to the Indies. England promptly clamped a blockade on the key French ports (Boulogne, Brest, and Toulon). Napoleon ordered 100 vessels to be ready to sail from Dunkirk in mid-August, but only 21 were ready. He impatiently postponed the enterprise until 1804. To carry out his daring scheme, he calculated the need for at least 100,000 troops, which would require a transport fleet of 1,300 craft assembled at Boulogne. In the spring of 1804, there were over 900 flatboats available, but during a rehearsal, a storm broke up the formation. In any event, the fleet could not be deployed from Boulogne on a single tide.

In 1804, the British Admiralty prepared a sanguine assessment of England's chances if the French attempted to "leap the ditch": "This seems a very desperate attempt, and is likely to terminate in the destruction of their fleet."[14] However, if Napoleon did decide to risk everything in an invasion attempt, the Admiralty astutely recognized that "we are not at liberty to calculate solely on what is rational or probable, but we must likewise keep in view such contingencies as may be barely possible, and such as passion and intemperance may give rise to." To guard against the "contingencies as may be barely possible," the Admiralty placed the main blockading force in a central position off Brest. From there, Cornwallis' squadrons could sail immediately in pursuit of a fleet moving toward the West Indies, reinforce the squadrons blockading lesser ports in the Bay of Biscay, or, in the event of highest alarm, concentrate with other forces to bar the crossing of the Straits of Gibraltar.

Meanwhile, Napoleon made grandiose plans, ordering the fleet at Toulon to evade Nelson's blockade, sail into the Atlantic, swing wide around Cornwallis' striking force, and drive for the Channel. "Let us be masters of the straits for six hours, and we shall be masters of the world."[15] The grand venture had to be postponed, however, when the commander of the Toulon fleet died. Napoleon then abandoned the invasion plan, turning again to commerce raiding, colonial enterprises, and his continental designs. Through the winter of 1804–1805 he negotiated separately with Prussia, Austria, and Russia while luring Spain into an alliance. Then, in March 1805, the Emperor abruptly decided to attempt an invasion in the coming summer. At the same time, continuing his expansionary policy, he accepted the crown of the Kingdom of Italy and, in June, annexed Genoa. This was one step too many for Austria, which now concerted with Russia for military operations against the House of Bonaparte.

Even with the massive *Correspondance de Napoleon I* at their disposal, historians are not in agreement on Napoleon's exact intentions in the summer of 1805. Why did he challenge Austria in Italy at the same time he planned to invade England 600 miles away? To provide an alternative outlet for war if his naval strategy failed? Or simply to retain the initiative simultaneously on all fronts? On the other hand, was the camp at Boulogne, with its 93,000 soldiers, 2,700 horses, and supporting vessels, merely a demonstration to deceive all of Europe, rather than a force designed to conquer England? Did he plan from the beginning to strike for Vienna rather than London?

The answer to the last question, at least, seems to be no. This immensely complex individual preferred to maintain alternatives, considering and discarding each as the odds shifted. However, his orders to his naval commanders were unmistakable: to combine the Brest and Toulon fleets for a diversionary dash to the West Indies, followed by a combined trans-Atlantic drive on the Channel where they would rendezvous with the Boulogne flotilla. Once again, French troops and their restless commander waited only for favorable winds "to carry the imperial eagle against the Tower of London." *(See Atlas Map No. 14.)*

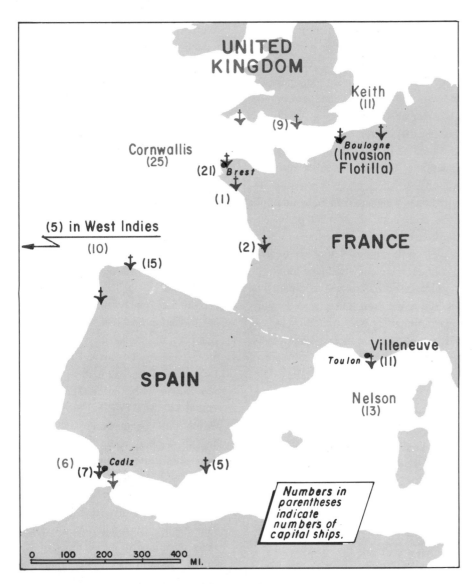

The Naval Situation, March 1805

Favorable winds were not enough. Although Admiral Pierre Villeneuve, the commander of the Toulon fleet, made good his escape and threw Nelson completely off the scent, the Brest fleet could not slip away from Cornwallis' watchdogs. Napoleon jeopardized Villeneuve's complicated and perilous task by dispatching repeated changes of mission to him. One message directed him to return by way of Scotland; the next, to wait in the West Indies for the Brest fleet, and, in the event it failed to appear, to proceed to Biscay, release the Brest fleet, and sail for the Channel.*

While Napoleon was maneuvering ships on the map, Nelson at last terminated his fruitless search of the empty Mediterranean, disobeyed standing orders to return to the

Channel if the French fleet escaped, and set out in hot pursuit of Villeneuve. The Frenchman departed from the West Indies with a one-month lead and eluded Nelson on the return crossing by sailing a northerly route. After this harrowing experience, Villeneuve's courage failed. Instead of following Napoleon's latest orders to sail for Brest, he retired to Cadiz. Nelson finally caught up with him and, at Cape Trafalgar on October 21, 1805, British superiority in tactics and Nelson's daring leadership brought about a classic battle of annihilation.[16] Suddenly, the threat of invasion was eliminated, and the seas again became a British imperium, never again to be contested directly by Napoleon.

Two months before the Battle of Trafalgar, however, the French Emperor had decided to turn the French ground forces eastward against Austrian concentrations that were building up in southern Germany, thereby negating any serious plans

---

*Since Nelson's thrashing of the French fleet at Aboukir Bay, French admirals —especially Villeneuve—were no match for England's hardy sea dogs.

Viscount Horatio Nelson

From the Channel to the Rhine

A blast of trumpets announced the change of mission to the troops, ending their two-year vigil on the Channel coast. Napoleon wrote: "My mind is made up. My movement has begun; by September 17, I shall be in Germany with 200,000 men."[17] Even the most experienced soldiers must have been unsettled by the confusion that attended the breakup of the Boulogne camp. One non commissioned officer, a veteran of fighting at Marengo, wrote in his memoirs that the artillery in his camp was on the march within an hour. Hussars contested with dragoons for the right of way, while *fusiliers** of the line regiments, slower to assemble, repacked their knapsacks, drew on their black felt hats, and threw away the accumulated debris that clutters every peacetime bivouac. Months of training, rehearsals, practice loading drills, and occasional forays onto rough Channel waters were soon to be forgotten as 50 infantry regiments and 180 cavalry squadrons began one of the most wearing marches in history.[18]

For three weeks, marching soldiers filled three main routes from the coast to the Rhine. This grand movement was far from the clockwork deployment that Helmuth von Moltke and the German General Staff perfected half a century later. Traffic clogged and blocked the routes through some of the smaller towns, especially those in the restricted Alsatian hill country.

*Hussars were light cavalrymen; dragoons originally were mounted infantry, but they gradually came to be considered a special form of cavalry; *fusiliers* were the standard infantrymen.

for an invasion of England. The resounding victories the *Grande Armée* was to win in southern Germany and Austria during the last three months of 1805 would overshadow Nelson's pivotal victory at Trafalgar, concealing for a time the French naval weakness that was important and enduring.

Napoleon Awards the Legion of Honor at the Camp of Boulogne

Arrangements for quartering were incomplete. Artillery and engineer units arrived in Strasbourg without their full complement of men and equipment. Cavalry squadrons were so short of horses that many of the dragoon squadrons moved on foot. As a result, by September 17 the *Grande Armée* was not in Germany, as the Emperor had willed, but was crowded into a number of assembly areas, strung along the Rhine from Mainz to Strasbourg. *(See Atlas Map No. 14.)*

One officer, whose unit was billeted in Strasbourg, later recalled that "men and horses were bivouacked in the streets; the wagons of the artillery and the heaps of stores and equipment choked them; there was such a muddle that one hardly knew where one was."[19] Prince Murat, commander of the Reserve Cavalry, wrote to the Emperor: "Sire, we are far from being organized . . . no hospital wagons; the battalions of the train are still en route; our artillery is being hauled by requisitioned horses."[20] Napoleon arrived in Strasbourg on September 26, too late to reorganize his administrative services and put order into the chaotic supply system. Nevertheless, in spite of shortages in horses, pontoons, and guns, his subordinates were already carrying out his orders; downstream from Strasbourg, the corps of Marshals Michel Ney, Nicolas Jean Soult, and Louis Nicolas Davout had begun crossing the Rhine.

In view of these material shortcomings, how could Napoleon have launched the campaign without serious misgivings? The answer to this quesiton lies partly in his buoyant, impetuous nature, and partly in his understanding of men—a factor often overlooked by war ministries that concern themselves largely with the development and procurement of weapons, while neglecting to ready their soldiers. Combat readiness, in Napoleon's mind, was a matter of confidence. He had every reason to be assured, because, in spite of its many technical defects, the *Grande Armée* was far superior in experience and vitality to any other fighting force in Europe.

The Grande Armée

The proud little Army of Italy had never counted more than 50,000 men in its ranks. Records of the *Grande Armée* for July 1805 show a total of 446,000, including units disposed in Hanover, Holland, France, and Italy. In September, Napoleon's main battle force available for deployment numbered roughly 200,000 men,* and included troop units stationed

*By comparison, the Duke of Marlborough never commanded more than 60,000; Frederick the Great usually operated with 30,000 to 40,000; Robert E. Lee commanded no more than 90,000 in the Civil War; each of Moltke's armies numbered roughly 100,000 in 1870; and the strength of George Patton's Third Army ranged from 200,000 to half a million in 1944 and 1945.

from Hanover in the north to points in France as far south as Brest.[21] Thus, the most striking features of Napoleon's *Grande Armée* were its size and its reach. In addition to these obvious assets, the army was vibrantly professional.

The Manpower

At least one-fourth of the army's manpower consisted of veterans of the wars fought under the Republican regime, while another quarter had fought at Marengo or Hohenlinden. The remainder were conscripts. Few were volunteers. From 1803 on, recruits entered the army, not for a fixed term of service, but for the duration of the war. In 1805, the army was, therefore, neither wholly regular nor largely citizen. Discipline was primarily functional. The recruit looked to the veteran for advice and guidance, but neither recruit nor veteran paid much attention to the trappings of barracks and parade ground. On the battlefield, they followed orders because they trusted their leaders and their leaders understood them. Perhaps this mixture of veteran and conscript was ideally suited to promote the enterprise and daring that then characterized French military professionalism. After the campaigns of 1805 and 1806, the percentage of veterans increased and the army became more regularized. Whether it became more professional is open to question.

In some respects, the officer corps had less expertise than the soldiery. The most common method of becoming an officer was by appointment from the ranks. Bravery and daring

Marshal Michel Ney

were the principal criteria for selection, and subsequent advancement depended entirely on merit, not on noble birth, as had been the case in the monarchial regime. This allowed a number of able individuals to make an astonishingly rapid climb in rank,* especially in the Revolutionary years, when over half of the 9,000 officers on active duty fled from the country.[22] In later years, however, younger officers encountered a decided obstacle to promotion, since the incumbents, having been promoted early to the top positions, were still young enough to hold their jobs ten or fifteen years later. There was little incentive within the officer corps for self-preparation and improvement. Satisfied with their remarkable record of victories, most officers saw no reason to devote the leisure time between campaigns to any extensive program of education or training.

The Weapons

The weaponry of the *Grande Armée* was superior to that of other European armies, but it still left a great deal to be desired. The principal characteristics of French gunpowder weapons were that they were muzzle-loading, smooth-bore, short-range, and inaccurate. Also, they were generally cheap, which eased the financial burden of arming the large numbers of troops making up the mass army. The Charleville Musket, Model 1777, was only effective against individual targets out to a range of 50–100 yards, and against formations to 200 yards. It used a large charge of black powder, which created a kick hard enough to dislocate a shoulder, and caused the first few volleys to shroud the battlefield in smoke. The weapon was slow to load and troublesome to keep clean. Such a firearm was hardly an improvement on the Prussian model used by Frederick's "walking batteries" half a century earlier. The *fusilier* carried between 40 and 50 rounds in his cartridge box, and to complete his armament, he also carried a bayonet. The standard bayonet was about 15 inches long

*Michel Ney, for example, was a sergeant major in 1792, a colonel in 1794, a general of brigade in 1796, a general of division in 1799, and a marshal of France in 1804. It took Marshal Soult six years to make sergeant; after gaining his commission, however, he needed only two years to become a general.

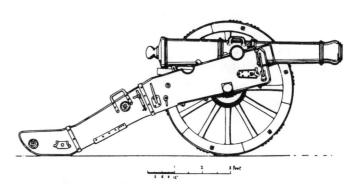

French Artillery Piece

and was equally dangerous to its owner and his enemy—indeed, more so to the former when he was trying to load his musket. No doubt, it was the sight of cold steel, as much as its actual employment, that caused an enemy to evacuate the battlefield. Napoleon's surgeon general, Doctor Larrey, discovered that less than five percent of the wounds inflicted in one engagement were caused by the bayonet. The rest were caused by bullets and the resultant infections.[23]

Although artillery weapons were of somewhat better construction than those used in the Seven Years' War, the many minor improvements in metallurgy, carriage construction, and gunpowder had done little to enhance the capability of the standard pieces. The 12-pounder cannon could fire shot at no greater range than 1,800 meters, and its maximum effective range was only one kilometer.* Ammunition was designed for a loose fit, recoil mechanisms were still unknown, and sights were crude. As a consequence, artillery fire was not very accurate. However, thorough training of artillery crews contributed to some spectacular displays of shooting. A few gunners learned to handle their weapons well enough to enable them to hit buildings, bridges, or even small groups of men at maximum range. At close range, fire with canister or grape† can only be described as murderous.

Cavalry weapons included an assortment of lances and long thrusting swords for the heavy cavalry (*cuirassiers*);

*Tube and carriage for this piece each weighed nearly a ton.

†See Glossary, under "artillery ammunition," p. 171.

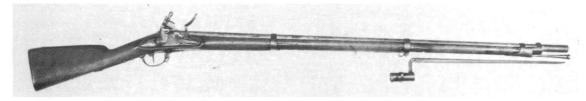

The Charleville Musket

heavy, curved sabers for the light cavalry (hussars and *chasseurs à cheval*); and various modifications of dragoon muskets, musketoons, and carbines. The firearms were light, short, and highly inaccurate. Probably the major factor bearing on the effectiveness of cavalry weapons was the degree of training given to man and horse.

The Tactics

These were the resources on which French commanders had to depend as they formulated their tactical methods— weapons little improved by a century of relatively stable technology, large numbers of patriotic troops, an unwritten doctrine of improvisation, and the imagination of men. Almost all of the regimental, division, and corps commanders had served during the Revolutionary War and had observed the fearful casualties that resulted from the use of the rigid, linear system of tactics. At the same time, they appreciated the value of the new open-order tactics, which placed a screen of skirmishers in front of the advancing battalion columns. *
Yet no one was willing to give up entirely the firepower of battalions firing from the line formation. Most officers preferred to use the *ordre mixte* formation, which was a combination of the best features of column, linear, and skirmisher formations. A demi-brigade in *ordre mixte* formation would usually deploy its three battalions behind a line of skirmishers, two being in battalion column formation while the third was formed linearly (its companies in line). Under the tactics of this system, a swarm of skirmishers moved forward and commenced sniping from covered positions to fix the enemy's attention. Under cover of this energetic fire and accompanying artillery fire, battalions in column formation advanced to close-in positions from which the assault was launched. When the division commander timed his movements properly, the attacking columns sometimes covered the distance from assault position to enemy line without coming under fire. Depending on the terrain, assaulting formations could expect to suffer sustained fire across less than 200 yards of ground. It was, therefore, essential that these last 200 yards be covered as quickly as possible, on the run, and preferably without stopping to fire. A successful attack was more often the product of vigor on the part of assaulting columns and initiative on the part of skirmishers than, as in the case of Frederick's well-drilled Army, the culmination of the steady advance of a rigid line of volley-firing infantry.

Napoleon held his cavalry forces in reserve for employment in mass. However, he did not keep his cavalry squadrons on as tight a leash as did Frederick. Once the cavalry units were committed, the cavalry commander (Murat or Bessières) controlled the charge, while the commander-in-chief observed, rather than directed, the action. Napoleon frequently used his *cuirassier* squadrons to countercharge the Austrian cavalry. Dragoons either formed on the flanks to guard against surprise attacks, or served as security in the rear. Hussars performed their traditional functions of providing a screen or reconnoitering, a role in which French cavalry outshone all its European counterparts.

French cavalry commanders labored under two severe handicaps. The flight of the nobility during the Revolution had eliminated most of the cavalry's leaders. These were gradually replaced by men from the ranks and some returned émigrés. The second problem was that of horse supply. Napoleon's principal source of horses lay outside the country, with the exception of several large horse farms in France. However, horses were almost prohibitively expensive, and the impoverished French treasury never could afford to buy enough horses to satisfy the needs of cavalry, artillery, and logistic trains. Considering the relative importance of these three consumers, perhaps Napoleon decided correctly in accepting shortages in his cavalry.

The Emperor would not accept shortages in cannon, having stated that "it is with artillery that war is made." He clearly believed his own precept, and personally supervised the management of his artillery resources. His goal was to supply 5 guns per 1,000 men, but he rarely had more than 3 per 1,000. Heavy and medium guns (12- and 8-pounders) and some light artillery (6-pounders) formed the artillery reserve and the artillery with the corps. Light artillery, including some captured guns, was attached to the divisions.* Napoleon abolished the regimental artillery, which had been a standard feature of Gustavus' and Frederick's Armies, in order to gain greater centralization and heavier weight of fire. However, as the quality of his infantry declined (beginning in 1809), he was forced to return to the regimental artillery system. Like Frederick, he steadily substituted massed firepower for tactical expertise. French artillery fired massed concentrations at Friedland in 1807, Wagram in 1809, Leipzig in 1813, and Waterloo in 1815. At Leipzig alone there were 600 French cannon.† Compare this number with the meager total of 60 with which the Army of Italy had begun its spectacular campaigns.[24]

---

* A battalion column was a formation in which the eight companies of the battalion were deployed in a column of four divisions, each division consisting of two companies abreast. The two companies in the division were deployed in line in three ranks; divisions of the two companies were about three yards apart in depth, thus creating the column.

*Normally, a company (battery) of foot artillery consisted of six guns and two howitzers. A horse artillery company contained six guns, but no howitzers.

†In spite of this tremendous increase in artillery, Napoleon was habitually inferior in numbers of guns on the battlefield, even at Leipzig.

In theory, it is a simple matter to combine infantry, artillery, and cavalry formations in such a way as to stage a coordinated, combined-arms attack. The history of warfare, however, is a record of the rarity of such occurrences, suggesting that it may well be one of the most difficult tasks of the general officer. A comparison between the tactical procedures employed by Frederick and Napoleon is instructive. Frederick sought to coordinate the attack by gaining dominance over every part of his enemy. His subordinate commanders were instantly responsive to his direction. Napoleon strove for the same goal by the assignment of tasks to orient his subordinate commanders on a common objective and plan. Napoleon rarely interfered in tactical execution, leaving that to corps and division commanders, except in a few setpiece battles like Austerlitz in 1805 and Friedland in 1807. Napoleon believed in thorough planning, but never passed up a chance to damage his enemy just because the occasion did not fit his original scheme. As a consequence, in many fluid engagements, Napoleon committed forces piecemeal, sacrificing coordination to exploit larger opportunities. The Battle of Jena in 1806 is a classic example of a highly successful piecemeal attack.*

There were other significant differences between Frederician and Napoleonic tactics. Frederick built his tactical method around the infantry, which formed the backbone of his army's defense and the spearhead of its attack. Cavalry and artillery complemented the infantry. There were no clearly distinguishable main and supporting attacks, and no reserve, although Frederick did weight the part of his force he expected to hurl against the decisive point in the enemy's line. Essentially, Frederick's army was a rigid body of troops that marched and fought in one massed formation. He relied on speed during deployment and discipline during the assault to overpower his opponent. Napoleon's army fought in loose, articulated formations, in which subordinate commanders had at their command all the resources—infantry, cavalry, and artillery—needed for semi-independent action. All three combat arms were equally important, although on certain occasions one or the other may have played a predominant role, such as the infantry at Arcola in 1796, or the cavalry at Eylau in 1807. Also, Napoleon usually retained a strong reserve for commitment to clinch the victory. The Imperial Guard—an elite, combined-arms team, heavy in cavalry—served this function admirably.

Perhaps the most significant difference between the two tactical doctrines lay in the conception of the battle itself. The typical battle of the eighteenth century was a formal, setpiece affair. Napoleon, however, thought of battle as a sort of

meeting engagement. The side that reacted quickest and with the firmest grasp of the situation could achieve a decisive victory, like an author ending a drama with a sudden, unexpected twist of plot. Strategy and tactics merged in Napoleon's conception of war. Campaign and battle developed as a whole, since "it is often in the system of campaign that one conceives the system of battle."[25] However, Napoleon rarely expected decisive battle to occur at a predetermined time and place. His common sense told him that a thousand accidents of human nature, weather, and geography could spoil the most elaborate plan. He was fully prepared to react to the offerings of chance, as long as he had his army firmly in hand.

The Corps System

The device with which Napoleon steered the *Grande Armée* was an elaborate organizational arrangement known as the corps system. In 1805, the *Grande Armée* consisted principally of seven *Corps d'Armée*, each staffed the same, but composed of varying combinations of troop units. Essentially, the corps was a control headquarters to which a number of combat divisions and support units were assigned. The corps was a combined-arms formation, including sufficient infantry, artillery, cavalry, engineer, and service units to operate independently for several days. In theory, a corps with two or three infantry divisions, a light cavalry division, several companies of artillery and engineers, and its own trains was expected to hold off an entire army of the old unitary type, at least until the rest of the *Grande Armée* could reinforce. The table on page 34 gives some idea of the varied composition of corps on the day in 1805 when the French army crossed the Rhine.[26]

The corps marched dispersed, a condition dictated by the requirement for foraging. A cavalry screen moved ahead of the formation to cover the advance of the army and to seek out the enemy's main strength. During the march to contact, all corps remained within supporting distance, a range that Napoleon himself plotted on the map when planning each day's moves. Napoleon concentrated the army when contact was made with strong enemy forces, or when reliable intelligence disclosed the enemy's exact location and strength.

The key to the corps system thus lay in the capability it gave the *Grande Armée* to march dispersed and to concentrate for fighting. In place of the detailed regulations for maneuver and deployment prescribed by most European armies, the French corps operated by what might be called standing operating procedure (SOP). Corps commanders trained their divisions, to be sure, using the drill regulations of 1791. Nonetheless, they kept an open mind regarding march tech-

---

* A piecemeal attack is one in which the various units of a force are employed as they become available.

Corps	Commander	Infantry Divisions	Cavalry Divisions	Battalions	Squadrons	Strength
I	Bernadotte	2	1	18	16	17,737
II	Marmont	3	1	25	12	20,758
III	Davout	3	1	28	12	27,452
IV	Soult	4	1	40	12	41,358
V	Lannes	2	1	18	16	17,788
VI	Ney	3	1	25	12	24,409
VII	Augereau	2	—	16	4	14,850
Cavalry	Murat	—	6	8	120	23,415
Guard	Bessières	—	—	12	8	6,278
						194,045

The *Grande Armée* in September 1805

niques and battle formations, altering regulations and devising new procedures to fit the situation. Although Napoleon rarely interfered in the tactical domain of corps and division commanders, he insisted that subordinate units follow his march instructions explicitly. Only by planning the pattern of movement in advance could he conceive campaign strategy as a whole; only by demanding that units adhere to his march schedule could he feel free to alter his strategy without throwing the army into hopeless confusion. Once a corps engaged an enemy force, control of the battle passed largely to the corps commander. The corps commander was expected to maneuver aggressively to fix the enemy and to develop the situation. Meanwhile, the nearest corps was under strict standing orders, "to march to the sound of the guns," not to wait for detailed instructions. Until such time as the Emperor received the first fragmentary reports of the engagement, corps commanders were, therefore, expected to react on their own and support each other. This policy reduced reaction time and contributed to the offensive spirit that distinguished the French Army from its more lethargic adversaries.

If Napoleon expected his corps commanders to handle their corps semi-independently, it was essential that this select group of leaders be endowed with special talents. Foremost among their qualifications was courage. The corps commander had to lead by example. In a hot fight on the outskirts of a Bavarian town, Marshal Lannes grabbed a scaling ladder from his men and shouldered his way to the forefront of the action, exclaiming to his troops, "I was a grenadier before I was a marshal!"[27] With such dramatic leadership, there was little the French soldier would not attempt.

The successful marshal also had to have enough resourcefulness to overcome the many obstacles that topography, climate, and enemy conspired to place in his way. The crossing of the Rhine in 1805 was an improvised operation, since the engineers were late in installing pontoons; the passage of cannon past Fort Bard in 1800 was accomplished by moving them at night directly down the road after spreading straw on the road and wrapping the wheels in rags to deaden the sound

of their movement. Napoleon accepted no excuses for a corps' failure to arrive on time. It was up to the corps commander to demonstrate the necessary initiative, guided by the Emperor's profound encouragement: "In war, all that is useful is legitimate."[28]

Armed with these traits of character and a certain flair, an ambitious soldier could go a long way toward becoming a marshal of the Empire. However, it was also important for a corps commander to refrain from asking questions. "I alone know what I want done," Napoleon wrote to Berthier in 1806.[29] All too many times, this proved to be true. Only a few of the marshals possessed the intellect and instinct to divine Napoleon's intentions. Consequently, while they were all excellent tacticians, only Davout and Massena were capable of the kind of judgment needed for independent command. By contrast, hotheads like Ney and Augereau occasionally jeopardized the larger goal by their overly zealous actions, and Murat's vanity was frequently the cause of error on a grand scale.

Any accurate assessment of this curious and colorful collection of warriors must grant their human weaknesses, as Napoleon surely allowed for them. He was willing to put up with their foibles and confer upon them titles, riches, and glory, if only to have their impetuous leadership at his call during those moments of crisis when the fate of the Empire depended on the daring feats of a few brave men.

Imperial Headquarters

One of the hazards of high command is the inherent tendency of a large staff to form a barrier between the general and his troops. When the *Grande Armée* slipped across the Rhine in September, there were over 400 officers serving in the *Grande Quartiers Général*, and this was only a fraction of the strength it attained in the next five years. Napoleon himself encouraged the growth of his headquarters, especially as his dual task as Emperor of an expanding empire and general of

Marshal Louis-Alexandre Berthier

an undefeated army became more demanding. However, Napoleon's personal manner of command guarded against the dangers of staff bureaucracy. The army definitely responded to its commander, rather than to his staff.

Imperial headquarters was primarily an operational, rather than an administrative, agency. The Intendant General, who was responsible for the administrative services of the army, was physically and functionally separate from Napoleon's military household. The headquarters proper was divided into two groups—the *Maison*, which worked directly for Napoleon, and the General Staff, which was supervised by Marshal Berthier, Prince of Neuchâtel. The *Maison* included two main branches: the Cabinet, in which were located three offices (the Intelligence Bureau, the Topographical Bureau, and the Emperor's personal secretariat), and a platoon of aides and orderlies who performed a variety of special functions, such as reconnaissance, the delivery and explanation of important orders, diplomatic negotiations, and even the temporary command of task forces for critical missions. The Cabinet was the closest thing to a war room in the headquarters, and the Emperor favored its members with a personal relationship of the kind reserved only for the dedicated and select group of men who work in intimate, daily contact with high-level commanders. The aides and orderlies were chosen for their demonstrated abilities as troop leaders. Napoleon placed more trust in their judgment and intelligence than he did in any other group on his staff. These dashing officers rode to every corner of the Empire representing the extension of Napoleon's command.

Berthier personally supervised the General Staff, which was a large and rather loosely organized body of personnel that performed a variety of military and diplomatic functions. A staff officer was expected to handle a number of different tasks, rather than become an expert in any one area. There was none of the extreme specialization that began to characterize military staffs during the nineteenth century. A certain amount of duplication and inefficiency was accepted in return for the flexibility afforded by this more unstructured arrangement. The chief purpose of the staff was to maintain a fund of information on various subjects of interest to the Commander-in-Chief. The cheerful and punctual Berthier managed his domain so well that he was rarely at a loss when the Emperor needed to know some obscure fact. He could always find, somewhere in the staff's elaborate card files, detailed information on such diverse subjects as the condition of roads; the number of artillery pieces in each depot; and the status of each regiment, including the name and record of its commander, its strength, and its latest recorded location. Berthier also supervised the issuance of orders, although it may be doubted that he always understood exactly what Napoleon intended by them.

Although Napoleon used his staff in the decision-making process, he refused to let the staff channel his thinking. He also discouraged original thinking by his staff officers. His mind was the source of all decisions; he alone formulated and updated the courses of action under consideration, determined their feasibility, and calculated odds. The staff merely produced the information needed to fill gaps in his estimate. He first consulted his intelligence bureau and his maps. Then, in the words of an admiring disciple, Baron Henri Jomini, he proceeded to dictate "those instructions which are alone enough to make any man famous."[30]

However, issuing orders is only the bare beginning of a commander's responsibility. To insure full compliance with his will, Napoleon exercised the magnetic power of his personality on his subordinate commanders. When campaigning, he moved his headquarters as often as necessary in order to be near the front. Each day he rode out to visit corps commanders, regimental officers, and soldiers of the line. He personally checked the condition of his army, and he inspired as many men as possible with his own driving energy. To facilitate his supervisory efforts, he normally used a small tactical command post, which included selected members of the staff, two or three aides, and an escort of several cavalry squadrons. If urgent business developed elsewhere, an aide galloped to the appropriate commander with written orders, an understanding of the Emperor's desires, and the authority to make changes on the spot. Meanwhile, routine reports flowed from corps to army headquarters, and by midnight, the staff compiled the detailed information of unit dispositions on which Napoleon based his orders for the next day's operations. Napoleon issued guidance in those orders, but he directed by his personal presence.

During the first Italian Campaign, many astonished observers believed that Berthier was the guiding brain behind Napoleon's success. This opinion gained some credibility among advocates of the staff process, who pointed to Napoleon's loss at Waterloo as proof that, without his chief of staff, the commander could not control his army. There were other more important causes for Napoleon's defeat, just as there were more important reasons for his victories. The staff system was an adjunct to his dynamic method of command; Napoleon exercised generalship as much from his carriage as from his headquarters. However, the very able men on his staff, especially Berthier and aides like Generals Rapp and Savary, were important assistants. Because of Napoleon's highly centralized method of command, the staff never developed into a modern, deliberative agency, but remained an effective instrument of execution.

There is no way to know for sure what ultimate goal Napoleon had in mind when he marched the *Grande Armée* eastward in 1805. Historians have debated vigorously and inconclusively over whether Napoleon planned to resurrect the kingdom of Charlemagne or only to chastise Austria for defying him; whether he still viewed England as his main antagonist or only as a support to the Third Coalition; whether he intended to withdraw his legions from Germany or maintain a military presence east of the Rhine. Regardless of historical interpretations, one fact must have been evident in 1805: when French troops marched across the natural boundary, Napoleon was continuing a process of expansion that was becoming increasingly difficult to restrain. In the years of the Republic and the Consulate, France could justify its offensive strategy by claiming the need of *La Grande Nation* for suitable protective boundaries. When the *Grande Armée* marched across the Rhine in the summer of 1805, no rationale excused French aggression, other than a desire to expand the French empire.

Notes

[1]Robert R. Palmer, *The Age of the Democratic Revolution* (2 vols.; Princeton, 1959, 1964), II, 10–16, 64–65; Jacques Godechot, et al., *The Napoleonic Era in Europe*, trans. by B. Hyslop (New York, 1971), pp. 107–110; Crane Brinton, *A Decade of Revolution, 1789–1799* (New York, 1934), pp. 94–102, 164–189; Carl von Clausewitz, *On War*, trans. by O. J. Matthijs Jolles (New York, 1943), pp. 580–584.

[2]Miot de Melito, *Memoirs*, trans. by C. Hoie and J. Lillie (New York, 1881), p. 167. See also Louis Madelin, *The Consulate and the Empire*, trans. by E. F. Buckley (2 vols.; New York, 1934–1936), I, 35–41.

[3]Madelin, *The Consulate and the Empire*, I, 94.

[4]John E. Howard (ed.), *Letters and Documents of Napoleon* (1 vol. to date; New York, 1961–), I, 384.

[5]Sir Walter Scott, *The Life of Napoleon Buonaparte, Emperor of the French* (3 vols.; Philadelphia, 1827), I, 463.

[6]Felix Markham, *Napoleon* (New York, 1963), p. 95.

[7]Madelin, *The Consulate and the Empire*, I, 108–109.

[8]Harold Deutsch, *The Genesis of Napoleonic Imperialism* (Cambridge, 1938), pp. 29–36.

[9]George Lefebvre, *Napoleon: From 18 Brumaire to Tilsit, 1799–1807*, trans. by H. F. Stockhold (New York, 1969), p. 131.

[10]For a thorough explanation of the interaction of Bonaparte's foreign policies and domestic reforms, see Madelin, *The Consulate and the Empire*, I, 101–163; and Leo Gershoy, *The French Revolution and Napoleon* (New York, 1964), pp. 348–381. On the subject of control of the media, see Godechot, *The Napoleonic Era in Europe*, pp. 44, 170, 256–257; Pieter Geyl, *Napoleon: For and Against*, trans. by O. Renier (New Haven, 1949), pp. 19–22; Leo Gershoy, *The French Revolution and Napoleon* (New York, 1964), pp. 356–357; Madelin, *The Consulate and the Empire*, I, 38, 51–54.

[11]Godechot, *The Napoleonic Era in Europe*, pp. 76–78: The quote in the footnote is taken from the biographical sketches in Vincent J. Esposito and John R. Elting, *A Military History and Atlas of the Napoleonic Wars* (New York, 1964).

[12]Lefebvre, *Napoleon: From 18 Brumaire to Tilsit, 1799–1807*, p. 169.

[13]In October 1802, Great Britain had 39 ships of the line in commission, compared to France's 13. One year later, the figures were 111 and 60 respectively, but France could get only 14 under way by January 1804, and 23 by March. See William L. Clowes, *The Royal Navy* (7 vols.; London, 1897–1903), V, 10, 48; J. Holland Rose, *Pitt and Napoleon: Essays and Letters* (London, 1912), pp. 117–118.

[14]Rose, *Pitt and Napoleon: Essays and Letters*, p. 128.

[15]*Ibid.*, p. 129.

[16]The best accounts of the Trafalgar Campaign are in Clowes, *The Royal Navy*, V; Oliver Warner, *Trafalgar* (New York, 1960); E. B. Potter and Chester Nimitz (eds.), *Sea Power: A Naval History* (Englewood Cliffs, 1960); J. F. C. Fuller, *A Military History of the Western World* (3 vols.; New York, 1954–1956), II.

[17]*Correspondance de Napoleon I* (32 vols.; Paris, 1858–1870), XI, No. 9130, p. 133.

[18]Loredan Larchey (ed.), *The Narrative of Captain Coignet*, trans. by M. Carey (New York, 1890), p. 117. Figures interpolated from P. Alombert and J. Colin, *La Campagne de 1805* (Documentary Annex) (Paris, 1902); Maurice Dumolin, *Precis D'Histoire Militaire* (3 vols.; Paris, 1906–1913), II, 119–121.

[19]Jean Baptiste Barres, *Memoirs of a Napoleonic Officer*, trans. by B. Miall (New York, 1925), p. 57.

[20]Frederic L. Huidekoper, "Napoleon's Concentration on the Rhine and Main in 1805," *Journal of the Military Service Institution of the United States*, XLI (September–October, 1907), 212.

[21]Dumolin, *Precis D'Histoire Militaire*, II, 119–121. The figures in the footnote are taken from Vincent J. Esposito, *West Point Atlas of American Wars* (2 vols.; New York, 1964); Department of History, *The Art of War in the 17th and 18th Centuries* (West Point, 1970).

[22]Gershoy, *The French Revolution and Napoleon*, p. 207.

[23]David G. Chandler, *The Campaigns of Napoleon* (New York, 1966), p. 344. According to Lefebvre, *Napoleon: From 18 Brumaire to Tilsit, 1799-1807*, p. 227, the number of men killed in action accounted for a small percentage of the dead—2 percent at Austerlitz and 8 percent at Waterloo. The rest died from disease, wounds, and exposure.

[24]Fuller, *A Military History of the Western World*, II, 417; Chandler, *The Campaigns of Napoleon*, pp. 332–367; and Esposito and Elting, *A Military History and Atlas of the Napoleonic Wars*, Introduction, are the principal sources for the factual material regarding tactics and weapons.

[25]*Correspondance*, XII, No. 10032, p. 230.

[26]Dumolin, *Precis D'Histoire Militaire*, II, 120–121.

[27]Archibald G. MacDonnel, *Napoleon and His Marshals* (New York, 1930), p. 188.

[28]Chandler, *The Campaigns of Napoleon*, p. 142.

[29]*Correspondance*, XII, No. 9810, p. 44.

[30]Antoine H. Jomini, *The Art of War*, trans. by G. H. Mendell and W. P. Craighill (Philadelphia, 1877), pp. 139–140. The principal source for this section is a series of personal interviews with Colonel John R. Elting, USA (retired).

PART II
EXPANSION
OF THE
EMPIRE

Whose game was empires and
whose stakes were thrones,
Whose table earth—whose dice were human bones.
                                        Byron

The Ulm and Austerlitz Campaigns

3

In May 1805, Napoleon journeyed from Paris to Milan to receive the crown of the Kingdom of Italy. On the way, he stopped off to revisit the plain of Marengo. Seated on a raised dais with Josephine, he reviewed 30,000 troops in battle dress, many of whom were veterans of the memorable but flawed victory that had fired the pride of France. The soldiers roared their approval when they saw their Emperor in the same faded uniform he had worn on that battlefield five years before. Marshals Murat and Lannes were also there to lead the troops through a re-enactment of the battle. It was an awe-inspiring scene—the blare of trumpets and the din of cannon and musketry beat at the spectators, while a dense cloud of smoke and dust blanketed the plain. It was more than a mere impulse that led Napoleon back to the scene of his closely contested victory over the Austrians. Great battles require commemoration to revive the spirit of glorious achievement and to remind soldiers that victories are purchased with sacrifice. The pageant also served notice that France would fight again to protect the prizes she had won.

Austrian Preparedness for the War of the Third Coalition

Of all the European monarchies, Austria was probably the least inclined to risk the hazards of a major war. Hapsburg rulers had painstakingly built their sprawling empire over a period of five centuries with a judicious blend of diplomacy, guile, political marriages, and the measured use of force. It was Austrian policy to favor the idea of a strategy of maneuver to win a small border district or parry an enemy invasion, but normally to renounce a major confrontation which in the event of defeat on the battlefield might lose an entire province or duchy. Negotiation and the threat of war thus seemed infinitely preferable to the uncertain outcome of a bloody battle —especially in 1805, when serious flaws in administration,

training, and command responsibility impaired the Army's combat readiness. Beaulieu, Würmser, Alvintzi, and Melas had all met defeat against Bonaparte in Italy. This unpromising record reinforced the conservative outlook of the Austrian Cabinet.

After the loss at Marengo, Emperor Francis had appointed his brother, the Archduke Charles, as head of the *Hofkriegsrat* (The Supreme War Council), and asked him to study the problem of renovating the Austrian Army. Charles was the most reform-minded of the Austrian generals, and he plunged

Napoleon, Emperor of the French

enthusiastically into his task. Taking his cue from the French, he planned to reorganize the army into divisions and corps, to institute national conscription, and to open the officer profession to all social classes. These ideas were too liberal for the aristocratic Hapsburg officer corps, however, and Francis himself was hesitant to give Charles' reforms the sweeping endorsement needed to make them fully effective. Charles was unable, for example, to change the basic tenets of the old drill manual which flatly stated, "Regular, well drilled and steady infantry cannot be impeded by skirmishers. All the shooting and skirmishing decides nothing."[1] The great Frederick had fought off Austria and her allies for seven years using linear tactics, and soldiers now refused to abandon the old system, in spite of what had happened in Italy. The tradition of the eighteenth century and the circumspection of the Hapsburg monarchy held military doctrine in a grip that even a member of the royal family could not break.

It was bad enough that the Austrian Army was armed with an outdated tactical doctrine. Worse, the Government neglected to supply its troops adequately because of a failing supply of money. Lack of funds deprived the entire royal artillery of its horses, and a large percentage of the cavalry was on foot, as well. Stockpiles of food stuffs and ammunition were adequate, but insufficient transport limited the supplies actually delivered to the troops.[2] Governmental inefficiency inevitably contributed to unreadiness in the Army.

Strategic planning in the high command was also faulty, primarily because of the Emperor's uncertain policies. In spite of the obvious unpreparedness of the Army, Austrian policy drifted from appeasement of France to military alliance against her. Ignoring the pessimistic advice of the *Hofkriegsrat*, Francis accepted the advice of his diplomats to sign a secret military convention with Russia in November 1804. Charles protested this decision, which placed the burden of the coalition on Austria's unready Army. But Russian assistance and the promise of British subsidies seemed to offset the weakness of the Hapsburg Army. Moreover, Francis believed that Napoleon's assumption of royal status might cause him to come to terms with the other monarchs. To the contrary, French expansion continued at Austria's expense, and while Austria's political leaders edged closer to war, her military leaders were unable to prepare for it.

The events of the preceding five years had steadily eroded the outlying Hapsburg dominions in the Netherlands, northern Italy, and southern Germany. *(See Atlas Map No. 13.)* Napoleon now trumpeted warlike noises again. His coronation as King of Italy violated the understanding of the Treaty of Lunéville. His incorporation of Genoa into the French Empire was as clear a statement of aggrandizement as was his blunt assertion that France and Austria were like two bulls competing for two cows, the cows being Germany and Italy.[3]

Russia and England had prodded Austria into joining the coalition in 1804; now, in the summer of 1805, a thoroughly alarmed Francis finally overcame his last hesitations for fear that the monarchy would lose everything without ever offering resistance. In July, Austria and Russia concerted a strategic plan.

A lively debate took place within the Austrian Cabinet over where the main theater of operations would be. Charles' opinion was that Austria's major interests lay in Italy; he recommended that the apportionment of combat power between Germany and Italy be calculated accordingly. Although it overlooked the important factor of Russian support, his plan received the Emperor's approval. The main Austrian field army, numbering 94,000, deployed to Italy under Charles' command, while a secondary force of some 72,000 men marched into Bavaria under the nominal command of his brother, the Archduke Ferdinand. *(See Atlas Map No. 14.)*

The Austrian Invasion of Bavaria

Ferdinand was a particularly bad choice to command the ill-supplied, poorly-trained force that advanced into Bavaria. The archduke was only 25 years old, which by itself did not necessarily serve as a bar to command. In fact, Ferdinand had served with some distinction in the campaigns of 1799–1800, and might have been a promising candidate for high command at a later time. However, the young prince lacked self-confidence, and Emperor Francis prescribed that he follow the advice of his chief of staff, Karl Mack, who was a proven staff officer and a veteran of much campaigning in Germany and Italy. Mack was known for his ability to work hard, his talent for administration, and his zealous willingness to accept responsibility. However, he was not a man of vision, nor even of imagination; he never fully comprehended the explosive power of the revolutionized French Army. Napoleon met Mack, who was then a prisoner, after the Marengo Campaign, and rendered this fateful judgment of him:

> Mack is a man of the lowest mediocrity I ever saw in my life; he is full of self-sufficiency and conceit, and believes himself equal to anything. He has no talent. I should like to see him opposed some day to one of our good generals . . . and, besides all that, he is unlucky.[4]

At the very hour when Napoleon was imperatively issuing another directive to his despondent admirals from Imperial Headquarters at Boulogne, Mack and Ferdinand met in Vienna to discuss the plan of campaign drawn up by the Archduke Charles and the Russian military staff. *(See Atlas Maps Nos. 14 and 15.)* The Allied concept of operations can be summarized as follows: while the main army under Charles advanced into Italy to seize the area around Milan, Ferdinand's supporting force was to move into Bavaria along the south bank of the Danube as far as the Iller River to await the arrival of a Russian army, which was supposed to reach the Inn River by mid-October. Ferdinand's immediate task was to coerce Bavaria into a military alliance with Austria while avoiding a major engagement with the French main army. How Ferdinand's troops were to avoid confronting the battle-seeking *Grande Armée* seems never to have been considered by the Austro-Russian high command.

The Archduke John's 22,000 men in the Tyrol were to remain on the defensive until Charles' advance secured his southern flank. Meanwhile, England and Russia planned two amphibious feints—in Hanover and in Naples—to draw off French forces and to encourage neutral Prussia to join the coalition. After the Russians joined Ferdinand's army in Bavaria, the combined army, presumably under the Austrian Emperor's command, would advance on Strasbourg, seeking a decisive battle. At that time, Charles' army would advance into France from Switzerland.[5]

Ferdinand expressed the opinion that Napoleon could probably march to Munich with 150,000 men before the Russians could arrive on the Inn. He suggested sending only a corps of 40,000 men into Bavaria, while the rest of his force occupied a stronger more easterly position to facilitate concentration with the Russian army, commanded by Mikhail Kutusov. Mack confidently predicted that Napoleon could never bring more than 70,000 men out of France. The Emperor of the French had to protect the Atlantic coast, keep order in Paris, and guard his lines of communication. Attrition alone would subtract 20,000 men from Napoleon's strength.[6] For once, Emperor Francis was optimistic and overruled the youthful Ferdinand.

On September 2, 1805, Mack set his troops in motion. Within one week, the elaborate plan started to break down. While the Bavarian foreign minister conversed amiably with an Austrian envoy, the Bavarian Prince and Army hurried away to Würzburg and shortly joined the French invasion force.

Meanwhile, friction began to affect the Hapsburg war machine. It had long been standard practice for Austrian forces to resupply from pre-established depots and magazines. Although this system insured continuity of supply, it stripped an army of mobility and flexibility and left the commander virtually at the mercy of his logistical system. Mack now attempted to change this procedure in an attempt to match the French Army's mobility. Shortly before the opening of hostilities, he directed that his force should live off the country. It was a bold decision, but troops rarely become proficient at new techniques without some time for

Francis I, Emperor of Austria

training and practice. Thus, the Austrians, unskilled at foraging and unorganized for requisitioning supplies, were forced, like the French, to improvise as they began the campaign.

Undeterred by the mounting pressure of accumulating problems, Mack pressed ahead with his plans to put his force into a forward posture. He hastened the flow of transport wagons toward the Iller River and personally reconnoitered the defensive positions he planned to entrench at Memmingen and Ulm. Worried over the risk incurred by pushing the army so far to the west, Ferdinand requested that Mack return to headquarters to confer on troop dispositions. Mack ignored the request and accelerated the forward movement of troops. On September 19, the lead units arrived on the Iller, virtually determining the pattern of the campaign.* It would not unfold in the manner envisioned by Mack. *(See Atlas Map No. 15.)*

On the following day, Mack met with Archduke Ferdinand and Emperor Francis to discuss the possibility of a threat across the plains from the north. Mack discounted the likelihood that Napoleon would violate the neutrality of Ansbach, a possession of Prussia. Had not Prussia declared that access would be denied to the French? He intimated that it was a diplomatic, not a military problem. Besides, the Lech River could be turned as easily as the Iller; if Austria abandoned the Lech, all of Bavaria must be evacuated. So reasoned Mack in

---

*Just one day later, Napoleon received Murat's report of the arrival of Austrian forces on the Iller.[7]

his justification after the war.[8] How Mack reasoned during those fateful weeks when he thrust Ferdinand's army westwards toward the Black Forest can only be surmised. Possessed with optimism, energy, and the resolve to carry out his carefully considered plan, he apparently lacked only the gift of prescience—that tiny whisper of doubt that tells one in moments of impending crisis that all is not as it should be.

The French Strategic Envelopment

While the Austrians prepared their defenses on the Iller River, the *Grande Armée* moved swiftly from the Rhine to the Danube, cut off the Austrian escape routes to the east, and encircled Ferdinand's army at Ulm. The speed and power of this scythe-like maneuver has evoked admiration from generations of students of the military art. How was it done?

After abruptly reversing his grand strategy in August, Napoleon's first move had been to deploy the army to the Rhine and Main Rivers. Even while dictating the march orders for this move, he was already thinking of the battle that would be the logical outcome of the campaign. (In his view, an operation should be thought out in advance and conceived as a whole; but execution of the plan was progressive, guided by developments as the campaign unfolded.) As more precise information on enemy dispositions became available, he was

Austrian Dragoons

then fully prepared to alter the main thrust of the army's advance. *(See Atlas Maps Nos. 14 and 15.)*

Next, the Emperor dispatched an aide to the King of Prussia to offer an alliance with Prussia and to gain at least the assurance of freedom to operate against Austria in southern Germany. Meanwhile he collected intelligence—from the ambassador to Saxony, from spies, from his voluminous notebooks, and from his library. At this time, Napoleon also sent Murat and two key aides—Anne J. Savary and Count Henri Bertrand—on a detailed reconnaissance of the terrain over which he expected to advance. Murat rode from Mainz to Bamberg and Passau, and returned by way of Munich, Ulm, and the Black Forest. Bertrand made a careful inspection of Ulm and the Inn and Lech River valleys. While the *Grande Armée* hurried toward the Rhine, Napoleon stayed at Boulogne, gathering information and pondering the various plans that were turning over in his mind.

On September 3, the Emperor left Boulogne and traveled to Paris, his itinerary known to all the world. The following week he instructed Fouché to suppress all information on the location of the *Grande Armée*: "let it be as if it did not exist at all."[9] Hussars and dragoons began to watch the roads in the Black Forest and to patrol toward the Iller. By mid-September —before the *Grande Armée* reached the Rhine—reports started filtering in from Napoleon's long-range reconnaissance teams: the Austrians had crossed the Inn on September 10; the Bavarians had retired to Würzburg. One week later, he had a fairly accurate picture of the enemy deployment toward Ulm and Memmingen.[10] *(See Atlas Map No. 15.)*

On September 17, Napoleon issued a preliminary directive, projecting his strategic plan to the Danube. The guidance was specific, including instructions for the crossing of the Rhine by the cavalry reserve and the corps of Davout, Soult, Ney, and Lannes; the routes of advance for each of these corps through Baden, Württemberg, and Bavaria; the desired date of arrival and march objective for each corps. Davout was to reach Nördlingen by October 10, Soult to reach Aalen by October 9, Ney to be on the heights overlooking Ulm by October 7, and Lannes to reach Ulm by October 9. Bernadotte and Marmont were to depart from Würzburg on or about September 30, and to be within a day's march of Donauworth by October 9. Napoleon laid out a general scheme with specific objectives for each corps; the rest was up to the marshals—the most irresistible, hard-driving team Europe had seen since the Golden Horde swept toward Vienna from the East, 500 years earlier. The Emperor gave more detailed instructions to his brother-in-law, Prince Murat.* The cavalry's major role was to penetrate in strength into the

---

*Murat had married one of Napoleon's sisters, the vivacious Caroline, in 1800. The marriage proved to be a poor match—for the Murats and for the Empire.

Black Forest and attract the Austrians' attention with a dazzling demonstration.[11]

Several days later, Napoleon received more accurate information in an intelligence dispatch forwarded by telegraph from Strasbourg: the Austrians had crossed the Lech and were closing on Ulm. He now issued a fragmentary order to correct the course of the army. Ney, Lannes, Soult, and Davout were to angle more to the east; the mass of the army, more closely assembled, was to aim for a point downstream from Ulm.[12]

On September 24, Napoleon left Paris for Strasbourg, accompanied by Josephine for part of the journey. After reaching that city, he gloated in a message to Bernadotte:

The Emperor of Germany has made no detachment onto the right bank of the Danube, and the Russians have not yet arrived. . . . if I have the good fortune to catch the Austrian Army asleep on the Iller and in the Black Forest for three or four more days I shall have outflanked it, and I hope only the debris will escape.[13]

At Strasbourg, Napoleon discovered also that his supply system was barely organized. However, it was too late to correct it. Besides, French troops could live off the countryside; in fact, they expected to do so. For several days, Napoleon remained in Strasbourg, taking advantage of the telegraphic center there to expedite coordination with Eugène de Beauharnais* and Massena in Italy, with Fouché in Paris, and with Augereau, who now began to move from Brest. At the same time, Murat's cavalry screen sifted through the Black Forest. Napoleon now wanted prisoners to tell him which way Mack was heading.

On September 26, the *Grande Armée* crossed the Rhine. *(See Atlas Map No. 16 .)* Four days later, the troops heard the Emperor's proclamation, which he ordered each of his corps commanders to have read to their troops:

Soldiers, the war of the third coalition has commenced. The Austrian Army has passed the Inn, violated treaties, attacked and driven our ally from his capital. You yourselves have been compelled to hasten by forced marches to the defense of our frontiers. But you have already passed the Rhine. We shall not pause again until we have assured the independence of the Germanic people, succored our allies and humbled the pride of unjust aggressors. We shall not make peace again without guarantees.

Soldiers, your Emperor is in your midst; you are but the vanguard of a great people. If it becomes necessary, it will rise as one at my voice, to confound and dissolve this new league which has been fabricated of hate and

*Eugène was the son of Josephine and her first husband, Alexandre de Beauharnais.

Donauworth, Looking Toward Ansbach

English gold. But, soldiers, we shall have to make forced marches, endure all sorts of hardships and privations. Whatever obstacles we confront, we shall overcome, and we shall not rest until we have planted our eagles on our enemies' territory.[14]

This spirited pronouncement was more accurate as a prophecy than as history.

Napoleon further refined the course of his onrushing formations during the last few days of September. With the latest intelligence available fixing Ferdinand's army at Ulm and Memmingen, Napoleon now aimed his army farther eastwards, directing its center of mass at Donauworth. Berthier's harassed staff officers erased planned routes from the map and plotted new ones, while aides and orderlies filled the back roads, dashing from one headquarters to another to coordinate changes in march routing.

Inevitably, certain problems arose, most of them being human. Murat complained to Napoleon that Berthier had issued him contradictory orders. Napoleon smoothed over the dispute by personally and explicitly restating Murat's mission:

You are to flank my entire advance, which is a delicate operation, as it is an oblique march on the Danube. It is necessary therefore that if the enemy attempts to take up the offensive, I should be warned in time to take action and not be compelled to accept that which the enemy forces upon me.[15]

Soult complained that Davout had taken more than his share of biscuits from the magazines, and Murat quarreled with Lannes over the right of way at Rastatt. Marmont worried Berthier over the inadequacy of supplies.

The most serious incident of all occurred at Ansbach. When Bernadotte's I Corps neared the little medieval fortress, the gates were found to have been closed by the Prussian garrison. Bernadotte followed Napoleon's instructions to the letter—to "offer many assurances favourable to Prussia, and testify all possible affection and respect for her, and then rapidly cross her land, asserting the impossibility of doing anything else."[16] It took every bit of the Gascon's spirited persuasion to convince the Prussian commander to open the gates, and there were some tense moments before the impatient French soldiers were allowed to resume their march. When news of the incident reached Berlin, Frederick William III first threatened to declare war, but finally settled for the milder revenge of allowing Russian columns to cross Silesia on their way to reinforce the Austrian Army.

These troubles were primarily the concern of commanders and staffs; for the troops, as yet, the war had not begun. Ahead of the relentlessly marching columns lay gentle Bavarian terrain—a patchwork quilt of rolling farmland and dark green forest. Pleasant fall weather and the recently gathered harvest invited the French soldiers; there could hardly have been a more ideal time for campaigning.

There could have been no worse time for the Austrian Army to take the field. Ferdinand's hastily assembled force was short of transportation and ill-trained for living off the country. Several days were lost waiting for Bavaria's reaction to the invasion; when Mack finally was able to move the army on toward the Iller, stragglers and deserters began to drop from the ranks. In spite of the faltering step of his army and the almost total lack of information about his enemy, the unimaginative Mack remained secure in the conviction that his forces were protected from major attack by his scouts in the Black Forest and by the strength of their positions on the angle of the Danube and Iller Rivers. Throughout the week, as the French net settled gently onto the Danube, Mack's gaze remained riveted on the Black Forest defiles. Only when Murat's patrols disappeared from view on October 3 did Mack begin to suspect that the French main advance would come from the north instead of the west.

Mack promptly made the courageous decision to concentrate his dispersed forces at Ulm, and to hold out until the Russians arrived. One can hardly fault his decision to resist, but he allowed his subordinates four days to complete a maneuver requiring marches of no more than 50 miles. For Napoleon, whose strategy was calibrated in hundreds of miles, that was enough time to pour five corps across the Danube at four different crossing sites, from Donauworth to Ingolstadt.

By October 9, the fate of Ferdinand's army was sealed, although Mack still seemed unable to realize it. *(See Atlas Map No. 17.)* His 55,000 troops, which clustered around Ulm, op-

posed almost 200,000 Frenchmen, nearly 150,000 of whom lay squarely across his line of retreat. Rain and sleet began to fall. Ferdinand promptly lost heart and urged Mack to order a retreat to the south.

The Fights Around Ulm

On October 19, shortly before Mack's capitulation, Napoleon wrote to Josephine, "I have achieved my objective; I have destroyed the Austrian army by sheer marching."[17] However, the historical record of what occurred during the preceding week clearly indicates that, having won a great advantage by his brilliant strategic maneuver, the Emperor nearly threw it away by heeding his growing misconception of the enemy situation south of the Danube. Napoleon's letters during the first week in October show that he was well aware of the state of high confusion present in Ferdinand's force, and that his confidence was growing with every day's march. Sometime during this period, he apparently began to indulge in overoptimism, particularly after his lead units had crossed the Danube, almost unopposed, and headed first south and then east across the Lech. Napoleon, arriving at Donauworth on October 7, sent this message to Ney:

> It is probable that our crossing of the Lech and occupation of Augsburg, which will occur during the course of the day, will bring the enemy to his senses. . . . It is impossible that the enemy, when he learns of our crossing of the Danube and the Lech, together with the terror which must have possessed his troops on the other side of the Lech, will think seriously of anything but retreat.[18]

This inexplicable, near fatal conviction—that the enemy thought only of retreat through Augsburg—persisted for almost four days.

On October 8, Soult's corps pressed south toward Augsburg. Murat and Lannes fanned out to the southwest in search of enemy formations, and collided with an Austrian covering force that had just received orders to hold open the road from Ulm to Augsburg. The French promptly drove this detachment back toward Ulm, taking nearly 1,500 prisoners, several of whom stated that over 60,000 Austrians were located to the west, near Ulm. Incredibly, Napoleon persisted in his belief that a decisive battle was still to be found on the Lech. During the evening of October 8 and the following day, orders were dispatched directing Soult, the Imperial Guard, Davout, and Marmont to concentrate on Augsburg. Only Murat and Ney, with roughly 30,000 troops, remained to drive the Austrians out of Ulm. Napoleon's conception of the

Gunzburg on the Danube

situation at that time is revealed in a message sent by Berthier to Ney later that day: "Concerning Ulm, it is impossible that the enemy occupies it in force; if it is occupied with 3,000 or 4,000 men, take a division and chase them out; if it is occupied with larger forces take your entire force, storm the town and take a lot of prisoners."[19] *(See Atlas Map No. 18.)*

Ney, who received this message shortly after a stout fight for the bridge at Gunzburg, promptly reported, "the enemy at Ulm appears stronger than we had supposed."[20] Napoleon continued to be obsessed with Augsburg and called for more speed from Marmont and Bernadotte, whose corps had become entangled north of the Danube and still had not crossed. On October 10, he placed Murat in temporary control of the forces at Ulm, in order to free his full attention for the situation at Augsburg and the anticipated interception of Russian reinforcements near Munich. Thus, while Mack and Ferdinand argued over whether to retreat into the Tyrol or break out to the north, Napoleon turned his back on Ulm and heedlessly sent a fraction of the *Grande Armée* to do battle with the bulk of Ferdinand's army.

On October 11, Lannes, also, came under Murat's control to help clear out Ulm. Murat, however, seemed unable to comprehend the situation, even after part of the Austrian army crossed to the north bank of the Danube and stunned a division of Ney's thinly stretched corps, which was vainly trying to surround the city on the north. On the same day, Soult, having found nothing in Augsburg, pressed south along the Lech, while the Emperor remained in Augsburg with Marmont and the Guard.

Napoleon finally began to revise his mental picture of the enemy situation on October 11, as is indicated by his letter of that morning written to Murat: "I still do not think matters are

settled in your direction. The enemy, surrounded as he is, will fight." But with 50,000 men under his command (Ney's and Lannes' corps), Murat should have combat superiority—provided the troops march tightly assembled "so that they can concentrate within six hours."[21] The assumption that Murat was capable of handling the group of corps around Ulm perhaps deserves to be questioned. On the other hand, Murat could hardly be held entirely responsible for the failure to take Ulm when the Emperor himself continued to insist that Mack intended to retreat, either toward Augsburg or the Tyrol. If this were not his belief, then why was Marshal Soult, with over 30,000 men, slogging around the circuitous southern route along the Lech River valley and thence to Memmingen? *(See Atlas Map No. 19.)*

On October 12, Napoleon finally read the situation properly and made two important decisions. First, he wrote to Murat that he was ordering an encirclement of the Austrians at Ulm that would commence with the arrival of Soult's corps from the south. Second, he decided to go to Ulm and take personal command of the forces there.[22] That evening he rode out from Augsburg into the stinging rain, which had not ceased for five straight days. On the same day, captured orders apprised Mack of the weakness in Ney's positions north of the Danube. Accordingly, he ordered an advance across the Danube to attempt a breakout and linkup with the Russians near Ratisbon. Mired in the wet clay of the Swabian Scarplands, the Austrian troops made slow progress, but unfounded rumors of a revolt in France and a British landing on the Atlantic coast buoyed Mack's spirits. This euphoria lasted only until the morning of October 14, when his troops fell back before a vicious attack on Elchingen led by Michel Ney.

Elchingen and Terrain to the East

Combat at Elchingen, October 1805

Napoleon had arrived at Gunzburg the day before to discover a total lack of information in Ney's headquarters concerning the situation north of the Danube. Murat's staff offered no more information than Ney's. Napoleon quickly ordered Lannes' and Marmont's corps to take positions along the eastern circumference of the encirclement, and then went to deliver four days of accumulated wrath on the head of Marshal Ney. The decisive part of this imperial reprimand charged the hotheaded marshal to take possession of the bridge at Elchingen and the heights commanding it the next morning. Thus began the epic career of the Duke of Elchingen, "the bravest of the brave."*

On October 14, Ney's spirited attack captured the bridge at Elchingen, overran the heights overlooking the Danube, shut off the Austrian retreat, and drove Ferdinand's army back into Ulm. Mack took one hard look at the disaster, which finally stared him in the face, and decided not to fight. Ferdinand escaped with a small detachment of horsemen, and the formal capitulation took place at Ulm one week later.

*Ney was to fight in a dozen major campaigns across the entire map of Europe, the saga finally ending before a firing squad in Paris 10 years later.

The French Advance on Vienna

In an Imperial order of October 20, Napoleon announced the conclusion of the campaign and congratulated his soldiers on their achievements: the surrender of 5,000 Austrians at Memmingen to Soult's IV Corps, the capitulation of Mack at Ulm with 25,000 men, the daring seizure of the bridge at Elchingen by Ney's corps and his capture of the formidable position at Elchingen resulting in 3,000 more prisoners, and Murat's subsequent pursuit to Nördlingen, yielding 5,000 more. The order concluded: "The Emperor announces that he is pleased with his army."[23]

In spite of these assurances of satisfaction, all was not well with the *Grande Armée*. The 500-mile march from the coast to the Danube had sorely tested the hardiest of the French veterans. Of the march to the Rhine, Sergeant Jean R. Coignet, a member of the Imperial Guard, had this to say: "Never was there such a terrible march. We had not a moment for sleep, marching by platoon all day and all night, and at last holding on to each other to prevent falling."[24] The incessant marching

Marshal Auguste Frédéric Marmont

and the heavy rains and sleet that had begun in October wore the shoes right off the men's feet; the improvised logistical system hardly sufficed to sustain 200,000 men in the field.

Some corps commanders, like Davout and Soult, were able to supply their units by careful planning, expertly-managed foraging, and outright thievery.* Others, like Marmont, entered the campaign less prepared, and complained loudly about shortages of food and the lack of pre-established depots. Berthier's response to Marmont's criticism is suggestive of Napoleon's philosophy of logistics:

> . . . in the war of invasion and of rapid movements which the Emperor is waging there can be no depots, and the commanding generals have to see to it themselves that they procure the necessary supplies from the countries which they traverse.[25]

In the midst of the campaign, Marmont finally had to halt at the Danube—in spite of the Emperor's entreaties to press the advance—to feed his famished soldiers.

Inadequacy of supply inevitably led to serious disciplinary problems. The authorization to procure supplies from the countryside soon became interpreted as the right to pillage. In spite of Napoleon's orders to apprehend and court-martial looters, hungry soldiers often took matters in their own hands and wrecked a number of villages along the main routes of march. "At no other time, save in the Russian campaign,"

*Nicolas Jean Soult and Louis Nicolas Davout were two of Napoleon's youngest marshals (36 and 35, respectively). They were also two of the most competent. Both were excellent tacticians; both administered their commands well. Davout possessed the stronger character and also had the better grasp of strategy.

wrote one officer, "have I seen the army in such a state of disorder."[26] Napoleon threatened to throw looters in the stockade, and some of his officers even had offenders shot on the scene; but there was only one effective solution to the problem—to bring the campaign to a successful conclusion as swiftly as possible and return the army to garrison.

Speed was necessary for other compelling reasons. Kutusov was nearby with over 40,000 Russian and Austrian troops, and Generals Frederick Buxhowden and Levin A. Bennigsen were approaching with at least 60,000 more. The Archdukes John and Charles could muster over 100,000 in the south. Napoleon was also uncomfortably aware that Russian and British diplomats were hard at work trying to convince the vacillating Frederick William III that the moment for Prussian intervention had arrived. Frederick William was anxious to avoid the war, but he also coveted Hanover—which Bernadotte had just evacuated and Napoleon now offered as the price of alliance. Above all, although England still remained untouched and aloof from the turmoil on the Continent, she was active on the seas and busy sending money to Vienna, Berlin, and St. Petersburg to keep armies in operation against Napoleon. Given enough time to ready her forces, England might even launch an invasion against France's weakly defended coastline.

Time has always been the ally of the vigorous, active general, and the enemy of the slothful. To Napoleon, time was more than an ally; it was a resource to be managed and exploited, just like his cannon, horses, and soldiers. On the other hand, time was also a tyrant. To Napoleon, the passing of one hour without an aide galloping forth from headquarters with an order to quicken the tempo of the action was worse than the perpetration of a crime. It was the curse of Napoleon's destiny and character that he never was able to remain still.

After Mack's surrender, the Emperor worked feverishly for five days to restore order to his army. Augsburg became the site of a major advance depot, patrols hunted down stragglers and deserters, and supply trains brought forward new reserves of munitions. Augereau's VII Corps arrived in November and took over the occupation of the territory along the Danube in Bavaria. At the same time, Ney's corps pushed into the Tyrol to protect the army's south flank from an attack by Archdukes John and Charles.

Learning of the defeat at Ulm from the paroled Mack, who was on his way to Vienna, Kutusov promptly withdrew behind the Inn River, burning the bridges behind him. His strategy appears to have been to delay the French advance along the Danube until Russian, Austrian, and Prussian reinforcements could arrive. The *Hofkriegsrat* at Vienna urged him to defend on the Inn, rather than withdraw. Meanwhile, Charles fought Massena to a draw in northern Italy and then began to fall back, pausing for a week to cover John's withdrawal from the mountains south of Salzburg. Ferdinand gathered the remnants of his army at Prague, while the Russian reserve army under Buxhowden marched slowly toward Vienna. Thus, it appeared that all the ingredients were at hand for another climactic encounter. *(See Atlas Map No. 20.)*

The *Grande Armée* moved out again on October 26, led by Murat's cavalry and Lannes' grenadiers. Ignoring Austria's plea for him to hold the Inn River line, Kutusov readily retired before the fast moving lead units of the French army, which crossed south of the strong positions at Passau, the gateway to Vienna. French forces steadily advanced on parallel roads through the rough, cut-up country south of the Danube. Kutusov—who later gained the nickname "The Old Fox" from his countrymen—withdrew one step ahead of Murat's dragoons.

Napoleon's rapid advance caused a serious division between the Allies. Francis saw the French advance primarily as a threat to Vienna, and repeatedly urged Kutusov to stand and fight on the south side of the Danube to protect the city. Kutusov held the safety of his army to be more important than the protection of Vienna, and laid plans to mislead the French by crossing the river west of Vienna and withdrawing north to link up with Buxhowden's army.

The Emperor of the French now expected the Allies to stand and offer battle before Vienna. A stiff rearguard fight that developed between General Peter Bagration and Murat on November 5 seemed to confirm his expectations; nonetheless, he allowed the *Grande Armée* to become divided. To cover his south flank, Napoleon sent Marmont to defend against Charles and John. Meanwhile, he had gathered two divisions and detachments of artillery and cavalry from other corps, formed a new command (VIII Corps, under Marshal Adolphe E.C. Mortier), and sent it across the Danube in case Kutusov attempted to escape across the river to the north. Once Mortier assembled his full complement, his new corps would number nearly 17,000 men and 26 pieces of artillery;[27] but he never got them all together.

One of Napoleon's most dangerous habits was his practice of allowing his subordinates nearly free rein during a pursuit. During the advance to contact, he expected corps commanders to adhere closely to his march orders. In the pursuit, he estimated the enemy to be less capable of doing serious damage; therefore, decentralization better allowed his subordinates to retain the initiative, which in turn magnified the disorder of the enemy's retreat. However, it remained essential for corps commanders to report their dispositions accurately, in order that no individual unit be caught unexpectedly out of supporting distance before the Commander-in-Chief could reinforce it. This was exactly what befell Mortier's corps, largely because Napoleon momentarily forgot about Mortier's exposed position north of the Danube. *(See Atlas Map No. 20.)*

Kutusov crossed the Danube at Krems on November 9 and promptly captured several stragglers from Mortier's corps, who readily disclosed the strength and location of their unit. On November 11, the VIII Corps blundered into a defile at Dürrenstein, where Kutusov had set a trap, and suffered heavy casualties before withdrawing to safety on the other side of the Danube. At the same time, Murat ignored the chase of Kutusov's army and thoughtlessly rode pellmell for Vienna and the supposed glory of being first to enter the city.

Napoleon's anger at Murat may be attributed at least partly to his chagrin at his own neglect. Nonetheless, the sentiments he expressed to Murat were genuine:

> My Cousin, I cannot approve of your manner of advancing; you plunge ahead thoughtlessly and you do not follow the orders I give you. The Russians, instead of covering Vienna, have recrossed the Danube at Krems. This extraordinary circumstance should have made you realize that you should not have moved without new instructions.[28]

While Napoleon reprimanded his errant subordinates, activity quickened along the French lines of communication. Napoleon himself noted that but for the substantial potato crop in Bavaria that year, the *Grande Armée* might have been in desperate straits. Accordingly, he arranged for the safeguarding and defense of major fortresses and post-stations along the army's route of advance at Augsburg, Braunau, Passau, and Linz.[29] He also organized a special flotilla on the Danube in order to have a means of lateral communication across the river. It was not enough simply to race ahead to Vienna. The army had to have its minimum operating level of supplies, and had to be capable of reacting to its commander's orders.

Having failed to catch Kutusov west of Vienna, Napoleon now gave Murat and Lannes free play and prepared to throw a wider lasso around the elusive Russians. First, he had to seize a bridge. In places, the Danube was nearly a half mile wide,* but beyond Vienna, to the east, lay the great Bridge of Tabor. It was here that an extraordinary scene took place—an event that illustrates better than any other action in the campaign the freedom of judgment and independence of mind with which Napoleon's marshals sometimes operated. No other contemporary army could have executed the dazzling ruse that Murat and Lannes perpetrated on November 13 to capture this valuable bridge.

The two marshals arrived at the bridge slightly ahead of the infantry, marched up to the Austrian commander of the

---

*Today the Danube is considerably tamed by the elaborate embankments and flood control apparatus that direct the waters along a generally smooth course. In the early nineteenth century, however, the river meandered along several channels. While the current was slower than it is today, the obstacle was more difficult to negotiate.

bridge site in plain view of the artillery and infantry posted at the far side of the bridge, and announced that Napoleon had concluded an armistice with the Austrian Emperor. The Austrian commander, Prince Auersperg, was baffled by the news, but gentlemen as finely dressed as the two French marshals could hardly have been expected to lie to a nobleman, so he prepared to let them pass. Murat overcame the suspicions of one incredulous Austrian non commissioned officer by the simple expedient of distracting him with conversation. While the officers were talking, French *grenadiers* rushed forward and took possession of the bridge.[30] Not a man was lost.*

It is worth more than just a passing commentary to note that at least one of the individuals on the scene who recorded an account of the deed—an aide-de-camp to Lannes by the name of Marcellin de Marbot—declaimed the use of trickery. No matter how many lives were saved, he said, it was wrong to practice deceit on one's enemy. Just two days later, Murat himself became the victim of a similar trick when he halted his advance for the offer of a truce by the Tsar's aide-de-camp. While Kutusov's army filed toward safety, the pursuing French troops rested—until an aide galloped madly up to the unfortunate Murat and delivered another installment of Napoleonic fury:

> It is impossible for me to find words with which to express my displeasure to you. You have command of my advance guard only and you have no right to conclude

---

*Four years later, Napoleon fought two pitched battles, Aspern-Essling and Wagram, at a cost of more than 50,000 casualties, to cross the same river.

Marshal Joachim Murat

an armistice without my orders; you are causing me to lose the fruits of a campaign. Break the armistice at once and march on the enemy.[31]

Meanwhile, Augereau and Bernadotte, too, were exasperating the Emperor. The former failed to keep in contact from Bavaria. Irritated, Napoleon concluded a message to Ney with "find out whether Marshal Augereau is dead or alive."[32] One day earlier, Bernadotte had earned a rebuke for his inertia:

> The Emperor is displeased that, while Marshals Lannes and Soult are fighting at two days march beyond Vienna, you have yet to get a single man across the Danube . . . By the return of my staff officer the Emperor expects you to inform him that the whole of your corps has crossed, that you are pursuing the Russians, and keeping the bayonet at their backs.[33]

The Emperor's ill humor was hardly improved two days later by the news of Villeneuve's defeat at Trafalgar. However, Murat at last resumed the advance and attacked the Russians commanded by Bagration, who fought a gallant rearguard action about 30 miles north of Vienna.† Kutusov subsequently evacuated Brünn and retired to Olmütz. *(See Atlas Map No. 21.)*

Napoleon's troops replenished their food and ammunition supplies from the vast stores in Vienna, but having been on a long, uninterrupted campaign they also needed rest. Many of them wondered how much farther Napoleon could advance across a snow-covered countryside, against an enemy who preferred not to fight. Meanwhile, the Archduke Charles, with 80,000 men, slowly retired from Italy before Massena's languid march, and edged north toward Vienna. As the pursuit slowed and the main armies settled in and around Olmütz and Brünn, Napoleon assessed his lengthening line of communication, the lack of forage, the difficult weather, the Prussian threat, the menace posed by the Archduke Charles at his rear, and his tired troops. Sensing that the decisive moment of the campaign was at hand, he chose to seek battle with the Russians.

The Battle of Austerlitz

Exactly one year after his glittering coronation at Notre Dame, the Emperor of the French fought his greatest battle in the frozen back-country of Moravia. Fully 11 days before, he had devised a scheme to break the stalemate at Brünn and Olmütz. On that day, Murat's light cavalry outposts ad-

---

†This fight has been immortalized in Leo Tolstoy's *War and Peace*. Reprinted in Ernest Hemingway's *Men at War*, it is worth reading more as a study of character than as precise history.

Napoleon and His Staff at Austerlitz, 1805

vanced nearly 30 miles beyond the positions of Soult and Lanne at Brünn. This isolation of the cavalry caused no small anxiety among the French dragoon and hussar leaders. Their positions were considerably closer to the 86,000 enemy troops at Olmütz than to the 43,000 French troops at Brünn. However, Napoleon had no more intention of defending this position than he had of attempting to carry the fortress at Olmütz by assault. On the other hand, how could he accept an extended stalemate during which his army would remain stretched out 250 miles from north to south and over 300 miles from east to west, vulnerable to attack from Prussia? Accordingly, he resolved to lure the Austro-Russian army into attacking him, choosing the piece of ground on which he would fight during a reconnaissance on November 21.*

Although not a particularly striking terrain feature, the Austerlitz area fitted the Emperor's needs precisely, and therefore deserves description. *(See Atlas Map No. 22.)* Bounded on two sides by sluggish streams and on the north by irregular hills and the Brünn-Olmütz road, the plain of Pratzen is roughly triangular in shape. At the apex of the triangle, in the south, there were several well-defined but

---

*According to several eyewitnesses, including his aide, Ségur, Napoleon stopped along the Olmütz-Brünn road on the return from his reconnaissance of the outpost line and said to the officers accompanying him, "Gentlemen, examine this ground carefully; it is going to be a battlefield." It was the plain of Pratzen, west of Austerlitz.[34]

shallow ponds, the closest to the plain being called Satschan Pond. On the western side of the triangle, the ground rises gently from Goldbach Brook, which in those days was a marshy rivulet hardly noticeable from any distance except for the numerous small settlements, patches of woods, and orchards that marked its course. On the eastern side of the triangle the ground dropped sharply into the more substantial Littawa River. Two fair-sized hills overlooked the plain: next to the highway was Bosenitz Hill, which the French nicknamed Santon, in memory of a similar prominence they had encountered in Egypt; a dominant rise in the northwest corner of the triangle near Schlappanitz was the other hill, which Napoleon chose as the site for his command post. One might visualize this combination of terrain features as a tapered sock, into which Napoleon planned to compel the Russian high command to stuff the better part of its army.

Deception played the leading role from the moment Napoleon decided on his tactical scheme until Tsar Alexander's bitter revelation on December 2. Although Kutusov was actually the commander of Allied forces, Alexander, who was not yet 30 years of age, had the ultimate responsibility for deciding whether to fight. Kutusov had firmly stated his opinion that by fighting a major battle with the French, the Allies would risk losing the war at one stroke. He preferred to wait, retreating if necessary, and reinforcing the army so as to outnumber Napoleon decisively before resuming the offensive. Alexander ignored the 60-year-old Kutusov's advice in deference to the opinions of his younger advisers. These hot bloods urged offensive action, claiming that Prussia might otherwise intervene and steal the glory of victory from the Tsar. It was obvious, they exulted, that the outnumbered Napoleon feared a battle, because he had halted his advance. To help convince his enemies that he feared their attack, Napoleon had dispatched General Savary, a clever man who was expert at intelligence work, to negotiate with the Tsar; from his horse, Savary was to observe carefully the Russian dispositions. On November 24, the Allies had already decided to attack to cut the French army's line of communication with Vienna. By the twenty-seventh, both armies had thoroughly stripped the "Moravian Corridor" of food and firewood. On that date, the Allied army began to move.

Savary returned on November 28 with Alexander's reply "to the head of the French government": the French must evacuate Italy. More important, Savary reported the advance of the entire Allied army. The bait had been taken. Napoleon immediately sent his aide back to request a meeting of the two emperors and to call for a suspension of hostilities for 24 hours. At the same time, he ordered Murat and Soult to withdraw their forces behind Goldbach Brook, surrendering the dominant Pratzen Plateau.

Reports from outposts early that evening confirmed that the Allies were indeed making a major advance along the road to Brünn. Napoleon had already gauged their strength, and therefore knew that the troops of Soult, Lannes, Murat, and the Guard (totaling less than 50,000) were insufficient to achieve a decisive victory. He had displayed a weak front as long as he dared. Three hours after dark, he sent messengers flying with the call for reinforcements—for 11,000 of Bernadotte's men nearly 50 miles away, and for Davout's III Corps, which lay east of Vienna, 80 miles away.[35]

Napoleon's order to Davout occasioned one of the most stirring forced marches in history. The order reached III Corps Headquarters in Vienna the afternoon of November 29; Davout was away, supervising the occupation of Pressburg. His chief of staff in Vienna immediately dispatched march orders to the units of the corps that were stationed in the Vienna area; they began their trek at 9:00 p.m. The lead division, commanded by General Louis Friant, marched all night at full speed, and by 9:00 p.m. the following evening had covered 53 miles. It arrived in its assembly area at Raigern, four miles from the battlefield, at 7:00 p.m. on December 1, trailing stragglers but having marched *78 miles in 46 hours*. The exhausted soldiers slept six hours and were then launched into the most desperate fighting that was to take place during the entire course of the battle.[36]

Napoleon's evacuation of the Pratzen Plateau caused the Allies to feel even more certain that the French were withdrawing. On November 29, they began to displace into attack positions south of the highway, while the Russian advance guard, commanded by the rugged Bagration, deployed at Raussnitz to cover the sideslip of the rest of the army. Partly because of bad roads, partly because of bad staff work, but mostly because of uninspired generalship, the columns became entangled and the move took all of three days—until the evening of December 1—to complete. Throughout those three days, Napoleon impatiently rode from one end of the line to the other, peering across the gloomy landscape to observe the movements of his enemy and waiting for news of Davout. On November 29, Savary returned from his final mission through the Russian lines, accompanied by the Tsar's favorite aide-de-camp. The young Russian was pleased with himself, and with scarcely-concealed insolence he announced the Tsar's terms: the evacuation of Italy, Belgium, and the west bank of the Rhine. Hiding his rage, Napoleon calmly refused Alexander's offer.

On the thirtieth, as the ponderous Allied deployment continued, Napoleon began to wonder whether his reinforcements would arrive before the enemy could attack. By December 1, French strength had increased to 60,000. This was still not sufficient. "What news from III Corps?" Napoleon

anxiously inquired at noon. "Still nothing from Marshal Davout, Sire," was the reply.

Meanwhile, the Allies occupied the dominant plateau that Napoleon had offered them. Late in the afternoon, from an observation post just south of the highway, the Emperor of the French and his staff watched the gradual shift toward the ponds in the south. "They are walking into the trap," Napoleon exclaimed, "before tomorrow night this army will belong to me."[37] At that moment, a tired officer arrived with the welcome news that Marshal Davout's advance guard had just completed its march and was pitching camp in Raigern.

The French were now in or near their positions for the fight that would take place on the morning of December 2. Lannes was on the left, to bar the Brünn Road and deliver a supporting attack on Bagration; Davout was on the right, reinforced by one division from Soult's corps, to hold the Russian main effort; Soult, located in the center, was to launch the main attack north of Pratzen, supported by Bernadotte; Murat and the Guard were in reserve, prepared to exploit success either on the left or in the center. This was Napoleon's most carefully planned battle, and it was a bold plan that required perfect coordination to make it work. To insure that coordination did not break down, Napoleon directed his marshals to assemble at his command post at 7:30 a.m. on December 2.

The events of that evening (December 1) proved the wisdom of Napoleon's precaution. While General Albert Weyrother, an Austrian staff officer, briefed the Allied commanders on the plan of attack,* Russian and Austrian troops shuffled confusedly through the darkness toward Tellnitz and Sokolnitz Castle. The noise of this movement alerted the French outposts, which commenced a brisk fusillade. In response to Napoleon's inquiries regarding the meaning of the noise, an aide returned with the news that the enemy was concentrating a sizable force near Telnitz and Sokolnitz. It was there that a substantial gap in the French lines existed, since Davout's reinforcements still rested at Raigern before a final early morning displacement into their battle positions. Thus, at the very hour when Kutusov slept in the Allied staff briefing, Napoleon rode through the cold December night to examine the terrain and decide how his dispositions should be readjusted in the morning. Upon his return to headquarters at 3:00 a.m., he dictated a change in orders for Marshal Soult's attack, directing the main thrust of the advance more to the south, through Pratzen.

The Emperor then went to sleep in a bearskin that had been tossed on a pile of straw, while outside the crude hut that

---

*One of the better Allied commanders, a French émigré named Langeron, noted in his memoirs that the pedantic Weyrother read the order like a school teacher reading a lesson to his students. During the harangue, Kutusov fell into a sound sleep.

Napoleon Orders the Main Attack at Austerlitz, 1805

served as headquarters, sentries exchanged the password for the night: RIVOLI—ARCOLA.

The Russian attack opened on Tellnitz shortly after 6:30 a.m. on December 2. Although it made some progress, General Andrault Langeron's attack on Sokolnitz had to wait for Prince John of Lichtenstein's cavalry, which had become lost in the darkness, to clear the assault positions. Heavy fighting continued on this flank all morning, with Davout's troops counterattacking to retrieve Sokolnitz, losing it again, and then holding the line of the Goldbach while Generals Adolph Kienmayer, Langeron, and D.S. Doctorov jammed 40,000 troops into the bottom of the "sock."

Meanwhile, Soult, Lannes, Murat, and Bernadotte waited fretfully at Napoleon's command post, hearing the heavy firing off to the south. The mist completely hid Soult's troops, but the hilltops were plainly visible, and it was apparent that the Allies were steadily moving southward down the Pratzen Plateau. Normally imperturbable, Soult was agitated and wanted to attack at once; it would take time to set his troops in motion. "How long to climb the plateau from Goldbach bottom?" the Emperor inquired. "Less than twenty minutes," the marshal responded. "In that case," said Napoleon, "we will wait another quarter of an hour."[38] At 9:00 a.m., the decisive attack began, and within 30 minutes the Pratzen Plateau and victory belonged to Napoleon. *(See Atlas Map No. 23.)*

Several bloody fights occurred as the desperate Allies tried to retrieve the plateau. Kutusov, who was following Kollowrat's southward advance, shouted to these troops to change front and hold off the line of bayonets bearing down on their northern flank. Only two battalions responded at once, and these promptly caved in before the weight of General Count L.V.J. St. Hilaire's division, which slammed clear through the town of Pratzen. Farther north, General Dominique Vandamme's division swung around this clash and charged Kollowrat's formation from the rear. By 9:30 a.m., the weak Allied center was a wreckage of men, horses, and equipment.

During the same period of time, along the highway to the north, nothing had happened. No one had bothered to tell Prince Bagration to attack, and Marshal Lannes had stood firm, silently daring the Russians to advance against his entrenched strongpoint on the Santon. A distant crescendo of fire clearly told them that the crisis of the battle was in the south.

Davout's men, with one of Soult's divisions attached, fought for their lives. The struggle swayed back and forth, fierce charge and countercharge surging among the marshes and stone walls around Sokolnitz. At 10:00 a.m., Friant's footsore division arrived, having marched directly to the sound of guns.* Friant had four horses killed under him and lived to tell about it. He also lived to see his wasted division take heavy casualties, first capturing and then losing Sokolnitz. By noon, however, the Allied offensive had spent itself against Davout's block of granite.

In the north, Bagration finally lost his patience and moved against Lannes' southern flank. Simultaneously, Lichtenstein's cavalry charged the French light cavalry; the French horsemen withdrew through Lannes' infantry, which had been precisely formed in squares. With two cannon for every one of Lannes', Bagration had a chance to force the issue along the highway. However, French infantrymen knew how to die, and they were not prepared to abandon either their defenses on the Santon or their valiant commander, who personally positioned his cannon under a hail of fire. At this point Murat found his chance to strike, and launched 1,000 steel-clad *cuirassiers*. Within minutes, the Austrian and Russian cavalry gave way and the initiative passed to Lannes, who

---

*Friant's division had started from its assembly area at Raigern for its original march objective in a reserve position, but a staff officer overtook its commander with orders for the division to reinforce the threatened positions in the south.

Marshal Nicolas Jean Soult

The Battle of Destruction: Austerlitz, 1805

steadily forced Bagration back down the highway. *(See Atlas Map No. 24.)*

Shortly after noon, watching from his new vantage point on the Pratzen Plateau, Napoleon correctly sensed that the battle had been won. Bagration's 14,000 men were slowly losing ground along the highway and were already separated from the forces on the plateau. Soult's two divisions were firmly on the plateau behind the Russian main body. Davout was hard-pressed, but showed no signs of breaking. To exploit his advantage, Napoleon now released Bernadotte to sweep the ground south of Lannes. Moreover, he calmly sent part of the Guard Cavalry to rescue an isolated brigade of Vandamme's division, which was under heavy attack by the Russian Guard Cavalry—Kutusov's last reserve.

These diversions were over within an hour, at which time the main attack resumed its southward swing, pressuring the survivors of the Allied main attack out onto the ice of Satschan Pond. Cavalry, artillery, and infantry intermingled in flight, while the French artillery fired shot from the bluffs to break the ice around the Allied troops. Finally, Napoleon himself ordered the guns quiet. The Emperor had his win, and as he had hoped, it was "no ordinary victory," but a battle of destruction. Nightfall and a fresh snow served to forestall an immediate pursuit."[39]

Austerlitz was one of Napoleon's most decisive battles, both in a military and political sense. By destroying Alexander's army, Napoleon forced Russia back to the East and was able to impose a peace on Austria and Prussia. From the standpoint of the purely military art, he left a model battle for military leaders to emulate. The tactical maneuver was as nearly perfect—considering the terrain and the enemy—as was Frederick the Great's maneuver at Leuthen. By deceiving his opponent beforehand, Napoleon set up the decisive counterblow. His untiring supervision insured the proper timing of the counterattack, which achieved superiority of combat power by striking the disorganized Russians from an unexpected direction. In every respect, Austerlitz belongs in company with Cannae, Breitenfeld, Blenheim, and Leuthen—all masterpieces of tactics and generalship, all decisive wins that shattered enemy strategies.

It had taken just 100 days for the Emperor of the French to lead the *Grande Armée* from the Atlantic coast to the threshold of the East. In that brief time, many of his soldiers marched nearly 1,000 miles. Baden, Württemberg, Bavaria, the Tyrol, and Moravia had fallen under the lash of the French Imperium. Ulm, Augsburg, Munich, Passau, and Vienna now lay under the Napoleonic heel. The Holy Roman Empire was dead; Austria was powerless. In what direction would the French Empire next expand? The answer was readily apparent. After agreeing to a truce with Austria, Napoleon harshly dictated a treaty to the Prussian envoy at Vienna. Prussia would soon regret its failure to join the Third Coalition.

Notes

[1] Gunther E. Rothenberg, *The Military Border in Croatia, 1740–1881* (Chicago, 1966), p. 94.

[2] Georges Lefebvre, *Napoleon: From 18 Brumaire to Tilsit, 1799–1807*, trans. by H. F. Stockhold (New York, 1969), pp. 237–238.

[3] Geoffrey Bruun, *Europe and the French Imperium, 1799–1814* (New York, 1938), pp. 44–46.

[4] Louis de Bourrienne, *Memoirs of Napoleon Bonaparte*, ed. by R.W. Phipps (4 vols.; New York, 1885), I, 318.

[5] Vincent J. Esposito and John R. Elting, *A Military History and Atlas of the Napoleonic Wars* (New York, 1964), p. 46.

[6] Maurice Dumolin, *Precis D'Histoire Militaire* (3 vols.; Paris, 1906–1913), II, 26.

[7] *Correspondance de Napoleon I* (32 vols.; Paris, 1858–1870), XI, No. 9244, p. 225.

[8] P.C. Alombert and J. Colin, *La Campagne de 1805 en Allemagne* (3 vols.; Paris, 1902–1904), III, 138–142.

[9] *Correspondance*, XI, No. 9202, pp. 188–189.

[10] *Ibid.*, Nos. 9207–9208, p. 191.

[11] *Ibid.*, No. 9227, pp. 211–214.

[12] *Ibid.*, No. 9244, p. 225; 9245, pp. 225–226.

[13] *Ibid.*, No. 9274, pp. 251–252.

[14] *Ibid.*, No. 9293, pp. 263–264.

[15] *Ibid.*, No. 9313, p. 276.

[16] J. Holland Rose, *The Life of Napoleon I* (2 vols.; London, 1901–1902), II, 20.

[17] *Correspondance*, XI, No. 9393, p. 336.

[18] Alombert and Colin, *La Campaigne de 1805 en Allemagne*, III, 17.

[19] *Ibid.*, 391.

[20] *Ibid.*

[21] *Correspondance*, XI, No. 9364, p. 308.

[22] *Ibid.*, No. 9372, pp. 315–316.

[23] *Unpublished Correspondence of Napoleon I Preserved in the War Archives*, pub. by Ernest Picard and Louis Tuetey and trans. by Louise S. Houghton (3 vols.; New York, 1913), I, 134–135.

[24] Loredan Larchey (ed.), *The Narrative of Captain Coignet*, trans. by M. Carey (New York, 1890), p. 117.

[25] Count Yorck von Wartenburg, *Napoleon as a General*, ed. by W.H. James (2 vols.; London, 1902), I, 229.

[26] Lefebvre, *Napoleon: From 18 Brumaire to Tilsit, 1799–1807*, p. 239.

[27] Dumolin, *Precis D'Histoire Militaire*, II, 213.

[28] *Correspondance*, XI, No. 9470, p. 392.

[29] *Ibid.*, No. 9425, p. 355.

[30] Baron Marcellin de Marbot, *Memoirs of Baron de Marbot*, trans. by A.J. Butler (2 vols.; London, 1892), I, 180–183.

[31] *Correspondance*, XI, No. 9497, p. 415.

[32] *Ibid.*, No. 9500, p. 417.

[33] *Ibid.*, No. 9491, p. 410.

[34] Louis de Segur, *An Aide de Camp of Napoleon*, trans. by H.A. Patchett-Martin (New York, 1895), p. 238.

[35] Dumolin, *Precis D'Histoire Militaire*, II, 246.

[36] Frederic Huidekoper, "Austerlitz: A Most Remarkable Forced March," *Journal of the Military Service Institution of the U.S.*, XXIX (July–August, 1906), 38–46.

[37] Segur, *An Aide de Camp of Napoleon*, p. 238.

[38] Wartenburg, *Napoleon as a General*, I, 259.

[39] The foregoing description of the battle is constructed from Esposito and Elting, *A Military History and Atlas of the Napoleonic Wars*, pp. 53–56; Wartenburg, *Napoleon as a General*, I, 250–262; and Claude Manceron, *Austerlitz, The Story of a Battle*, trans. by G. Unwin (New York, 1966).

The Jena and Friedland Campaigns

4

On October 25, 1805, approximately one month before the Battle of Austerlitz, the Tsar of Russia concluded a personal agreement with King Frederick William III of Prussia at Potsdam. Alexander promised to negotiate with the King of England to obtain Hanover for Prussia and subsidies to support the Prussian Army. In turn, Frederick William pledged to join the Austro-Russian alliance if Napoleon refused to grant independence to conquered territories in Holland, Germany, and Italy. Meanwhile, 180,000 Prussian troops would occupy a flanking position to menace the rear of the *Grande Armée* while it advanced eastward. To seal the bargain, Alexander accompanied the Prussian King and Queen in a secret midnight visit to the vault where the body of Frederick the Great lay entombed. In a simple ceremony lit by a flickering torch, the two monarchs grasped hands and swore their common cause at the grave of Europe's most renowned soldier. In so doing, they prepared the grave of the Prussian Army.

The Isolation of Prussia

Until the Battle of Austerlitz, there was still reason to believe that Napoleon's intrusion across the Rhine might only be temporary. The over-extension of the *Grande Armée* into Moravia had placed France in a dangerous military position. At the same time, a financial crisis in Paris had weakened the Government's capacity to support its military forces. For these reasons, Napoleon had been faced with a difficult choice—either precipitate a risky battle in Moravia to destroy the Third Coalition, or retire to a more tenable position nearer France. Alexander helped him resolve that dilemma with the ill-considered attack at Austerlitz. From that point on, Napoleon appeared bent on expanding the French Empire as far as possible. To be sure, ever since Marengo, he had increasingly thought of power on a European rather than a French

scale. Once he crossed the Rhine, it would have been difficult to retire behind it, and Austerlitz clearly encouraged him to accelerate the tempo of his aggressive enterprises. In fact, his triumph inspired the Emperor to define even more broadly his concept of *le Grande Empire*.

Napoleon moved swiftly to capitalize on his victory over the Austro-Russian Army. He forced Austria to sign a treaty (the Treaty of Pressburg, December 26, 1805) that divested

Frederick William III and Queen Louise of Prussia Meet With Alexander I of Russia at the Tomb of Frederick the Great, 1805

the Hapsburg Crown of its possessions in Italy and southern Germany, and demanded the cession of Austria's part of Venice, Istria, and Dalmatia. Later, he occupied Ragusa. As if to emphasize the finality of Austria's withdrawal from Germany, Napoleon subsequently promoted the Electors of Bavaria and Württemberg to the rank of King, while arranging the marriages of his stepson, Eugène, to a Bavarian princess, and his younger brother, Jerome, to a princess of Württemberg. Thus, France now considered Vienna a vanquished opponent, and could concentrate on Berlin.[1] *(See Atlas Map No. 25 for territorial changes that occurred between December 1805 and September 1806.)*

Prussia, which had anxiously observed the latest battle from the sidelines, hastily signed a treaty dictated by Napoleon at Vienna. With this treaty (the Treaty of Schönbrunn, December 15, 1805) the Prussian minister agreed to the transfer of the troublesome province of Ansbach to Bavaria,* and several small Rhineland duchies to France. In exchange, Prussia received temporary possession of Hanover, but at the expense of her relations—and trade—with England. Thus, at one stroke Napoleon provoked war between Prussia and England, weakened Austria and Prussia, and strengthened French relations with Bavaria, Baden, and Württemberg. At this point, there was no indication that Napoleon sought war with Prussia. To the contrary, he preferred to draw her into his imperial orbit by cutting her off from her former allies.[2]

While the French Emperor was subduing Austria and humiliating Prussia, he resolved to take over entirely the Kingdom of Naples, which was ruled by a Bourbon. From Vienna, he issued the following decree: "The Neapolitan dynasty has ceased to reign; its existence is incompatible with the peace of Europe and the honor of my crown." On the last day of 1805, he ordered his older brother, Joseph, to take command of the armies of Marshal André Massena and General Gouvion St. Cyr and to occupy the Kingdom of Naples. This was soon accomplished, and, in March 1806, Joseph received the formal title of King of Naples. At the same time, Napoleon gave his brother-in-law, Murat, possession of the Duchy of Berg on the east bank of the Rhine. In June, another brother, Louis, became King of Holland. Napoleon was now well on the way toward proving the validity of a private boast he had made in January: "I am making a family of kings attached to my federative system."[3] That same month, William Pitt—Napoleon's most stalwart adversary—died in office, discouraged by England's inability to halt the stride of the new Charlemagne across the Continent.

Far off in the Mediterranean, however, there was a glimmer of hope that Napoleonic aggression might yet be checked. On

July 1, a force of 5,200 British Regulars landed on the western shore of Italy, about 150 miles south of the city of Naples. A French division promptly attacked, using the bayonet. English infantry, firing well-ordered volleys, repulsed the Frenchmen, but the arrival of Massena with reinforcements forced the British to withdraw to their well-established base in Sicily. This show of force against French rule triggered a popular insurrection in Naples, which lasted for three years—until Murat finally quashed the last resistance in 1809. Napoleon, however, viewed guerrilla war as being secondary to his larger interests in European affairs; his lieutenants could handle popular uprisings, while he concerned himself with building his empire.

These changes in the old territorial order formalized several trends that had become apparent before the French victories at Ulm and Austerlitz. Three of these trends were the crumbling of the Holy Roman Empire, which formally ceased to exist in August 1806; the withdrawal of Austria from western Europe; and the expansion of the French Empire beyond the Rhine. The occupation of Naples, the forced transfer of Hanover to Prussia, and the crowning of a Bonaparte as King of Holland represented clear threats to British mercantile interests in the Mediterranean and North Seas, while French troops on the Dalmatian Coast posed a threat to longstanding Russian claims to the Dardanelles. Throughout the period during which these developments occurred, Prussia remained aloof from the fighting, but steadily became involved in the struggle for power. Eleven years of peace had brought French dominance in Germany and French troops to the borders of Prussia.

At first, the Prussian King and his ministers in Berlin viewed Napoleon's efforts to acquire territory along the Rhine as natural moves to provide buffer states as defense against an invasion of France. The strengthening of Bavaria and Württemberg was made primarily at Austria's expense. Prussian anxiety mounted, however, as the *Grande Armée* remained in southern Germany throughout the spring of 1806. Meanwhile, Talleyrand began negotiations with 15 west German princes to whom Napoleon had offered his protection. In July, the Confederation of the Rhine came into being. It was a typically Napoleonic creation that replaced the waste and inefficiency of the Holy Roman Empire with a territorial simplicity that facilitated modern government, while enhancing French influence in Germany.[4]

It now became apparent to Prussia that there could be no profit in negotiating with Napoleon. News of double dealing concerning Hanover reached the Prussian Government from British diplomats, and rumors of French concentrations along the Rhine and Main Rivers added to Frederick William's apprehensions. Prussia had maintained its neutrality in order to further peace and prosperity. The likelihood of both now

---

*It should be noted that this move was against the wishes of the Ansbach citizens, who had locked their gates against Bernadotte's corps in the Ulm Campaign, and the desires of the Prussian royal family.

seemed remote. High ranking officials openly criticized the King's policy. Louise, Prussia's vivacious and spirited Queen, led the war party, which finally persuaded Frederick William to stand firm against Napoleon's encroachments. Encouraged by this advice and trusting in the Tsar's promise of support, Frederick William decided in August to mobilize the Army again.

Apparently, Napoleon did not divine Frederick William's intentions for nearly a month. As late as September 10, he wrote to Talleyrand, "The idea that Prussia could take the field against me by herself seems to me so ridiculous that it does not merit discussion." But on the same day he observed more soberly to Berthier, "My Cousin, the movements of the Prussians have continued to be quite extraordinary. They need to receive a lesson."[5]

The Prussian Military System and State of Readiness

In 1781, five years before the death of Frederick the Great, a perceptive British general who had observed much of the Seven Years' War, wrote the following commentary on the Prussian Army:

The Prussian army, being composed chiefly of strangers of different countries, manners, and religion, are united only by the strong chain of military discipline; this and a most rigid attention to keep up all the forms and discipline established, constitutes a vast and regular

Louise, Queen of Prussia

machine, which being animated by the vigorous and powerful genius of their leader, may be justly accounted one of the most respectable armies in Europe; but should this spring, however, languish but for an instant only, the machine itself, being composed of such heterogeneous matter, would probably fall to pieces, and leave nothing but the traces of its ancient glory behind.[6]

Henry Lloyd's respect for the army of Frederick the Great thus included an implied criticism that helps explain Prussia's defeat a quarter of a century later.

Frederick's system, built on the premise that the state could only afford to send a few of its productive young men into military service, featured a highly trained standing army, nearly half of which was composed of foreign mercenaries. These men learned their business by incessant drilling. Like the Macedonians, they relied on the solidarity of a compact formation to break their opponent's line, rather than on the skill of the soldier, as did the Romans. The Prussian infantryman was, therefore, not an individual fighter, but a part of a smoothly running machine. Carefully balancing the limits of the Government's war treasury against the soldier's needs, Frederick economized on new equipment, but compensated with strong discipline and rigid training.

This philosophy of war relied on willpower as much as firepower to produce a favorable decision on the battlefield, a rationale that was valid only as long as the Prussian Army faced enemies that used similarly rigid, linear formations. The brilliance of the great King, whose position as Commander-in-Chief was guaranteed both by legal right and demonstrated skill, insured the best possible employment of the Army, both strategically and on the battlefield. However, Frederick's successors were unfit to replace him. For over a generation, they and the Prussian officer corps had gained little firsthand experience in war, and so were unable to interpret the latest doctrine and the Revolution in France. The *Ober Kriegs Collegium*, a council of old soldiers that supervised the Prussian military establishment under Frederick William III, assumed that all was right with the Army as long as the great Frederick's instructions were strictly followed. Governed by this philosophy, the hard-fighting officer corps that had built the Brandenburg-Prussian kingdom became soft—tamed by the reputation of past glories and the luxuries of peacetime.

During the two decades between Frederick's death and the Jena Campaign, the Prussian Army received many warnings that time was passing it by. A number of European theorists besides Lloyd criticized the formal style of war practiced in the eighteenth century. Maurice de Saxe, the victor of Fontenoy, had written in his *Reveries*, long before, that armies should be divided into subordinate formations of combined arms, and that part of each infantry regiment (or legion, as he proposed) should consist of light infantry capable of semi-independent fighting. The famous French theorist, Count de Guibert, went even further, calling for an entirely new kind of army in *Essai general de tactique*. Guibert proposed an army freed from reliance on fortified depots, trained to maneuver and fight decisive battles, and led by a general who departed from established convention. He also urged the reform of tactical formations, suggesting an *ordre mixte*—a combination of line, column, and skirmisher tactics—to replace the unwieldy linear array.[7]

There was ample precedent to support the feasibility of these ideas in the contemporary experience of European forces that fought in the American colonial wars* and the frequent successes of Austrian light troops during the Seven Years' War. The Prussian defeat at Valmy in 1792 might have suggested the bankruptcy of the old system to the losing commander, the Duke of Brunswick, who outmaneuvered his opponent and then, uncertain of success, withdrew without ever launching the final attack.† Gerd von Scharnhorst, an influential Hanoverian officer who gained a Prussian commission in 1801, had already begun to analyze the causes of French success in the early Revolutionary campaigns. Tactically, he observed, the French skirmisher could "profit from all advantages offered by the terrain and general situation, while the phlegmatic Germans, Bohemians, and Dutch form on open ground and do nothing but what their officer orders them to do . . . "[9]

Unhappily for reformers, men have usually felt more secure in established patterns of thought and action than in untried ways. Although Scharnhorst continued to call for more flexible tactical formations and the establishment of a militia to exploit patriotic feeling, he was unable to overcome the conservatism of the Prussian officer corps. One influential general emphatically stated that patriotism was incompatible with the discipline of the monarchial standing army: "What motive to fight for a fatherland, which to him does not exist, could possess the soldier who lives on his pay alone? He recognizes no other home than the company to which he belongs!"[10] Some officers conceded that changes were probably necessary, but none felt certain of the general direction these reforms should take. The following letter, written by a Prussian officer at the end of the Rhineland Campaign of 1794,

probably summarizes the opinion of the officer corps concerning Prussia's military readiness:

> What you as a Prussian might especially celebrate is the glory our brave warriors have proven again in this campaign . . . they are, believe me, still the same Prussians who in the unequal contests of the Seven Years War defended and preserved the state against half of Europe . . . the officers have lost nothing of their former energy. . . . Also the soldier is, in general, better, more loyal and no less brave. The supply and hospital services are in better condition. It is thus possible with this army to do even what Frederick the Great did.[11]

One may excuse such shortsightedness among the rank and file of an army that was still recognized in many quarters as the model of European military professionalism. However, one could hardly excuse the King, the titular Commander-in-Chief, for failing to update his professional cadre in a time of widespread and revolutionary changes. Perhaps Frederick William had too long counted on neutrality for safety. Neutrality may have been an effective safeguard in the short run, but it was a poor guarantee that Prussia would not have to fight again for its survival.

Mobilization and Deployment of the Opposing Armies

Nothing distinguishes the outlook of Napoleon from that of Frederick William III as completely as the following com-

Frederick William III, King of Prussia

---

*August Gneisenau, a Prussian light infantry officer, served in America, but his experience in the New World did not seem to have as much effect on the reform of Prussian tactics as did the thinking of other officers who had served only in Europe.

†Johann Goethe, who witnessed the battle, clearly saw that times had changed. To his stunned companions he prophesied: "From this place and from this day forth commences a new era in the world's history, and you can all say that you were present at its birth."[8]

ment of the French Emperor in December 1805: "Peace is a meaningless word; it is a glorious peace that we want."[12] Napoleon used diplomacy in his policy as he used his cavalry in strategy: to throw dust in the eyes of his opponent and to set him up for a decisive confrontation. When his strategy was successful, it left his adversary only two choices—to fight or to surrender. By contrast, when Bernadotte had bullied his way through the Prussian territory of Ansbach in October 1805, Frederick William had mildly retaliated—not with force, but with the threat of force, by mobilizing his long dormant battalions. At length, when Napoleon continued on his way to Ulm and then on to Vienna, it appeared that the danger had passed. Soothed by Napoleon's protestations of peace, the Prussian monarch demobilized his army several months later. Napoleon, on the other hand, did not demobilize, but maintained the *Grande Armée* in southern Germany, where it drew most of its support from Bavaria while threatening both Prussia and Austria. Napoleon's army was in a relaxed but ready posture in this favorable position when Frederick William decided to mobilize his army again.

The immediate cause of war was Frederick William's realization that Napoleon was offering Hanover to England behind his back. This final insult to the much trampled Hohenzollern honor required more than a conventional diplomatic response, and on August 9, the Prussian cabinet ordered the Army from its garrisons. At last, Prussia had emerged from her neutrality. However, she could no longer count on support from England, it was unlikely that Austria would face Napoleon again, and Russian help was far away. *(See Atlas Map No. 26.)*

In Paris, Napoleon heard of these developments, but at first interpreted Prussian movements as another bluff. On September 5, he ordered Berthier to begin reconnaissance of routes from Bavaria to the north, but on the same day he authorized Augereau 20 days' leave in Paris. One week later he warned Prussia that coercion of Saxony would be cause for war.[13] This was the final straw. On September 25, a messenger was dispatched from Berlin with an ultimatum from Frederick William III: all French troops were to withdraw behind the Rhine, and France was to leave Prussia free to organize a North German Confederation.[14] The bearer of this ultimatum arrived in Paris on October 1—one week after Napoleon had departed to join the *Grande Armée* in Germany.

As usual, both to give the appearance of pacific intentions and to give necessary attention to matters of state policy, the Emperor had stayed in Paris as long as possible before taking the field. Berthier remained in Munich, in nominal command of the *Grande Armée*, a responsibility for which he felt supremely unfitted. During this tense transition from peace to war, Napoleon bombarded his harassed subordinate with a flurry of dispatches on every conceivable subject.* On September 9 he wrote, "If I make war against Prussia, my line of operations will be: Strassburg, Mannheim, Mainz and Würzburg . . . " On the next day he asked, "How many days will it take for the artillery park at Augsburg to assemble at Würzburg? How much time will it take to send to Strassburg, the greatest part of the artillery pieces that are at Augsburg?" Without waiting for an answer, he dashed off another letter, designating Mainz as the main supply depot in place of Augsburg, and giving detailed orders on a variety of subjects: wagons for the transportation of bread, regimental ambulances, and money for the purchase of horses.[15]

The hardest matter to coordinate at long distance concerned the exact conditions under which the army was to deploy. On September 13, Napoleon defined his conception precisely: "I have sent orders to my minister at Berlin to leave at once if Prussia invades Saxony." On receipt of this news from the French Ambassador at Berlin, Berthier was to move his headquarters and the corps of Marshals Ney, Augereau, and Davout to Würzburg, the assembly area for the army. Two days later, Napoleon restricted Berthier's initiative: he was not to make any movements until the Ambassador actually left Berlin, and once notified of the Ambassador's departure, he was to assemble the army at Bamberg. Responding to the exact intention of these fast-changing orders was no simple matter. Dismayed by the task of interpreting Napoleon's desires under pressure, and fearful of acting wrongly, Berthier sent a plaintive appeal: "The Prussian Army . . . is advancing on Hof. . . . What is certain, Sire, is that all Germany is at the point of war. I am waiting from moment to moment for news from you and for your arrival . . . there is no time for your Majesty to lose . . . "[16]

By this time, Napoleon had become resigned to the fact that it would be impossible to avoid a decisive confrontation. He had already received a letter from Murat warning that everything pointed to war. On the same day, he confided in a frank newsletter to Eugène in Italy, "Prussia continues to arm. I hope that it will disarm quickly or it will soon repent."[17] Meanwhile, the Emperor actively pressed his ministers and staff to prepare Mainz as a base of supply, and Würzburg as his base of operations. He now had enough information to decide on a massive advance on Berlin from the Würzburg-Bamberg area.

On September 18, the Emperor received the news that Prussian troops had entered Saxony. He waited until that evening, and then ordered Berthier to concentrate the army. In a herculean effort, Napoleon worked all night dictating de-

---

*It is necessary to bear in mind that a courier required four days to travel from Paris to Munich.

tailed orders to coordinate the movement. At the same time, 400 miles away, Berthier chafed in frustration; he had learned of the invasion of Saxony but had not yet received the necessary signal from the Ambassador at Berlin. Berthier's urgent report did not reach Napoleon until five days later: "It appears that the Prussians are assembling at Hof, . . . at Magdeburg, where their main force is, and at Hanover."[18] Napoleon's reaction was immediate and predictable. He accelerated the northward movement of the *Grande Armée* and, especially, the displacement of Soult's corps from the region of the Inn River. Before dawn on the following day, he left Paris, accompanied by Talleyrand and the Empress Josephine. By the time the imperial entourage arrived at Mainz three days later, Napoleon had conceived the outline of the bold strategy he would employ.

The Emperor's first thought after arriving at Mainz was for information on Prussian movements. The latest intelligence available indicated that Berthier's earlier report had exaggerated the progress of Prussian deployment. Time was precious, but there was no need for unnecessary haste. Throughout the twenty-eighth, Napoleon busied himself with the inspection of troops and the communication of his greetings to various German kings and princes of the Confederation of the Rhine, who now required his promised "protection." There was even time for a customary bit of bravado, which the Emperor tossed defiantly back to Paris: "Hardships and dangers are nothing to me. I will regret the loss of my soldiers, if the injustice of the war which I am obliged to sustain does not result in causing humanity to experience so much mischief caused by feeble kings." Then, in another spasm of prolonged overnight dictation, Napoleon cast the shape of the coming campaign, beginning with a key order for Bernadotte's I Corps to occupy the southern exits from the Thuringian defile, northeast of Bamberg.[19]

In the Prussian camp, preparations were equally feverish, but hardly as well coordinated. Now that the King had decided on war, there was a curious lack of energy in the preparations for it. The mobilization itself was inefficient; out of a potential strength of over 200,000 men, nearly half remained in garrisons, depots, and fortresses, while 30,000 troops stayed in East Prussia. In addition, the King placed no pressure on the small German states for support, thus forfeiting another 38,000 men. No attempt was made to raise funds for emergency procurement, and no one thought to organize a reserve of munitions and weapons. Worst of all, after provoking the French to battle by his untimely mobilization, Frederick William allowed his senior officers to believe that there was still a chance for accommodation to Napoleon. Thus, at the hour when the most superhuman efforts were required of Prussia, the Army and the nation responded feebly and slowly.

If the political leadership of Prussia was inept because of the weakness of its head, the Army had a more egregious problem because it was burdened with three heads. The formations that deployed into Saxony were commanded by generals who operated almost independently of each other. The King entrusted overall command to the aged Duke of Brunswick, who also commanded the main army. However, Prince Hohenlohe, who had considerable experience commanding a corps in 1794, decided not to subordinate his army to the Duke, and proceeded on a semi-independent course of action. General Ernest Rüchel commanded a corps-sized force, only half the size of Brunswick's. Hence the Prussian Army was in fact divided into two uncoordinated main armies, a weak third element, and a distant reserve at Magdeburg.

Each of these armies was subdivided into divisions, which had recently undergone reorganization into the combined-arms pattern of the French corps. However, none of the Prussian commanders had any experience in handling this new kind of organization, and all persisted in the Frederician convention of issuing detailed orders to every regiment. In addition to this outdated method of tactical organization, there was no question that the higher generalship of the Prussian Army had fallen far below the lowest acceptable standards of the past. Brunswick refused to make a major decision without referring the problem to councils of war, in which the King's many advisers played an argumentative and disruptive role. Hohenlohe offered noncompliance, if not outright disobedience, to Brunswick's orders. Furthermore, Frederick William determined to stay at Brunswick's headquarters, thus superimposing his sizable military and diplomatic suite on an already overburdened operational agency. The result was confusion and indecision.[20]

On September 25, the day the Prussian Cabinet dispatched its ultimatum to Paris, the Duke of Brunswick submitted his plan to the King, recommending an advance against the French line of communication. (Several plans had already been considered and rejected.) Hohenlohe, urged on by his chief of staff, had already submitted a counter plan for an offensive on the east side of the Saale River. The scheme that was finally adopted was for 10 divisions to advance through the Thuringian Forest onto the French left flank near Würzburg; however, as Carl von Clausewitz, the Prussian critic, acidly noted, "One had good reason to fear that this plan of attack . . . was no longer practicable. . . ."[21] By the end of September, information on French dispositions began to materialize, and it was apparent that the *Grande Armée* was not waiting to be caught in its cantonments. Obviously, Napoleon was not going to allow the Prussians to cross the border first. *(See Atlas Map No. 26.)*

By October 4, Brunswick had abandoned the idea of attacking the French, and convened a meeting of the royal staff to seek advice. The discussion became heated and ended without a decision. On the following day, Scharnhorst, Brunswick's chief of staff, offered to reconcile the opposing ideas, suggesting approval of Hohenlohe's concept: "Let us carry out the march towards the left, suggested by the Prince, but let us do it immediately and with maximum energy."[22] However, the meeting ended in wrangling; the troops remained stationary and fatally dispersed over a 60-mile front. Disunity of effort and the irresolute high command had nearly paralyzed the Prussian Army before the French had even fired a shot. Scharnhorst, probably the most clear-sighted officer on the Prussian staff, bitterly deplored the dangerous posture of the divided army: "What ought to be done, I know right well; what will be done, only the gods know."[23]

The French Advance

On the same day that Scharnhorst tried to persuade his superiors to act, Louis Nicolas Davout squinted out at the divisions of his corps passing in review at Bamberg.[24] Davout was one of those men who command attention not because of striking appearance or glittering attire, but rather because of unpretentious manner and unshakeable character. In fact, Davout had a rather odd appearance; at 36 he was bald, slightly stooped, and severely nearsighted. On the battlefield, he had to wear a pair of special combat glasses that fastened behind his head. None of these impediments seemed to affect his leadership. In garrison he was a thorough trainer; in battle he was coldly efficient.

Marshal Louis Nicolas Davout

Altogether, III Corps included nearly 29,000 officers and men, although Davout admits in his memoirs that somewhat fewer actually made it to the battlefield. Under his command were three infantry divisions, a cavalry division, an artillery reserve of 70 pieces, and a company of engineers. It was a proud moment for an officer who had been thrown out of the Army during the Revolution for insubordination, although it is unlikely that the quiet, methodical Davout would have shown much enthusiasm anyway. He was more concerned with looking after the condition of his troops and arranging the billeting of the Guard, which, for some reason, Napoleon

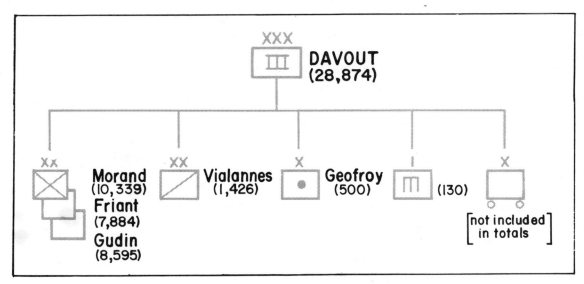

Davout's III Corps Organization

The Thuringian Forest, North of Coburg

had ordered him to prepare.[25] Besides, Davout's corps was well to the rear of Bernadotte's and the cavalry of Murat. It appeared that I Corps or IV Corps would probably have the first brush with the enemy.

The orders Davout received from Berthier early on October 7 seemed to confirm this supposition. He was to move his corps forward and enter Kronach on the following day, ready to support Bernadotte's advance to the Saale on October 9. The rest of Berthier's message spelled out the general formation for the army's advance: Soult, followed by Ney on the right flank, was to advance through Bayreuth; Bernadotte, Davout, and the Guard were to advance in the center through Kronach; Lannes, followed by Augereau on the left, was to move through Coburg; and the Imperial Headquarters was to move from Bamberg to Kronach on October 9.[26]

Now the grand design unfolded. "With this immense superiority of forces assembled in such a limited space," Napoleon wrote to Marshal Soult, "you will understand that I am determined to hazard nothing and to attack the enemy wherever he may stand with double his strength." Napoleon was confident of his strategy before the *Grande Armée* began to move through the rough, densely wooded Thuringian Forest,* where lateral communications would be difficult. *(See Atlas Map No. 27.)* By moving two corps on each route, he planned to have quick reinforcements at hand for each of the advance elements. While these units moved as rapidly as possible through the narrow passes, the thickly wooded terrain would deny maneuver room to the Prussian cavalry. On the other side of the defile, however, infantry would have to rely on their square formations to repulse the highly regarded Prussian *cuirassiers*. "After having arrived at Hof your first care will be to establish communications," the Emperor continued in his message to Soult, "I cannot too strongly recommend to you to correspond very frequently with me and to

keep me advised of all that you learn along the highway to Dresden." This was Napoleon's most immediate concern: to maintain supporting distance between his corps. The columns were separated by 20 to 30 miles of untraveled highlands. To further offset the danger of defeat in detail,† Napoleon counted on vigorous action by corps advance guards and the frequent exchange of information between himself and the commanders of the leading corps. "You will surely appreciate," he concluded, "that it is a fine thing to advance through this place in a battalion square** of 200,000 men. However, all that demands a little skill and some luck."[27]

Like the plans for the Marengo and Ulm Campaigns, Napoleon's strategy in 1806 accepted substantial risks for the promise of higher gains. Several days earlier, he had written to his brother Louis from Mainz: "My intention is to concentrate all my forces on the extreme right, leaving the entire area between the Rhine and Bamberg unoccupied so as to permit the concentration of 200,000 men on the same battlefield. My first marches will menace the heart of the Prussian monarchy."[28] To insure superiority of combat power in Saxony, Napoleon thus left France nearly defenseless along the Rhine. However, it is one thing to oppose weakness to enemy strength and quite another to expose a vulnerability that the enemy can only exploit by taking a large risk himself. Napoleon was too familiar with Frederick William's charac-

*On inset, Map 27, the Thuringian Forest runs generally from Eisenach to Ilmenau to Hof.

†Defeat in detail occurs when one part of a force is defeated before it can be reinforced by other parts of the force. In this case, the individual corps of the *Grande Armée* were potential subjects for such a defeat.

**The battalion square was the term Napoleon used to describe the formation in which he marched the several corps of the *Grande Armée* when approaching the enemy. They were positioned in the form of a square (or diamond) so that they could turn in any direction to repulse an enemy attack; they were also positioned so that they could reinforce each other rapidly.

ter to believe that the Prussian King would attempt a bold stroke toward the Rhine. Anyway, he had no intention of granting the enemy enough time to take the offensive. Within two weeks he planned to fight a battle on the Saxon plain, trusting that Prussia had neither the capability nor the comprehension to carry out a decisive offensive within that time.

There were interesting similarities between Napoleon's strategy for 1806 and those of his previous campaigns. In each case, he assembled his army behind the screen of a protective terrain feature (the Alps in 1800, the Rhine in 1805, and now, the Thuringian Forest); in each case, he avoided the enemy's main strength and struck for his rear to cut him off from his line of communication and his homeland; in each case, information of the enemy was limited. At the same time, the campaign of 1806 was a unique operation in which a number of conditions were different from those of either 1800 or 1805. From top to bottom, the *Grande Armée* was more experienced than it had ever been; hence it was more resilient to unexpected shocks, as well as more responsive to Napoleon's touch. The Emperor could therefore take chances with more confidence in his subordinates, even though he warned them that the Prussian Army would be a tougher competitor than the Austrian or Russian Armies had been. Trusting in his corps commanders, and mostly in himself, Napoleon was willing—in fact, preferred—to accept a certain element of chance, while forcing his less flexible enemy to make mistakes on which he could capitalize. Napoleon's strategy was not a fixed script, but an inventive art in which the flexibility of his veteran army perfectly complemented the fast-paced movement of his mind. *(See Atlas Map No. 27.)*

Bamberg to Saalfeld— The French Initiative

Marching swiftly behind a light cavalry screen on October 9, Bernadotte's troops encountered a Prussian covering force of about 7,000 men that was falling back to avoid pressure from Soult's advance farther to the east. The Prussians offered a brief resistance to I Corps before withdrawing, hotly pursued by Murat and a regiment of hussars. This first action between opposing forces cost the enemy nearly 400 casualties, but was not sufficient to confirm Napoleon's opinion that the Prussian main body lay on his left. To carry out the task of uncovering the enemy's strength on that side, Napoleon called on Jean Lannes.

Lannes' V Corps had moved through Coburg on October 8. After a difficult march on October 9—27 miles over an atrocious road—V Corps advanced out of the Thuringian defile and prepared to attack the Prussians. That evening,

Marshal Jean Lannes

Lannes received news from Berthier that Saalfeld was probably held in strength by the enemy. If this proved to be the case, he was to wait for Augereau before attacking.[29]

Meanwhile, a Prussian reconnaissance team had reported to Brunswick that the *Grande Armée* was streaming north from Bamberg. Subsequent reports indicated that Napoleon had left no combat troops to protect his line of communication through Würzburg to Mainz. Brunswick saw his opportunity. In perfect eighteenth-century form, a token force of 11,000 men would break through the Meiningen Gap and threaten the French line of communication along the Main River. Casting aside Scharnhorst's recommendation to mass the army east of the Saale River, Brunswick ordered the rest of the army to concentrate west of the Saale. Hohenlohe's new scheme—to attack along the east bank of the Saale—was simply ignored, allowing Hohenlohe to advance on the assumption that his plan had been approved.[30] Thus, while the compact French Army rapidly crossed the Thuringian barrier, the ill-coordinated Prussian and Saxon forces achieved a further state of dispersion.

A short but decisive engagement at Saalfeld on October 10 shattered Hohenlohe's optimism and Brunswick's illusions. Prince Louis Ferdinand, the hot-blooded nephew of Frederick William,* commanded the advance units of Hohenlohe's army. Hohenlohe's intention to press an attack in this area reinforced Louis' burning desire to wage his own private war

*Prince Louis was one of the leading members of the Prussian war party, which had convinced Frederick William to declare war.

with the hated French. Late on October 9, after superfluous correspondence with Brunswick, Hohenlohe had finally acknowledged that Brunswick expected him to obey orders, and had ordered Louis to hold his positions along the
Saale River, south of Jena. Louis, who had been watching
Lannes' campfires in the foothills, either ignored these orders
or did not receive them in time. Unaware that French units
moved in corps of 15,000–30,000 men, he advanced to Saalfeld with 8,300 men to meet the French advance personally.
The uneven action lasted less than four hours as Lannes
promptly deployed cavalry, artillery, and skirmishers to fix
the Prussian defenders, while a division maneuvered through
the woods to envelop the Prussian right flank.[31] In desperation, Louis led a cavalry charge to try to restore his line. He
was killed in the fighting, and his force dissolved. The news
of this setback and of Louis' death spread consternation
throughout the army. *(See Atlas Map No. 28 .)*

The sharp skirmish at Saalfeld was less important tactically
or strategically than it was for the psychological effect it had
on the defeated soldiers and the Prussian high command.
After confused marches and countermarches, which seemed
to have no other purpose than exhausting the soldier's
energy, the poorly supplied Saxon troops began to wonder
whether they had joined the wrong cause. Stories spread that
the Prussian generals planned to sacrifice the Saxons to cover
their own retreat. While Brunswick concentrated the main

The Death of Prince Louis at Saalfeld, 1806

army near Weimar, Prussians and Saxons at Jena fought over
supplies, firewood, and bivouac areas. Suspicion quickly
turned to an outright lack of confidence. During a march
through Jena, one column panicked at the totally groundless
report that French troops were between Jena and Weimar. At
nightfall, on October 12, Hohenlohe, having settled his
troops in reconnoitered assembly areas, began preparations to
defend against Lannes' driving advance from the south. No
one knew for sure where the French army was; rumor ruled
the Prussian camp. In the confusion, both Hohenlohe and
Brunswick failed to act on the one most important piece of
news the Prussians received that day: French cavalry was in
Naumburg, 15 miles *north* of Jena.[32]

From the beginning, Napoleon had planned to throw the
mass of the *Grande Armée* to the east of the Saale. Early on
October 10, he had reviewed the situation and decided that
the rapid advance of Bernadotte and Lannes had definitely
thrown the enemy off balance, but he still had no clear conception of his enemy's pattern of movements. The Prussian
plans to attack had been temporarily thwarted, but which of
his two remaining alternatives was Brunswick most likely to
adopt: an offer of defensive battle west of the Saale, or a retreat via Magdeburg?

To clarify that important issue, Napoleon ordered Murat to
reconnoiter vigorously along the east bank of the Saale, and
reproached him for scattering his cavalry on minor tasks. To
Soult he expressed hopes that the enemy would stand and
fight:

> If he attacks me, I will be delighted; if he allows me to
> attack him I will not fail to do so; if he withdraws to-
> ward Magdeburg, you will be at Dresden before him. I
> greatly desire a battle. . . . After this battle, I will be at
> Dresden or at Berlin before him.[33]

Napoleon had hardly finished this dictation when a message
arrived from Soult, reporting that the enemy had evacuated
Plauen and was falling back on Gera. Napoleon now lacked
information only from the left column to support his half-
tested hypothesis that Gera was the enemy concentration
point. In a postscript to Soult's orders, he stated this belief,
but pointed out that further supposition would have to await
the judgment of the day's events.

Three hours later, Napoleon heard the noise of Lannes'
fight 15 miles away. He correctly sensed from the magnitude
and short duration of the artillery fire that Lannes had won,
but wrongly concluded that Hohenlohe was covering the
Prussian withdrawal toward Gera. Without waiting for a report from Lannes, Napoleon anxiously dispatched orders to
Soult, Murat, and Bernadotte to head for Gera; to Davout to
take over the lead of the center column; and to Augereau
(who was still waiting for orders near Coburg) to catch up

with Lannes by forced marches. The heavy cavalry of Murat's corps and the Guard were still strung out between Bamberg and the Thuringian divide. Napoleon ordered them forward in anticipation of a battle on the plains somewhere east of the Saale.[34] All the evidence indicates that Napoleon's misinterpretation of the erratic Prussian movements lasted only until the morning of October 12, when a succession of reliable intelligence reports caused him to revise his estimate.

The most decisive news, forwarded by Murat during the evening of October 11, reported the capture of 100 Saxons in a convoy bound for Gera. These prisoners claimed that the King was at Erfurt "with 200,000 men."[35] Napoleon received this note at 1:00 a.m. on October 12, sat down to study the situation, and two hours later began to dispatch the flurry of orders that led to the envelopment of Jena. To Lannes went delayed congratulations for his bold action at Saalfeld and an update on the enemy situation. "All the letters intercepted prove that the enemy has lost its head. They hold councils night and day, and do not know what to do. . . . The game today is to attack everything we encounter, in order to beat the enemy in detail while he is uniting his forces." Within half an hour, the hard-working Berthier dispatched a followup letter with the details of Lannes' mission: he was to proceed to Jena and obtain all possible information on the enemy's activities. To Murat went typical Napoleonic exhortations: "Attack boldly everything which is on the march. These forces on the move are columns endeavoring to concentrate, and the rapidity of my movements prevents them receiving counterorders in time." In a supplement to this message, Berthier wrote simultaneously that if the enemy re-

mained near Erfurt, Murat should proceed to Naumburg, "where Marshal Davout will be." Bernadotte received brief instructions to support Murat's movement. Finally, Napoleon sent orders to Davout to proceed directly to Naumburg and prepare for a fight.[36] This last was the decisive order that sealed the Prussians' fate. On the evening of October 12, after a march of 28 miles, the most reliable of Napoleon's lieutenants—the "Iron Marshal"—slept serenely at the bridgehead, his corps now occupied at Naumburg, squarely across the Prussian escape routes to Leipzig.

The next day brought a respite for the French lead units while Napoleon sharply ordered the Guard cavalry, artillery, and trains to close up for battle. By mid-morning the Emperor received Davout's evening summary, which pinpointed the Prussian main army at Weimar. Another intelligence report located Hohenlohe at Jena. Napoleon promptly took action to reinforce Lannes' isolated corps, ordering Ney to march as far toward Jena as possible before dark, and Murat and Bernadotte to move from Naumburg to Dornburg. *(See Atlas Map No. 29.)* "At last the veil is torn aside, the enemy having begun its retreat to Magdeburg."[37]

Jena: Closeup of a Commander

If the French troops received a rest on October 13, their commander decidedly did not. His entire day and most of the night was spent in feverish activity. At 9:00 a.m., he de-

The Commander and His Staff

parted from Gera on horseback to determine the exact situation on the Saale. En route, he located a new position for Soult in reserve, and hurried off a dispatch to order the necessary displacement. Hearing the crackle of musket fire from the direction of Jena, Napoleon headed for the noise and met a courier from Lannes who brought news that "the enemy has . . . 30,000 men one league from here on the road to Weimar. He will probably want a fight." This occasioned Napoleon to speed the moves of Soult and the Guard infantry. At the same time, he sent orders to Davout and Bernadotte covering two contingencies. If they heard heavy firing at Jena that evening, they were to march via Naumburg and Dornburg on the east bank of the Saale to envelop the enemy's left flank. If no enemy attack developed that night, early morning orders would direct their movements.[38] Having settled affairs to the north, Napoleon galloped on to Jena for a personal reconnaissance of what he felt sure was the Prussian main army.

Thanks to the Prussian surrender of the heights on the west bank of the Saale, Napoleon was to see a great deal. Hohenlohe's covering force had given up this difficult terrain feature and withdrawn in search of more level ground for fighting. Lannes, arriving at daybreak with his advance guard, promptly took possession of the Landgrafenberg, a high plateau overlooking Jena to the south and dominated by a round hill, the Dornberg, to the north. At 4:00 p.m., the Emperor arrived, dismounted, and walked forward over this ground with Lannes until they came under fire from the enemy outposts. Napoleon had a clear view to the west where nearly 30,000 Prussian troops were visible, but he now committed an error in judgment that was to have a decisive effect on the course of the battle. He estimated that Hohenlohe's troops comprised the entire Prussian force opposing him. Without checking this presumption, he immediately ordered all of Lannes' corps and the Guard infantry to occupy the Landgrafenberg that night. Apparently, he was counting on the corps of Augereau, Soult, Ney, and Bernadotte for the fight that would take place on the high plateau west of the Saale.

Unknown to the French, a Prussian council of war had decided to withdraw, Davout's threatening position at Naumburg having finally become too obvious to overlook. Orders went out on October 13 for the retreat of the main Prussian army to Merseburg (*see Atlas Map No. 28*) along the road on the west bank of the Saale, while Hohenlohe's smaller force covered the withdrawal from positions near Jena. In contrast to the vigorous French advance, the Prussians failed to send out security forces to clear the intended escape route, and were accordingly ill-informed of Davout's dispositions. Thus, on the evening of October 13, Napoleon was maneuvering to bring the bulk of the *Grande Armée* to bear on the Prussian rearguard at Jena, while Brunswick and 63,000 men struggled along a single road toward Auerstädt and Davout's thoroughly aroused III Corps.

Meanwhile, in accordance with Napoleon's instructions, Murat rode for Jena, ahead of his hussars and dragoons. Bernadotte, puzzling over his discretionary orders, finally decided to halt his tired troops for the evening near Naumburg.

Toward the end of the day (October 13), French units began to arrive on the Landgrafenberg. In the darkness, a certain amount of confusion was unavoidable. Lannes' artillery failed to appear, and Napoleon descended the slope to look for it. At this point, several houses in Jena caught fire. The glare blinded Prussian outposts, but illuminated the entire valley, helping Napoleon to find the V Corps artillery column. It had jammed itself into a dead-end ravine, and the exit was blocked by a cannon that had become wedged in the narrow trail. No officers could be found to untangle the snarl of cannon, limbers, and caissons. Napoleon, calmly taking charge, organized a work party to free the gun, and, lantern in hand, got the column back on the proper road.

By midnight, elements of four corps and the Guard were in the Jena area. Convinced that the entire Prussian Army lay in the darkness before him, an impatient and tired Napoleon had already decided to launch the attack at dawn. It appeared to be an enormous gamble; a bold counterattack by the entire Prussian Army might easily have driven his scattered lead units back down the hill. However, the victor of Arcola, Rivoli, Marengo, and Austerlitz was certain that the odds favored him. Even if he did not have a numerical advantage, he knew that his troops had moral supremacy, and was confident that his own personal superiority would tip the scales. All other factors became secondary to the paramount consideration: to attack the Prussians with whatever troops were available before the enemy could get away. Almost as an afterthought, Napoleon sent Davout his orders for the battle—to attack toward Apolda against the flank of the Prussian army. Berthier, working in haste and trying to clarify the Emperor's intentions, added a note: "If Marshal Bernadotte is with you, you can march together, but the Emperor hopes that he will be in the position indicated to him, at Dornburg."[39]

Napoleon and Berthier formed an extremely competent team of commander and staff officer, but they did not always work at maximum efficiency. Napoleon formulated ideas so rapidly that he sometimes failed to articulate his completed thoughts; nor was he often willing to divulge his inner thinking. Communicating with subordinate units, governmental agencies, and imperial princes thus posed problems of coordination that Berthier alone could not completely solve. However, the chief of staff tried valiantly, making every effort—short of reading Napoleon's mind—to transmit not only Napoleon's orders but also the intentions behind those orders, and, when he could foresee them, the coordinating instructions required to facilitate the army's movements. By staying near his master's elbow at critical times, Berthier at least managed to catch most of what Napoleon said, and thus was able to check on the myriad of details that inevitably complicated every imperial wish. On the hectic evening of October 13, however, there was a dangerous lapse in communication. *(See Atlas Map No. 29.)*

Perhaps it is too much to expect that men who had worked for weeks with inadequate sleep, under the crushing weight of life-and-death responsibilities and with the difficult task of making swift decisions based on incomplete and often incorrect information, should not occasionally make mistakes. Maybe, for once, Napoleon failed to keep a corner of his mind attuned to distant events while attending in person to the compelling business that lay close at hand. Undoubtedly, Napoleon's tactical judgment was affected by the same boundless overconfidence that had driven him to near fatal misjudgment on the eve of Marengo. Whatever the reason, there was a false move in the otherwise coordinated effort of shifting French combat power from bearing on a target previously assumed to be east of the Saale River, but now known to be in a location west of Jena. Napoleon certainly intended to attack on October 14 with only the lead elements of four of his seven corps (25,000 men). This was a dangerous but necessary move if he were to retain the initiative and fix the Prussian force for a decisive engagement. The Emperor could count on reinforcements of 70,000 men by noon, and 60,000 more by evening. But it was never his intention that any of his forces within 24 hours marching distance should miss the battle entirely. And yet, that was what happened.

At 3:00 a.m. on October 14, Davout received the Emperor's order, promptly gave instructions to his division commanders, and then rode to Bernadotte's headquarters to deliver Napoleon's message and personally confer with the I Corps commander. After a short discussion, Bernadotte announced that he was marching for Dornburg.[40] Not knowing for certain where the enemy's main strength would be found, Davout could not have realized the magnitude of the task he would have to undertake; but he now knew for certain that he would have to carry out his mission alone. With his thoughts well concealed behind his natural icy reserve, Davout rode back to his corps.

While Davout was conferring with Bernadotte, Napoleon concentrated on preparing the order for the attack at Jena. He made a final reconnaissance at about 1:00 a.m. and then returned to the one large fire he had permitted his Guard to build on the Landgrafenberg. There he dictated his plan. It was a badly written order;* place names were entirely omitted

*One must assume that Napoleon amplified the instructions in the written order in his discussions with several of the marshals that night—especially during his reconnaissance with Lannes and Soult.[41]

because of inadequate maps, and no mention was made of Davout's attack toward Apolda. However, this was a veteran army, which required no detailed instructions. Even in the dark, the order made sense: "The important thing today is to deploy on to the plateau; the dispositions necessitated by the enemy's maneuvers and forces will be fixed afterwards, in order to drive it from the positions it occupies and which are necessary for the deployment."[42]

The attack was keyed to Lannes' progress in clearing room for Augereau and Ney to form their troops on his left and right, respectively. Soult was to place his corps on the extreme right flank as space became available. To be sure of success, it was necessary for the assault to begin at dawn, before Hohenlohe had time to launch a spoiling attack; however, a dense fog delayed Napoleon's signal to begin the advance until about 6:00 a.m. By then, the Prussians had already commenced firing. *(See Atlas Map No. 30.)* When the troops left their positions, it was still too dark to determine direction, and Lannes' attack swerved too far to the left, blocking Augereau's deployment. Soon, Prussian and French troops were locked in close combat between Lützeroda and Closwitz. Neither Napoleon nor Lannes could see enough to discern the situation. Prussian artillery fired aimlessly, exploding a Saxon ammunition wagon in Lützeroda and occasionally felling a clump of French soldiers. At the same time, Soult's men were climbing the steep slopes on the right, while on the left Augereau's troops were cursing their way upward through difficult ravines, all of which seemed to run the wrong way. Unseen in the fog-shrouded action, Ney's advance guard then showed up, and without waiting for orders, plunged into the melee on the left side of Lannes' hard-pressed troops, entirely contrary to Napoleon's intention. By mid-morning, the fog had sufficiently burned off to reveal to French commanders two disturbing facts: their disarranged assault forces were wearing out, and Prussian cavalry was forming on the Dornburg, preparing to strike.

On the Prussian side, activity ranged from near panic among the Saxons to pure sloth on the part of Hohenlohe, but there were displays of uncommon bravery as well. Hohenlohe's forward defenses were alert and ready for the attack, repulsing several of Lannes' assaults in hand-to-hand fighting around the Closwitz Woods. The Prussian division commander engaged there sent back several calls for help, but Hohenlohe only responded after an intrepid attack by Lannes and Ney had already captured the western slopes of the Dornberg and the burning town of Vierzehnheiligen. Prussian infantry, attacking in rigid waves, was badly mauled by a battery of 25 guns that had been personally assembled by Napoleon on the Landgrafenberg. Throughout the morning, Brunswick's troops had slowly moved through Auerstädt; 13,000 men under Rüchel had trudged through Weimar; Saxe Weimar's

11,000 men were 30 miles away; and the Duke of Württemberg, with 15,000 men in Halle, would have been no farther removed from the battle if he had stayed in Berlin. *(See Atlas Map No. 31.)*

Toward noon, Hohenlohe at last mounted a coordinated counterattack on Vierzehnheiligen. Prussian troops swung forward, band playing and flags flying, as precisely aligned as if the troops were marching on the parade field. Napoleon's large battery could not be brought to bear on them, but Lannes' light artillery took them under fire, while the French infantry scrambled to take cover in the debris of the ruined town. A concerted push by Hohenlohe's infantry, which was well supported by artillery, might have flushed the skirmishers of Ney and Lannes from the town. However, Hohenlohe's men were untrained for street fighting, and their commander failed to understand that he was authorized to launch a sustained attack. Confronted with a dilemma for which their doctrine and training had not prepared them, Prussian commanders halted their tightly ranked lines and ordered what they could do best—battalion volley on command in the open. For two hours, 20,000 infantrymen remained exposed to French marksmen, who were nearly untouched behind the cover of garden walls and tumbled down masonry.

One more disaster occurred even after Hohenlohe finally ordered the retreat:

> Now Rüchel came tramping onto the lost battlefield, plowing his way with difficulty through the rout. Stout of heart and arm (if thick of head) certain that Frederick the Great's teaching encompassed the whole art of war, highly disdainful of French fighting qualities, he did not seek merely to cover Hohenlohe's retreat. Instead . . . he threw his little army into a wedge-shaped formation and marched on Gross Romstadt to win his own battle.[43]

Murat Leads a Cavalry Charge at Jena, 1806

Rüchel's attack staggered the French infantry and gained the plateau, but the Prussians then halted and began to deliver the conventional volley fire, exposing themselves to the withering fire of nearly the whole French army. By mid-afternoon, Rüchel's troops had broken, and the battle became a rout. Clausewitz has best critiqued the Prussian generalship at Jena: "When the Prussian generals . . . all threw themselves into the open jaws of destruction in the oblique order of Frederick the Great, and managed to ruin Hohenlohe's army in a way that no other army has ever been ruined on the actual field of battle—all this was due not merely to a manner which had outlived its day, but to the most downright stupidity to which methodism has ever led."[44]

Auerstädt: The Making of a Marshal

By the time the battle between Napoleon's main force and the Prussian rearguard was nearing its climax, Marshal Davout had already beaten the main Prussian army under Brunswick. *(See Atlas Map No. 30.)* Napoleon had left the III Corps commander considerable latitude in his mission, stating only that he must engage in the battle, but specifying neither route nor timing. After crossing the Saale River, Davout discovered that there was no way to march on the enemy other than by the long, steep slope to the Hassenhausen Plateau. This road, which crossed the Heights of Kösen opposite Naumburg, ran directly into the road to Freiburg, which was the escape route prescribed by Brunswick for the Prussian army. Davout quickly decided that it was necessary to seize the heights of Kösen if he were to deploy his corps for any fight that might erupt on the plateau.[45]

The lead French division marched at 4:00 a.m. on October 14, crossed the Kösen Bridge at 6:30 a.m. in thick fog, and collided with the Prussian advance guard shortly thereafter. Cavalry led by a flinty 66-year-old general named Gebhard Leberecht von Blücher charged Davout's lead units repeatedly, but was unable to penetrate the quickly formed infantry squares. As successive Prussian units came into action to support Blücher, Davout fed his trailing divisions into the battle. Friant's division double-timed across the bridge, labored up the incline, and proceeded directly into battle in battalion column on the right flank. By 8:30 a.m., Blücher had been sent pounding back toward Auerstädt with heavy losses. Davout's cavalry, consisting of three light regiments, arrived next and took position on the extreme right flank. Meanwhile, two divisions of Prussian infantry made a strong effort against the French positions along the road, nearly enveloping the French left flank until Davout's third division

Davout's Infantry Squares

raced into battle and beat off the Prussian cavalry on the left. At that point, Prussian determination faltered, partly because it was now becoming known that Brunswick had been badly wounded. In this extremity, Frederick William took command of the Hohenzollern Army. *(See Atlas Map No. 31.)*

Around noon, the last Prussian attack lapped around the hard-pressed French corps. The imperturbable Davout, having committed all his resources—one battalion remained behind to guard the Kösen Bridge—rode to the critical left flank to command personally. After breaking a ferocious cavalry charge led by Prince William of Prussia, the left flank division slowly began to advance into the teeth of intense Prussian artillery and infantry fire. The movement of one regiment, noted Davout in his memoirs, "was traced on the ground by the brave men who had fallen."[46] At the same time, Friant's division, in firm command of the high ground to the north, also began a steady advance. By 12:30 p.m., the spirit of the Prussian troops had been broken, and there were no grenadiers who could do for Frederick William what they had done for his illustrious ancestor at Mollwitz. The battle was over even before the army disintegrated into a rabble of scattered fugitives and running, fighting men.

Realizing that his army was crumbling, Frederick William lost heart and ordered the retreat from Auerstädt. The order was superfluous, but the King hoped to fall back on Hohenlohe for support. From that quarter, however, there was to be no support—only the wreckage of a dispirited army pouring west across turnip patches and potato fields through Weimar, every man for himself. On the other side of the Saale and Ilm Rivers, the two streams of fugitives intermingled, rendering impossible any positive control by their commanders. Once the elaborate apparatus of discipline was demolished, the primordial instinct of survival reasserted itself, and each man bent his remaining energies to insuring that he remained a survivor, rather than becoming a casualty. A proud army had lost its title to greatness; an era had been conclusively ended.

But what of Bernadotte, Prince of Ponte Corvo, the commander of the lead French corps that had struck first through

Thuringia onto the Saxon plain? Bernadotte departed from Naumburg early on the fourteenth and marched for Dornburg, which he reached at about 11:00 a.m. En route, he could hear the noise of III Corps' desperate fight behind him, but refused to countermarch to Davout's aid. His orders were to march to Dornburg, he later claimed, and that is where he steadfastly proceeded. As a consequence, the 20,000 men of I Corps, reinforced by two divisions of cavalry, took part in neither of the battles fought that day. This misunderstanding may well have cost many of Davout's soldiers their lives—out of the 26,000 men engaged, III Corps lost nearly 8,000.[47]

Even late on October 4, Napoleon had no idea of the totality of Prussia's defeat. The Emperor knew that he had routed an army nearly 50,000 strong, but that left a sizable portion of his opponent's troops unaccounted for. Apparently, because of the din of fighting on the plateau west of Jena, he had heard no sounds of the action at Auerstädt. Until he received Davout's report the next morning, he was uncertain of the overall outcome of the battle and had as yet ordered no immediate tactical pursuit. Later on the fifteenth, Napoleon wrote to Murat, "Marshal Davout has had a superb fight; alone he defeated 60,000 Prussians."[48]

Pursuit to the Oder

Shortly before learning of Davout's magnificent action, Napoleon began to throw the *Grande Armée* forward to exploit the victory. *(See Atlas Map No. 32.)* Murat and Ney pushed to the west, while the remainder of the army received orders to stand ready until the direction of the Prussian retreat became known. Early on the following morning, the marshals began to feel the imperial lash again. To Murat went orders indicating that he was to pursue the enemy with his sword at their backs, and later in the day Napoleon wrote again: "I presume you are not losing a minute in pursuing the enemy . . ."[49] Meanwhile, Bernadotte began to move toward Halle, while Soult advanced to the northwest toward the Harz Mountains. Now the chase was on!

Frederick William's thoughts wavered between collecting the still unused parts of his army and gathering the remnants from Jena and Auerstädt. Napoleon's intention was to push him hard, denying him the opportunity to halt in safety. On the night of October 14, Murat took the fortress at Erfurt without a fight, harvesting 10,000 prisoners. Two days later, Bernadotte fought a sharp action at Halle, dispersing Württemberg's army and taking 5,000 more prisoners. Murat, Soult, and Ney followed in Hohenlohe's tracks, while Bernadotte, Lannes, and Augereau moved toward Magdeburg and Berlin to cut the retreating Prussians off from

Russian reinforcements. Meanwhile, Napoleon released all Saxon prisoners and sent an emissary to Dresden to soothe the Saxon Government and separate Saxony from her Prussian alliance.*

Ten days after the battle, French troops were at the outskirts of Berlin, and Frederick William had fled to East Prussia. Davout's corps received the honor of entering Berlin first. An observer noted with surprise that these were "lively, impudent, mean-looking little fellows" who had beaten the Prussian Regulars.[50] Just three days earlier, Hohenlohe, hounded by Ney and Soult, had pulled out of Magdeburg with 40,000 men. Blücher, who had slipped across the Harz Mountains with the Prussian heavy artillery, now fell in with Hohenlohe, after having abandoned most of the cannon in difficult terrain.

Hohenlohe's retreat to the northeast might have resulted in an epic escape if Napoleon had not switched Murat's cavalry from the western axis to the east. Nipping at the Prussian's heels all the way, these enthusiastic harriers finally ran down the last of Hohenlohe's exhausted force 25 miles from the Oder River. Blücher, who had kept up a stout rearguard presence behind Hohenlohe, heard of the Prince's surrender, and quickly changed direction to the northwest, intending to run for a neutral haven. Murat, Soult, and Bernadotte finally cornered the aggressive cavalryman near Lübeck, where he surrendered on November 7. Murat's laconic report wrote the end to one of the most active pursuits in history: "Sire, the combat ends for lack of combatants."[51]

The Continental System

One of the most interesting and frequently recurring themes in the history of war is the way extended conflicts inevitably become altered by unexpected circumstances. Every battle— won or lost—creates a different situation in the political and geographic sense, thereby producing new enemies or allies, new constraints to policy and strategy, and often new objectives—which sometimes lead to new wars. So it was after Jena and Auerstädt. Forced prematurely into war by Prussian intransigence, Napoleon suddenly discovered tremendous opportunities after his devastating win. In his mind, he had long since renounced any intention of retiring behind the Rhine. Now he had no intention of halting at the Elbe. Less than a month later, most of Europe west of the Oder River lay under

his control, and Napoleon could seriously entertain the idea of excluding England altogether from the European Continent.

Throughout Napoleon's rise to power one may trace a continuing thread of competition with and hatred of England, beginning even before the Italian Campaigns in 1796. No doubt, the young Corsican learned early to respect the British squadrons that brazenly patrolled off the rocks of Genoa; he championed the expedition to Egypt, at least in part, to demonstrate that France might challenge British naval and commercial supremacy. His attempt to invade England in 1805 marked a further escalation of hostility, and the defeat at Trafalgar added a final bitter element that remained until the end of the struggle. However, to attribute Napoleon's advance against Russia in 1807 solely to a rising curve of anti-British sentiment is to oversimplify the wars of Napoleon. Napoleon fought against Prussia and Russia in 1806 and 1807 for many of the same reasons he had fought against England and Austria; but mostly he fought because they resisted his expanding empire. In 1807, his feud with Great Britain converged with his larger imperial aims. Unchecked conquest on land now made feasible the subjugation of all of Europe.

Germany was the first to learn of these unparalleled schemes of conquest. In Berlin, Napoleon swiftly recast the shape of the expanding *Grande Empire*. Dukes, electors, and princes who had been allied with Prussia now joined the Confederation of the Rhine. Prussia ceded all its hard-won territory west of the Elbe. A special envoy travelled to Vienna to check any attempt at rearmament along the Danube. By the end of November, the *Grande Armée* had advanced to the Vistula, and French troops entered Warsaw, provoking a squall of Polish national feeling against their Russian, Prussian, and Austrian despoilers. Meanwhile, advancing French troops systematically closed the Hanseatic towns to British merchants, and, on November 21, 1806, Napoleon crowned his achievement by announcing the Berlin Decree.

This proclamation established a continent-wide blockade of the British Isles by closing all ports within the Empire to shipping of British origin. In addition, Napoleon ordered British merchandise seized, and forbade all travel, commerce, and communication with Great Britain and the British colonies. Even letters "written in the English language shall not pass through the mails . . ."[52] Lacking the naval power to enforce his paper blockade, Napoleon was forced to rely on the cooperation or control of commercial agents along the coast to impose his will. The war of conquest had become reinforced by all-out economic warfare.

Whether Napoleon could have enforced the blockade solely by land conquest remains an open question. The British retaliation on January 7 with an "Order in Council" forbidding neutral trade with France seems not to have bothered the Emperor. He saw very clearly, however, that his Continental

---

*Napoleon allowed his troops to deal more severely with Prussia, as is suggested by Marshal François J. Lefebvre's proclamation to a small German town: "We have come to bring you Liberty and Equality, but don't lose your heads about it; for the first one of you that moves without my leave will be shot."

System had little chance of successful application without Russian acquiescence. He had already given the order to call up 80,000 conscripts, and now was planning a spring campaign in Poland to enforce his will on Russia.

Eylau: Winter War

Napoleon remained in Berlin while Murat, Bernadotte, and Soult extinguished the last Prussian resistance on the Danish border. Now it was time to continue the war against Russia. First, the Emperor ordered his pursuing forces to reverse their direction and advance to the Vistula River—the next defensible obstacle to the east. There, he planned to seize sufficient room on the east bank of the river to allow for the protection of his troops in winter quarters, where they would prepare for the resumption of active campaigning in the spring. *(See Atlas Map No. 33a.)* Over 150 miles of nearly trackless wasteland separated the Oder from the Vistula. Rain, snow, frost, and thaw combined to obliterate the few serviceable roads that Napoleon planned to use in traversing that difficult ground. Nonetheless, the *Grande Armée* covered the distance in three weeks, although not without speculation by the troops as to how much farther their Emperor would lead them from Paris.

Napoleon planned to hold the prize of Warsaw throughout the winter, but he needed more territory on the far side of the Vistula to secure it. Davout and Ney fanned out to the north to cover the crossing of the rest of the army. On December 25, a strong Russian counteroffensive was shattered by the spearhead of Lannes' intrepid attack on Pultusk. Such victories were bought, however, at the expense of much suffering. Sergeant Coignet described the ordeal of the common French soldier:

> We sunk down up to our knees. We were obliged to take ropes, and tie our shoes around our ankles. . . . Sometimes we would have to take hold of one leg, and pull it out as you would a carrot, carrying it forward, and then go back for the other . . . and make it take a step forward also. . . . Discontent began to spring up among the old soldiers; some of them committed suicide. . . . We lost about sixty of them in the two days previous to our arrival at Pultusk, a miserable thatched village. . . . Here we came to the end of our misery, for it was impossible to go any further.[53]

The dire condition of the troops and the inability of the French supply system to operate in the barren spaces of eastern Europe finally convinced Napoleon to bring the campaign to a close.

Once again, unexpected actions—in this case, on the part

of Napoleon's own commanders—precipitated unwanted hostilities. Avid for glory, Ney gradually extended his troops to the northeast, in the hope of making a surprise assault on undefended Königsberg—the largest city in East Prussia. Bennigsen noted Ney's extended positions and, eager to profit from his dispersion, planned to break through to relieve Danzig, which now lay behind the French lines. On January 10, 1807, Bennigsen advanced, scattering Ney's cavalry but failing to rupture the main French positions.

While Ney was looking toward Königsberg and the Russians toward Danzig, Napoleon was thinking only of Bennigsen and how to get at his army. After rebuking Ney for his rash maneuver and ordering him back to his winter positions, Napoleon examined the developing situation. To prepare for a possible breakthrough, he formed a new corps under Marshal Lefebvre,* and instructed him to take up a reserve position at Thorn. Meanwhile, Bennigsen had continued his advance toward Danzig, driving Bernadotte southward toward Thorn. On January 27, Napoleon decided that Bennigsen's dispositions invited a counteroffensive, and ordered his troops from their winter bivouac to concentrate on the Russian south flank.

Bernadotte was instructed to fall back on Thorn while absorbing the enemy offensive. The bulk of the army prepared to attack to the north with the objective of severing Bennigsen's communication with Königsberg and forcing his army against the coast. It was to be a typically Napoleonic maneuver—a strategic envelopment in which minimum essential combat power protected the flanks while the bulk of the army assembled stealthily to deliver a hard blow to the enemy rear. Misfortune, however, intervened when Cossacks captured a newly assigned staff officer carrying Bernadotte's orders. Before the *Grande Armée* began the offensive, Bennigsen had learned Napoleon's entire plan. Immediately, he prepared to fight off the French counteroffensive.

While Bennigsen's army withdrew to protect its escape routes, Napoleon's army stumbled forward over bad roads made worse by several feet of snow. Tenuous communications made reliable information scarce, which in turn complicated Napoleon's task of coordinating his army's movements. On February 3, after a number of indecisive clashes with Cossacks, Murat collided with large formations of Russian infantry on the north side of the Alle River. Napoleon burned to come to grips with the Russians, but Bennigsen beat off all attempts to hold his army in position, and escaped

---

*The career of François Lefebvre illustrates Napoleon's desire to combine men of different talents in his new imperial nobility. Lefebvre was a man of humble origins who rose to the rank of Sergeant Major in the monarchial army. He became a staunch Republican after the Revolution, commanded the Imperial Guard at Jena, and received command of X Corps to besiege Danzig, apparently in order to justify his appointment to the Marshallate.

to the east. The impatient Emperor pronounced the action a
success. He might well have returned his shivering soldiers to
their winter bivouac, but a partial victory was inadequate
gratification for an imperial ambition.* Without hesitation,
Napoleon ordered his troops forward through blinding drifts
in pursuit of his elusive prey.

On February 8, Napoleon overtook Bennigsen at Eylau. In
an indecisive struggle fought in a blizzard, Napoleon enveloped both Russian flanks, but could not produce the final
thrust to destroy his opponent. Both armies suffered terribly,
and Bennigsen finally withdrew during the night, leaving
Napoleon in possession of a bleak, snow-covered field littered with frozen corpses and the debris of two suffering armies. Both sides claimed a victory, but veterans of Marengo,
Austerlitz, and Jena noted that after Eylau, Napoleon had to
deactivate Augereau's decimated corps. This was the first
time a major French unit had become ineffective for combat.

*It is perhaps significant that when the Emperor apparently refused to recog-
nize any limits to his empire, he also began to abandon propriety in his personal life. Since arriving in Warsaw, he had openly enjoyed a love affair
with Countess Marie Walewska in spite of Josephine's protestations. "You
must submit to all my whims," he brazenly wrote the unhappy Empress.

Friedland: Decisive Victory

After the fearful losses at Eylau, the war subsided into the
classic pattern of cavalry skirmishes, feints, withdrawals, and
local repositioning of reserves. Both sides planned to renew
their offensives in June. Napoleon, hindered by the necessity
to simultaneously conquer the Silesian fortresses—Danzig
fell on May 27—finally gathered his strength for a general
offensive on June 10. Meanwhile, Bennigsen had begun his
offensive, but soon lost the initiative when he was unable to
break through Ney's resilient defenses. *(See Atlas Map No.
33b.)*.

Napoleon's strategy contained the essence of subtle persuasion. By advancing along the left bank of the Alle River,
he threatened Königsberg and forced Bennigsen to make a
painful choice: remain on the west side of the river to fight
and protect the city, or withdraw to the east, surrendering
Königsberg and the rest of East Prussia. Napoleon guessed
that Bennigsen would stay and fight, but he was never sure—
until Lannes' brilliant independent action lured the Russians
into a fight at Friedland.

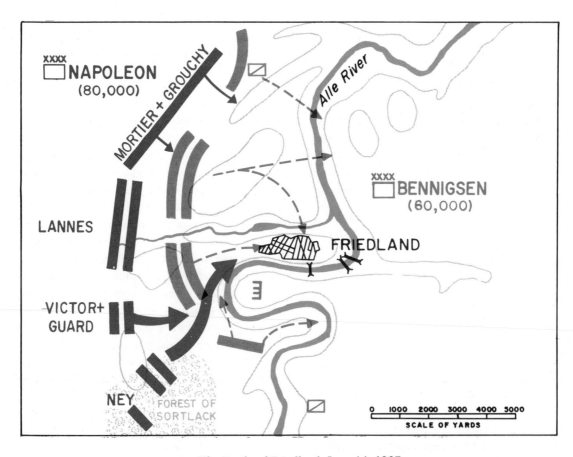

The Battle of Friedland, June 14, 1807

Early on June 14—the anniversary of Marengo—Lannes, with just 26,000 men, approached Friedland. Bennigsen had rushed to that town to prevent the French from seizing crossings over the Alle River. Hesitant to withdraw and uncover Königsberg, he gradually moved his army across the river in an attempt to destroy Lannes' isolated corps. By shifting his troops from one sector to another, Lannes managed to hold his ground. More important, he held Bennigsen on the west bank of the Alle for nine hours, while Napoleon raced toward Friedland with reinforcements to fight a decisive battle.

Joining Lannes on the heights overlooking Friedland at noon, Napoleon immediately perceived the incredible opportunity with which Bennigsen had presented him. The Russian army lay almost entirely on the wrong side of the river with an unfordable obstacle to its rear, and the town choked its withdrawal routes to pontoon bridges. To further aggravate this dangerous posture, a stream divided the Russian positions, making any lateral movement difficult. Several of Napoleon's generals suggested that it might be safer to delay the attack until next day, by which time more reinforcements might arrive from Königsberg. "No, no," exulted the Emperor, "we can never hope to trap them in such a mistake again."[54]

The supreme opportunist issued orders for the attack. By 4:00 p.m., Napoleon had gathered a force of 80,000 men; an hour later, he launched the attack, which was aimed at cutting the enemy escape routes to the river and destroying the isolated Russian army. Ney (reinforced) delivered the main attack, emerging from Sortlack Forest against the unsuspecting troops on Bennigsen's left (commanded by Bagration). For about 3,000 yards, the attack went well. Just short of the town, Ney's force recoiled, blasted by Russian artillery on the opposite bank of the river. At this point, Napoleon committed the reserve—I Corps, now commanded by Victor*—which had swung in close behind Ney's advance.

Victor's artillery commander shrewdly decided to mass 30 of his guns against the enemy line. In order to insure maximum effect at the decisive time and place, he ordered his crews to roll the pieces forward, along with the attacking troops. As Bagration's men emerged to halt Ney's attack, they met a storm of canister fire that shattered their formations and drove them back into the clogged streets of the town. Encouraged by this sight, Ney's men reformed and surged into Friedland while the town and the bridges burned. Once Friedland fell, Napoleon ordered his center and left flank forward to destroy the trapped remnants of Bennigsen's army. Many Russian soldiers who had escaped death in

---

*Although a man of somewhat dubious character, Claude Victor was valued as an audacious tactician. Originally a musician in the monarchial army, he became an officer after the Revolution, and later rose to be a brigade and division commander in Bonaparte's Army of Italy.

Friedland drowned in the Alle River; 11,000 bodies were found, but total Russian losses were undoubtedly much higher.

Tilsit

After Austerlitz, Friedland was Napoleon's best-coordinated battle, and it was clearly a bona fide victory. It erased the bad memories of Eylau, and was also a decisive victory in the strategic sense, bringing Russian resistance to an end. Two days after the battle, Soult occupied Königsberg and Alexander offered to negotiate. In a well-staged meeting on a raft moored in the middle of the Niemen River, the Emperor of the French and the Tsar of all the Russias divided Europe between them. *(See Atlas Map No. 34.)* Alexander joined the Continental System, surrendered his properties in the Mediterranean, and allowed Poland to become the Duchy of Warsaw under French supervision. A kingdom of Westphalia was created out of former Prussian territories, to be ruled by brother Jerome. The winner of the greatest amount of territory was clearly Napoleon, but Alexander may have won the more valuable and lasting rewards—peace and time for recovery. The biggest loser was Frederick William. While he waited—dismal and unbidden—on the shore of the Niemen, his erstwhile ally agreed to the reduction of Prussia to less than

Napoleon, Frederick William III, Louise, and Alexander I at Tilsit, 1807

her size in the Seven Years' War. Thus was the descendant of Hohenzollern greats rewarded for his feeble attempts to keep the peace.

Tilsit marked the high tide of Napoleonic conquest—the Empire's farthest expansion to the East. Within a month, however, Great Britain responded with a bold amphibious raid that damaged Copenhagen and destroyed the Danish fleet. In strategic terms the raid was significant—a vital fleet had been snatched from the conqueror's hand. Henceforth, Napoleon's Continental System was forced onto the defensive. The raid signified a psychological turn as well. As long as England lived, hope remained for the enemies of the French Empire. Amidst the shambles of the old order, Copenhagen became a signal of the resurgence of Europe.

Notes

[1] C.W. Crawley (ed.), *The New Cambridge Modern History* (14 vols.; Cambridge, 1966–1971), IX, 266–267; Leo Gershoy, *The French Revolution and Napoleon* (New York, 1933), p. 405.

[2] Georges Lefebvre, *Napoleon: From 18 Brumaire to Tilsit, 1799–1807*, trans. by H.F. Stockhold (New York, 1969), pp. 254–255.

[3] *Correspondance de Napoleon I* (32 vols.; Paris, 1858–1870), XI, No. 9625, p. 509; J. Holland Rose, *The Life of Napoleon I* (2 vols.; London, 1901–1902), II, 63.

[4] H.A.L. Fisher, *Studies in Napoleonic Statesmanship: Germany* (Oxford, 1903), pp. 118-121.

[5] Geoffrey Bruun, *Europe and the French Imperium, 1799-1814* (New York, 1938), p. 122; *Correspondance*, XIII, No. 10757, p. 162.

[6] Henry Lloyd, *History of the Late War in Germany* (London, 1781), p. xxvii.

[7] Maurice de Saxe, *Reveries on the Art of War*, trans. by T.R. Phillips (Harrisburg, 1944), pp. 36–37; R.R. Palmer, "Frederick the Great, Guibert, Bülow: From Dynastic to National War," in *Makers of Modern Strategy*, ed. by E. M. Earle (Princeton, 1943), pp. 62–68.

[8] J.F.C. Fuller, *The Conduct of War, 1789–1961* (New Brunswick, 1961), pp. 30–31.

[9] Peter Paret, *Yorck and the Era of Prussian Reform* (Princeton, 1966), p. 77.

[10] *Ibid.*, p. 91.

[11] Curt Jany, *Geschichte der preussischen Armee vom 15 Jahrhundert bis 1914* (4 vols.; Osnabrück, 1967), III, 307–308.

[12] *Correspondance*, XI, No. 9561, p. 472.

[13] *Ibid.*, XIII, No. 10744, p. 152; and No. 10765; H. Bonnal, *La Manoeuvre d'Iena* (Paris, 1904), pp. 27–28; *Unpublished Correspondence of Napoleon I Preserved in the War Archives*, pub. by Ernest Picard and Louis Tuetey, trans. by Louise S. Houghton (3 vols.; New York, 1913), I, 329.

[14] R.B. Mowat. *The Diplomacy of Napoleon* (London, 1924), p. 171.

[15] *Correspondance*, XIII, Nos. 10756–10758, pp. 160–164.

[16] *Ibid.*, No. 10773, p. 177; No. 10786, p. 188; Bonnal, *La Manoeuvre d'Iena*, pp. 56–58.

[17] *Correspondance*, XIII, No. 10789, p. 191; No. 10800, p. 198; No. 10803, p. 200.

[18] Bonnal, *La Manoeuvre d'Iena*, p. 105; *Correspondance*, XIII, No. 10881, p. 264.

[19] *Correspondance*, XIII, No. 10889, p. 266; No. 10893, pp. 269–270.

[20] Carl von Clausewitz, "Nachrichten über Preussen in seinen grossen Katastrophe," in *Kriegsgeschichtliche Einzelschriften*, ed. by the Military History Section of the Great General Staff (9 vols.; Berlin, 1885–1914), II, No. 10, pp. 481–485; Oscar von Lettow-Vorbeck, *Der Krieg von 1806 und 1807* (4 vols.; Berlin, 1892–1899), I, 99–100.

[21] Clausewitz, "Nachrichten über Preussen in seinen grossen Katastrophe," pp. 487–489.

[22] *Ibid.*, p. 491.

[23] Lettow-Vorbeck, *Der Krieg von 1806 und 1807*, I, 170.

[24] Louis Nicolas Davout, *Operations du 3d Corps, 1806–1807* (Paris, 1896), p. 7.

[25] *Ibid.*, pp. 8–11; *Correspondance*, XIII, No. 10943, pp. 311–312.

[26] Davout, *Operations du 3d Corps*, pp. 11–12.

[27] *Correspondance*, XIII, No. 10941, pp. 309–310.

[28] *Ibid.*, No. 10920, pp. 292–293.

[29] Maurice Dumolin, *Precis D'Histoire Militaire* (3 vols.; Paris, 1906–1913), II, 377–379.

[30] Clausewitz, "Nachrichten über Preussen in seinen grossen Katastrophe," pp. 502–503.

[31] Dumolin, *Précis D'Histoire Militaire*, II, 384–386.

[32] Clausewitz, "Nachrichten über Preussen in seinen grossen Katastrophe," pp. 502–503.

[33] *Correspondance*, XIII, No. 10976, p. 332; No. 10977, p. 333.

[34] Bonnal, *La Manoeuvre d'Iena*, p. 388.

[35] *Ibid.*, p. 399.

[36] *Ibid.*, pp. 406–407; *Correspondance*, XIII, Nos. 10981–10983, pp. 336–337; No. 10986, p. 338.

[37] *Ibid.*, No. 11000, p. 348; No. 11003, p. 349; Bonnal, *La Manoeuvre d'Iena*, pp. 412–413.

[38] Bonnal, *La Manoeuvre d'Iena*, pp. 415–416.

[39] *Ibid.*, p. 421.

[40] Davout, *Operations du 3d Corps*, p. 30.

[41] Paul-Jean Foucart, *Campagne de prusse, 1806* (2 vols.; Paris, 1887–1890), I, 625.

[42] *Correspondance*, XIII, No. 11004, pp. 350–351.

[43] Vincent J. Esposito and John R. Elting, *A Military History and Atlas of the Napoleonic Wars* (New York, 1964), p. 65.

[44] Carl von Clausewitz, *On War*, trans. by O.J. Matthijs Jolles (New York, 1943), p. 91.

[45] Davout, *Operations du 3d Corps*, p. 33.

[46] *Ibid.*, p. 41.

[47] Dumolin, *Précis D'Histoire Militaire*, II, 426; Hubert Camon, *La Guerre Napoleonienne* (2 vols.; Paris, 1903), I, 183.

[48] *Correspondance*, XIII, No. 11011, p. 360.

[49] Foucart, *Campagne de Prusse*, II, 34–35; *Correspondance*, XIII, No. 11017, p. 363.

[50] J. Holland Rose, *The Life of Napoleon I* (2 vols.; London, 1902), II, 101.

[51] Foucart, *Campagne de Prusse*, II, 757.

[52] *Correspondance*, XIII, No. 11283, pp. 555–557; Department of History, *Documents of the French Revolution* (West Point, 1970), pp. 71–73.

[53] Loredan Larchey (ed.), *The Narrative of Captain Coignet*, trans. by M. Carey (New York, 1890), p. 138.

[54] Camon, *La Guerre Napoleonienne*, I, 228.

The Resurgence of Europe

Another year! . . . Another deadly blow!
Another mighty Empire overthrown!
And we are left, or shall be left, alone;
The last that dare to struggle with the Foe.
                                        Wordsworth

PART III
DEFENSE OF
THE EMPIRE

There's a divinity that shapes our ends,
Rough-hew them how we will.
                        Shakespeare—Hamlet

Defensive on the Danube and in Spain

5

In December 1806, in the midst of an exhausting winter war in Poland, Napoleon sent orders back to Paris for the erection of a memorial building. This temple was to be inscribed with the following dedication: "The Emperor Napoleon to the soldiers of the *Grande Armée*." He further directed that the names of all the men who had fought at Ulm, Austerlitz, and Jena be engraved on marble tablets, "and on heavy tablets of gold the names of all those killed on the battlefield."[1] Even when on campaign, Napoleon always remembered that the seat of his imperial power lay in Paris. His power depended on his reputation, which in turn was nourished by the promise of *gloire*—the magic tonic that fired his legions to overrun Western Europe. Ultimately, the conquered nations learned to adopt the aggressor's methods. Finally, they took his empire away from him. But no one has ever succeeded in depriving him of his glory.

The French Continental System Versus English Command of the Sea

The Peace of Tilsit failed to bring peace to Europe. Napoleon and Alexander had met on a raft in the Niemen River and agreed to divide Europe between them. *(See Atlas Map No. 35.)* King Frederick William disconsolately accepted the reduction of his plundered Prussian kingdom by one half, and Emperor Francis of Austria maintained a wary neutrality to protect what was left of the Hapsburg domains. Smaller kingdoms, duchies, and protectorates saw their frontiers redrawn and their princes dispossessed without complaint, while Napoleon's relatives enjoyed newly created thrones in Holland, Italy, Naples, Westphalia, and Warsaw. England, however, remained unconquered and implacable. In May 1806,

the British Government had announced a blockade of the coast from Brest to the Elbe. After Jena, the new British Foreign Minister responded to Napoleon's Berlin Decree, which declared the British Isles to be in a state of blockade, with a counter order that escalated the commercial war: all neutral ships must carry a British license or risk seizure on the high seas. *The Times* mirrored public support of this active policy with its derisive comment on Napoleon's embargo: "His decree will have as little effect on British commerce as his navy has."[2]

At first, it appeared that the new French maritime policy was indeed only an empty threat. The British task force that raided Copenhagen in September 1807 carried off 61 Danish vessels, 15 of which were ships of the line that Napoleon had planned to incorporate into his renovated imperial fleet. Thus, while the Continent lay relatively quiet during the last half of 1807, British frigates ploughed relentlessly through uncontested waters all around the periphery of Europe. As long as England maintained command of the seas, the French

Temple de Gloire—Monument to the *Grande Armée*

The Meeting at Tilsit, 1807

blockade remained largely a paper embargo, primarily dependent for success on events outside the frontiers of the Empire.

In July 1807, after an absence of 11 months, the Emperor
had returned to Paris and begun to strengthen his despotic
control of the Government. He ruthlessly eliminated any individuals or agencies that resisted him, such as the judiciary
and the Tribunate, which he abolished entirely. Talleyrand
received an empty promotion, removing him from the field of
diplomacy which Napoleon resolved to bring under closer
supervision.* At the same time, Napoleon cultivated his personal creations: the new French university, which was to furnish the future officials for his empire, and the aristocracy of
merit, which executed his current designs. These domestic
projects were crucial for the permanence of his regime, and in
no way intruded on his immediate and overriding aim—the
enforcement of the Continental System.

Before the Berlin Decree, over two-thirds of Britain's markets were in America and India. Only one-third of British exports went to Europe, and part of this European trade was
with Sweden, northern Germany, and Portugal. Stalled in his
attempt to gain control of the Baltic, Napoleon determined to
seal the other gaps in his commercial defenses. Inspectors
and customs officials traveled to the Hanseatic towns of
northern Germany to crack down on the inefficient regulation
of imperial customs. At the same time, Napoleon demanded
that Portugal close her ports to British shipping.

In 1807 and 1808, the embargo began to undermine Britain's
economy. English exports fell from a declared value of 40.8
million pounds in 1806 to 35.2 in 1808. Signs of this decline
in trade encouraged Napoleon to increase the pressure on

England by occupying every corner of Europe not yet subser-
vient to his will. In November 1807, he wrote to his brother
Joseph in Naples, "I see that you have 27,000 men present
under arms. It is inconceivable that with this number of
troops you should suffer the English to remain at Scylla and
Reggio."[3] In December, the Congress of the United States
forbade American shipping to call at French or English ports
without presidential authorization. The effect of this ruling,
combined with Britain's loss of trade in Europe, reinforced
Napoleon's opinion that by closing the last commercial
loopholes he might finally destroy British trade and morale.

In fact, he judged incorrectly, for while British trade with
Europe declined, it rose just enough in the Levant and in
South America to keep merchants and manufacturers solvent.
Furthermore, British credit proved more elastic than France
mercantilist policies in meeting financial crises. Thus, British
industrial productivity, although hurt in 1808, soon revived
and steadily expanded thereafter.[4] In the final analysis, the
effectiveness of the Continental System depended on its vigorous and steady application all over Europe.* In 1808, it
seemed that France might prevail. In 1809, however, Napoleon's commercial war measures suddenly relaxed as a result
of a series of unexpected events precipitated by his own attempts to seal the Continent against England. The crux of the
conflict lay in Spain.

The Spanish Insurrection

Portugal was the only country in Europe that refused to close
its ports to British trade. Linked to England for centuries by
commercial treaties, this conservative country debated the
unpleasant alternatives confronting it and chose to evade the
Emperor's demands. Retaliation was swift. On October 29,
1807, France concluded a treaty with the Spanish Government, giving French troops free passage through Spain and
providing for the partition of Portugal. Within one month, a
French army, commanded by General Andoche Junot,† was
in Lisbon, and the royal family had fled to Brazil. *(See Atlas
Map No. 36.)*

If Napoleon's only aim had been to enforce the Continental
System, the tragedy that followed might have been averted.
However, it soon became apparent that not only Portugal but
all of the Iberian Peninsula lay within his sights. At the same
time, he was corresponding with Alexander on the question

---

*Since Austerlitz, Talleyrand had favored a more lenient policy toward de-
feated enemies—particularly toward Austria—and had thereby incurred the
Emperor's disfavor.

*One other factor hindered the effectiveness of the Continental System—
smuggling. British merchants quickly discovered ingenious ways of infiltrat-
ing their products into northern Europe.

†Junot was one of Napoleon's most faithful followers. He participated in the
siege of Toulon, served as Napoleon's aide-de-camp in Italy, and even
fought a duel for his master in Egypt. He was wounded many times, which
contributed to his mental debility; he committed suicide in 1813.

of dividing the Ottoman Empire. Perhaps the Emperor had Justinian in mind and hoped to carve out a domain to rival that of the Byzantine ruler. Certainly, he had not abandoned his visions of invading India.[5] In any case, he had long distrusted the ability of the Bourbon family to rule in Spain. He knew that neither Charles IV nor Marie Luisa, but Manoel Godoy, a frustrated soldier who won influence in Madrid via the Queen's bed, held real power in Spain. Godoy wanted a part of Portugal as his fiefdom. However, the Crown Prince of Spain, who hated Godoy, was the popular choice of the Spanish people. When French troops began to occupy the strongpoints in Spain, ostensibly for the purpose of military security, Spaniards became alarmed and accused Godoy of selling out to the conqueror from the north. In February 1808, Napoleon appointed Murat commander of the Army of Spain. One month later, revolts broke out and Murat occupied Madrid.

As tempers rose, Napoleon chose to believe that only a change of government—in fact, a complete modernization of the country—could calm Spain's unrest. In April, he summoned the entire Spanish royal family and Godoy to Bayonne, just across the border. There, he quickly formed his opinion of the incompetent King and Queen, and their foolish son.* Playing off each against the other, alternately bribing and threatening, at length the Emperor forced the Crown Prince, Charles IV, and his adviser to sign away all rights to Spain and its colonies in the West Indies. In return, Charles received several handsome châteaus and a large pension, while his son received a castle. Of his ill treatment of the deposed family, Napoleon said, "My action is not good

*Of the Queen, Napoleon callously observed, "her heart and history are written in her physiognomy." Of the Crown Prince, he contemptuously remarked, "He eats four times a day and has no ideas of anything."

Goya's "Dos de Mayo" (The Second of May)

People's War in the Siege of Saragossa, 1808

from a certain point of view, I know. But my policy demands that I shall not leave in my rear, so near to Paris, a dynasty hostile to mine."[6]   In the long run, this miscalculated treachery was one of his worst mistakes; immediately, it began to cost the French Army.

Napoleon's rough handling of the Spanish royalty aggravated the already bad feelings in Spain just at the time French troops were settling in Madrid. On May 2, French soldiers were attacked in the streets; Murat retaliated with firing squads. Before order could be restored, several hundred Spaniards and Frenchmen were dead. Within three weeks, the entire country had exploded into revolt. Cries of "Death to the French" rang throughout Spain. The insurrection developed along local lines, exacerbated by local grievances: unemployment and factory shutdowns caused by the blockade, the nobility's fear of reforms that would deprive them of their privileged position, and the clergy's calls to resist French assaults on the country and its orthodox religion.[7] Remote from it all, Napoleon seemed unaware that he was confronting something new, a kind of opposition that could not be overwhelmed by gunfire and modern tactics. To Murat, he had already written, "Make the grandees and other influential persons of the country thoroughly understand that the fate of Spain depends on their behavior, that if Spain is

aroused, and the safety of my troops compromised, the country will be dismembered."[8] And then, to complete his error, the Emperor committed a cardinal blunder: he summoned his elder brother, Joseph, from Naples and crowned him King of Spain.

Throughout the summer, Spanish rebellion expanded into insurgency. Napoleon ordered Marshal Bessières to open the road to Madrid, and on July 20, 1808, Joseph entered his new capital. Meanwhile, the Emperor had ordered another task force, composed of 13,000 men under the leadership of General Pierre Dupont,* to seize Cadiz. Harassed by insurgents and lacking supplies and water, Dupont advanced to Cordova, defeated one Spanish army, and then retired toward Baylen pursued by two others. On July 20, he was trapped on the road to Baylen with only 3,000 effectives. His Spanish-Swiss component had deserted, and many of his men were sick or wounded. On the next day, Dupont surrendered.

Panic-stricken, Joseph immediately ordered a withdrawal of French forces north of the Ebro River. At the same time, Napoleon was writing fiery messages to encourage him:

---

*Dupont had fought savagely when cut off from Ney's Corps on the north bank of the Danube during the Ulm Campaign. Until the surrender at Baylen, Napoleon considered making him a marshal.

"You should not be surprised at having to conquer your kingdom. Philip V and Henry IV hd to conquer theirs." And, on July 31, "There is no question of dying, but of fighting and being victorious. I shall find in Spain the pillars of Hercules, not the limits of my power."[9] Unknown to their Emperor, however, French soldiers were already encountering a new form of war that was setting definite limits to Napoleon's power. Guerrilla knives had begun to dispatch individual French soldiers, while imperial messengers were running a gauntlet of ambuscades along lonely country roads.

The most striking example of the effectiveness of this people's war was the siege of Saragossa. Early in June 1808, a French task force defeated a small army commanded by the Captain General of Aragon near Saragossa. Thereafter, the Spanish commander decided to abandon Saragossa (the capital of Aragon), to revive his army, and to return to Saragossa later if the town managed to hold out. Hold out it did! The French commander was astounded to see men, women, and children resisting his heavy cavalry, which broke through the gates of the city only to be forced back out again in confusion. Priests, retired army officers, and a few soldiers fanned the flames of the resistance. The attack of the famed French lancers was repulsed by inspired civilians after nine hours of confused street fighting.

The battle for the town subsided into a siege. While townspeople enthusiastically turned their homes into fortifications, the French commander brought up reinforcements and siege artillery. The bombardment started late in June and lasted into July, when the assaults began again. Peasants, clergy, and soldiers led the defenders. The most heroic feat was performed by a young woman whose husband fell while manning a cannon at the city walls. Nearly all the gun crew was dead or wounded. She picked up a smoldering match from one of the dead crewmen and fired the cannon herself into the teeth of the French assault. Crying "Vive España!" the courageous girl then led a party of soldiers back to restore the defensive positions. Unable to break the will of the Spanish people, the French finally withdrew on August 14.[10] The aroused citizenry of Saragossa had defeated the French Regulars.

One individual clearly saw how to profit from the welter of intrigue and confusion that gripped the Iberian Peninsula. In London, Lord Castlereagh, British Foreign Secretary, swiftly responded to the pleas of the insurgents by granting subsidies to support them. More important, he sent troops. On August 1, the vanguard of a British expeditionary force landed in Portugal. It was commanded by Arthur Wellesley, who before leaving Spain would earn the title of Duke of Wellington and a reputation as England's most renowned general since Marlborough.

Wellington and the British Army

Arthur Wesley* was born in Dublin in April 1769. His father, a nobleman, died when the boy was 12, and the widow raised her son with the intention of placing him in the Army as quickly as possible. With the assistance of his elder brother, a member of the Treasury, Arthur gained a commission shortly before his 18th birthday. He purchased a lieutenancy in 1787, a captaincy in 1791, and became a lieutenant colonel in command of a regiment nearly a year before he first saw action in the Netherlands in 1794. In 1796, his regiment was ordered to India, where the young officer received nine years of rigorous schooling in the practice of war.

Wellington was fortunate that his eldest brother was appointed Governor General in Calcutta in 1798. Henceforth, British civil-military relations in India flourished, as did Wellington's career, for his brother turned to him for counsel on most military matters. In 1799 and 1800, Wellington participated in campaigns against brigands, insurgents, and Mahratta armies that resisted British colonial rule. During these colonial campaigns, the young officer learned to adapt his tactics to difficult terrain, to respect native customs, and most of all to organize adequate supply trains for independent task forces. After being promoted to major general in 1802, he served in the campaigns of 1803 as an independent commander, and won a costly victory at the Battle of Assaye by

*The family name changed to Wellesley in 1798. "Wellington" was adopted in September 1809. The name Wellington will be used hereafter.

Arthur, Duke of Wellington

a combination of audacity and flexibility in altering pre-established plans. One of his staff officers submitted this report on Wellington's performance at the crisis of the battle: "I never saw a man so cool and collected as he was the whole time."[11] Two months later, Wellington enhanced his reputation by winning an even more decisive triumph at Argaum. In this action, it was his personal presence on the battlefield that rallied shaken formations and converted defeat into victory. In 1805, he sailed for England. At 35 years of age, he had profited from his experiences as a young general officer, but he had no clear idea of how to capitalize on his well-earned renown.

Wellington arrived in England amidst the great alarms of invasion that preceded the Battle of Trafalgar. In December, his regiment was sent to northern Germany, but it re-embarked in February without seeing action after Napoleon's decisive conquests in southern Germany and Moravia had destroyed the Third Coalition. In 1806, Wellington was elected to Parliament, and in 1807 he went to Ireland as Chief Secretary. Shortly thereafter he learned of a secret expedition that was forming and applied for leave to take a command. As a consequence, he served in the famous raid on Copenhagen—a highly successful military venture for England in a year of disappointments, and another notch of excellence on Wellington's growing combat record. After this exploit, in which he personally negotiated the Danish capitulation, Wellington returned to Ireland where he received a promotion to lieutenant general in April 1808.

Events now moved swiftly. Napoleon's legions had overrun Portugal and were closing in on Gibraltar. Spanish representatives met with Lord Castlereagh, who promptly decided on armed intervention. At that moment, a force numbering 9,000 was in Ireland preparing to embark for South America. Castlereagh placed the expedition under Wellington's command, reinforced it to a strength of 17,500, and charged Wellington with employing the force in "counteracting the designs of the enemy, and in affording the Spanish and Portuguese nations every possible aid in throwing off the yoke of France."[12] Soon afterwards, another force of 12,000 men (destined for the Iberian Peninsula) sailed from Sweden, where its commander had vainly attempted to land his forces to counter Russian and French influence in the Baltic. The dizzying pace of global war—reaching from the Levant to the Baltic, from the Mediterranean to South America—called for commanders who could maintain their balance amidst the most unsettled of circumstances, under changes of geography and mission. In selecting Wellington to command in Portugal, it is apparent that Castlereagh knew his man.

Wellington's task was no easy one. As he was soon to learn, England's alliance with Spain and Portugal was more a hindrance than a help when it came to strategic coordination. The reputation of French arms was not to be taken lightly either. Austrian, Russian, and Prussian armies had fallen before Napoleon's swift sword. What reason did the British Army have to believe that it might improve on the dismal record of its continental allies?

King George's Army represented precisely the outlook of British society in the early nineteenth century. Edmund Burke had said that "an armed disciplined body is, in its essence, dangerous to liberty; undisciplined, it is ruinous to society."[13] Having learned too well the bitter lessons of Cromwell's dictatorship and concurring with Burke's opinion, Parliament had resolved that no king should maintain a large standing army. Such an army as was allowed came under close parliamentary controls. One could only become an officer, for example, if one had sufficient means to purchase a commission. Since command of a prestigious regiment might cost as much as 15,000 pounds, the commission became a sort of investment; ultimately, a comfortable retirement might be financed by the sale of one's final commission. The purchase of a commission thus served as a guarantee of an officer's loyalty. A military adventurer had no way to gain a commission; the propertied members of society had everything to lose by revolution.[14]

The Army was also shaped by the global interests it served. Whereas the French, Austrian, and Prussian armies were large armies designed to protect the frontiers of the homeland or to invade a neighboring state, the British Army was fragmented into a number of small expeditionary task forces. These armies operated far from the capital of the British Empire; hence, field commanders had to exhibit some measure of independence. However, since the responsible ministers were remote from the action, London often failed to properly coordinate the operations of armies in the field, and supply and administration usually became a local responsibility. Coordination with naval forces and strategic decisions were frequently left to British commanders in the field.

To a great degree, British imperial strategy was determined by commerce. By 1800, London had become the financial center of Europe, with connections in Vienna, Naples, Frankfurt, and even Paris. Power was very much a function of wealth, and wealth depended on trade. Thus, it was natural for ministers to see the wisdom of deploying small expeditions all over the globe to protect British trading outposts and maritime bases. This only served to accentuate the division of strategic authority as well as the dispersion of Great Britain's limited military resources.[15] *(See Atlas Map No. 35.)*

No British statesman ever solved the problem of mobilizing the country's manpower—partly because no one ever resolved the continuing conflict between the need for militia and that for Regulars. During the invasion scare of 1805, William Pitt had managed to produce nearly half a million

G. III R.
LXXIX. REGIMENT
OR,
CAMERON VOLUNTEERS.

All VOLUNTEERS, who wish to Serve his Majesty
KING GEORGE THE THIRD,

Have now an opportunity of entering into present Pay, and free Quarters, by Enlisting into

The LXXIX Regiment, or, Cameron Volunteers.

COMMANDED BY

Major *ALLAN CAMERON* of *ERCHT.*

Who has obtained his *Majesty's* Permission to raise a *Regiment* of *Highlanders;* which he does at his own private Expence having no other View connected with the undertaking, except the Pride of Commanding a Faithful and Brave Band of his Warlike Countrymen, in the Service of a King, whose greatest Happiness is to reign as the Common Father and Protector of his People.

ALL ASPIRING YOUNG MEN

Who wish to be serviceable to their *King* and *Country* by Enlisting into the *79th Regiment,* or, *Cameron Volunteers,* will be Commanded by the *Major* in *Person,* who has obtained from his Majesty, that they shall not be draughted into any other Regiment; and when the Reduction is to take place, they shall be marched in to their own Country in a Corps, to be therein disembodied.

The past and well known Generofity of Major *Cameron* to all his *Countrymen* who have applied to him on former occasions, is the strongest Pledge of his future Goodness to such as shall now step forward and Enlist under his Banner.

Any Young Man who wishes to Enlist into the *Cameron Volunteers,* will meet with every Encouragement by applying to the Major in Person, or, to any of the Officers, Recruiting for his *Regiment.*

GOD SAVE THE KING
AND
CONSTITUTION AMEN

British Recruiting Poster, Circa 1795

militia, but these untrained, unarmed volunteers only served to siphon off the men sought by the Regular Army recruiter. Inevitably, the dregs of British society—the criminal element, the indolent, the unwanted—ended up in the ranks. Wellington himself expressed distaste for the rabble that he commanded, calling them "the scum of the earth." The obvious solution to his problem had already occurred to the small unit leaders—harsh discipline to keep His Majesty's soldiers in the ranks. However, the many failures of the British Army since 1794 showed ample cause for a substantial program of reform in many areas.

From 1801 to 1803, the Duke of York—the Commander-in-Chief of the British Army—managed to institute a number of reforms. He revised the purchase system, which had become riddled with abuses; restricted promotion of line officers to those who had demonstrated adequate service; and improved the soldier's life by raising pay and providing better clothing, rations, and equipment. He reformed the medical service and paid close attention to his men's welfare. These were necessary correctives to halt the steady decline in British military professionalism. However, the British Army did not modernize in the sense that the French Army had reformed itself. The British Army—like Wellington—was thoroughly conservative in theory and practice. Being conservative, it had much less to fear from the challenge of revolutionary ideas, and much more to gain by adhering to traditional practices. Wellington's judgment of the French style of tactics accurately reflected this traditional attitude:

> As to the enthusiasm about which so much noise has been made even in our own country, I am convinced the world has entirely mistaken its effects. I believe it only creates confusion where order ought to prevail.[16]

Order was the hallmark of Wellington's tactics, strategy, and generalship. Whereas Napoleon preferred to "break the equilibrium" and then take advantage of unexpected opportunities, Wellington sought regularity in a system founded on more conventional principles. Napoleon accepted risks in return for decisive victories; Wellington sought to minimize risk through careful logistical and administrative preparations, followed by a methodical execution of his strategy.* Napoleon energized his subordinates with personal leadership, frequent visits, and colorful messages. Wellington bolstered his lieutenants not with words but with steady supplies, and he insisted on strict obedience to his instructions. Wellington probably centralized control even more than Napoleon. His pattern of command thus resembled more closely that of Frederick the Great than that of Napoleon.

---

*William Pitt said of Wellington that he "states every difficulty before he undertakes any service, but none after he has undertaken it."[17]

Fate would delay the meeting between Wellington and Napoleon for seven more years, but there could be no delaying the confrontation of their armies.

Wellington's forces landed at Mondego Bay, just north of Lisbon, during the first week of August 1808. *(See Atlas Map No. 36.)* One week later, British cavalry contacted French outposts. The first battle of the Peninsular War fought between British and French troops occurred on August 21 at Vimiero. While covering the disembarkation of British troops near Lisbon, Wellington's army repulsed a headlong but uncoordinated attack by an inferior force under the command of Junot. Wellington prepared to exploit the victory with an advance toward Lisbon. At this point, however, he was superseded in command by a 74-year-old general who had been appointed several weeks earlier to satisfy the requirement of seniority. This cautious gentleman (Lieutenant General Sir Harry Burrard) forbade a pursuit, in spite of Wellington's urgings, but the pessimistic Junot settled the situation for him. He offered to evacuate Portugal if the British would transport his men back to France. Wellington subsequently returned to England, dissatisfied with the outcome of what had initially been a promising campaign. His first brief but highly successful foray into the Peninsular War was over.

The Spanish Campaign, 1808–1809

The disaster that befell Dupont at Baylen, the failure to conquer Saragossa, and Junot's evacuation of Portugal, combined to trigger an uncontrollable Napoleonic rage. To Berthier he lamented, incredulously, "Are we going back to the cordon system again? After ten years of war, must we return to such stupidity?"[18] When told that Dupont had surrendered to save the lives of his starving men, Napoleon burst out, "Better, far better, to have died with arms in their hands. Their death would have been glorious: we should have avenged them. You can always supply the place of soldiers. Honour alone, when once lost, can never be regained."[19] Perhaps he was right. The French imperial structure was on trial in Spain, and all of Europe was sitting in judgment.

To restore his lost prestige, Napoleon decided to escalate the war in Spain. "I will conduct this war of peasants and monks myself," he said to Fouché, "and I hope to thrash the English soundly."[20] To stiffen Joseph's spine, he sent Ney to Spain; however, he would need to strengthen the 150,000 men then stationed in the Peninsula. He now decided to commit more divisions. This decision posed a problem for imperial policy: how to guard against a renewal of hostilities by

Austria or Prussia once French forces were removed from southern Germany and dispatched to Spain? His solution was to call on Alexander to fulfill the pledge of friendship made at Tilsit.

The second meeting of the two emperors took place in Erfurt and lasted from the end of September until the middle of October. Again, the meeting was staged as a spectacle. Kings and dukes were invited; there were lavish dinners, military reviews, balls, and "each evening, in a din of rolling drums, the two Emperors led a regiment of kings into a lighted hall to listen to plays by Corneille, Racine or Voltaire."[21] Napoleon spoke with Goethe and presented him with the star of the Legion of Honor. Behind this dazzling display of civility, Napoleon and Alexander maneuvered adroitly against each other. Everyone present knew that the fate of Europe hung in the balance.

The outcome of the conference assured Napoleon of peace in Germany throughout the winter, giving him just enough time to transfer the *Grande Armée* to Spain for a decisive campaign. But Alexander refused to submit entirely to Napoleon's demands. According to Prince Clemens von Metternich, the Austrian Ambassador to Paris, Talleyrand spoke privately with the Tsar and encouraged him to stand firm against Napoleon's irrational ambition. Talleyrand is supposed to have said, "France is civilized, but its sovereign is not."[22] Napoleon could not have realized that the time he was

The Road to Madrid, 1808

granted at Erfurt to intervene in Spain would ultimately enmesh him in a two-front war that would have staggering consequences for his imperial system.

Fresh from this apparent diplomatic triumph, Napoleon rode for Bayonne, trumpeting his intention to "terminate the war by a single blow." Characteristically, he added, "and for this my presence is necessary." At Bayonne, he was greeted with an immense logistical breakdown, and met it with his usual vigorous display of dissatisfaction. "I am in want of everything," he wrote to the War Office, "nothing can be worse than the clothing. My army will begin the campaign naked."[23] French supply deficits notwithstanding, Spain was ripe for a decisive Napoleonic attack. Although Spanish in-

Napoleon Leads the French in Pursuit of Moore's British Army , December 1808

surgents actively opposed the French, there was no coordination between their efforts and those of the five Spanish armies in the field. Nor was there any effective Spanish central government to coordinate the various provincial chieftains. The military force in the Peninsula that posed the greatest danger to the French was the British force led by a new commander, Sir John Moore. As it would develop, his army was too small to cope with a sustained French drive, although it was to play a decisive role, indirectly. Moore assumed command in October and promptly invaded Spain. Unfortunately, he was ill-advised about the condition of the roads leading east into the hinterland, and thus sent his cavalry and artillery over a route separated from that of his infantry by 100 miles. On November 13, 1808, he reached Salamanca and decided to wait there until his cavalry and guns arrived. *(See Atlas Map No. 37.)*

Meanwhile, Napoleon had launched his offensive from Bayonne. Many of his most famous marshals crossed the frontier with him—Soult, Lannes, Victor, and Gouvion St. Cyr.* (Ney and Bessières were already in Spain; Murat was now comfortably situated as King of Naples, far from the battle area.) The man the Emperor probably needed most—the ruthless Davout—remained in Germany to command the widely dispersed Army of the Rhine, which consisted of 90,000 Frenchmen reinforced by contingents from the Confederation of the Rhine.

In a military sense, the campaign resembled some of Napoleon's decisive offensives, especially the Italian Campaign of 1796. However, from the standpoint of imperial policy, Napoleon's intervention in Spain marked the beginning of a steady dispersal of French war resources. In 1808, almost imperceptibly, the Emperor began to lose the initiative. Beginning with the invasion of the Iberian Peninsula, he was gradually forced on the defensive to maintain his sprawling empire. Although he could not foresee the consequences in November 1808, Napoleon knew that invasion involved certain risks. He knew that he must rapidly stamp out the Spanish resistance in the Peninsula in order to prepare for Austria in the spring. There was every reason to assume that Spain would fall, just as all his previous enemies had fallen. In fact, the Emperor was not far wrong in his assumption as it concerned the Spanish Regular forces. By November 23, the last of the Spanish armies had been defeated. A gallant but costly charge by a squadron of Polish calvary at the Pass of Somo Sierra opened the road to Madrid, and the Emperor triumphantly entered the capital on December 4, 1808.

Moore had learned of Napoleon's intervention during the middle of November and had considered pulling his 22,000

troops back to Portugal. He was tortured by the thought of deserting the Spaniards, realizing that "we have no business here, but being here it would never do to abandon the Spaniards without a struggle."[24] On December 5, he decided on a bold stroke to the north in the hope of striking at Napoleon's line of communication. It was a risky decision, but Moore saw clearly that "what is passing at Madrid may be decisive of the fate of Spain."[25] A token blow against an isolated French force might give heart to the insurgents; in any event, it was far better than a tame withdrawal—unless Napoleon reacted by concentrating against the British.

Napoleon received little information of the British for two weeks after his entry into Madrid. With the first part of the campaign successfully completed, the Emperor began to disperse his corps to subdue the insurgents. Once this pacification program was underway, he planned to march on Lisbon to drive the outnumbered British army into the sea. Moore learned of the fall of Madrid on December 10, and marched for Valladolid the next day. Several days later, a captured dispatch gave him positive information that a small French force under the command of Soult was nearby. Hoping to catch Soult and defeat him before Napoleon could react, Moore ordered his men to advance. Within a few days, however, his lead regiments turned back with new orders, for Napoleon had learned of Moore's advance and had immediately launched a vigorous counterthrust with all the forces he could assemble (over 80,000 men). Personally leading his troops through snow-clogged mountain passes, the Emperor vowed to drive the British from Spain and Portugal, and exulted at the thought of making 20,000 British mothers "feel the horror of war."[26]

Tormented by visions of a major defeat, Moore retreated toward Corunna. "It would only be losing the army to Spain and to England to persevere in my march on Soult. Single-handed I cannot pretend to contend with the superior numbers the French can now bring against me."[27] He had already signaled the fleet to be prepared to receive his army near there. During the retreat, discipline broke down. Men became drunk, broke into convents, and insulted their officers. They had come to fight, not to run away. Camp followers clung to the retreating columns, which struggled through icy passes. Moore drove his men hard, determined to stay ahead of his pursuers; the sick, the wounded, and much baggage fell into enemy hands. On the night of January 11, 1809, the ragged army struggled into Corunna. Five days later the French attacked. Moore was killed defending his port of embarkation, but the last elements of his army embarked on January 18.

Moore's defeat cost the British 6,000 of the 25,000 men committed. However, his bold strike for Napoleon's rear had diverted the Emperor's attention from further conquest in Spain. The French had been forced to lift the second siege of

---

*St. Cyr had been an artist at the outbreak of the Revolution. He volunteered for duty in 1792, and served mostly on the Rhine. He would win his marshal's baton in Russia in 1812.

Saragossa, and Cadiz remained securely in Spanish hands. The morale of the Spanish began to rebound, and in the midst of his pursuit of Moore, Napoleon received a message that upset all of his plans—Austria was arming, and Paris stirred with rumors of conspiracy.

Napoleon promptly turned the pursuit over to Soult and rode for Paris to retrieve the reins controlling his empire. There, he confronted Talleyrand with evidence of his duplicity. In a violent tantrum, he shouted, "You are a thief, a coward, and a traitor . . . " After threatening to hang his former foreign minister, the Emperor spat profanely that "he was nothing but so much dung in a silk stocking."[28] After his dismissal from the room, the imperturbable Talleyrand murmured to his astonished friends, "What a pity that such a great man should be so ill-bred."

Nationalism and Reform in Germany

While Napoleon's attention had been turned toward the Mediterranean, developments elsewhere in Europe boded ill for the French. Fifteen years earlier, the French Revolution had marshaled considerable support outside of France, especially among British poets such as Coleridge and Wordsworth, Polish noblemen seeking assistance in re-creating their nation, and the leaders of public opinion and intellectual life in the Rhineland. Most of the enlightened elements of European society had seen the fall of the Bourbon dynasty as a symbol of freedom from tyranny. In 1808, however, these same elements soon became embittered with Napoleon's substitution of his own dynasty for local despotism, and were disgusted with his proscription of the individual rights that the French Revolution had fervidly proclaimed. It is not surprising, therefore, that the appeal of the Revolution served the interests of the men who now began working to undermine the French Empire.[29]

At first, opposition was fragmented. The defeats of Austria, Prussia, and Russia had evoked little response from their peoples. Beethoven had angrily struck Napoleon's name from the dedication of his famous *Eroica* symphony when the Duke of Enghien was murdered in 1804, and Wordsworth had deplored with poetic vehemence the invasions of Switzerland and Spain. The Pope vented his wrath over the confiscation of church properties throughout western Europe; but during the critical times when Napoleon was ransacking Italy, he remained little more than an outraged spectator to the crime. It was in Germany that the most profound psychological currents started to wash away the foundations of the Napoleonic Empire.

The leaders of the German movement were writers. During her exile, Madame de Staël wrote a famous book extolling German culture and history. At the same time a number of pamphlets, journals, and folksongs appeared, arousing German national feeling. The coincidence of this spirit of nationalism with Napoleon's domination of Germany stimulated uncommon hatred for the French oppressor. The celebrated lectures of Johann G. Fichte (*Addresses to the German Nation*)* capitalized on this emotion to inspire the idea of resistance to foreign domination. The thought of achieving personal liberty also began to appeal to the middle class, once Napoleon's economic restrictions started damaging trade.

At the same time that German discontent began to rise, a trio of capable reformers worked to reshape Prussia for a rematch with Napoleon. It was probably no accident that none of the three was Prussian. Baron vom Stein, a Rhinelander, sought to promote the citizen's respect for his country by urging reforms in the Government. Stein opposed the idea that only the nobility knew what was good for the state. He argued that the monarchy must take the initiative by capturing

*An idea of Fichte's appeal may be gained from the following excerpt, which was taken from lectures delivered in Berlin, literally under the noses of French occupation troops:

> In this way men become accustomed even to slavery, if only their material existence is not thereby affected, and in time they get to like it. It is just this that is the most dangerous thing about a state of subjection; it makes men insensitive to all true honor, and moreover, for the indolent man it has its very pleasant side, because it relieves him of many a care and of the need of thinking for himself.

> Let us be on our guard against being taken unaware by this sweetness of servitude, for it robs even our posterity of the hope of future emancipation. . . . Let us not allow our spirit, as well as our body, to be bent and subjected and brought into captivity.[30]

Baron vom Stein

the loyalty—not merely the blind obedience—of its subjects, and thus create a healthy atmosphere of cooperation between peasant, burgher, and aristocrat. Stein bitterly denounced the French occupation and championed a reformed Prussian nation that could lead all of Germany to overthrow French rule. His ardent advocacy of Napoleon's overthrow led the French Emperor to outlaw the fiery baron, who fled to Bohemia with only a few of his proposed reforms enacted. At length, Stein accepted an invitation from Tsar Alexander to continue his work against Napoleon in Russia. Stein's radical ideas, however, were never entirely accepted by the timid Frederick William or the inherently conservative officer corps, one member of which exulted after Stein's dismissal: "One mad head is already smashed; the remaining nest of vipers will dissolve in its own poison."[31]

Stein's political reforms were endorsed by Prince Friedrich von Hardenberg, who, understanding what the King might accept, adopted a more realistic approach. Hardenberg saw very clearly that reforms were necessary if Prussia were to survive, but realized that he must compromise with the aristocracy, since authority for reform had to come from above. His assessment of Prussia's situation in September 1807 was a masterful political and military critique:

> The French Revolution, of which the current wars are an extension, has brought the French people a wholly new vigor, despite all their turmoil and bloodshed. . . . It is an illusion to think that we can resist the Revolution effectively by clinging more closely to the old order. . . . Thus our objective, our guiding principle, must be a revolution in the better sense, a revolution leading directly to the great goal, the elevation of humanity through the wisdom of those in authority and not through a violent impulsion from within or without.[32]

Prussia was fortunate that the "wisdom of those in authority" extended into the military sphere as well as the political. Gerhard Johann D. von Scharnhorst, a Hanoverian commoner who had earned his reputation through his military writings and his reorganization of Hanover's military college, accepted an invitation to join the Prussian Army in 1801. Scharnhorst, who had fought in the Rhineland campaigns and studied the French system carefully, concluded that Prussia's goal must be "to bring army and nation into close union."[33] Scharnhorst, like Stein and Hardenberg, saw that Prussia's survival depended on its ability to mobilize all the psychological, economic, and political energies of the state. The 1806 defeat proved that only a modern, national army could compete with the *Grande Armée*. To modernize the Army it was therefore necessary to revolutionize the state.

Scharnhorst's recommendations to the King marked an important turning point in modern European history. To bring the Prussian Army and nation together, he urged Frederick William to adopt universal conscription without regard to class restrictions and to establish a militia. At the same time, he argued that the Frederician system of brutal discipline was incompatible with the concept of a citizen army. (After Jena, Prussia no longer had access to foreign mercenaries anyway.) Discipline should now depend, not on the corporal's cane, but on the commitment of an informed citizenry to a popular cause.

These ideas amounted to strong medicine, and they were not particularly palatable to the King or the Army. When Scharnhorst proposed offering officers' commissions to all social classes, though only to men of the requisite talents, mutters of disapproval greeted the suggestion. One old soldier put the monarchial issue squarely on the line. "If your Royal Highness deprives me and my children of my right, what is the basis of yours?"[34] The logic of this objection notwithstanding, Scharnhorst's argument prevailed, and the new regulations read: "From now on, a claim to officer rank shall in peacetime be warranted only by knowledge and education, in time of war by exceptional bravery and quickness of perception." However, because of its revolutionary undertones, the militia concept failed to gain the King's approval.

Even these modest advances in political and military institutions could only have occurred after the shock of defeat. It remains, however, a miraculous occurrence that Prussia should have found the men of vision and courage to press for the necessary reforms. Unfortunately for the Prussian people, their vacillating King continued to temporize; in 1809, as in 1805, he refused to declare against Napoleon. In 1809, even after the Spanish example, Prussia yielded the leadership of opposition against Napoleon to Austria.

Austria was a most unlikely candidate for leadership in Germany. The monarchy operated on a tradition of conservatism. This tradition was reinforced by the sprawling, multiracial character of the Hapsburg Empire, which touched nearly every European interest. By its geographical position alone, Austria intruded into Poland, threatened the Balkans, opened into the Mediterranean, incorporated a substantial portion of Germany, guarded the north-south communications through the Alps, and was vulnerable to invasion via the Danube. The variety of peoples encompassed within the Hapsburg dominions (Slavs, Germans, Italians, Magyars, Croats, and Serbs) ruled out the possibility of national feeling. A revolution would fragment the Empire like a bombshell. (*See Atlas Map No. 38.*)

The Emperor Francis was a fearful, suspicious man, living in a precarious age. The French Revolution had doomed his army to perpetual obsolescence, unless he sanctioned the political reforms necessary to give it new life. However, unlike his enlightened forebears, Maria Theresa and Joseph, he resisted any attempts to liberalize education, to open new channels of ideas, or to reform state economics. In spite of these reactionary tendencies, his brother, the Archduke Charles, persuaded him that some military reform was unavoidable if the monarchy were to be saved. In imitation of France, semi-independent corps were formed, a *Landwehr** was authorized, and field artillery was assembled and trained in batteries. These were hardly reforms, but strictly military improvements. The *Landwehr* never developed its full potential because popular feeling never became fully spontaneous, except in the German-speaking regions; the artillery batteries proved devastating to French infantry, but fiscal deficits limited the number of cannon that could be fielded; and in spite of their new combined-arms structure, the corps were no match for their French counterparts because their commanders were appointed on the basis of social rank, not talent.[35] In short, the revolutionizing of Austria along the lines pursued by Prussia was impossible without the virtual abdication of the Austrian throne. Since six centuries of expansion had preceded Francis' rule, it is hard not to feel sympathy for his inclination to retrench. Francis, and the whole bureaucracy of his government, stood for stability.

Although most of Francis' key advisers were unalterably opposed to revolution, in foreign affairs they were equally opposed to the status quo, which seemed to surrender the initiative to Napoleon at unacceptable Austrian expense. The talented Prince Clemens von Metternich, Austria's Ambassador to France, believed in the eighteenth century concept of the balance of power, but in 1809 he sensed that the time had come to redress that balance through war. From Paris, Metternich sent a steady stream of intelligence indicating that the growing demands of the war in Spain had swayed French public opinion against the Emperor. When Napoleon transferred the *Grande Armée* from Germany to Spain, the time seemed ripe for Austrian intervention.

The man to whom Francis entrusted command of the Austrian armies was the Archduke Charles, a man with a great deal of experience in war, much of it gained campaigning against Napoleon. Charles' upbringing was unusually cosmopolitan. Born in Florence, he spent his youth in Tuscany, Vienna, and the Austrian Netherlands. He commanded a brigade in the Low Countries in 1793, and distinguished himself at one of the early Austrian wins over Revolutionary France. From this point forward, he was marked for high command. His campaign of 1796 against Moreau and Jourdan was a masterpiece of strategic maneuver. Even his skillful retreat toward Vienna in 1797 brought fresh accolades for his excellence as a general. In 1797, he defeated Jourdan in

the Tyrol, and then invaded Switzerland and defeated Massena. His final campaign that year drove the French across the Rhine before ill health necessitated his temporary retirement. From 1801 to 1805, Charles worked tirelessly to update the Austrian Army, and in 1805 he fought Massena to a draw in Italy.[36] After the defeat of the Third Coalition, he resumed his duties as head of the *Hofkriegsrat* and championed most of the reforms mentioned above. In spite of all these successes, Charles was opposed to war in general, and was especially opposed to it in 1809. The motivation of this reluctant warrior is instructive.

The renowned German historian, Hans Delbrück, claims that Charles was a member of the attrition school of strategy.† According to Delbrück, Charles had studied Fred-

---

† Delbrück defines two chief modes of strategy in the history of war: the strategy of annihilation and the strategy of attrition.

The Archduke Charles of Austria

---

*Landwehr has meant slightly different things at differing periods of time. At this time, it was a reserve group of men who had already served actively and sometimes in a first-line ready reserve, as well. They formed an older, experienced reservoir of strength for an army.

erick's strategy of the Seven Years' War and deduced that his success was due to the possession of certain strategic points. These terrain features were decisive for the occupation of an area, "because by their possession was earned the key to the area . . . "[37] Indeed, Charles' voluminous theoretical writings reveal a marked concern for position-type warfare and maneuver strategy.

In a book entitled *The Principles of War*, Charles declared in true eighteenth century style that "war is the greatest ill which can befall a state or a nation." In another work, he elaborated:

> The events of war have such decisive results that it is the first duty of the *Feldherr* to be concerned for the greatest assurance of success. But this can only occur where the necessary means for the conduct of the war are available; consequently, only where an army is in possession of the area from which these means are procured—and that route by which they are transported.[38]

Charles then proceeded to caution that strategy must guarantee security for the army's base of operations and for its communications. The main army should never be so disposed that "the enemy can be nearer to our communications line, to our magazines, supplies, etc., than we." Thus, the core of Charles' strategic philosophy was concerned with safeguarding the army's communications and magazines while "forcing an enemy to abandon his strategic points" by menacing his rear area.

This restrained form of strategy, so typical of eighteenth century war, was an extension of Austria's inability to liberate its Army from the shackles of the monarchial state system. The accompanying influences of mercantilism, the mercenary system, the aristocracy, the Church, and the geographic configuration of the state, all conspired to limit strategy and hinder the reform of the Army. These constraints in turn insured that the army Charles commanded remained tied to the logistical system used in the Seven Years' War. There was little to be gained from adopting Napoleonic concepts of strategy as long as the Army depended on magazines and depots for its supply. Logistics, more than any other factor, was to hamper Charles in the campaigns of 1809.

Campaigns on the Danube, 1809

In 1797, Napoleon had rendered an interesting critique of his vanquished opponents by comparing the Austrian concept of stategy with his own. "There are many good generals in

Europe; however they see too many things at the same time. I only see one thing, that is the masses. I seek to destroy them, because I am then certain that all else will soon fall."[39] Apparently, this judgment was still valid 12 years later; but one of the "good generals in Europe" came close to breaking the spell that the Emperor of the French had cast over the art of war.

At first, Charles persisted in his long-held belief that Hapsburg interests were best served by a strong defensive to cover mobilization of reserves, fortification of the frontiers, and completion of those tasks involving logistics and communications. Charles was not entirely opposed to war, but he was against a premature offensive which would force the Army to fight before it was ready. He knew that Austria's full might could be put into play only gradually. At the earliest, the line troops needed until the end of March to finish arming; it would take the *Landwehr* and the first-line reserves even longer to mobilize. Emperor Francis, however, was swayed by the advice of a vibrantly confident war party that hoped to encourage Prussian support by an early victory. British subsidies, also, depended on visible signs of success. In February 1809, Francis made his decision, overruling Charles. Several days later, he appointed the Archduke to command the entire Austrian Army.[40] *(See Atlas Map No. 38.)*

Charles knew that success depended on rapid movement. His plan specified that the attacking forces must strike the French army in Germany before it could receive reinforcements from the Rhine, "in order to win as much territory as possible on the upper Danube." Charles selected a position in western Bohemia for his army's main assembly area, from which he planned to launch the offensive into Bavaria. The main attack would aim for Bamberg; however, the Bohemian position also offered the option of a thrust to the north, depending on French reactions. At the same time, forces under the Archduke Ferdinand would operate in Poland to protect the homeland against a threat from Russia, while the Archduke John was to lead an army of 65,000 men to the southwest to recover the Tyrol and northwest Italy.[41]

Napoleon was grimly aware that Austria's threatening attitude meant war. Charles' formation of a *Landwehr* the year before had served notice that the Hapsburg monarchy contemplated revenge for its losses at French hands in four previous wars. The issue of propaganda appeals from Vienna, the presence of Madame de Staël and Baron vom Stein in Vienna, and the recall in February of troops on furlough were ominous signs that could hardly be ignored. In March, Metternich notified the French foreign minister that the Austrian Army had been placed in full readiness for war "as a simple precautionary measure." At the same time, French agents working out of Munich began watching the roads to Vienna and Prague, and quickly picked up the Austrian deployment into Bohemia. On March 22, a French courier was detained at Passau, an act virtually tantamount to a declaration of war.[42]

Napoleon duly noted all these hostile signals. More than likely, he had planned to deal with Austria earlier, but the war in Spain had diverted him. He had committed his best troops to the Peninsula and could not retrieve them quickly. The situation was no more dangerous militarily than those he had faced at Castiglione, Arcola, and Rivoli. However, it was the most perilous hour for *le Grande Empire*, which was simultaneously troubled by internal disturbances and beset on all sides by enemy powers that only waited for the right moment to intervene. "In war one sees one's own difficulties," the Emperor of the French wrote to Eugène, "and does not consider those of the enemy; one must show confidence."[43] In March, Napoleon masked his fears with an outward display of nonchalance and self-confidence.

At first, the Emperor estimated that Austria could not advance before the end of April 1809. This left time to improvise a new army in western Germany. There was no comparison, however, between this hastily conscripted, multi-national army and the superbly professional formations of 1805 and 1806. Weapons, clothing, and transport were in short supply, key commanders were in Spain, and many new recruits were half trained. As in 1800, the burden of victory lay almost entirely on Napoleon.

While Davout's expanded corps of 67,000 men occupied northern Bavaria, Massena* received a summons to take command of a new corps forming at Ulm, and Lefebvre readied the Bavarian Corps south of the Danube. At the same time, the Imperial Guard marched from Spain, and Napoleon sent word to Lannes to join him in Bavaria. Berthier departed for Strasbourg on March 31 to oversee the army's assembly, but Napoleon remained in Paris—to give the impression that he desired peace. (Paris was also the best place to deal with the manifold problems requiring his attention in other parts of the widespread Empire.) *(See Atlas Map No. 39.)*

Napoleon formulated a strategy based on two specific contingencies. The most likely contingency was that the Austrian attack would come after April 15. While Lefebvre's Bavarians (VII Corps) formed a covering force south of the Danube, Davout's III Corps would assemble and cover the area between Bamberg and Nürnberg; Massena's IV Corps would concentrate at Ulm; and Oudinot's II Corps (intended for Lannes' command) and the Guard would concentrate at Ratisbon. "My goal is to place my headquarters at Ratisbon and to assemble my whole army there," Napoleon advised Berthier. If, however, the enemy attack developed sometime

before April 15, the army was to assemble behind the Lech River. In either case, the citadel of Passau ("an important post, above all for the offensive") would be well stocked and tenaciously defended.[44] Similarly, in either case, Napoleon's intention was to cover the mobilization of the Confederation of the Rhine by concentrating his army as far forward as possible.

Unexpected complications quickly destroyed the Emperor's plan. To begin with, there were unavoidable weaknesses even in the excellent French communications system. In clear weather, a brief telegraphic message required less than 10 minutes for transmission from Napoleon's office in Paris to the communications center at Strasbourg.† When bad visibility rendered the telegraph unusable, relays of couriers needed two days to carry the same message to Strasbourg, and a day and a half or more to reach forward headquarters at Donauworth. Almost as soon as Berthier departed for Strasbourg, Napoleon received new intelligence indicating that enemy forces were moving from Bohemia toward the Tyrol.[45] Were the Austrians going to attack across the Inn River?

Obsessed with the risks of attacking from Bohemia, Charles had decided to reposition his forces for a more conventional advance along the south bank of the Danube. He left two of the eight corps to advance out of Bohemia, and transferred the other six corps south for a direct move from Austria to Ratisbon. On April 6, Charles informed his troops of their mission: "The freedom of Europe has sought refuge under your banners. Your victories will break her chains." Four days later, the Austrian army crossed the Inn, preceded by a warning to the Bavarian authorities that all who resisted the advance would be treated as enemies.[46] Thus began Austria's fifth war with France in less than two decades. For once, Napoleon had been too slow.

Uncertain of the exact meaning of the Austrian moves, Napoleon had already dispatched a barrage of messages intended to help Berthier concentrate the army. Berthier, who had never displayed independence of mind in strategic matters, soon discovered that his original orders did not cover all eventualities. As in 1806, Berthier looked to Paris for detailed guidance. The events of the succeeding two weeks would graphically illustrate the dangers of command by remote control. *(See Atlas Map No. 39.)*

Berthier learned of the enemy crossing of the Inn on April 11, promptly ordered the appropriate westward assembly, and left Strasbourg to supervise the execution of his orders (i.e., the second contingency—concentration behind the Lech). Meanwhile, still ignorant of the invasion, Napoleon

---

*Massena had been recovering from the loss of an eye suffered in a hunting accident caused by Napoleon's careless discharge of a firearm.

†Employing a form of semaphore, messages were transmitted by line of sight between successive stations located on prominent terrain heights.

had dispatched two followup messages to his chief of staff. The first was a telegram essentially confirming his original orders to concentrate behind the Lech. A storm blocked transmission of this message. The second was a hastily drafted letter, apparently based on Napoleon's reassessment of Austria's capacity for rapid movement. The latter directive ordered Massena to assemble his corps at Augsburg, and Davout to position his forces in the vicinity of Ratisbon, "in spite of anything that may happen." This message, which reached Berthier at Donauworth on April 13, defies historical understanding, for it was written on the tenth, after Metternich had broken diplomatic relations in Paris, and after Napoleon had received an intercepted dispatch indicating that *an Austrian offensive was imminent.*[47]

Davout's withdrawal toward Ingolstadt was already in progress. Berthier informed him of the Emperor's desires, resolutely overriding the corps commander's justifiable remonstrations. The troops had already begun to carry out these new orders when the delayed telegram arrived from Napoleon, reiterating the Emperor's original guidance, which prescribed the concentration behind the Lech.

Meanwhile, Charles' offensive progressed methodically, only slightly delayed by Lefebvre's retrograde action. The Austrians were almost entirely uninformed of French dispositions because of inferior intelligence and communications services, as well as energetic French security measures. The army's ponderous logistical apparatus slowed the advance, and unusually hard rains washed out roads and swelled the Danube. Wishing not to anger the Bavarian people by quartering troops in villages, Charles ordered his men to find shelter in the open. March discipline broke down as soon as the troops crossed the Inn. Riding forward to inspect, the Archduke found livestock jamming the intervals between regiments, and officer's baggage cluttering the roads.[48] Four years of reforms had done nothing to break habits ingrained by generations of practice.

On April 13, Charles ordered a day of rest so that he could restore order among the confused columns. This pause undoubtedly saved the French. On the same day, Berthier was in a state of great confusion, well on the way to placing the French army in a posture far more disordered than that of Austria. By the fifteenth, Lefebvre and Davout had obediently, though with growing frustration, ordered two countermarches, and were thoroughly outraged by Berthier's inability to control the situation. Finally, the Emperor realized that the worsening strategic situation in Bavaria took precedence over political demands in Paris. He departed early on April 13. Reaching Strasbourg two days later, Napoleon learned that the Tyrol had risen in revolt. *(See Atlas Map No. 40.)*

Early on April 17, Napoleon arrived at main headquarters in Donauworth. Worried and impatient, he demanded to be briefed on the situation. Berthier was with Massena at Augsburg; the General Staff was ill-informed. Reading the latest dispatches from the field, Napoleon deduced that Davout was probably at Ratisbon and that Charles was advancing from Landshut toward Ratisbon. (Actually, at that very moment, Charles was ordering an assault crossing of the Danube to take place near Neustadt.) Realizing for the first time that his army was divided into two masses separated by more than 50 miles, the Emperor promptly ordered Davout to move to Ingolstadt along the south bank of the Danube, and Lefebvre to defend near Abensberg as long as possible in order to cover the withdrawal of III Corps. Massena's IV Corps and Oudinot's II Corps were directed to advance to Pfaffenhofen. To Massena, Napoleon wrote, "Activity, activity, speed! I am counting on you."[49] On the morning of April 18, as more information on Charles' advance became available, Napoleon altered Davout's mission: to speed up his march through the forest trails south of the Danube, but to hold the bridge at Ratisbon if possible. By now the Emperor had viewed the river. It was in full flood. Throughout the eighteenth and nineteenth, Austrian pressure against Davout increased. It had already become apparent to the "Iron Marshal" that he was on his own again.

Meanwhile, Charles' ponderous attack ground to a halt before Lefebvre's defenses along the Abens River. Austrian columns jammed the roads, and the Archduke sought to clear the constriction near Abensberg by shifting part of his force to the north. At this time, hussar patrols began to give him his first reliable intelligence of the campaign—Davout was in Ratisbon in strength. He at once abandoned the plan of striking across the raging Danube and, true to Napoleon's criticism, began to "see too many things at the same time." He ordered three of his six corps* to patrol to the north and prepare for an attack on Davout's strong positions. Two corps were to remain near Pfeffenhausen to cover the Austrian left flank, and one was to cover Landshut. Later on April 18, the Austrians captured a courier en route from Lefebvre's headquarters to Davout. This source revealed that the two French corps were in motion, attempting to unite. Charles now decided to fix Lefebvre with 25,000 men and fall on Davout with the weight of his main force (67,000), while 20,000 of General Heinrich Bellegarde's troops struck at Ratisbon from north of the Danube.[50]

This complicated scheme had little chance of success without aggressive execution and energetic coordination. Until this time, Napoleon's original dispositions had been dispersed, while Charles' were relatively concentrated. On April 19, however, combat superiority shifted to Napoleon as the

---

*The two corps under Bellegarde still wandered aimlessly north of the Danube.

Austrian dispositions suffered from the centrifugal effect of Charles' orders. Furthermore, Charles failed to strike decisively to deprive Davout of the critical Abensberg-Ratisbon road. As a result, Davout's men, who were on the march at 5:00 a.m. on April 19, were able to seize the southern exits from the forest. The entire day's action, and much of that of the succeeding two days, consisted of small unit skirmishes in which the French maintained their positions in the face of repeated but futile Austrian attempts to dislodge them. By April 20, the corps of Davout and Lefebvre had made contact. More dangerous for the Austrians, Charles had lost control of his entire left wing. *(See Atlas Map No. 41.)*

During the next few days, Napoleon refused to recognize the strength of Charles' assault on Davout's corps, just as he had misjudged the strength of Ney's opponents at Ulm, and Davout's at Auerstädt. Satisfied that Lefebvre could maintain his position at Abensberg, the Emperor busied himself with managing the envelopment of Charles' left flank by Massena and Oudinot. A series of sporadic fights occurred all across the battle area—from Pfaffenhofen on the south to Ratisbon on the north, where one of Bellegarde's corps finally appeared on April 19. This was a fluid, dispersed battle consisting of as many as six disconnected engagements at one time—the kind of battle no one could have imagined 20 years earlier. It was a preview of modern, mobile warfare, and the victor would prevail by his ability to discern the true situation, control the action, and capitalize on unexpected opportunities.

Napoleon's opportunities became apparent on the morning of April 20. Lefebvre still held his position along the Abens River; Davout was in firm control of the hills west of Eggmühl; Massena was on his way to Landshut to cut the Austrian escape routes; and most important of all, the redoubtable Lannes had arrived from Spain. Napoleon turned over five divisions to him, two of which had been detached from Davout's corps, and ordered him to drive for Landshut.[51]

At this point, Charles irretrievably lost the initiative. He had never been entirely sure of French dispositions and strength. He had failed to break Davout's stronghold in the Brixner Forest after two hard days of fighting. His left flank commanders were rapidly losing heart for the fight, and began falling back on Landshut. Sensing that he had lost his early advantage, Charles decided to seize Ratisbon, from which position he could still threaten the French on both sides of the river. On April 21, the French regiment, clinging to the bridge at Ratisbon, finally surrendered. The capture of the bridge gave Charles an escape route, further encouraging him to shift his effort toward Ratisbon.[52]

Napoleon did not learn of the fall of Ratisbon for two days. Furthermore, he remained secure in his conviction that Lannes' attack on Landshut would force Charles into a pre-

cipitate retreat to cover Vienna. In spite of Davout's warning that III Corps was holding off the Austrian main body at Eggmühl, the Emperor exhorted him to attack, assuring him that the events of the day would yield "another Jena." Meanwhile, Lannes' force had knifed rapidly to the Isar. There, three Austrian corps slipped across the river, leaving the bridge in flames. Massena's weary troops had halted 10 miles from Landshut and failed to cut the Austrian escape routes. At the same time, the divisions of St. Hilaire and Friant, under Davout's steady command, beat off renewed Austrian attacks around Eggmühl. Late on April 21, after three successive messages from Davout reporting Charles' northern envelopment, Napoleon called on Lannes for another attack. "The Duke of Auerstädt is at grips with the enemy," he wrote from Landshut, "You are to march on Eggmühl and attack the enemy on all sides."[53]

Within the 750 square miles of territory that lay between the Danube and the Isar, the battle had now been raging for nearly a week. In the previous century, armies had taken the better part of a day to line up in plain view of each other, and usually blasted away until darkness almost always put an end to the brief but bitter fighting. In the age of Napoleon, soldiers had to march and fight and keep marching and fighting for days and nights, over an extended area. The exertions required in this kind of campaigning could and did ruin many a man's health forever. The will to keep going and the inspiration and example of his commander were all that kept a soldier in the ranks. In the Austrian Army in 1809, both the will and the inspiration were lacking. On April 22, the final action at Eggmühl showed it.

Lefebvre and Davout were solidly emplaced along the wood line overlooking the little farm town of Eggmühl. As Lannes' attack began to take effect on Charles' left flank, the Archduke gave up his assault on Davout's north flank and began to fall back on Ratisbon.[54] *(These actions are not shown on Atlas Map No. 41.)* He might still have made a fight of it, but French soldiers, inspired by their fighting commanders (Lannes, Davout, and Lefebvre), pressed hard and threw the exhausted Austrians back. After darkness fell, one of Lannes' cavalry divisions took up the pursuit with some success, but during the night of the twenty-second, Charles withdrew across the Danube and avoided Massena's lackadaisical attempt to cut him off through Straubing the next day.

The battle at Eggmühl climaxed a thoroughly Napoleonic campaign. There had been improvisation in logistics and strategy, a nearly fatal dispersion of the army, frantic orders for concentration, man-killing forced marches to compensate for earlier miscalculations, and the Emperor's last-minute arrival on the scene to pull it all together. Napoleon's deployment in 1809 was far inferior to those of 1800, 1805, and 1806, but his adjustment on the battlefield was typically superb. (At St. Helena, he asserted that the maneuvers of Abensberg and Eggmühl were the finest of his entire career.)[55] Even so, the Emperor did not obtain the decisive victory he sought: Charles' army was still at large; the Empire was aflame with uprisings in Prussia, Westphalia, and the Tyrol; and Wellington was reported to be back in Portugal. Balancing the requirements of his empire with those of his army, Napoleon decided to pursue along the familiar road to Vienna. That city fell on May 13, but the precious bridges across the swollen Danube were destroyed. *(See Atlas Map No. 42.)*

For a few days, the army commander paused to deal with problems of governing. On May 17, in imitation of Charlemagne, Napoleon issued a decree annexing the Papal States to the Empire, declaring Rome an imperial city, and reducing the Pope to the status of a mere bishop. This was a mistake that only compounded his earlier errors in misgauging European public opinion. He explained the seizure of Rome as a means to insure "the security of our armies, the tranquility and good will of our people, the dignity and integrity of our empire."[56] However, the news of the Pope's ill treatment was bound to stir Catholics in Spain, Austria, and even in France against his imperial rule. Refusing to admit the strength of any opposition, Napoleon professed contempt for anyone who resisted him—especially the Archduke Charles. Perhaps he was too concerned with ruling his empire to give full attention to the military situation in Austria. At any rate, he acted with extraordinary negligence while in Vienna. Overconfident, he ordered a quick crossing of the Danube in the face of Charles' reinforced army, which lay within 10 miles of the river.

On May 18, the crossing began at Lobau Island—a mosquito-infested tract of woods and swamp. Two days later, Charles marched to attack the crossing site, now held solely by Massena's corps. On May 21, Austrian shock troops ran up against the French bridgehead, which was tightly anchored to the stone buildings of Aspern and Essling. That

Massena's Troops on Lobau Island, May 1809

night, Lannes' corps and the Guard infantry crossed on pontoon bridges that were lashed by a fierce current and floating debris. While Massena held the left side of the bridgehead, Lannes dug in on the right against heavy artillery fire. Napoleon lacked only Davout's III Corps to achieve sufficient strength to overpower the enemy. Early on the morning of May 22, the Austrians released a large, floating grain mill upstream that smashed the tenuous string of pontoons. Davout would never reach his embattled fellow marshals, and ammunition was beginning to run low. The French troops stood up against a shattering cannonade and held their fire to conserve ammunition. Years later, a soldier of the guard remembered those terrible moments: "Time is very long when one awaits death without being able to defend oneself. The hours are centuries."[57] Sometime during those indescribable hours, the steadfast Jean Lannes fell, mortally wounded—both legs torn by a cannonball.*

Napoleon never admitted that he had suffered defeat at Aspern-Essling. During the early evening of May 22, he held a meeting on Lobau Island with Davout, Berthier, and Massena to discuss the pros and cons of withdrawing. The marshals all advised retreat, to which Napoleon replied, "Shall we say thus to the enemy, to Europe, that victors today are vanquished?" His mind was already made up. "We must remain here [in the Lobau]. We must threaten an enemy accustomed to fear us . . . " According to eyewitnesses, the marshals nodded in agreement, exclaiming, "the Danube alone has conquered us, and not the Archduke!"[58] This was surely one of the epic moments of Napoleon's career. Threatened by disaster, the Emperor resolved to win. He had convinced his marshals; now he had to convince his troops.

After each battle, Napoleon made a point of inspecting the combat divisions. Massena's units received his attention during the pursuit to Vienna. Marching up to the colonel of the 26th Light Infantry Regiment, Napoleon demanded in a voice that carried to the rear rank: "Who is the bravest soldier in your regiment?" The colonel hesitated, but a battalion commander prompted him: "Baionnette." "What a name for a soldier!" the Emperor exclaimed, "Have him come forward." Baionnette emerged from the formation, and, while standing before his comrades, received the following acclaim from his Emperor: "You are the bravest soldier in the regiment. I name you chevalier of the Legion of Honor and I grant you, with the title, an annual endowment of 1500 francs, which you may bequeath to your children."[59] A lifetime of hard work in a civilian occupation could not have earned the common soldier that title and the respect from his peers which accom-

---

*Among a number of generals and marshals who died in action, Lannes was probably Napoleon's most irreplaceable loss. St. Hilaire, a hard-fighting division commander to whom Napoleon had promised a marshal's baton several weeks earlier, also died at Essling.

panied it. Napoleon's instinctive way of capitalizing on the soldier's ego needs still electrified the regiments. His inspirational leadership surely accounts in large part for the French recovery after the difficult fighting during the battle at Aspern-Essling.

Napoleon's attempt at a hasty river crossing* had failed, but the French still held the Lobau bridgehead and commanded the waterway itself with a squadron of gunboats. Napoleon knew that an all-out effort would be necessary to gain superior combat power for the next encounter. He immediately began to reinforce his battered army, calling up reserves from along the Danube, and ordering Eugène's Army of Italy, Bernadotte's IX Corps (in Saxony), and Marmont's XI Corps (in Dalmatia) to join him at Vienna. While Jerome suppressed uprisings in Westphalia and Saxony, Davout marched on Pressburg to secure the French east flank from the threat of raids from Hungary. The Emperor built up his artillery strength and ordered the construction of multiple bridges for the next crossing. With an iron will, he personally supervised these preparations for battle. *(See Atlas Map No. 43.)*

The river crossing and the battle were two distinct actions—largely because of Charles' decision to occupy the high ground six miles north of the Danube and to virtually surrender the crossing either to the north or to the east. Fearful of being surprised and wishing to avoid being caught in the open by French artillery, which was superior both in numbers and caliber of guns, he elected to conduct a mobile defense from the plateau north of the Russbach River in the hope of cutting the advancing French formations off from their bridges. However, the Archduke was lethargic in his preparations. He apparently felt that Napoleon might eventually tire of war and sue for peace. He made no effort to fortify the positions behind the Russbach, and he disagreed with those of his advisers who believed that a sizable force should be left to oppose the French assault crossing. (Out of a total strength of 136,000 men, 24,000 stayed at Aspern-Essling.) It is doubtful that Charles really contemplated a decisive action. In fact, he gave as much attention to choosing his line of retreat—toward Prague—as to preparing for the battle.[60]

Charles' planning also suffered from the effects of the unfavorable situation on other fronts. Because Polish forces were making considerable headway against Ferdinand in Galicia, Francis ordered detachments from Charles' army to hold the line. Moreover, the expected cooperation of Prussia had failed to materialize, and Hungary remained passive in-

*Doctrinally speaking, a hasty river crossing is an operation that is attempted as a continuation of an ongoing offensive, in the hope of achieving surprise and advancing without loss of momentum. Conversely, a deliberate river crossing occurs when the enemy defenses are strong or when the river obstacle is severe; such a crossing requires a buildup of forces, delay, loss of momentum, and detailed planning.

The French Assault Crossing of the Russbach, 1809

stead of reinforcing the Archduke John's hard-pressed army as it withdrew from Italy. Finally, members of the Austrian Cabinet expressed dissatisfaction with Charles' conduct of the war, especially his failure to exploit the victory at Aspern-Essling.

On the French side, there were no such reservations concerning either generalship or strategy. On July 2, orders were dispatched for the crossing; during the next two days, French troops moved in strength to Lobau Island; then, on the stormy night of July 4, French assault forces crossed under cover of a heavy artillery bombardment that set the town of Gross Enzersdorf on fire. Bypassing the fortified line of Aspern-Essling-Gross Enzersdorf, the corps of Massena, Oudinot, and Davout reached the north bank of the Danube with only minor losses from artillery fire, and by early afternoon were advancing against light cavalry resistance toward the high ground to the north. Napoleon's second crossing of the Danube had been professionally planned and executed. Hyperactive after two nights without sleep, the Emperor burned to come to grips with Charles' main force. *(See Atlas Map No. 43.)*

Charles' moment of truth had arrived. His personal direction of a heroic counterattack combined with nightfall to bring the French assault to a halt along the Russbach. (The brook was only about one meter wide, but its sharp banks created an effective obstacle to horse and cannon.) Earlier, Charles had started concentrating his forces between Wagram and Markgrafneusiedl, but now he reverted to his original plan for an envelopment, and ordered his two western corps to attack toward Aspern and Essling on July 6. He called on John to attack from Pressburg against the French east flank. Napoleon himself could not have conceived a more decisive scheme of maneuver. But success hinged on execution, and by the time the fight along the Russbach had stopped, it was nearly midnight. Less than four hours of darkness remained to conceal the Austrian move to the west.

Napoleon spent another sleepless night concentrating his forces for an all-out assault on the following day. His verbal orders suggested that he planned to renew the attack along the entire front, seeking a penetration somewhere between Wagram and Markgrafneusiedl. At 4:00 a.m. on July 6, the roar of artillery announced that Davout had already joined battle with Charles' left flank corps.

The Battle of Wagram developed into a series of uncoordinated local attacks and countercharges along the 5-mile line of contact. Within two hours, Davout had stamped out Austrian hopes in his sector, and his men had begun to work their way around the cluster of buildings at the base of the plateau. Meanwhile, Austrian forces had materialized on the French left, sweeping around Aderklaa, which Bernadotte had arbitrarily abandoned during the night. Massena counterattacked to restore the line, but was driven out of Aderklaa by a surging Austrian thrust. Bernadotte urged his faltering Saxons back into the battle, only to see them break in panic at the sound of artillery fire. While Frenchmen and Austrians struggled for the plateau behind Wagram, Charles' main attack swept in behind Massena's left flank and drove the army's flank guard (one division of Massena's corps) back into the old bridgehead, south of Aspern-Essling.

By 11:00 a.m., the battle had reached its crisis. The force making Charles' envelopment had reached Aspern and required only a final reinforced thrust to deliver its full effect. However, Charles' attention was now riveted on his left flank, where Davout's resolute advance had steadily forced the Austrians back through Markgrafneusiedl and up the hill. The outcome of the battle hung on whether Davout's attack would succeed before Charles' weakening envelopment could strike into the French army's rear.

Napoleon now intervened by massing 100 guns against Aderklaa and mounting a counterattack with one of Eugène's corps. The corps commander, Jacques MacDonald, formed three divisions into a huge hollow rectangle, open on the end that was farthest from the Austrians.* The pressure from this massive assault paralyzed the entire Austrian right wing. By early afternoon, Davout's attack had become an envelopment

of its own, and Charles had lost the initiative. The Austrian Commander-in-Chief gradually drew off his right flank units and skillfully extricated his army by falling back while covering his moves with his center. Thus ended a battle marked by the largest concentration of troops seen on one battlefield up to that time. (Altogether, over 300,000 men and nearly 1,000 guns saw action at Wagram.) The loss ended Austria's hopes of challenging Napoleon's widespread empire with direct military action, and also ended the military career of the one man who had been able to defeat Napoleon in battle.[62]

Napoleon's victories on the Danube cast a pall over the entire German resistance movement. Andreas Hofer, the spiritual leader of the Tyrolean insurgency, was eventually captured and executed. A revolt in Prussia led by an army officer failed to strike a spark, and finally ended in defeat at Straslund. Napoleon virtually ignored the Prussian uprising, observing with disdain, "Prussia today counts for very little; I have sufficient means to keep it under."[63] But the spirit of the reformer and the nationalist patriots in Germany remained alive—largely because of Napoleon's continuing inability to extinguish the Spanish insurgency.

Guerrilla Warfare and the Spanish Ulcer

The war in Spain alternately simmered and flared for four more years. On the average, 250,000 French soldiers were occupied with the combined efforts of the Spanish and British armies and the ever present local *guerrilleros*. This ultimately proved to be a drain that the French Empire could not tolerate. Obsessed with maintaining his empire, however, Napoleon refused to cut his losses and withdraw from the unprofitable venture. The war in Spain had become a battle for the mind of Europe. It was a struggle in which the primary stake was the reputation of Napoleon. *(See Atlas Map No. 44.)*

There were four main elements involved in the war: French occupation troops, Spanish armed forces, Spanish resistance forces, and elements of the British Regular Army. As it turned out, the British determined the fate of the contestants. On the advice of Wellington, the British Cabinet decided to resume operations in Portugal in the summer of 1809. Wellington himself received the command and remained on the Peninsula until the British swept into France in 1814. The concept of operations evolved by Wellington was a masterpiece of strategy founded on common sense, the advantages of British naval superiority, and logistical necessities.

---

*The German critic, General Rudolf von Caemmerer, notes that this tactical formation was a throwback to the Swiss column and observes that "the thirty thousand combatants could just as well have been armed with pikes as with flintlocks."[61] He calls the formation a large square column. John Elting, in *A Military History and Atlas of the Napoleonic Wars*, p. 106, strongly objects to "the massive column commonly described," and points out that MacDonald formed the hollow, three-sided formation because he would need to fight in three directions as he penetrated the Austrian line.

Essentially, Wellington's strategy was to hold Portugal as a base of operations and, with a modest investment of British ground strength, to tie down as many French troops as possible, while keeping the hopes of Spanish patriots alive. With 25,000 British troops initially at his command (augmented by a small Portuguese force), Wellington planned to conduct judicious forays into Spain, draw the French away from their harassed and tenuous land supply lines, and, if attacked, fall back on his relatively secure base at Lisbon. The threat of British amphibious landings would force the French to maintain a cordon defense* around the entire perimeter of the Peninsula. Wellington could rely on sea transport for resupply or, in the event of great danger, for evacuation. The cost effectiveness of his strategy proved the correctness of his calculations. With never more than 60,000 men at his disposal, Wellington managed to tie down as many as six times that number of French troops by combining limited objective attacks, timely withdrawals, and methodical sieges.

The turning point in this crucial war of attrition occurred in 1810 and 1811. After defeating the Austrians at Wagram, Napoleon sent Massena to Spain with orders to attack the British and bring the war to a conclusion. There were 360,000 French troops on the rolls in Spain; Massena should have been able to assemble at least 130,000, but rear area security consumed all but 60,000.[64] Massena steadily forced Wellington back. Then, in September 1810, he launched a headlong attack at Busaco. Wellington fought off Massena's assault and then retired behind the entrenched lines of Torres Vedras, which protected his well-stocked base at Lisbon. For five months, the British remained behind their fortifications, while Massena'a ill-supplied troops hunted for food in a barren countryside and helplessly watched British supply ships come and go. In March 1811, after Soult had repeatedly failed to come to his aid, Massena withdrew in frustration. Henceforth, Wellington possessed the initiative. Alternately besieging Badajoz and Ciudad Rodrigo, he expertly outmaneuvered Soult and Marmont, who relieved Massena in 1811. In 1812, he defeated Marmont at Salamanca. In 1813, he defeated Joseph at Vitoria.

The Tagus River

Napoleon's decisive victories on the battlefield had failed to eliminate resistance to his empire. He had not heeded the admonishment of Henry IV that "Spain is a country where small armies are beaten and large ones starve." Even worse, he had failed to appreciate the inherent limits of military power. In 1811, Wordsworth summed up Napoleon's dilemma exactly:

> The power of armies is a visible thing, formal and
>   circumscribed in time and space;
> But who the limits of that power shall trace
> which a brave people into life can bring or hide, at will,
> —for freedom combating by just revenge inflamed?[65]

Napoleon had neither the temperament nor the time for such a war. Nor was he able to devote full attention to the Peninsula, especially after Tsar Alexander began to turn against him. Spanish, British, Germans, and Russians now threatened his Continental System. After another frustrating year of fighting the elusive foe in Spain, he decided on a final solution to his predicament—he would march eastwards in quest of one more decisive battle. Once more the Emperor would entrust the fate of his Empire to the sword.

*A cordon defense is one in which the defender disposes his units all along the line of defenses, seeking to leave no area undefended. In such a defense, the defender will seldom have much strength remaining as a reserve.

Notes

[1] *Correspondance de Napoleon I* (32 vols.; Paris, 1858–1870), XIV, No. 11353, p. 14.

[2] Felix Markham, *Napoleon* (New York, 1963), p. 143.

[3] Georges Lefebvre, *Napoleon: Tilsit to Waterloo, 1807–1815*, trans. by J.E. Anderson (New York, 1969), p. 11; Napoleon Bonaparte, *Confidential Correspondence with His Brother Joseph* (2 vols.; London, 1856), I, 276.

[4] Eli Heckscher, *The Continental System* (Oxford, 1922), pp. 175–180.

[5] *Correspondance*, XVI, p. 498.

[6] J. Holland Rose, *The Life of Napoleon I* (2 vols.; London, 1901–1902), II, 167.

[7] Jacques Godechot, et al., *The Napoleonic Era in Europe*, trans. by B. Hyslop (New York, 1971), pp. 140–142; Gabriel H. Lovett, *Napoleon and the Birth of Modern Spain* (New York, 1965), pp. 130–132.

[8] Mary Loyd (ed.), *The New Letters of Napoleon I* (New York, 1897), p. 83.

[9] *Correspondance*, XVIII, No. 14218, p. 407; *Confidential Correspondence with Joseph*, I, 340.

[10] Lovett, *Napoleon and the Birth of Modern Spain*, pp. 239–245.

[11] Michael Glover, *Wellington as Military Commander* (London, 1968), p. 44.

[12] Arthur Wellesley, Duke of Wellington, *The Dispatches of Field Marshal the Duke of Wellington . . . From 1799 to 1815*, comp. by Lieutenant Colonel Gurwood (12 vols. plus index; London, 1834–1839), IV, 16.

[13] Edmund Burke, *Speech on the Army Estimates, 1790*, in *The Works of Edmund Burke* (8 vols.; London, 1906–1914), III, 277.

[14] Cecil Woodham-Smith, *The Reason Why* (New York, 1960), pp. 21–22.

[15] C.W. Crawley (ed.), *The New Cambridge Modern History* (14 vols.; Cambridge, 1966–1971), IX, 47–48.

[16] Philip Guedalla, *Wellington* (New York, 1931), p. 194.

[17] *Ibid.*, p. 124.

[18] Wolfgang von Groote and Klaus-Jürgen Muller (eds.), *Napoleon I und das Militärwesen seiner Zeit* (Freiburg, 1968), p. 50.

[19] Rose, *The Life of Napoleon I*, II, 170.

[20] Joseph Fouché, *The Memoirs of Fouché* (2 vols.; Paris, 1903), I, 270–271.

[21] Octave Aubry, *Napoleon*, trans. by M. Crosland and S. Road (New York, 1964), p. 254.

[22] Lefebvre, *Napoleon: From Tilsit to Waterloo, 1807–1815*, p. 28.

[23] *Correspondance*, XVII, No. 14378, p. 556; *Confidential Correspondence with Joseph*, I, 370–371.

[24] Christopher Hibbert, *Corunna* (New York, 1961), p. 63.

[25] Donald Goodspeed, *The War in the Peninsula, 1807–1814* (Ottawa, 1958), p. 57.

[26] Hibbert, *Corunna*, p. 93.

[27] *Ibid.*, p. 94.

[28] Aubry, *Napoleon*, p. 224; Duff Cooper, *Talleyrand* (Stanford, 1967 [1932]); p. 187.

[29] George Rude, *Revolutionary Europe, 1783–1815* (New York, 1964), pp. 180–181.

[30] Godechot, *The Napoleonic Era in Europe*, pp. 146–148; J.G. Fichte, *Addresses to the German Nation*, ed. by G.A. Kelley (New York, 1963), pp. 176–177.

[31] Peter Paret, *Yorck and the Era of Prussian Reform, 1807–1815* (Princeton, 1966), p. 4.

[32] Geoffrey Bruun, *Europe and the French Imperium* (New York, 1938), p. 173.

[33] Hajo Holborn, *A History of Modern Germany, 1648–1840* (3 vols.; New York, 1959–1969), II, 415.

[34] Paret, *Yorck and the Era of Prussian Reform*, pp. 131, 133.

[35] Carlisle A. Macartney, *The Hapsburg Empire, 1790–1918* (New York, 1969), pp. 157–169; Moriz Edlen von Angeli, *Erzherzog Carl von Oesterreich als Feldheer und Heeresorganisator* (5 vols.; Vienna, 1896–1897), IV, 7–8.

[36] *Encyclopaedia Britannica* (29 vols.; Cambridge, 1911), V, 935–936.

[37] Hans Delbrück, *Geschichte der Kriegskunst im Rahmen der politischen Geschichte* (4 vols.; Berlin, 1900–1920), IV, 503.

[38] F. von Waldenstaetten, *Erzherzog Carl; Ausgewählte militärische Schriften* (Berlin, 1882), pp. 16, 57–73; W. Nemetz, "Erzherzog Karl" in *Klassiker der Kriegskunst*, ed. by Werner Hahlweg (Darmstadt, 1960), p. 299; H. Ommen, *Die Krieg-ührung Erzherzogs Karl* (Berlin, 1900), pp. 47–48, 57.

[39] Delbrück, *Geschichte der Kriegskunst*, IV, 496–497.

[40] Angeli, *Erzherzog Carl*, IV, 8–11.

[41] *Ibid.*, pp 22–23, 25–26.

[42] Maurice Dumolin, *Précis D'Histoire Militaire* (3 vols.; Paris, 1906–1913), III, 11–13.

[43] *Correspondance*, XVIII, No. 15144, p. 525.

[44] Dumolin, *Précis D'Histoire Militaire*, III, 20–23; *Correspondance*, XVIII, No. 14828, p. 296; No. 14965, p. 397; No. 14975, p. 406.

[45] Dumolin, *Précis D'Histoire Militaire*, III, 22, 28–29.

[46] Angeli, *Erzherzog Carl*, IV, 41, 46.

[47] Dumolin, *Précis D'Histoire Militaire*, III, 29–30; *Correspondance*, XVIII, Nos. 15047–15048, 459–460.

[48] Angeli, *Erzherzog Carl*, IV, 48–50.

[49] Dumolin, *Précis D'Histoire Militaire*, III, 43–45; Angeli, *Erzherzog Carl*, IV, 76–77; *Correspondance*, XVIII, No. 15087, p. 484.

[50] Angeli, *Erzherzog Carl*, IV, 79–90, 107.

[51] Dumolin, *Précis D'Histoire Militaire*, III, 51–52.

[52] Angeli, *Erzherzog Carl*, IV, 134.

[53] *Correspondance*, XVIII, No. 15100, p. 491; No. 15106, p. 496.

[54] Angeli, *Erzherzog Carl*, IV, 171–172.

[55] Count Yorck von Wartenburg, *Napoleon as a General* (2 vols.; London, 1902), II, 54.

[56] *Correspondance*, XIX, No. 15219, p. 1516.

[57] Loredan Larchey (ed.), *The Narrative of Captain Coignet*, trans. by M. Carey (New York, 1890), p. 250.

[58] Harold T. Parker, *Three Napoleonic Battles* (Durham, N.C., 1944), p. 74.

[59] Jean Morvan, *Le Soldat Imperial* (2 vols.; Paris, 1904), II, 512–513.

[60] Angeli, *Erzherzog Carl*, IV, 439–443.

[61] Rudolph von Caemmerer, *The Development of Strategical Science During the 19th Century*, trans. by Karl Donat (London, 1905), p. 41.

[62] The foregoing account of the Battle of Wagram is constructed primarily from Vincent J. Esposito and John R. Elting, *A Military History and Atlas of the Napoleonic Wars* (New York, 1964), pp. 104–106.

[63] Heinrich von Treitschke, *History of Germany in the 19th Century*, trans. by Eden and Cedar Paul (7 vols.; London, 1915–1919), I, 404.

[64] Lefebvre, *Napoleon: From Tilsit to Waterloo, 1807–1815*, p. 103.

[65] William Wordsworth, *Poems*, ed. by Philip Wayne (3 vols.; London, 1955), I, 326.

Offensive Into Russia

6

"From the day when peace is signed," wrote Metternich to Emperor Francis after the Austrian defeat at Wagram, "we must confine our system to tacking and turning, and flattering. Thus alone may we possibly preserve our existence, till the day of general deliverance."[1] Already the tacking and turning had started: Napoleon had decided to renounce his wife. The Empress had borne him no heir, which the legitimacy of his regime demanded. He made overtures for the hand of Alexander's youngest sister, but the Tsar was evasive. (The Russian court had never wholly favored the alliance of Tilsit.) Metternich was quick to pounce on the opportunity. The Hapsburg Archduchess, Marie Louise, was eligible and, although barely eighteen, would serve admirably as a sacrifice to the needs of Austrian policy. The marriage, celebrated in April 1810, bought time for Austria to re-

The Marriage of Napoleon of France and Marie Louise of Austria, April 2, 1810

cover. It also dramatized the abrupt turn of Napoleon away from Alexander and confirmed the growing enmity between France and Russia.

The Clash Between the Continental System and the Russian Empire

French and Russian hostility had not developed suddenly, nor was the cause of the enmity purely the eastward drive of Napoleon's armies. The enmity, which culminated in war in 1812, grew out of conflicting policies, competing economies, and the growth of national feeling all across the face of Europe. French and Russian interests were only the immediate causes that drove France and Russia to war. The major powers of Europe were all involved, Paris and Moscow becoming the two centers of polarity after Austria and Prussia had exhausted their resources fighting off Napoleon's aggressive actions to expand his empire.

Throughout the seventeenth and eighteenth centuries, the Russian Empire had tried to solve the same problem that Louis XIV had faced—the lack of natural boundaries. Moreover, since Muscovy had no topographical frontiers on any side, expansion was directed against all of her neighbors. Peter the Great's victory in the Great Northern War gave Russia a Baltic boundary. Then, during the greater part of the eighteenth century, Russian armies warred on the Prussians, Poles, and Ottoman Turks in attempts to secure a strong position in western Europe and on the Black Sea.

For most of the Seven Years' War, the Romanovs chose to ally themselves with Bourbons and Hapsburgs against Frederick the Great. After Elizabeth's death, however, her successor reversed this policy, and in the latter part of the eighteenth century, Catherine II linked Russia more closely with Prussia in order to gain territory in Poland and Turkey. Polish patriots such as Thaddeus Kosciusko resisted this encroachment, but a Russian army commanded by Alexander Suvorov finally occupied Warsaw in 1794, and Poland submitted—for the third time—to division among Austria, Prussia, and Russia. By the end of the century, Russia had become a large multi-ethnic empire with a reputation for aggressiveness and a serious interest in the affairs of western Europe.[2]

As long as the wars of western Europe were fought between semi-related dynasties, the westward drive of Russia (and the eastward drive of France) remained confined to the classic pattern of monarchial conquest—drawn-out wars and negotiations punctuated by occasional battles or sieges that ended in territorial trade-offs.* When the French Revolution expanded the scope of these wars and accelerated the velocity of campaigning, a host of new forces was set in motion. French national armies now roamed the Continent. Showing no inclination to halt at the borders of neighboring states to allow supply convoys to catch up, these hordes requisitioned supplies from the lands they invaded. A campaign that might have lasted through the entire summer during the Seven Years' War might now be finished in a few weeks, when fought by a commander of consummate skill. When that same talented commander showed no respect for the rights of monarchies, the areas he occupied began to rise against their princes. When he began to redefine the boundaries of nations, the entire balance of European power fell into disorder.

The rapidity of French conquests in 1796 and 1797 so endangered European stability that Russia joined the Second Coalition—thus extending Muscovite influence even farther to the west. *(See Atlas Map No. 10.)* Russian armies under the skillful Alexander Suvorov invaded Italy and Switzerland, gaining astonishing successes.† However, France was only one of Russia's foes, and Tsarist policy was soon diverted by conflicts with other powers. Great Britain's Mediterranean fleets and bases posed a challenge to Russia's hopes of acquiring Constantinople. The Ottoman Empire still governed the ancient Byzantine dominions, and thus posed an immediate obstacle to southern expansion. The sprawling Hapsburg Empire, suffering reverses in the west, was recoiling to the east, and Poland was making efforts to regain its political status as an independent kingdom. In Scandinavia, Sweden still blocked the outlets from the Baltic, and Prussia's obstinate neutrality offered little opportunity for any

further Russian gains along the Vistula or Oder Rivers. By 1800, France had withdrawn behind its natural boundaries, and the coalition had dissolved.[3] But neither Bonaparte nor the revolutionary forces he championed had retired permanently behind the Rhine. Just when European princes had begun to take their favored status for granted, the Corsican struck into Italy again and won at Marengo.

Alexander's accession to the throne in 1801 temporarily brought Russian foreign policy into line with reality. He came to terms with Great Britain and France and resumed relations with the Hapsburg monarchy. In 1802, he established a personal friendship with the Prussian royal family. Above all, Alexander wanted peace in order to proceed with domestic reforms; but the brief tranquility of 1802 was disturbed by a series of disconcerting events—Great Britain's refusal to evacuate Malta, the forced restructuring of Germany by France in 1803 *(see Atlas Maps Nos. 12 and 13)*, and the murder of the Duke of Enghien. (The French violation of neutral Baden to kidnap the Duke angered Alexander, not only because the

Alexander I, Tsar of Russia

---

*Russian wars against Sweden, the Tatars, and the Turks were more savagely total, in the ideological sense. Since the tenth century, Russia's experience with its steppe adversaries had been very similar to French revolutionary war.

†Bonaparte was acting out his high adventure in Egypt at this time.

Tsar's wife was a princess of Baden, but also because the assassination seemed to confirm Bonaparte's contempt for the legitimate authority of all nobility.) In 1804, diplomatic relations between France and Russia were severed. From this point forward, the basis of Alexander's foreign policy was often enigmatic.

In domestic affairs, the Tsar has been pictured as being enlightened. Apparently, his plans to offer the Russians a constitution were a product of his rational desire for a more efficient, effective government. In foreign relations, however, he had an uncanny facility for concealing his intentions. Exactly what influence his licentious grandmother, Catherine, had on his upbringing is uncertain. It is apparent that Alexander cultivated the art of deception in order to simultaneously satisfy his father and his grandmother, who were at odds with each other. It is also well known that Alexander was capable of great personal charm and that he had strong religious convictions. After repeated confrontations with Napoleon, he gradually became convinced that it was his destiny to save Europe from the ravages of war.[4]

The consequences of Russia's military miscalculations— the ill-considered attack at Austerlitz and Bennigsen's disastrous stand at Friedland—left Alexander's grand mission unfulfilled. After having suffered two major defeats at Napoleon's hands, Alexander developed a war policy that aimed not at fighting against the French nation, but at overthrowing the French Government, which was "as tyrannical for France as for the rest of Europe."[5] This idealistic attitude was counterbalanced by a strong conservative tendency which emphasized belief in natural boundaries and a balance of power on the Continent. The Treaty of Tilsit (1807) seemed to offer these advantages by dividing Europe between France and Russia roughly along the Vistula. *(See Atlas Map No. 34.)*

The events that followed Tilsit prove how widely men's actions can differ from the calculations of statesmen. Alexander had thought that Napoleon would digest the conquered territories of western Europe and leave Constantinople and the Baltic to Russia. In February 1808, however, Napoleon wrote to the Tsar, stating that he now envisaged a joint Franco-Russian expedition to India, by way of Constantinople. Before Alexander could assess the meaning of this grandiose plan, the Emperor of the French had become thoroughly embroiled in the Iberian Peninsula. At Erfurt, in September 1808, Napoleon requested the Tsar to restrain Austria while he personally vanquished the peasants and priests in Spain. Then, in 1809, beset by even greater crises on the Danube, Napoleon appealed to Alexander to move against Austria; but Russian reactions remained confined to a slow advance aimed chiefly at occupying Krakow and other cities before the Poles could liberate them from Austrian rule.

Napoleon resented Alexander's evasion of his Tilsit obli-

gations, while his peremptory decision to marry the Austrian Archduchess obviously irritated the sensitive Alexander. The Emperor's territorial aggrandizements further exacerbated matters by bringing French troops into confrontation with Russian influence. In December 1810, he incorporated the entire north German coast into the Empire,* and one month later he annexed the Duchy of Oldenburg. (The Duke was related to Alexander by marriage.) But the most immediate and pressing cause for antagonism was Alexander's decision not to enforce the French embargo on neutral trade. Russia had been one of Great Britain's most important customers for manufactured products, and had served as a key source of naval stores for British shipbuilders. At the end of 1810, Alexander imposed special taxes on luxury goods imported by land—an obvious blow to French commerce. The implication of this opposition was evident: the most powerful ruler in Europe could not enforce his own decrees. *(See Atlas Map No. 45.)*

---

*Louis had already despaired of simultaneously satisfying the aspirations of his Dutch subjects and the imperious desires of his brother, and had fled into exile. Napoleon's heavy-handed response was to annex Holland to France.

L'Empereur

By 1811, the French Empire had achieved its greatest size. Including the annexed territories, it consisted of about 43 million people.[6] More than likely, *le Grande Empire*, which included German, Italian, and Spanish vassal states, had expanded far too rapidly to allow time for the development of an efficient administrative government. Clearly, the continental embargo and the British blockade had played havoc with normal patterns of European trade. Unrest in Westphalia, periodic uprisings in Italy, and the unresolved insurgency in Spain reinforced the general concern among Napoleon's imperial family that he must take some positive action to bring peace to Europe. In December 1811, Napoleon's brother Jerome summarized the dissatisfaction that plagued all of Germany:

> . . . if war breaks out, all the countries between the Rhine and the Oder will rise as one man. The cause of unrest is not simply a strong impatience with the foreign yoke; it lies deeper in the ruin that faces every class of people, the crushing taxation; the war levies, the billeting of troops; all the military coming and going; and a constant series of harassments . . .[7]

Napoleon's problem was not with Russia alone, but with all of Europe. Yet he persisted in believing that England would tire of the struggle and make peace on French terms, if only Russia would adhere to his Continental System. In June 1811, he discussed the possibility of war with his former ambassador to Russia, Armand Caulaincourt. "Admit frankly," said Napoleon, "that it is Alexander who wants to make war on me." Caulaincourt replied that he would stake his life on Alexander's not firing the first shot. The Emperor blandly stated that he had no intention of invading Russia, to which Caulaincourt responded that he should explain his intentions "so that every one may know why your Majesty's troops are concentrating in Danzig and the north of Prussia." "Bah," exclaimed the Emperor, "One good battle will see the end of Alexander's fine resolutions." Caulaincourt then related to his master Alexander's exact words:

> If the Emperor makes war on me, it is possible, even probable, that we shall be defeated, assuming that we fight. But that will not mean that he can dictate a peace. The Spaniards have often been defeated; and they are not beaten, nor have they submitted. But they are not so far away from Paris as we are, and have neither our climate nor our resources to help them. We shall take no risks.[8]

Napoleon's reply to this clear warning has not been recorded. In any event, he had already made up his mind to use force in dealing with Russia. He had suffered what amounted to a serious reverse on the Peninsula in March 1811, when

Massena finally withdrew, unsuccessful in his attempt to force Wellington's Lines of Torres Vedras. All of Europe was in the grip of a severe economic depression, and there was mounting evidence that Russian merchants were receiving British products via neutral shipping. Napoleon refused to compromise on the issue of trading with England, and rejected Alexander's requests that French troops withdraw from Prussia. Moreover, in spite of these mounting military, political, and economic difficulties, the Emperor's belief in his own destiny remained unshaken. By August 1811, Napoleon had decided to "convince Europe of the impossibility of further resistance."[9] However, he misjudged his enemy badly.

Russian Generalship and Art of War

Armies often seek to repeat that which has been a part of their most recent experience, especially if that experience included victorious combat. The theories of the winning commanders are usually translated into doctrine, which in turn shapes future military organization and training. Of course, there have been some armies that consciously discarded doctrinaire theories derived from their immediate past, and sought a broader basis for the modernization of their military thought and practice. Resounding defeat gave impetus to that sort of reform in Prussia, while Revolution helped to quicken the conversion of the French Army into an organization more responsive to the national will. A tradition of borrowing foreign institutions dominated Russian military history; but the Army was distinct from other European armies, and it was rich in original ideas.

Peter the Great had begun the modernization of his army early in the eighteenth century. An experimenter, he was also a realist who rejected unnecessary trappings and procedures that were incompatible with Russian attitudes and ideals. Peter relied on foreign officers to train the Army because the Russian nobility lacked the necessary education, but at the same time he upgraded the position of the common soldier in society. Whereas the serf remained in bondage, the soldier became a relatively free man, still subject to the customary brutal discipline, but nonetheless a respected member of the state. Peter's system of recruitment required each province to provide its quota of trainees to the regular regiments. Religion and the justice of the cause, thought Peter, would inspire the soldier to fight for his country. His concept of officer procurement was to offer commissions to men of all classes, and he encouraged an unusual camaraderie between officer and soldier. Thus, at a time when most rulers were increasing

A Russian Artillery Crew in Action

their reliance on mercenaries, Peter was evolving the concept that military duty was expected of every man. The Russian Army, like the state, was becoming a national entity.[10]

After Peter's death, the continual wars of the eighteenth century helped reverse the trend toward Russianizing the Army. As more Russian officers came into contact with conventional European military practice, especially during the Seven Years' War, there was a natural tendency to adopt many of the foreign practices encountered. Prussian influence was especially significant, perhaps because of Frederick's success using the linear system of organization and tactics. Frederick's reliance on the nobility for officers reinforced the caste system, which was traditional in most monarchial armies. Not all Russian officers, however, accepted without question the need for parade ground drill, formal maneuvers, and siegecraft. Some commanders examined the problems of their army with a critical eye and trained their men in methods that departed substantially from the formal European style of tactics and strategy. The most important of these men was Count Alexander Suvorov, a little known general in the Western World, but a legendary hero and an influential theorist in Russian military history.[11]

Suvorov was a man of simple manner, who knew his men well and shared their discomforts in the field. Consequently, he was an effective leader and trainer. He was merciless, placing little value on human life, but the ruthlessness he demonstrated in Turkey and Poland was more the result of his outlook on war than of personal cruelty. After lengthy combat experience, Suvorov pragmatically concluded that brutal violence produced quicker results than drawn-out maneuvers and sieges. Contrary to the philosophy of "maneuver strategy" practiced in France and Germany, Suvorov waged total war, the most extreme example of his method being the sack and destruction of Ismail (in Bessarabia) in 1790. Yet Suvorov was shrewd enough to recognize that "all wars are different."[12] The means he used to capture territory on the Danube differed from the strategy employed to conquer Poland.

Suvorov was an individualist in temperament and intellect. He was deliberately rude and coarse, shunning the manners of the nobility and displaying his contempt for their ignorance. Long before his campaigns in Italy, he had learned five languages and had studied the methods of Russia's potential enemies. The speed with which he ejected the French from Italy in 1799 is proof enough that he was a moving spirit in the Russian Army. Even more so, he was profoundly influential as a teacher of later generations of Russian generals. The terse and direct language of his writings captures the essence of his views on war. Two examples may be cited, both of which indicate how far apart Suvorov's experience and teachings were removed from conventional European practice. In an almost Napoleonic vein, he wrote: "a minute decides a battle, an hour a campaign, and a day the destiny of an empire." In another of his writings, collected in a manual entitled, *The Science of Victory*, he observed:

> The power of an army is not in its numbers,
> Nor is it in its arms and equipment,
> The strength of an army lies in its spirit and in its soul.[13]

These quotations suggest that Suvorov had thoroughly

Field Marshal Mikhail Kutusov

grasped the nuances of war, and may even have exceeded Napoleon in his understanding of war as an instrument of policy.

Suvorov's recipe for victory was utilized by another general, Mikhail Ilarionovich Kutusov, a shrewd officer who was Suvorov's close companion in the Turkish Wars for over three years.[14] At a conference held on the night before the Battle of Austerlitz, Kutusov had slumped in his chair and snored throughout the entire discussion of the battle plan. (It was not, of course, his plan; in fact, he had recommended to the Tsar that battle be avoided.) On the following day, the Russian Army suffered defeat, and historians have never forgotten the apparent indifference of Kutusov on the eve of that battle. Unfortunately, Kutusov's well-deserved reputation for dozing has lessened proper recognition of his decisive role in repulsing Napoleon's invasion in 1812. Kutusov's special qualifications for command of the Russian Army may be ascribed to three factors: first, his association with Suvorov; second, his active service in many wars during the reign of Catherine the Great—the golden age of the Russian Army; and third, his personal development of a concept of war that envisioned victory as the result of the enemy army's destruction.

Under Suvorov, Kutusov learned a great deal about the higher direction of war. Suvorov once commented that to one officer he had to give an order, to another a hint, "but there's no need even to speak to Kutusov—he understands it all by himself."[15] Equally as important, Kutusov had been reared on a diet of winning. Upon the accession of Catherine the Great in 1762, the Empress announced her intention to expand the Army, which gradually rose to a strength of half a million men. Not surprisingly, Catherine's wars against Poland, Turkey, Sweden, and the tribes in the Caucasus were successful wars. These were Russia's years of greatest expansion, and they were the formative years of Kutusov's career. He not only discovered the unpleasant reality of war during these wars—he lost an eye in action—but he fought well and also obtained important diplomatic posts—in Constantinople, Finland, and Berlin.

If the outcome of Austerlitz temporarily damaged Kutusov's reputation, it also hurt Russia's prestige and indirectly led to the general's rejuvenation. Encouraged by Russia's losses and goaded by Napoleon, Turkey resumed its war against Russia in 1806. The conflict was long and costly, and a series of commanders failed to subdue the stubborn Turks. Increasingly concerned with the threat of war with France, Alexander finally selected Kutusov to force a decision on the Danube in 1811. Kutusov concluded that the quickest way to end the struggle was to withdraw and lure the Turks from their strongholds across the Danube River. This imaginative strategy yielded a decisive win within three months, and Kutusov earned wide acclaim and the title of prince.[16] The destruction of the enemy army was Kutusov's goal, and withdrawal his initial strategy. Would Russia apply the same concept in defending the nation against invasion?

Shortly before the French invasion, Alexander was heard to say:

> I intend to follow the system which has made Wellington victorious in Spain and exhausted the French armies—avoid pitched battles and organize long lines of communication for retreat leading to entrenched camps.[17]

There was no mention of Kutusov, who had freed the Tsar from war on Russia's southern flank. Alexander disliked Kutusov—for obvious reasons stemming from the disastrous loss at Austerlitz. As the armies mustered, the hero of the Turkish war went quietly into retirement, at the age of 67.

Napoleon's Invasion of Russia

An understanding of the motives for Napoleon's 1812 invasion of Russia, discussed above, are important in judging his state of mind at the outset of his most ambitious campaign. It was more than the failure of the Continental System that drove him eastwards. Ever since Tilsit, and especially throughout 1810 and 1811, the Emperor had increasingly come to view Europe as his personal domain. There was insufficient room on the Continent for two major empires. Therefore, there was no reason to suffer any opposition, even on such issues as the reconstruction of Poland, which was more a matter of interest to Russia than to France. Napoleon may not have wanted war, but his massive self-indulgence and his arbitrary habit of subjecting every country and every person to his will were clearly leading to a conflict of gigantic dimensions.

And what of France, which had already borne the major burden of war for two decades and was now seeing its manpower steadily consumed by an apparently endless war in Spain? Napoleon had once been concerned for the glory of France; now he exploited the country. It is possible to trace the growth of his monstrous lust for power at least as far back as 1800. His attitude was never more clearly expressed than in a statement attributed to him in 1809:

> I have only one passion, only one mistress, and that is France. I sleep with her. She has never failed me, she has lavished her blood and her treasures on me. If I need five hundred thousand men, she gives them to me.[18]

In fact, his mistress was not France at all, but power. France merely supplied the resources for his aggression.

French Preparations

Even the French nation could not provide all the manpower and supplies needed to carry out the Emperor's grandiose plan for subduing Russia. Throughout 1811, he worked to mobilize the entire Continent against Russia. He not only levied the vassal kingdoms in Spain, Italy, and Germany, but also summoned Austria and Prussia to furnish their share of men and goods. (Crown Prince Bernadotte, newly attached to Sweden, avoided committing his country to Russia's support until Napoleon had forced the issue by occupying Swedish Pomerania in January 1812.) In February 1812, Frederick William III signed an agreement that furnished Napoleon with 20,000 soldiers for the war against Russia, and, in March, Austria grudgingly promised an auxiliary corps of 30,000 men.* Altogether, Napoleon could count on nearly

700,000 men of 20 different nationalities, of whom more than 600,000 crossed the border.[19] The *Grande Armée* had never included so many foreign contingents. Swollen far beyond its original size, the unwieldy army was difficult to assemble and hard to feed. Compared with the rapier-like force of 1805–1807, it was a bludgeon. Once Napoleon decided on war, sometime in 1811, it was impossible to turn back. All rational considerations now paled before the lure of the great adventure. Victory had become a narcotic, and the Emperor had become enslaved by his own immense ambition.

The supply of this vast army posed enormous problems. Correctly anticipating that the army could not live off the land in Poland and Russia, Napoleon ordered the establishment of a network of depots and magazines from which the advancing forces were to be supplied. *(See Atlas Map No. 46.)* General Joseph Poniatowski guarded the Vistula River line; Danzig became a huge base stocked with large quantities of materiel.† The Niemen River provided water transport to the forward base at Kovno, and 26 transportation battalions equipped with oxen and wagons followed the combat elements with ammunition and a three-week supply of provisions. Each soldier carried four days' rations in his knapsack—an emergency issue, as it were. As Napoleon pointed out in a letter to Davout, "we must carry with us all we need." To do the carrying, there were 90,000 draft animals—of which 20,000 were "traveling beef"—aside from the 30,000 artillery horses and the 80,000 cavalry chargers.[20] This unaccustomed and unwieldy logistic element was essential to the army's survival, but it promised to restrict mobility severely if it should become necessary for Napoleon's units to strike deeply into Russia.

---

†According to calculations of the German General Staff, the amount of bread and flour accumulated at Danzig was sufficent to feed half a million men for a year.

Rations on the Hoof

---

*Napoleon requested the Archduke Charles for this command, but Charles refused. Prince Karl Philip Schwarzenberg, a man of greater diplomatic than military talent, received the position.

Corps	Commander	Infantry Divisions	Cavalry Divisions	Strength	Nationality of Troops
I	Davout	5	1	72,051	French, with Spanish and Germans attached.
II	Oudinot	3	1	37,139	French, Swiss, and Portuguese.
III	Ney	3	1	39,342	French, Portuguese, and Dalmatian.
IV	Eugène*	4	1	45,798	Italian, with some French and Spanish.
V	Poniatowski	3	1	36,311	Polish.
VI	St. Cyr	2	1	25,134	Bavarian.
VII	Reynier	2	1	17,194	Saxon.
VIII	Jerome*	2	1	17,935	Westphalian and German.
IX	Victor	3	1	33,567	French, Polish, and German.
X	MacDonald	3	1	32,497	Polish, Bavarian, Westphalian, and Prussian.
XI	Augereau	5	1	50,000 (approx.)	French, German, and Neapolitan.
Cavalry Reserve	Murat (four corps, two detached to Jerome and Eugène)	—	11	40,153	French, Württenberg, Saxon, Westphalian, Prussian, Polish, and Bavarian.
Guard Cavalry	Bessières	—	—	(6,279)	French.
Old Guard	Lefebvre	—	—	} (41,004)	French.
New Guard	Mortier	—	—		French, Polish, Dutch, Swiss, and German.
Guard Total				47,283	
Austrian Auxiliary Corps	Schwarzenberg	4	1	34,148	Austrian.
Imperial Headquarters	Berthier	—	—	3,983	French.
Artillery and Engineers	Lariboissière (Artillery)	—	—	} 18,265	French.
	Chasseloup (Engineers)	—	—		
Total forces that entered Russia				550,800	

*Once the campaign was underway, Eugène controlled IV and VI Corps, plus one of Murat's corps; Jerome controlled V, VII, and VIII Corps, plus one of Murat's corps; and Napoleon personally controlled I, II, and III Corps, plus the Guard and Murat's remaining cavalry.

The *Grande Armée* in June 1812

Throughout the spring of 1812, Napoleon addressed himself to these problems while the various French and allied contingents made their way eastward. Davout pressed his 80,000 men forward from the Oder, Ney's corps crossed France from the camp at Boulogne, Jerome's German army followed Davout, and Eugène's Army of Italy wound its tortuous way across the Alps. The Emperor planned to have these formations in their assembly areas along the Nieman River by the end of May.

Meanwhile, Napoleon studied maps, books, and reports on Russia. He was particularly interested in the account of Charles XII's campaign in Poland and Russia. Characteristically, he neglected no opportunity to consume quantities of information on Russia's topography, people, and history. He was enraptured by the enormity of the vast enterprise he had set in motion. In 1805, the *Grande Armée* had traversed 400 miles from the English Channel to the Danube. Now, between Tilsit and Moscow, there lay over 600 miles of hostile, barren countryside. In 1805, the *Grande Armée* had numbered barely 200,000 men. Now, swollen by foreign reinforcements, it was three times as large. To Davout, Napoleon wrote at the end of 1811, "I have never made greater preparations."[21]

French intelligence had located the major Russian formations and estimated their strength at 200,000 men.* Napo-

*The combined strength of Bagration's and Barclay's armies was actually 175,000.

Marshal Michel Ney

campaign."[23] His intention, as he explained to Jerome, was to force the enemy either to stand and offer battle in the interior of Russia, or to undertake an offensive toward Warsaw. If the Russians offered battle, he explained in letters to Eugène and Berthier, he would employ a massive maneuver "upon their flank and rear with my whole army. The advance of the army is a movement which I will make with my left while refusing my right . . ."[24]

Thus, Napoleon planned to rupture the extended Russian front with a direct advance of the main army from Kovno to Vilna. Following the anticipated success of this maneuver, French forces would then defeat the fragments of the Russian armies in detail or, in the event of a Russian offensive toward Warsaw, swing to the south and envelop the enemy forces pressing towards the Vistula. Army-size formations under Eugène and Jerome would advance in echelon; MacDonald's corps, reinforced by the Prussians, was to advance along the Baltic coast; Schwarzenberg's Austrians would protect the southern flank. This was a lofty plan, appropriate for the high purpose of the venture. But what if the Russians failed to offer battle and retired to the east? There was no mention of this possibility in the voluminous letters Napoleon wrote on the eve of the invasion. His intention was to bring about a battle, defeat the Russian Army, and dictate a settlement. Apparently, neither he nor his soldiers, who cheerfully began crossing the Nieman on the evening of June 22, thought beyond that immediate goal.

Early Operations

On the Russian side, there was a good deal of confusion during the early weeks of the campaign. To begin with, Alexander had appointed no commander-in-chief to coordinate the actions of the three forward armies. He intended to play that role himself, but his understanding of war had improved little since Austerlitz, and his strategy was uncertain. On the main axis of Napoleon's advance, 127,000 Russian soldiers would meet over 300,000 French and allied troops. Michael Barclay de Tolly, descendant of a Scottish soldier of fortune, was charged with defending the roads to St. Petersburg and Moscow, and was authorized to withdraw to a fortified camp on the Dwina River, which presumably would draw out the French Army for a counterstroke from the south by Bagration. However, Peter Bagration, a soldier of proven courage and resolution, refused to cooperate. Critical of Barclay, who was viewed as a foreigner, his pointed comment was, "The headquarters is full of Germans . . . ."[25] While Bagration suggested an attack toward Warsaw, Barclay did not generate confidence when he promptly, though wisely, ordered a retreat. *(See Atlas Map No. 46.)*

leon's plan for concentration along the Vistula allowed the choice of several invasion routes, either to the south or to the north of the Pripet Marshes. However, the choice was a difficult one. For reasons of climate and grain supply, the southern route was preferable, but the main Russian army was undoubtedly covering the routes to Moscow and St. Petersburg. Russian forces were in fact dispersed to cover all these obvious avenues. *(See Atlas Map No. 45.)*

On May 25, the Emperor of the French arrived in Dresden, surrounded by imperial royalty. On the following day, he began to issue orders that revealed his plan of campaign. To Davout he wrote, "The result of all my movements will be to concentrate 400,000 men upon one point . . ."[22] The following week, he wrote to Jerome from Thorn, "I will cross the Nieman and seize Vilna, which is the first objective of the

By June 27, Murat's cavalry neared Vilna, Jerome moved on Grodno, and the army's flank guards advanced cautiously across the Niemen and Bug Rivers. With the exception of General Matvei I. Platov's Cossacks, which put up an occasional rearguard fight, no Russians were in evidence, and Napoleon seemed briefly unsure of what to do next. During these early days of the campaign, the troops suffered from the heat—even those who had fought in Spain and had become accustomed to a similar climate. One lieutenant described the marches as thinning the ranks to such an exceptional degree that "thousands of men disappeared within a very short time." The most unpleasant experience for the soldier was dust. As the same officer observed, thick dust "enveloped us on the march. . . . I recall that at one stage, so as to prevent anyone taking a wrong turning, a drummer was stationed at the head of each battalion."[26]

At the end of June, the weather abruptly changed. Heavy rainstorms began, slowing the advance of the main column. Sickness began to reduce the strength of horses and soldiers. Jean R. Coignet, a member of the Imperial Guard, told of seeing thousands of horses that had died because of inadequate forage and a sudden drop in the temperature. Also, the regular distribution of food ceased as soon as most units had crossed the Vistula. According to one officer in the Bavarian corps, the order of the day read, "Let each man take wherever he can find it, and live as well or as badly as he can manage it."[27] Napoleon's irritation with these unexpected problems found expression in letters to his subordinate commanders, especially to the incompetent Jerome: "I can only express my dissatisfaction at the small amount of information I have from you. I neither know the number of Bagration's divisions, nor their names, nor where he was, nor what information you obtained at Grodno, nor what you are doing."[28] Meanwhile, Napoleon made a key operational decision, deciding to move on Bagration with Jerome's group of corps while Davout's stripped corps swung south toward Minsk to cut off the slowly retreating Russian Second Army. The maneuver was well conceived, but Napoleon, far away in Vilna, was unable to coordinate his widespread columns, especially as Jerome's advance fell behind. On July 5, Napoleon told Berthier to inform Jerome "that all the fruits of my maneuvers and the finest opportunity in the war have been lost by his singular ignorance of the simplest notions of war."[29] Forced to abandon his failing plan, Napoleon conceived a new one. *(See Atlas Map No. 47.)*

Lacking adequate intelligence on Russian dispositions, the Emperor decided that Davout must advance toward Minsk in order to force Bagration to the south and, hopefully, trap the elusive Russian Second Army between Davout's and Jerome's formations. At the same time, Murat and Ney were to move on Barclay's First Army and attempt to fix him west of the Dwina. Meanwhile, Napoleon gathered a strong reserve consisting of the corps of Eugène, St. Cyr, and the Guard, and projected a bold move on Vitebsk to cut off Barclay's retreat. Occupying himself principally with this enveloping force, he implicitly delegated authority to Davout to take command of Jerome's forces "if the *corps d'armée* come together."[30] However, either he or Berthier neglected to inform Jerome of this contemplated change of command arrangements.

Meanwhile, Bagration continued his running feud with Barclay, writing to one of the Tsar's principal advisers:

Think of the Tsar and of Russia. Why do we offer no resistance to the enemy when we can so easily manage to do so? A man must really be a traitor to the Tsar and the country to lead us to destruction in this way.[31]

While the Russian generals continued to bicker and argue, the Russian troops steadily withdrew. Driving his men hard, Davout finally saw his chance to attack Bagration, and advised Jerome that he was assuming command of their combined forces. Resentful of his abrupt subordination to a mere prince, Jerome promptly resigned, leaving his subordinates without instructions for nearly a week. Before Davout could regain control, Bagration had slipped away, but not before delivering a savage onslaught at Mogilev. Meanwhile, General Alexei P. Tormassov's Third Army, which had remained in its original positions south of the Pripet Marshes, began sending raiding parties into Poland. Napoleon, furious at his inability to fix the retreating Russians, raged at Davout.

Persuaded by his sister, Alexander at last relinquished the high command to Barclay on July 18 and returned to Moscow to organize the national defense. Barclay now directed Bagration to join him near Vitebsk, but even as he wrote the order, he was already thinking of retiring to Smolensk. Napoleon pushed Murat forward in pursuit of Barclay, but forbade him to push too hard for fear of accelerating the Russians' retreat. At the beginning of August, Napoleon was in the enviable position of having gained the initiative in every way; but, already 300 miles inside Russia, he had as yet found no way to exploit his advantage. Unknown to the Emperor, Barclay, who was now empowered with supreme command of the Russian Army, was about to give the French their first opportunity by offering battle with the combined First and Second Armies in defense of Smolensk.

Smolensk: Point of No Return

The Emperor's original calculations of space and time had clearly forecast that the early part of the campaign would be critical. In programming the resources necessary to achieve his objective he had anticipated fighting a decisive battle within a month after crossing the Niemen,[32] after which negotiations would surely begin and the army would be able to recover from its exertions. Toward the end of that month, Napoleon began to recognize, if not accept, that events were disproving the validity of his estimates. Dying horses littered the roads, the advance guard found little forage as Russians everywhere abandoned their homes, and at Vitebsk he discovered that Barclay had blown up the magazines before withdrawing. The terrible condition of the French army was aggravated by straggling, water shortage, and the inability of the supply trains to keep up with the forward elements. Disorder prevailed, even in the Guard, which lost 9,000 men in two weeks without even seeing action. According to a captured officer, the united Russian army now lay near Smolensk, 80 miles away, but the weakness of French troops, the lack of horses—80,000 had perished already[33]—and ammunition shortages made an immediate advance impossible. The Emperor was forced to halt at Vitebsk to allow men, animals, and guns to catch up. This pause, to which Napoleon resigned himself with great ill-humor, was to cost him two more precious weeks. *(See Atlas Map No. 48.)*

Positive intelligence that Bagration had joined Barclay at Smolensk raised Napoleon's hopes. He still seemed to deceive himself regarding the severe wastage of Murat's cavalry, the true extent of which Murat kept to himself, but the scent of battle fired his imagination and his senses. He now planned an adroit maneuver, seeking to turn Barclay's flank by crossing to the south bank of the Dnieper and marching for Smolensk. Napoleon knew that he must move rapidly if he were to execute an enveloping maneuver like that of Ulm or Jena. Unfortunately, rapid movement was no longer possible in the French army. On August 10, Napoleon wrote to Davout, "it is probable that I will march on Smolensk with 200,000 men,"[34] yet when battle was actually joined one week later, only half that number of Frenchmen were immediately available for combat. Also, there were disturbing indications that the Emperor, who suffered from an irritation of the bladder when on long campaigns, was not sufficiently active, either.

After an abortive Russian offensive, which stalled because of the continuing feud between Barclay and Bagration, the French advanced. The advance guard, led by Murat and Ney, arrived at Smolensk on the morning of August 16. Napoleon rode up to the Russian lines, surveyed the city's protective fortifications, which had been constructed during the Tatar era, and decided to attack on the following day. However, the better part of the next day was gone before a limited attack by Ney, Davout, and Poniatowski probed the city's defenses. Sensing that Smolensk might become a trap, Barclay had already ordered Bagration to begin withdrawing while Barclay

himself covered the retreat from positions in Smolensk. Heavy French artillery fire set the town ablaze, and Barclay thereupon ordered Smolensk evacuated during the evening. Napoleon entered the burning town at daybreak and directed Ney to follow Barclay's army. He was too late.

Ney's pursuit resulted in a series of confused rearguard fights on the high ground overlooking the town, but the Emperor had failed to move quickly enough with an encircling force to the east. Nevertheless, by the end of August 19, elements of three French corps and Murat's cavalry had built up pressure against Barclay's rearguard. In perhaps his finest display of fighting, the Russian stoutly fought them off in a costly engagement contested over rough, wooded ground. Both Russian armies then again vanished to the east. *(See Atlas Map No. 49.)*

The fights in and around Smolensk had cost Napoleon roughly 20,000 men,[35] and he was still far from his goal of bending the Russians to his will. In retrospect, it may appear that he had won a strong position, and that he thus had the freedom to choose from various courses of action. Three such courses of action were: first, he could remain at Smolensk and perhaps, as an alternative, lure the Russians to attack him there; second, he could use the entire winter to reorganize his logistical system and, with this added time, seek the full support of Poland by acceding to Polish requests for unification; three, he could withdraw behind the Niemen and begin again in 1813. (In occasional, unguarded conversations with his closest associates, he spoke of a "Spring Campaign" to be renewed in 1813.)

There were serious drawbacks to all of these options, the first plan being the most problematic. Smolensk, a town with a population of 20,000, could hardly support an army of 10 times that number, particularly since artillery fire and flames had destroyed the main buildings. As for logistics, the major problem was transportation. The roads around Smolensk were certain to deteriorate in the autumn rains. Besides, having brought the *Grande Armée* into the depths of Russia to dictate a peace to Alexander, a lengthy halt would be an admission of weakness. News from Spain supported this conclusion. After having seized Badajoz and Ciudad Rodrigo in the spring, Wellington was stalking Marmont's army near Salamanca in July. Bad news from Russia on the heels of these defeats might have encouraged revolts all across the Empire. Napoleon probably relied as much on his intuition and his instinct—to seek out the enemy army—as on the cold calculation of relative advantages. However, before continuing the pursuit, he sent a message to the Tsar, declaring boldly that he was not waging war on Russia with animosity, but in order to deal with Great Britain. Alexander's response was devastatingly effective: silence.

After the battle at Smolensk, the strength of the main

The Battle of Smolensk, 1812

French army had shrunk to about 145,000 men.[36] The sick and wounded were cruelly condemned by the lack of medical facilities, the shortage of water, and the oppressive heat. This seemed not to affect the Emperor, who cheerfully announced, "within a month we shall be in Moscow, in six weeks we shall have peace."[37] Was Moscow now to be the objective, instead of the Russian Army?

It would be naive to assume that all was going according to plan for the Russians. It is true that in May, Alexander had

fervently resolved: "If the Emperor Napoleon is determined on war, and if fortune does not smile on our just cause, he will have to go to the ends of the earth to find peace."[38] However much a withdrawal may have confirmed his resolution, the surrender of Smolensk dealt a great blow to Russian pride. After its loss, Bagration resumed his sniping at Barclay: "You have no comprehension of our anguish caused by your insensate retreat which is causing Russia such grief." Barclay phlegmatically replied, "Hold your tongue; you are no more Russian than I."[39] On August 27, the Russians abandoned Vyazma in flames. At last, Alexander's patience was at an end. He sent for Kutusov, who was the overwhelming choice of both the people and the Army, to take command, halt the French advance, and save the sacred city of Moscow.

Borodino: A Lack of Resolve

Urged on by its eager commanders, the dwindling *Grande Armée* managed to cover the 280 miles between Smolensk and Moscow in 28 days. Considering its earlier performance, this was an extraordinary pace. During the same time, however, Napoleon was increasingly losing control of the situation. Although outwardly confident, privately he began to be haunted by the specter of failure. At the same time, he continued to suffer from various physical ailments, and he hounded his commanders and staff unmercifully. Caulaincourt, one of his closest companions, was driven to threaten resignation, while Berthier, as usual, suffered the most. "My cousin," scolded the Emperor, "the general staff is of no help to me; no more than the Provost Marshal of the gendarmerie, the baggage master, nor the officers of the staff, none serves as he ought to."[40] Even the dour, thorough Davout was subjected to scathing criticism for the way his troops marched. The Duke of Auerstädt, in turn, complained that Murat's in-

competence as an advance guard commander had caused most of the disorder on the march: "The King of Naples pays no attention to the time of day or the strength of the enemy. He rushes up among his skirmishers, makes himself hoarse by shouting orders, and dances about like a madman in front of the enemy line."[41] For his part, Murat accused Davout of refusing artillery support to one of his advancing regiments. Napoleon's admonishments neither resolved the conflicts nor improved relations between his temperamental subordinates. As the army neared Moscow, it was becoming apparent to those who knew him best that their chieftain was losing his composure and, with it, that fine touch so necessary in the makeup of a great commander.

The only major battle of the Russian Campaign proved that something was definitely lacking in Napoleon's judgment and personal vigor. Borodino was a battle of legendary proportions. It has been narrated and analyzed in history and literature.* Napoleon personally dedicated the action to posterity by his proclamation, issued before the battle and published in the *Moniteur* three weeks later: "Soldiers, here is the battle you have so long desired!"[42] The fight, however, was inconclusive and, at its end, Napoleon found himself the possessor, not of victory, but of a barren hillside and an increasingly compelling commitment to advance farther to the east.

*Most notably in Leo Tolstoy's epic novel, *War and Peace*.

Russian Cavalry and Infantry at the Battle of Borodino, 1812

The battle can be simply described. On September 6, the French army, now reduced to 130,000 men, came upon the Russians, who occupied a line of hills strengthened by field fortifications. Napoleon reconnoitered carefully and, after noting the locations of the key enemy redoubts, apparently decided to rupture the Russian lines with a massive assault by Ney, Davout, and Poniatowski. Possessing nearly 600 guns and a slight numerical superiority, he had reason to anticipate success. Throughout the next morning, however, Napoleon, who was suffering from a bad cold, remained at his command post, out of sight of the battlefield.* His subordinates failed to carry out their assignments aggressively, and the attack degenerated into an artillery duel, followed by a frontal assault in which every advantage accrued to the defender. Eugène's supporting attack failed to fix the Russian right flank, part of which moved to support the threatened sector. Poniatowski moved slowly on the right. Davout, superbly matched against the tenacious Bagration, was knocked unconscious by an exploding shell, and Ney took over the smoke-shrouded fight to gain a footing on the hill that anchored the Russian positions. After several attacks and counterattacks, Bagration received a mortal wound, and a gallant charge led by Ney captured the outworks. About an hour past noon, the Russian left was close to cracking, having been driven back to the next ridgeline by Eugène's savage attack; the moment for which the *Grande Armée* had marched all the way across Europe lay at hand. At that crisis in the battle—surely one of the decisive moments of the campaign—Napoleon hesitated.

The Emperor's hesitation was occasioned by the need to decide whether to commit the Guard infantry to the battle. Shortly before noon, believing that their assaults had created the opportunity for a decisive final blow, Murat, Davout, and Ney had repeatedly asked Napoleon to commit the Old Guard; he had refused their requests. Now, Ney and Davout, joined by Eugène, clamored for Napoleon to commit the Guard in order to deliver the finishing blow to Kutusov's left wing and win the Battle of Borodino decisively. Riding forward to judge for himself, the Emperor considered committing the New Guard. Berthier and Murat dissuaded him, however, arguing that he would need to employ the entire Guard to insure success. Napoleon refused to do this, perhaps influenced by Bessières, who reminded the Emperor, "Sire, you are 800 leagues from Paris." Thus, after 14 hours of intense combat, the fighting died out at nightfall, and Kutusov gratefully began to withdraw his troops. The Guard infantry had remained unused. Napoleon justified his failure to exploit his advantage by saying that he did not want to destroy the

Marshal Jean Baptiste Bessières

Guard, and that at so long a distance from France, "I dared not to risk my last reserve."[43]

Just as Napoleon's inaction angered his lieutenants (especially Ney), his apology has confounded the critics. For the first time in nearly two decades of campaigning, Napoleon found himself unable to face the risks of decision. Why did the Emperor fail to act? The tactical situation was no more difficult than dozens he had successfully confronted, among which Arcola, Jena, and Abensberg come most readily to mind. Exhaustion from prolonged field duty may have hindered his physical performance, but does not entirely explain his collapse of will. Although, in fact, the enormity of the stakes may have finally overwhelmed him, there could have been no worse time to falter. At St. Helena, Napoleon must surely have been recalling that fatal moment when he stated how important it was for a general to have "the strength of mind necessary to engage, with full consideration of its consequences, in one of those great pitched battles on which may depend the fate of an army or a country and the possession of a throne."[44] Perhaps the weight of his destiny had finally overcome his resolve. Although inexplicable, Napoleon's lapse in generalship was unpardonable, and was to contribute to his army's perilous overextension.

After the Battle of Borodino, in which losses on both sides

* By this time, Napoleon had learned that Wellington had shattered Marmont's army at Salamanca and was advancing toward Madrid.

totaled over 70,000 men,* Napoleon had 100,000 effectives remaining, while Kutusov probably had no more than 55,000. Both sides claimed a victory, whereas, actually, both sides had lost. However, while the Russian army filed disconsolately toward Moscow, the Emperor of the French acted the part of the victor. Indeed, within two weeks, French cavalrymen were entering Moscow; a revived Napoleon seemed to have rationalized his indecision at Borodino by contenting himself with the capture of the city. Alexander, on the other hand, was possessed by implacable resolution. "I would rather go and eat potatoes with the last of my peasants," he wrote to Kutusov, "rather than ratify the shame of my fatherland."[45] Caulaincourt had already judged the Russian resolve, noting uneasily after Borodino, "There were very few [Russian] prisoners."[46]

Moscow

Napoleon's arrival in Moscow† seemed to signal the climax, if not the end, of the campaign. The sight of golden domes and gleaming spires produced a miraculous change in the spirit of the sorely diminished *Grande Armée*. One member of the Guard reflected that the effect on everyone was magical: "It was indeed the great city; there we should rest after all our labours . . . "[47] To Murat, the natural showman who had alternately fought with and searched for the Cossacks all the way from the Niemen, the mere chance to ride into the city dressed in his glittering and plumed finery probably justified all the privations his men and horses had suffered. Napoleon commented simply, "It's high time!" Amidst shouts of joy and the beating of drums, no one seemed to take into account an undeniable fact of mathematics: out of the almost 600,000 soldiers who had crossed the Niemen, no more than 95,000 entered Moscow. *(See Atlas Map No. 50.)*

It is true that not all those missing soldiers had fallen in combat. At least 90,000 were very much alive, fighting against Russian detachments along the Dwina River on the north flank and around the Pripet Marshes to the southwest. Some 40,000 to 50,000 were strung out in the wake of the *Grande Armée*, guarding the French line of communication against bands of partisans, who had become increasingly active after the fall of Smolensk. But there could be no avoiding the solemn fact that when the Emperor of the French entered Moscow on September 14, he rode at the head of a fraction of the Empire's military strength.

Meanwhile, Napoleon's opponent had made a decision that

was to shape the remainder of the campaign. Kutusov, who had come out of retirement and had nominally lost the Battle of Borodino, made up his mind not to fight another battle in defense of Moscow. He knew he would meet the same opposition from his subordinates that Barclay had suffered at Bagration's hands. To lose Moscow was to lose the war, they claimed. At first, the one-eyed Kutusov had spoken of a decisive battle to be fought "under the walls of Moscow." The mayor of the city, Count Rostopchin, advised the army commander that the inhabitants were prepared to defend their homes, and that there were sufficient stockpiles of ammunition to sustain the defenders. When the army neared the city, however, Kutusov, without consulting Alexander, called a council of war, attended by his key generals and the town commissioners, to discuss whether to fight or to evacuate Moscow. The majority favored battle. Then Kutusov spoke:

> With the loss of Moscow, Russia is not yet lost. Our primary responsibility is to ensure the preservation of the army and to consolidate the forces which join us as reinforcements. The very act of giving up Moscow will prepare us to defeat our enemy. As long as the army exists and is capable of resisting the enemy we are safe in the hope that the war will conclude happily, but when the army is destroyed Moscow and Russia will perish. I order the retreat![48]

Rostopchin, although opposed to Kutusov's decision, ordered the city's population out into the countryside, released all the inmates from the city jails, and destroyed the city's firefighting equipment.

To appreciate the mental impact of these decisions on the invading commander, it is necessary to picture his arrival in Moscow. "Moscow deserted!" he shouted, "Impossible. Go bring the Boyars to me." But there were no Boyars; only a handful of the original inhabitants and several hundred criminals and lunatics remained, freely roaming and plundering the streets. That night, whether by design or by accident, fires sprang up in various parts of the city. Fanned by a strong breeze and fed by a few Russians who tossed incendiaries into the wooden structures, the flames quickly spread, and by the following morning it was apparent that the better part of Moscow had been consumed by fire. The next evening the wind increased, driving the conflagration directly toward the Kremlin, where Napoleon had established his headquarters. "The barbarians!" he exclaimed, hypnotized by the fire's glow. "This is a war of extermination. . . . To burn one's own cities! . . . A demon inspires these people."[49]

"Besieged by an ocean of flames," the Emperor and his suite fled from the Kremlin to the Petrovsky Palace, from which vantage point Napoleon watched the fire rage for several more days. Meanwhile, in their search for loot and trea-

---

*Ten French generals were killed, and 39 others were incapacitated.

†Although it was not the political capital of Russia, Moscow was Russia's cultural and religious center.

The Conqueror Surveys a Deserted Moscow, 1812

sure, French soldiers wantonly demolished many churches and private buildings which might otherwise have been spared. To discourage both Russian and French marauders, courts-martial began to operate, but the damage was already done. One of the greatest cities in Europe had been destroyed, and its conqueror—the master of the unforeseeable at Marengo, Ulm, and Jena—was unprepared for the consequences.

It is said that tears ran down Alexander's face when he learned of the devastation of Russia's ancient capital; that Rostopchin defiantly burned his country estate to prevent its seizure by the French; and that Kutusov wrote sadly to the Tsar that Moscow offered "no position from which it was possible to risk a battle . . . ,"[50] thereby severely straining relations between Alexander and Kutusov. Historical investigation of the war in Russia has never completely explained these stirring events; hence, interpretation of the exact Russian strategy must remain largely a product of conjecture. Clearly, however, the destruction of Moscow was one of those fortuitous events in history that opened up hitherto inaccessible lines of action. It is equally clear that Kutusov was the sort of opportunist who knew how to take advantage of such openings. After eluding Murat's pursuit, the Russian

army circled warily back to the west and assumed positions southwest of Moscow, just out of reach of the exhausted French cavalry patrols.

The situation facing Napoleon in the middle of September poses an intriguing problem for those who enjoy pondering unpleasant alternatives. There were essentially two choices: to stay in Moscow regardless of Alexander's response to his peace proposals, or to retire into a more secure and less devastated locality where the army might be reconstituted and better supplied. Neither option had a known outcome, as Clausewitz later noted in *On War*: "All action in war . . . is aimed only at probable, not at certain results. Whatever is lacking in certainty must always be left to fate . . . "[51] This observation coincides nicely with Tolstoy's notion that free will must inevitably submit to "the law of general necessity."[52]

Regardless of how one views this underlying—and unresolved—philosophical issue, it must be admitted that by the end of September, Kutusov's dispositions accorded more favorably with the realities of the situation than did Napoleon's. Possessing 120,000 men, a healthy cavalry, and all the resources in the interior, Kutusov could either wait while the French ate, quarreled, and finally abandoned the still smoldering city, or he could launch a limited offensive against their line of communication. Meanwhile, he stepped up partisan activity, thereby forcing French convoys and patrols to stay on the roads. While both armies settled into a waiting posture, the onslaught of winter neared, and the game of bluff between Napoleon and Alexander dragged on.

It was a game in which most of the advantages lay with the Tsar. While partisans intercepted French communications, Napoleon was discovering that there was insufficient fodder in the area around Moscow to feed his horses. (30,000 horses died during his stay in Moscow.)[53] Kutusov neither could nor needed to attack the ravaged city, whereas every time French foraging parties ventured too far from the city walls, Cossacks dealt them a bloody blow. Yet, Napoleon refused to order Moscow evacuated. His dilemma was discouraging. As field commander, he needed to break free from the destroyed city and reorganize his nearly mutinous army; as Emperor, he dared not leave Moscow in any semblance of retreat.

The Retreat from Moscow

Within a week after entering Moscow, Napoleon had sent peace proposals to Alexander. "The beautiful and superb city of Moscow no longer exists," he wrote. Its destruction was, of course, the work of Rostopchin, he avowed, and French soldiers had fought the flames. The *Grande Armée* had not pillaged Vienna, Berlin, or Madrid, and he found it impossible to believe that Alexander, with "his principles, his heart, the justice of his ideas, would authorize such excesses, unworthy of a great sovereign and a great nation."[54]

This was no way to bring the Russians to heel. Alexander ordered Kutusov to refrain from even discussing the word peace while Frenchmen remained on Russian soil. However, Kutusov and Murat worked out an informal truce that lasted until October 18. On that date, Kutusov's forward units emerged from the woods and dealt Murat's unwary outposts a sharp blow. Napoleon reacted by setting Ney's divisions in motion, as if to reinforce his brother-in-law's troopers. In actuality, he had begun to evacuate Moscow. *(See Atlas Map No. 51.)*

Napoleon's plan was to march via Kaluga and Bryansk. By returning along this untraveled route, he hoped to find forage for the horses, to avoid the appearance of a retreat, and eventually to settle the army in winter quarters somewhere between Smolensk and Minsk. He had already placed Victor in command of this area, and according to his logistical reports, the depots there were full. There appeared to be a good

The French Retreat From Russia, 1812

chance of reaching his destination before the first hard frost. Indeed, it was imperative to do so. Except for those mounts in the imperial suite, the horses were not shod for heavy snow, nor had the troops been issued any winter gear. To carry home a trophy of victory, Napoleon ordered the venerated iron cross atop one of Moscow's most famous churches removed, and as a final gesture of defiance he ordered the Guard to blow up the Kremlin before departing.

Kutusov followed up his first success, but missed his prey until October 24, when strong Russian forces ran into the main column headed by Eugène at Maloyaroslavets. After a series of attacks and counterattacks, during which Eugène's troops seized and lost the town several times, Kutusov finally drew off to the south, remaining squarely across the road to Kaluga. A determined attack might have cleared the road, but Napoleon was now beset by indecision. Most of his marshals endorsed an immediate withdrawal along the route used during the advance. Davout suggested using a back road that paralleled the main route, but Napoleon's nerve appeared shaken by his near capture at the hands of a Cossack troop. Without giving full consideration to all the alternatives, he abruptly abandoned the plan to retreat along the southerly route and ordered the column back onto the main road to Smolensk. Davout took over the rearguard.

The French withdrawal now began to turn into a stampede, especially after passing through Borodino. Here, the debris of the September battle and the decomposed bodies of thousands of men and horses offered not only a grim reminder of suffering on a grand scale, but also a chilling forecast of a fate even worse than death in battle. Kutusov appeared satisfied to shepherd the French formations along, relying mostly on Cossacks and militia to harass the French flanks and rear while raiding parties struck at depots in and around

The Rearguard

Smolensk. On October 31, Napoleon and the Guard reached Vyazma; Davout had just cleared Borodino. One week later, a heavy snow fell and, with it, morale. On the icy roads it was impossible for the starving horses to pull their loads. Tired men dropped in their tracks and, pushed to the side of the road, were lost forever. Artillery pieces, loot, and many of the wounded had to be left behind.

November was an unending catastrophe for the decimated *Grande Armée*. Numbed by events as well as by the cold, Napoleon increasingly left decisions to his subordinates, failing to alert Victor to the full extent of the deteriorating situation, and refusing even to take simple tactical measures for the security of his command. Men began to fight for scraps of bread and frozen horseflesh. Arriving at Smolensk to find the place in total disorder, the Emperor simply ordered the march continued. Caulaincourt observed that "as a soldier, Napoleon had touched his lowest ebb."[55]

As the *Grande Armée* began to fragment, there were extraordinary acts of individual heroism. Mere survival itself required superhuman strength of will. Many a man fell and simply refused to summon the courage to rise again and go on. Marching out of Smolensk, there was an air of desperation about this ragged, famished group of men, all of whom knew that they must sooner or later fight the Russians as well as the winter. They were now reduced in numbers to about 40,000. From all quarters, the news was bad. The rearguard lagged behind. At the same time, the depot at Vitebsk, astride the main withdrawal route, fell to the enemy.

On November 16, Kutusov finally decided to block the French escape routes. Eugène broke through in a running fight at Krasnoi, but Davout lingered to support Ney. The fiery Ney, who had assumed command of the rearguard, waited too long in Smolensk, and was intercepted by about 80,000 Russians barring his way. He immediately attacked, ignoring Davout's advice to circle around the enemy. The attack failed, and the Russians offered generous terms if Ney would surrender. "A marshal of France never surrenders!" Ney is supposed to have said. *(See Atlas Map No. 51.)* Then, overriding the protests of his staff, he countermarched towards Smolensk and made a daring cross-country march to the north, crossing the icy Dnieper at night and finally rejoining the main body near Orsha, where Eugène turned back to help him. This epic march of Ney's rearguard, survived by less than a thousand able men, caused a thrill of joy to run through the starving, frozen army. "It was a national triumph," said Caulaincourt.[56]

Meanwhile the Russians had captured Minsk, and Admiral Pavel Tshitsagov had seized the key defile at Borisov, over the Beresina River. Abruptly becoming himself again, Napoleon declared, "I have been Emperor long enough, it is now time that I acted as a general."[57] Gathering together the still

The Crossing of the Beresina, November 1812

able troops of Victor's and Oudinot's commands, on November 26 he forced a hasty crossing of the thawing Beresina, north of Borisov, and transported the remainder of the army across before Tshitsagov could react.* The French then eluded pursuit by turning northwest toward Vilna.

Even this success could not prevent news of the unfolding disaster from spreading throughout Europe. In Paris, trouble had arisen just as the retreat got underway. On October 24, a group of conspirators had attempted to seize control of the Government. After crossing the Beresina it became evident to Napoleon that he must leave the army and return to Paris if he were to preserve order in his empire. Command devolved on Murat, who received orders to hold along the Niemen River. Then, while the army staggered on through blinding snow, the Emperor rode for Paris, arriving at midnight on December 18.

Two days earlier, a lengthy bulletin composed by Napoleon had appeared in the *Moniteur*. "Until November 6," it read, "the weather was perfect, and the movement of the army was executed with the greatest success. But on the 7th the cold commenced . . . " So began Napoleon's justification. French officers and soldiers had fought bravely, and their

chief had fought expertly. The Russian winter—not the Russian Army—had defeated him. The article concluded with an item befitting a royal announcement: "His Majesty's health has never been better."[58]

The Arousal of Prussia

Meanwhile, as the main body of the French army was struggling painfully toward Vilna, the flank guards (MacDonald and Schwarzenberg) had gradually drawn back. Napoleon continued sending orders to both, requesting that they move "as slowly as possible," but Berthier's wistful message to Schwarzenberg took better note of reality: "we wish to hear from you as often as possible."[59] Schwarzenberg now remained a part of the French army only for the sake of form. He was actually taking his orders from Vienna, where Metternich considered the whole new range of possibilities—and dangers—Napoleon's reverse was posing to the Hapsburg Crown.

At the same time, the rest of Germany was in turmoil. Stein, who had become the Tsar's personal advisor for German affairs, had urged Alexander in November to place himself "at the head of Europe's powers." The enemy should be allowed no respite, he argued, pointing out that Alexander could now appear to be the benefactor of all of Germany—

*French troops (engineers, *pontoniers*, and naval troops) worked for hours in the icy waters to complete the bridge. General Jean-Baptiste Eblé, commander of the French bridge train during the campaign, personally set the example. Probably from exposure to the cold, he became ill and died at Königsberg within a month.

and of Europe. In Prussia, Frederick William III viewed events more soberly. Even the electrifying report from a Silesian postmaster that Napoleon and a small escort had been spotted on the evening of December 12 on the road to Dresden failed to move the King and his careful foreign minister, Hardenberg, to throw off the mask and mobilize the country against the French. Hardenberg did recommend, however, the calling up of reserves in East Prussia and the collection of all war material "which might be of value to the enemy."[60] It has been questioned whether Hardenberg interpreted "the enemy" as being French or Russian. Nonetheless, there was to be no sudden decision until the full extent of Napoleon's defeat became clear and the limit of Alexander's political ambitions was known.

Frederick William might well have remained undecided, and Murat might have held out on the Vistula had events not forced decisions. On December 23, the Prussian court received an authoritative report that the *Grande Armée* had been completely destroyed. General Hans D.L. von Yorck, the commander of the Prussian auxiliary corps that served under MacDonald, wrote that he had been approached by Russian emissaries, and requested specific instructions. He was told only "to act according to the circumstances."[61] Still afraid of Napoleon and suspicious of Alexander, the vacillating King of Prussia simply could not make up his mind to cast for independence. Yorck decided for him. On December 30, acting on his own initiative and without instructions from Berlin, he signed an armistice with the Russians at Tauroggen, having deliberately slowed his withdrawal as MacDonald's rearguard commander. This action exposed the north flank of the French army and upset MacDonald, who considered the act one of treachery. MacDonald also resented Yorck's delay in notifying him of his action, since he lost precious time waiting at Tilsit for Yorck, in the belief that the latter was in danger. Murat thereupon ordered most of his troops into Danzig and turned over the command of the army to Eugène. Meanwhile, Stein entered East Prussia, took control of the government there, and began to form a militia. The champions of revolt, such as General Blücher, who was "itching in every finger to grasp the sword," and Arndt, the fiery poet who cried, "the moment has come for plunging the steel into the enemy's breast," believed that restraint was a sign of weakness.[62] Hardenberg, however, advised the King to pursue the pretext of alliance, at least until the reserves could be mobilized and the active army established along the Oder River. *(See Atlas Map No. 52.)*

The political consequences of Yorck's defiant "disobedience" were immense.* Although Frederick William repudiated his action, it is clear that Yorck's deed emboldened him to make the final break with Napoleon. The very soul of Prussia was stirred, in turn putting more pressure on the Govern-

ment to cast off the French yoke. Hardenberg, however, refused to be rushed in his policy of steadily consolidating military and diplomatic strength under the guise of friendship with Napoleon. In his mind, the resurrection of the Prussian Army and an alliance with Austria were the twin conditions without which Prussia's liberation might turn into a premature, bloody, and unsuccessful conflict.

Schwarzenberg signed a separate peace in January and withdrew across the Vistula. Eugène subsequently withdrew from Posen, judging that French strength was too depleted to hold the Oder line. Hardenberg now more actively sought an alliance with Austria that would give Prussia some bargaining power against both Napoleon and Alexander. Austria, however, desired "to limit itself, for the moment, to words, and to seek advantage from the current conditions."[63] Metternich, too, was reluctant to join the lists against France too quickly. The bewildering sequence of events that accompanied this diplomatic sparring finally made it clear to the Prussian Government that the King must reach a formal understanding with the Tsar. Alexander himself persuaded his one-time friend with the words: "Friendship, faith, perseverance, and courage; Providence will take care of the rest."[64]

Kutusov had written to the Tsar, "Our mission is completed . . . let the Germans liberate themselves." But Alexander was now seized by the grandeur of his mission. At Vilna, he told his assembled generals, "You have not only saved Russia, you have saved Europe."[65] The campaign of 1812 was over, and Napoleon had failed in a colossal misadventure. But it was clear that the struggle for Europe was far from finished. Napoleon's return to Paris was no admission of defeat, but rather a statement of his intention to raise a new army.

Napoleon's letters to Murat and Eugène in December indicated that he had no intention of surrendering the eastern bastions of his empire. Rather, he hoped to piece together a defensive line along the Vistula, or at least along the Oder. As it turned out, he was forced to settle for the Elbe River line, as Yorck's defection, Schwarzenberg's retirement, and Alexander's advance successively uncovered his defenses. In March 1813, Frederick William finally overcame his fears and issued a proclamation "To My People," Scharnhorst's new army took up arms, and for the first time in Prussian history, the people volunteered for active service. It was a moment the patriots had long awaited and would never forget.

While reviving armies scrambled for position amidst the wreckage of the *Grande Armée*, the diplomatic duel between Austria and France continued. In cold fact, the nominal military alliance against Russia no longer existed. But, as late as April, the French envoy insisted that Austria must continue to

---

*Some writers called Yorck's act one of defection; others labeled it treason.

side with France against the newly forming coalition. Metternich refused, implying that Austria would fight if provoked. "But you are not ready," claimed the Frenchman, "it is my job to know this." "And mine to hide it," Metternich replied; "let us see who does his job better."[66]

The Campaign of 1812 into Russia ended in disaster for the French. Dangerously ambitious and blinded by a belief in his own infallibility, Napoleon had attempted a campaign that was beyond his means. The forces and distances were too great for the contemporary methods of supply and movement. Nor did the Emperor demonstrate his normal superiority as a general on the battlefield. His losses were too great to be replaced quickly, totaling over 400,000 men, 1,000 cannon, and 175,000 horses. Russia lost more than 250,000 men and many partisans. The disaster paved the way for a strong offensive against Napoleon—one that would be decisive.

Notes

[1]Clemens L.W. Metternich-Winneburg, *Memoirs of Prince Metternich, 1773–1835,* ed. by Prince Richard Metternich; trans. by Mrs. Alexander Napier (5 vols.; New York, 1880–1882), II, 365.

[2]Hugh Seton-Watson, *The Russian Empire, 1801–1917* (Oxford, 1967), pp. 41–50.

[3]Geoffrey Bruun, *Europe and the French Imperium* (New York, 1938), pp. 38–39.

[4]Seton-Watson, *The Russian Empire,* pp. 83–96, 142–143.

[5]*Ibid.,* p. 87.

[6]Bruun, *Europe and the French Imperium,* p. 137.

[7]Georges Lefebvre, *Napoleon: From Tilsit to Waterloo, 1807–1815,* trans. by J.E. Anderson (New York, 1969), p. 292.

[8]Armand de Caulaincourt, *With Napoleon in Russia,* ed. by J. Hanoteau (New York, 1935), pp. 4–5.

[9]Felix Markham, *Napoleon* (New York, 1963), p. 188.

[10]C.R. Andolenko, *Histoire de L'Armée Russe* (Paris, 1967), pp. 35–43.

[11]*Ibid.,* pp. 89–95, 135–139.

[12]Phillip Longworth, *The Art of Victory* (New York, 1965), pp. 305–311.

[13]Andolenko, *L'Armée Russe,* pp. 89–92.

[14]Longworth, *The Art of Victory,* pp. 312–317; *Encyclopaedia Britannica* (29 vols.; Cambridge, 1911), XV, 956.

[15]Longworth, *The Art of Victory,* p. 317.

[16]P.A. Zhilin, *Gibel Napoleonovs Koi Armii v Rossii* (Moscow, 1968), pp. 57–59.

[17]Alan Palmer, *Napoleon in Russia* (New York, 1967), p. 26.

[18]J.C. Herold, *The Mind of Napoleon* (New York, 1955), p. 257.

[19]Lefebvre, *Napoleon: From Tilsit to Waterloo, 1807–1815,* pp. 311–312; Hans Delbrück, *Geschichte der Kriegskunst im Rahmen der politischen Geschichte* (4 vols.; Berlin, 1900–1920), IV, 510.

[20]Freiherr von Freytag-Loringhoven, *Die Heerführung Napoleons in ihrer Bedeutung Fur unsere Zeit* (Berlin, 1910), p. 30; *Correspondance de Napoleon I* (32 vols.; Paris, 1858–1870), XXIII, No. 18725, 432; Hubert Camon, *La Guerre Napoleonienne* (2 vols.; Paris, 1903), II, 4.

[21]*Correspondance,* XXIII, No. 18400, p. 142.

[22]*Ibid.,* No. 18725, p. 432.

[23]*Ibid.,* No. 18769, p. 470.

[24]*Ibid.,* No. 18784, pp. 484–485; No. 18082, p. 482.

[25]Andolenko, *L'Armée Russe,* p. 181.

[26]Antony Brett-James, *1812: Eyewitness Accounts of Napoleon's Defeat in Russia* (New York, 1966), p. 21.

[27]*Ibid.,* p. 54.

[28]Mary Loyd (ed.), *The New Letters of Napoleon I* (New York, 1897), p. 263.

[29]*Correspondance,* XXIV, No. 18905, p. 20.

[30]*Ibid.,* No. 18911, p. 24.

[31]Brett-James, *1812: Eyewitness Accounts of Napoleon's Defeat in Russia,* p. 71.

[32]Camon, *La Guerre Napoleonienne,* II, 8.

[33]Freytag-Loringhoven, *Die Heerführung Napoleons in ihrer Bedeutung Fur unsere Zeit,* p. 182.

[34]*Correspondance,* XXIV, No. 19068, pp. 137–138.

[35]Carl von Clausewitz, *Der Feldzug 1812 in Russland und die Befreiungskriege von 1813–15* (Berlin, 1906), p. 63.

[36]*Ibid.,* p. 84.

[37]Jacques Bainville, *Napoleon,* trans. by H. Miles (Boston, 1933), p. 306.

[38]Caulaincourt, *With Napoleon in Russia,* p. 38.

[39]Andolenko, *L'Armée Russe,* p. 181.

[40]*Correspondance,* XXIV, No. 19173, p. 199; *Caulaincourt, With Napoleon in Russia,* pp. 66–72, 104–105.

[41]A.G. MacDonell, *Napoleon and His Marshals* (New York, 1934), p. 246.

[42]*Correspondance,* XXIV, No. 19182, p. 207.

[43]Camon, *La Guerre Napoleonienne,* II, 38.

[44]Count Yorck von Wartenburg, *Napoleon as a General* (2 vols.; London, 1902), I, 120.

[45]C.W. Crawley (ed.), *The New Cambridge Modern History* (14 vols.; Cambridge, 1966–1971), IX, 515.

[46]Caulaincourt, *With Napoleon in Russia,* p. 102.

[47]P. Cottin (ed.), *Memoirs of Sergeant Bourgogne, 1812–1813* (New York, 1889), p. 14.

[48]Zhilin, *Gibel Napoleonovs Koi Armii v Rossi,* p. 149.

[49]Eugene Tarle, *Napoleon's Invasion of Russia* (New York, 1942), p. 238.

[50]*Ibid.,* p. 245.

[51]Carl von Clausewitz, *On War,* trans. by O.J. Matthijs Jolles (New York, 1943), p. 105.

[52]Leo Tolstoy, *War and Peace,* trans. by C. Garnett (New York, 1931), pp. 1116–1125.

[53]Andolenko, *L'Armée Russe,* p. 192.

[54]*Correspondance;* XXIV, No. 19213, pp. 221–222.

[55]Vincent J. Esposito and John R. Elting, *A Military History and Atlas of the Napoleonic Wars* (New York, 1964), p. 122.

[56]Caulaincourt, *With Napoleon in Russia,* p. 230.

[57]Wolfgang von Groote and Klaus-Jürgen Muller (eds.), *Napoleon I und das Militärwesen seiner Zeit* (Freiburg, 1968), p. 38.

[58]*Correspondance,* XXIV, No. 19365, pp. 325–329.

[59]*Ibid..*

[60]*Urkundliche Beiträge und Forschungen zur Geschichte des preussischen Heeres,* ed. by German General Staff (Berlin, 1914), II, 366–367.

[61]Wilhelm Oncken, *Oesterreich und Preussen im Befreiungskriege, Urkundliche Aufschlusse uber die politische Geschichte des Jahres 1813* (2 vols.; Berlin, 1876–1879), II, 118.

[62]Ernest F. Henderson, *Blücher and the Uprising of Prussia Against Napoleon, 1806–1815* (London, 1911), p. 79.

[63]Oncken, *Oesterreich und Preussen im Befreungskriege,* II, 132.

[64]*Ibid.,* p. 251.

[65]Andolenko, *L'Armée Russe,* pp. 195–196.

[66]Henry Kissinger, *A World Restored* (New York, 1957), p. 66.

PART IV
LOSS OF
THE EMPIRE

The whole earth is the tomb of heroic men. And their story is not only graven in stone over their clay, but abides everywhere, woven into the fabric of other men's lives.

Pericles

Defeat at Leipzig and Napoleon's Abdication

7

Late in June 1813, Metternich and Napoleon held a private meeting at the Marcolini Palace in Dresden. Metternich offered peace. In reply, Napoleon flung his hat into a corner of the room, exclaiming, "If I am to accept your policy I am required to evacuate Europe, half of which I still hold, lead back my legions across the Rhine, the Alps and the Pyrenees and, signing a treaty which amounts to a vast capitulation, deliver myself like an idiot to my enemies." Metternich, who remained calm throughout the tirade, was unable to shake Napoleon's resolve. The Emperor was candid. "Your Sovereigns born on the throne," he complained, "can let themselves be beaten twenty times and still return to their capitals. . . . My domination will not survive the day when I cease to be strong and therefore feared."[1] The conference lasted nine hours, but produced no agreement. The Austrian minister finally prepared to leave. With the cool precision of an executioner preparing the blade, he predicted, "Sire, you are a lost man."

Battles in Saxony and an Uneasy Armistice

If Napoleon had accepted Metternich's terms, he might well have spared France two more years of agony. A retreat behind the natural boundaries offered many advantages compared to the cost of maintaining a far-flung multi-national empire. But that which best served the interests of France did not necessarily coincide with Napoleon's intractable ambition. It was perhaps difficult for Metternich to appreciate that the French Emperor's power depended on the sustained confidence not only of his own country's 40 million people, but of 40 million people in the vassal states as well. Victory secured that support; defeat quickly severed it. In 1812, all of continental Europe had allied itself with France against Rus-

sia. Just one year after the retreat from Moscow, Napoleon lost his empire and for the first time found himself confronted by the combined might of Europe.

The defeat in Russia, bad as it was, left most of Napoleon's empire intact. *(See Atlas Map No. 53.)* By the end of February 1813, he had lost only the Duchy of Warsaw, and he still planned to recover it. Then, on March 16, Prussia declared war, and active campaigning resumed. French troops clung grimly to fortresses along the Vistula and Oder Rivers while the countryside around them rang to the sound of men marching to liberate their homeland. Inspired by the example of Yorck's defection, Prussia showed uncommon spirit. The

Napoleon and Metternich's Meeting at Dresden, June 1813

Schlesische privilegirte Zeitung

No. 34. Sonnabends den 20. März 1813.

Se. Majestät der König haben mit Sr. Majestät dem Kaiser aller Reußen ein Off= und Defensiv=Bündniß abgeschlossen.

An Mein Volk.

So wenig für Mein treues Volk als für Deutsche, bedarf es einer Rechenschaft, über die Ursachen des Kriegs welcher jetzt beginnt. Klar liegen sie dem unverblendeten Europa vor Augen.

Wir erlagen unter der Uebermacht Frankreichs. Der Frieden, der die Hälfte Meiner Unterthanen Mir entriß, gab uns seine Segnungen nicht; denn er schlug uns tiefere Wunden, als selbst der Krieg. Das Mark des Landes ward ausgesogen, die Hauptfestungen blieben vom Feinde besetzt, der Ackerbau ward gelähmt so wie der sonst so hoch gebrachte Kunstfleiß unserer Städte. Die Freiheit des Handels ward gehemmt, und dadurch die Quelle des Erwerbs und des Wohlstands verstopft. Das Land ward ein Raub der Verarmung.

Durch die strengste Erfüllung eingegangener Verbindlichkeiten hoffte Ich Meinem Volke Erleichterung zu bereiten und den französischen Kaiser endlich zu überzeugen, daß es sein eigener Vortheil sey, Preußen seine Unabhängigkeit zu lassen. Aber Meine reinsten Absichten wurden durch Uebermuth und Treulosigkeit vereitelt, und nur zu deutlich sahen wir, daß des Kaisers Verträge mehr noch wie seine Kriege uns langsam verderben mußten. Jetzt ist der Augenblick gekommen, wo alle Täuschung über unsern Zustand aufhört.

Brandenburger, Preußen, Schlesier, Pommern, Litthauer! Ihr wißt was Ihr seit fast sieben Jahren erduldet habt, Ihr wißt was euer trauriges Loos ist, wenn wir den beginnenden Kampf nicht ehrenvoll enden. Erinnert Euch an die Vorzeit, an den großen Kurfürsten, den großen Friedrich. Bleibt eingedenk der Güter, die unter

---

Faksimile einer von der Verlagsbuchhandlung W. G. Korn in Breslau zur Verfügung gestellten Nummer der „Schlesischen privilegirten Zeitung" vom 20. März 1813, die zuerst den Aufruf König Friedrich Wilhelms III. brachte.

Frederick William's Declaration of War, 1813

pro-German historian, Treitschke, wrote of the Prussian people:

> Their souls were stirred by the great passions of public life, stormily moved as never before since the days of the wars of religion. The peasant left his farm, the manual worker left his workshop. . . . The King, too, with all the princes, had gone into camp. In a thousand moving traits the loyalty of the common people was displayed. Poor miners in Silesia worked for weeks without receiving pay, in order that their wages might equip a few comrades for the army. A Pomeranian shepherd sold his little flock, his only possession, and then went, well armed, to join his regiment.[2]

Treitschke undoubtedly exaggerated the depth of feeling in Prussia. There is no evidence that Prussian patriotism was spontaneous, except among certain segments of the middle and upper classes. There was no widespread guerrilla movement such as that which swept Spain. Until the King's declaration, there was no mass revolt; and after the declaration there was still no flood of volunteers for the Army. The Prussian revolt of 1813 was less a popular rebellion than a carefully planned and controlled change of sides, engineered by a relatively small group of intelligent, dedicated patriots. In fact, it was probably well that there was no popular uprising, which, if premature, would only have provoked bloody reprisals. The disciplined reserve of the Prussian people had not roused the King to action, but it had allowed Hardenberg and Scharnhorst time to work out plans for mobilization and deployment. According to treaty, Prussia was allowed to maintain an army of only 42,000 men, but in March 1813 the troop lists showed 131,000 soldiers in the field, including those in garrisons and depots. Within two weeks, these men were in action.[3] *(See Atlas Map No. 54.)*

Eugène's faltering Army of the Elbe clashed with a Russo-Prussian force near Magdeburg early in April. The indecisive outcome of this engagement, combined with news of Blücher's crossing of the Elbe at Dresden, prompted Napoleon to take the field again. By extraordinary efforts, he had managed to scratch together a new army, which was heavy in conscripts. The Emperor arrived at Erfurt on April 25 and ordered an immediate advance on Leipzig. This action quickly brought the Allies* together, resulting in a battle at Lützen. Although Napoleon's massed artillery drove his opponents back, the undermanned French cavalry was unable to exploit the advantage and proved ineffective both in pursuit and in determining the direction of the enemy's retreat.†

The Allies withdrew, surrendering the west bank of the Elbe to the French. One week later, Napoleon conducted an expert hasty river crossing at Dresden, outflanking the Allied defenses and forcing the Russians and Prussians to decide between defending Berlin and falling back to the Oder. The Prussians preferred to defend; the Russians to withdraw. Taking advantage of the Allies' obvious confusion, Napoleon drove his young conscripts forward in search of a fight. On May 19, French outposts discovered the main Russo-Prussian army near Bautzen. After two days of hard fighting, the French seemed to have won a climactic battle, but the decisive maneuver miscarried, largely because of Ney's failure to coordinate the enveloping attack. (Ever since the ordeal of 1812, Ney had not been himself; but Napoleon's unclear orders were also to blame for French mistakes.) Again, the Allies escaped.** In order to recover their balance, the quarreling Russians and Prussians requested a seven-week armistice, to which, surprisingly, Napoleon agreed.

Napoleon's decision to accept the cease-fire was probably one of his worst mistakes. By delaying the impending decisive confrontation, he permitted the coalition to reorganize, reinforce, and coordinate its plans. "I decided on it [the armistice] for two reasons," Napoleon wrote to the French War Minister, "my lack of cavalry, which prevents me from striking decisive blows, and the hostile attitude of Austria."[4] It is doubtful whether he could have replenished his supply of mounts in such a short time, but there is no question that he had every reason for concern about the threatening attitude of Austria. In March, Metternich had sent Prince Schwarzenberg to Paris to assure Napoleon of Emperor Francis' support. In April, however, there was a subtle and ominous change in the Hapsburg monarchy's stance. Whereas Metternich had maintained the guise of neutrality throughout January and February, in May and June, Austria's diplomats offered "armed" mediation. Whereas Austrian troops had fought as active partners in the war against Russia, now an Austrian army was assembling just south of the mountainous Bohemian frontier. To Napoleon, it was all very clear. His former ally was stalling for time to prepare for action against him.

---

*The term "Allies," as used here, refers to Russia and Prussia. The Sixth Coalition against France, however, was only a few months away from being completely formed. In March 1813, Sweden had accepted England's subsidy and the free hand the British had granted Sweden in Norway (then part of Denmark). In return, the Swedes had agreed to provide a 30,000-man army under Crown Prince Bernadotte to assist Russia and Prussia. On July 7, Bernadotte led Sweden firmly into the Allied camp. England technically did not join the alliance until June 15, when she gave 2 million pounds to Russia and Prussia to support the war effort. Austria was watching closely from the sidelines during the spring and early summer of 1813. At the secret Reichen-

bach Convention of July 19, Austria promised to join the alliance if Napoleon refused the terms then being discussed during the armistice following the May Battle of Bautzen. On August 12, 1813, Austria formally joined the Allies.

†Napoleon's problems continued to mount. At Lützen, Bessières died in action—the second marshal to lose his life in battle.

**Scharnhorst, the guiding brain and reorganizer of the Prussian Army, received a wound at Bautzen that became infected and caused his death in June.

Napoleon Plans for the Battle of Bautzen, 1813

If Metternich's intention had been simply to buy time for the Austrian armed forces to mobilize, Austrian diplomacy would have been transparent. However, Metternich's objectives were complicated by conflicting political purposes. It was necessary, in his mind, to do more than destroy Napoleon's empire. In fact, he would have been willing to see Napoleon retain his throne if the Emperor could have been persuaded to contain French aspirations within France's natural boundaries. Metternich's goal was to create a balance of power in which each European state remained within its proper sphere. The news of the *Grande Armée's* destruction in Russia had come as a severe shock in Vienna. The French retreat behind the Oder suddenly left Hapsburg interests in Poland unprotected against advancing Russian armies. Throughout the spring of 1813, only delicate and precise negotiations could resolve Metternich's dilemma: how to guard simultaneously against continued French imperial rule east of the Rhine and the expansion of Russia's empire west of the Vistula.

Metternich was in favor of a European equilibrium that would restore monarchial rule as well as limit territorial ambitions. He was deeply concerned with the danger posed by the revolutionary sentiment unleashed by Napoleon's restructuring of Germany and Italy. The Tyrolean Alps was a powder keg of popular dissatisfaction that endangered Austrian

objectives in Italy, while Baron Stein's talk of resurrecting a united Germany under Prussian (or Russian) leadership threatened Austria's plans for restoring Hapsburg influence in southern Germany. At the same time, recently awakened Polish national feeling haunted Metternich with the fear that parts of Austria itself might defect to Poland. The mere hint of revolution, anywhere in Europe, had always been of serious concern to the men governing the multi-ethnic Hapsburg Empire. Therefore, it was only natural for Metternich to be an advocate of not only the security of the Hapsburg Crown, but also the overall political and social equilibrium of Europe.

By contrast, Prussian policy aimed at liberating the homeland as rapidly as possible and regaining those territories seized by Napoleon. Napoleon's destruction could not come quickly enough for eager patriots like Scharnhorst and Gneisenau, who had been working covertly for six years toward the moment when liberation would be at hand. Once Frederick William overcame his fear of declaring against Napoleon, Prussia's next problem became the recovery of her Polish territories, which were now occupied by Russian troops. At the same time, Alexander had already decided that it was his right and duty to carry the war of liberation forward into western Europe.

While Russian, Prussian, and Austrian diplomats eyed

each other warily during the first week of the armistice, Great Britain decided to join the coalition. On June 15, an envoy from London arrived on the Continent and promised subsidies to support 80,000 Prussian troops and 150,000 Russians. In return, Castlereagh hoped to receive support for a policy that sought the complete destruction of Napoleon's government and his banishment from European affairs. Great Britain's main goal was freedom of the seas, and the best way to insure that goal was to restore the Low Countries. Throughout the summer of 1813, Castlereagh's resolve hardened. By the time hostilities resumed, he preferred not only to remove French soldiers from Holland, but also to set up barriers against any recurrence of French aggression. British policy, therefore, sought to restore a just balance of power by entirely dispossessing the dangerous and unpredictable Emperor of the French. France also had to lose her natural boundaries.[5]

There were now four distinct Allied policies that had to be reconciled before the coalition could begin its military work. Although Austria still remained nominally outside the alliance, toward the end of the armistice it was apparent that Hapsburg neutrality was fast becoming a fiction. To further complicate Allied policy, a fifth party had to be considered. The Crown Prince of Sweden—former French marshal, Count Bernadotte—saw his chance to help himself to a share of the spoils and, perhaps, take Napoleon's place on the French throne.

The Formulation of an Allied Strategy

Although the strategic problem facing the Allies in the summer of 1813 was complex, it was no more difficult than that confronting Napoleon. His main army, over 300,000 men strong, sat squarely between the Austrian army in Bohemia and the Allies in Silesia. The French had renewed their victorious tradition by inflicting two stunning defeats on the Allies at Lützen and Bautzen, but French troops were tired of incessant war, and the Emperor had dangers on all sides to consider. Military weakness and political uncertainty were his main grounds for seeking the armistice, but there were even more compelling reasons for not prolonging it. With his advance elements against the Oder, his main force in Saxony quartered among unfriendly people,* and enemies to the north and south, the French flanks and rear were vulnerable to decisive enemy thrusts. Napoleon had to either continue

the attack to the east until his opponents were driven out of the war, or fall back on the defensive. He finally elected to hold Saxony and the Elbe River line, positioning a strong central reserve near Dresden from which point it could march rapidly to northern Prussia, Silesia, or Bohemia. Napoleon's choice of position would thus facilitate a transition to the offensive if the Allies presented him with an opportunity for a sudden blow at either of their separate armies.† *(See Atlas Map No. 55.)*

The Emperor was well aware, however, that time worked to his disadvantage. Potentially, his enemies could muster superior forces. Also the expense of maintaining such a large army at a distance from its homeland placed the French at a disadvantage, for the Allies were close to their sources of supply. Furthermore, French fortunes were collapsing in Spain, where Wellington had again taken the offensive and defeated Joseph's main army at Vitoria late in June. Napoleon blamed his brother for the loss: "The English report shows, clearly enough, how incapably the army was led. . . . The King is not, of course, a soldier, but he is responsible for his own immorality, and the greatest immorality that can be committed is to exercise a profession of which you know nothing."[6] The Emperor knew that this loss would not only cost him Spain, but would also endanger his faltering empire in Germany. Now the Allies had every reason to stiffen their terms.

While Napoleon lamented his brother's blunders and tried to repair the damage by suppressing public announcements of the battle, the Allies were finding it difficult to agree on a plan of operations. Shortly before his death in June, Scharnhorst had written that the Allies should adopt an energetic concentric advance on all sides: "They [the Allies] attempt to approach the enemy where they find him; they attempt to attack him whenever the opportunity presents itself; incessantly seeking to strike him."[7] Scharnhorst's concept was for a dispersed advance followed by a vigorous concentration. This represented a striking departure from the school of thought that had governed Prussian strategy six years earlier.

On the other hand, Austrian strategic doctrine had not outgrown pre-Revolutionary constraints. The writings of the Archduke Charles, for example, emphasized cautious maneuver and the security of one's base of operations. Although

---

*The King of Saxony had fled to Austria in April.

†Earlier, in February and March, Napoleon had evolved a master strategy that he hoped would recoup his fortunes in eastern Germany and Poland. That plan envisioned a strong advance on Berlin, east of the Elbe River, under the Emperor's direction, while Davout screened the flank and protected the rear. After cowing Prussia, the French forces would then move east, threaten Russian communications with their armies in Poland and Silesia, and lift the sieges of French fortresses on the Oder (e.g., Stettin) and the Vistula (e.g., Danzig, Thorn, and Modlin).

Napoleon was never able to implement this plan because of a shortage of troops, and because the Russo-Prussian forces drove west so rapidly that he was forced to react at Lützen.

the Archduke had displayed considerable energy on the battlefields around Vienna, in strategic thought he was primarily a product of the Enlightenment, preferring artful maneuver to costly battles. This philosophy reinforced the ingrained prudence that historically had proven more effective in preserving the Hapsburg domains than had staking the fortunes of the Empire on the uncertain outcome of a decisive battle. Charles' influence on the Austrian officer corps was substantial. Even after his retirement in 1809, the hero of Aspern-Essling was accorded unusual respect, especially since his strategic ideas were in accord with the emphasis on restraint in Hapsburg foreign policy. Moreover, Charles was renowned as the most studious and knowledgeable member of the aristocratic officer corps.

The Austrian Chief of Staff, Count Josef Radetzky, was alert to his country's inability to liberate itself from the past.* In 1809, he had remarked somewhat wistfully that Austria had never based its military system on war, but only on peace. He noted, for example, that the conscription system was not designed to provide the largest possible combat force, but rather to spread the burden of war among competing political factions.[8] He might also have observed that the archaic state of the Government's finances further limited the monarchy's ability to mobilize its full resources rapidly.†

Radetzky's operational memoranda written in May and June clearly reflect the conservative philosophy of Hapsburg strategists. Although claiming "the destruction of the enemy" to be the proper objective of Allied maneuvers, he preferred to avoid the ultimate confrontation until success could be assured. Radetzky's approach was to wait and allow attrition of Napoleon's strength—a strategy that was likely to be more time-consuming than fighting. At a dramatic meeting with Scharnhorst just before the Prussian's death, Radetzky's plans received Scharnhorst's blessing, but agreement may have been more in the interest of apparent harmony than the resolution of substantive differences.

At the same time, Prince Schwarzenberg, the new Austrian Commander-in-Chief, asserted that the army in Bohemia should advance against the enemy's communications while "battle with a superior enemy main force should be avoided until the other Allied armies have united with us." After the union of all Allied forces "on the enemy communications," battle should be sought. The basic idea was "to force the enemy towards North Germany and to cut him off from South Germany, where he can accrue the greatest resources."[9] To further unity of effort, he recommended attaching Russian and Prussian forces to the Austrian army, emphasizing in a letter to Emperor Francis that "only unity in the spirit of maneuver can lead to victory."[10]

Alexander's principal strategic adviser was Count Karl von Toll, a man of German blood, fiery temperament, and no small strategic talent. He proposed several audacious plans, and vigorously urged the most impetuous execution of them. Toll was somewhat unpredictable, and exercised considerable influence not only over Alexander, who frequently asked for his advice, but also over the other Allied generals. Early in June, Toll authored the concept of a simultaneous advance by Austrian and Russo-Prussian forces. Should Napoleon turn with his main forces against either of the two armies, the other would promptly attack him in the rear. If Napoleon were to withdraw to the west bank of the Elbe before hostilities commenced, the Russo-Prussian army would pursue from Silesia, while the Austrians would advance through Eger and Hof to cut the French line of communication through Mainz.[11] (*See Atlas Map No. 55.*) Toll's ideas thus struck something of a compromise between the Austrian and Prussian schools of strategy. Yet, Russian military strategy, on the whole, appears to have been inconsistent, both in its purpose and its doctrine.

Several factors seem to have inhibited the development of the Russian philosophy of war. First, because of the general lack of education of the Russian officer corps, the high command was cosmopolitan rather than purely Russian. During the fall campaign of 1813, the Tsar's closest military advisers were Moreau (a Frenchman), Toll (a German), and, after his desertion from the French Army in August, Antoine H. Jomini (a Swiss).* Equally important, the disparate war experiences of the Russian Army had prevented the development of an integrated military philosophy. From the early eighteenth century until the Napoleonic era, Russian armies had fought four different kinds of wars—against Charles XII in northern Europe, the Chinese in Siberia, the Turks in the Crimea, and Frederick the Great in Europe proper. Each of these wars required a different strategic outlook, and each left different attitudes in its wake. The result was an ill-defined philosophy of military strategy, especially after the death in 1800 of Count Suvorov, who had been the most unifying intellectual force in the Russian Army.

The Tsar's decisions depended largely on the adviser whom he consulted at a given moment, rather than on a deep-rooted school of thought. Moreover, there was no well-trained staff to prevent the discord that inevitably developed within Russian headquarters.† On the one hand, the conser-

*Radetzky had the distinction of having served in every theater of war in which Hapsburg forces had fought for 20 years.

†Inflation was a governing fact of life in Austria. In 1811, the Government had gone bankrupt.

*Moreau had first fled to America and later emigrated to Russia after being implicated in Royalist intrigues. Jomini considered himself ill-used during the Russian Campaign, and had always harbored a grudge against Berthier.

†Note, for example, the conflicts between Kutusov and Alexander at Austerlitz, and between Barclay and Bagration in 1812.

vative generals, led by Barclay de Tolly, had waged a cautious, methodical war in both 1812 and the spring of 1813. On the other hand, aggressive staff officers, led by Toll, urged the Tsar to employ bold flanking movements and decisive strikes against the enemy rear. This could only result in a divided system of command, not only within the Russian Army but throughout the entire coalition, which looked to the Tsar for inspiration and guidance during the early part of the campaign.

As described at the beginning of this chapter, Metternich, in his role as a mediator between the Allies and France, met Napoleon in Dresden on June 26 to present Allied terms. The Austrian Foreign Minister also brought an Allied request to extend the armistice to August 10, which by mutual agreement meant that hostilities could not re-commence until the seventeenth. Napoleon agreed to the request. At this same time, representatives from Russia, Prussia, and Sweden were meeting at Trachenberg in Silesia to work out their common military strategy. The various streams of thought, each based on a different national policy and different strategic concepts, never completely merged. However, the Allies did make progress in cementing their cause. Unexpectedly, the unifier of the planning conference turned out to be the Crown Prince of Sweden.

If Napoleon turned against the Austrians, Bernadotte declared, he would relentlessly pursue from the rear, and "the center of the Austrian Monarchy will become the grave of the great Napoleon." Great strategical calculations were not needed, he repeated, "only brave colonels at the head of their regiments with orders directing them to march straight for the enemy."[12] In order to play his part, however, he would need an army, since 30,000 Swedes hardly sufficed for such stirring achievements. The Allies offered him 70,000 troops, in exchange for which Bernadotte agreed to advance forward of Berlin, cross the Elbe, and "then to advance towards Leipzig."[13]

The final accommodation of Russian, Prussian, and Swedish views prescribed that the Austrian army in Bohemia would be reinforced with 100,000 men from the Allied army in Silesia, forming a main force of over 200,000 men under Austrian command. *(See Atlas Map No. 55.)* This formation—termed the Army of Bohemia—would emerge through the mountains ringing Bohemia and, depending on the situation, would advance into Silesia, Saxony, or Bavaria. The Silesian army would follow the enemy toward the Elbe, being careful to "avoid a general action unless a favorable opportunity presents itself." The Bohemian army and the northern army were each to prepare for an advance on the enemy's rear in the event that Napoleon were to strike one of the two forces. In conclusion, it was agreed that "all the allied armies will take the offensive, and the camp of the enemy will be

Bernadotte, the Crown Prince of Sweden

their rendezvous."[14] The strategy of the dead Scharnhorst, the ringing phrases of Toll, and the political objectives of Bernadotte are all apparent in this plan. One voice was still missing, however—that of Austria—and it was characteristic of Hapsburg methods that the Austrian generals should have the final and decisive voice in shaping Allied strategy.

After learning of developments at the Trachenberg war council, Emperor Francis questioned Schwarzenberg on the status of Austrian mobilization. Throughout the month of June, Radetzky had been busy preparing estimates and attempting, as surreptitiously as possible, to influence the course of Allied military negotiations. His memorandum written early in July was the basis of both Schwarzenberg's answer to the Hapsburg Emperor and Austria's strategy:

> Most likely this attack of the French Main Army will be directed against the Austrian army. . . . Only an offensive by the Crown Prince of Sweden and by the Russo-Prussian Army will suffice to divert the French main force from the Austrian army, which by a well calculated defensive will be in a good position to keep its main forces assembled for the decisive combined blow.[15]

This plan was remarkable in that it required the two weaker Allied armies to "seize the offensive, and continue it in order to give the Austrians the opportunity, once united with them,

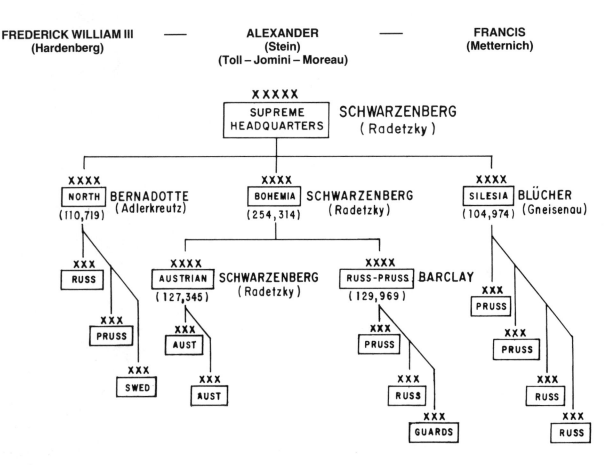

The Allied Command Structure in 1813

to strike the most decisive blow against the enemy." It has been argued that Austrian strategy aimed to maneuver Napoleon out of Germany rather than to destroy him, and that it reflected Metternich's policy of freeing the Confederation of the Rhine without destroying Napoleon's power entirely. Perhaps. However, the overall character of Radetzky's plan, which developed the situation by careful maneuver, clearly exhibits the typical Austrian striving for certainty and hesitancy to take chances. The strategy desired was thus one that sought an assured defeat of the enemy while leaving Austria's forces intact for any future contests that might ensue. The most important aspect of Austrian strategy was, therefore, its timing. The high command was willing to wait until the necessary strength was assembled "to strike the most decisive blow against the enemy."

There is no proof that the Russians and Prussians formally agreed to the final Austrian strategy. No written "Trachenberg Plan" has survived because there was none, oral agreements being easier to evade. On the other hand, there was a "Trachenberg Concept," which generally governed the strategy of the coalition. This concept, so strongly influenced by Radetzky, is best described in his own words: "To avoid any

unequal battle and so wear down the enemy, in order to fall on his weakened elements with superior forces and defeat them in detail."[16]

It is one thing to agree on the concept of a plan, and quite another to unite in its implementation. Radetzky's plan remained in force only until it came into conflict with the key personalities of the coalition—Blücher, Bernadotte, and Alexander I. Alexander's ambition was to be called to the supreme command of the Allied forces. Early in August, his advisers convinced him that it was inadvisable for a monarch to carry the military burden of command, and the Tsar reluctantly agreed to the selection of Prince Schwarzenberg for the post. That selection was a disappointment to Bernadotte, who harbored strong ambitions. However, Schwarzenberg's appointment was virtually meaningless, since all three monarchs decided that they and their advisers would be present at headquarters to assist the supreme commander in his duties. Of even more serious consequence was the fact that no directive delineated Schwarzenberg's authority and responsibilities. Thus, he soon discovered that while he had many of the latter, he had almost none of the former.

Blücher and the Reformed Prussian Army

No one individual shaped the character of the Silesian army more than its commander—Field Marshal Gebhard Leberecht Prince Blücher von Wahlstatt.* Blücher was an extraordinary man whose values were a product of the eighteenth century, but whose approach to war was decidedly unconventional. He had begun his military career in the Swedish service, had been captured by the Prussians in the Seven Years' War, and had then willingly agreed to become an officer in Frederick's famous army. After a disagreement with one of his superiors caused him to be passed over for promotion, he angrily submitted his resignation, thereby eliciting the remark from Frederick that he could "go to hell."

By the end of Frederick's regime, however, Blücher had recovered his commission and, with the outbreak of the revolutionary wars, found himself a general officer with a reputation as a bold cavalry leader. His ardent craving for excitement, however, remained unsatisfied. (Shortly after each of his exploits in the field, he would invariably repair to the nearest city for a night of gambling and drinking.) An intemperate man with strong likes and dislikes, he had deplored Prussia's neutrality, which lasted until 1806, and hated the French. Throughout Auerstädt and during the subsequent rout, Blücher had distinguished himself while commanding the rearguard covering Hohenlohe's retreat.

In 1813, Blücher was 70 years old, but he still possessed the energy of a lieutenant. The numerous arguments summoned against his selection to command the Silesian army provide an excellent summary of his personality:

> . . . he was too old, he had been mentally unsound,† his military methods were antiquated, he had no experience in commanding large forces; he had little real knowledge of strategy or tactics; he was illiterate to a great extent and would not be able to confer with his Russian subordinates either in their own language or in French; he was addicted to drink and to gambling.[17]

Aside from these distinguishing traits, however, he possessed an indomitable will and unfailing courage, inspiring his men to the greatest efforts, especially during moments of crisis. Perhaps his greatest asset was that he recognized his own failings in the art of planning and using maps, and had the good sense to delegate that function to someone who was more

Field Marshal Blücher

capable. This allowed plenty of room within which August von Gneisenau and his corps of general staff officers could operate.

Gneisenau, Blücher's chief of staff, perfectly complemented the aggressive, unreflective Prussian commander. Gneisenau had risen from the lower social order. He was born of an army family during a retreat in the Seven Years' War. Shortly after his birth, he slipped from the arms of his mother and was found on the trail by a Prussian cavalryman. From this moment on, his childhood was devoid of parental guidance, and evidently, of all happiness. He became a stoic, and sought refuge in the belief that a strong sense of duty afforded the best security against life's disappointments. He entered the Army and plunged vigorously into his work.

Gneisenau was not a thoroughgoing liberal, but a thoughtful, practical man who recognized from his experience that all men, regardless of their social status, were capable of making certain contributions to society. He was a believer in

---

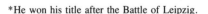

*He won his title after the Battle of Leipzig.

†On several occasions he suffered from severe psychoses, believing on one occasion that his head had turned to stone, and on another that he was pregnant with an elephant.

the native potential of each individual—a philosophy that came to have great value in the Prussian Army only after Jena and Auerstädt had revealed the fallacies of the fabled Prussian system of discipline. By 1807, it had become apparent to Gneisenau that France had been able to overrun Europe because the "revolution had aroused all the forces and had given to each its appropriate sphere of influence. That is why heroes took the places at the head of armies, the primary positions in administration were held by statesmen, and the greatest man rose out of the midst of a great nation to be its chief."[18] Gneisenau himself was a hero. During Prussia's darkest hour, he had taken over command of the fortress at Colberg and defended it tenaciously until the general peace was signed at Tilsit.

It is not surprising that Scharnhorst selected Gneisenau to serve on the reform commission. Originality of mind and the talent for penetrating analysis of complex problems are always rare qualities. Gneisenau had proved his right to participate in the work of reform with his bravery in battle, his dogged application of common sense, and his refusal to accept outdated methods when better ones were clearly available. Gneisenau had studied Napoleonic warfare carefully and concluded that Prussia should adopt the open-order tactics, national conscription, and system of promotion according to merit as practiced by the French. Within a few months, he became one of the most active and respected members of the commission.

During this same period, Scharnhorst had developed a program for the training and instruction of the General Staff. His program insured that commanders, also, would receive instruction on the function of the staff "so that every officer of the former [the staff] . . . should know exactly what he had to do and consider, and . . . the latter [the commander] should be informed of it, so that misunderstandings, wrong impressions, and conjectures or accusations should be avoided."[19] This was an essential step in the cultivation of Prussian doctrine. Henceforth, no general would lack doctrinal guidance. He need only turn to his general staff officer, who, schooled in the latest strategic and tactical theories, could provide immediate and trustworthy advice consistent with that of his fellow staff officers in other corps and brigades.

The Prussian staff system might have failed if Scharnhorst had not also reformed the war academy in Berlin and charged it with preparing officers for high level staff work. The emphasis of the academy's curriculum was on educating useful servants of the state, who would be capable of performing any function, rather than on educating men to perform a "strict mechanical duty." In this regard, Prussia's army carried the idea of professionalism far beyond that of Napoleon's command and staff system, which required simply that his aides and orderlies be ready at a moment's notice to ride forth

in quest of information or to transmit the commander's orders. Scharnhorst, the reformer, had in mind not only the training of staff officers, but the re-education of the Prussian officer corps.

It is unlikely that men even of Scharnhorst's and Gneisenau's stature and dedication could have carried their difficult work to completion if they had not found support in the idea of service to the Prussian nation. Formerly, the officer's sole loyalty had been to the *King*. The reformers altered this concept of duty, pledging the Army to the defense of the *nation*. In turn, they anticipated that the nation would willingly support the Army. This view of the military professional's relation to his country dealt a death blow to Frederick's policy of employing mercenaries, and at the same time eliminated any justification for the corporal punishment on which Prussian discipline had relied. From top to bottom, the army that took the field in 1813 bore little resemblance to the gallant but obsolete formation that had marched bravely to destruction in 1806.

Significantly, it was Gneisenau who took over Scharnhorst's duties after the latter's death, and, fortunately for the Silesian army, it was he who assumed the important position as Blücher's chief of staff in the field. One biographer has related that Blücher once remarked admiringly to Gneisenau that if only he (Blücher) had studied, instead of surrendering "myself to gambling, drink, and women . . . something could have been made of me."[20] After the war, when presented with an honorary degree at Oxford, he paid the ultimate tribute to his chief of staff when he said, "If I am to become a doctor, you must at least make Gneisenau an apothecary, for we two belong together." In 1806, this comment would have been ridiculed in any European army; in 1813, it could only have been made in the Prussian Army.

The Leipzig Campaign

As noted above, following the Battle of Bautzen, Napoleon elected to keep his army in Saxony, east of the Elbe River, where he could both move readily in any direction and exploit Dresden as a sizable base. Quite probably, also, the Emperor remained determined to position his troops farther to the east than his strength would seem to permit, because he still harbored hopes of retrieving the easternmost reaches of his old empire. *(See Atlas Map No. 55.)* One group of corps (eventually to be formed into an army under MacDonald's command) occupied positions opposing Blücher along the Katzbach River; another army-sized force under Oudinot faced Bernadotte near Berlin; Davout's corps (composed largely of garrison troops and raw recruits) was stationed at Hamburg, over 200 miles from Dresden; and the central reserve, under Napoleon's personal command, lay on the plains east of Dresden, near the mountain passes leading to Bohemia.

Napoleon formulated his plan of campaign on August 12 and 13, after Austria had declared war and the armistice had been terminated. He elected to assume the strategic defensive in southern Saxony, which would enable him to hold key points and guard his growing stock of supplies while watching the Allied armies in Silesia and Bohemia. At the same time, hoping to pull the Prussians northward and away from the Austrians and Russians, he planned an advance by Oudinot and Davout toward Berlin. This secondary offensive was probably also motivated by a Napoleonic desire to punish an erstwhile ally and strike at a treacherous ex-marshal. Regardless of the reason for the northward drive, it would accentuate the division of the Emperor's forces and provide an excuse for not mounting a vigorous offensive in the south, where more decisive results could be expected.

When Napoleon took the unusual step of asking his marshals for their comments on his plan, St. Cyr said that Napoleon was underestimating the strength of Bernadotte's army. Marmont deplored the badly stretched positions of the French, and urged the Emperor to pull back into a more tightly concentrated formation. "I fear greatly," he pleaded, "lest on the day on which your Majesty has gained a victory, and believe you have won a decisive battle, you may learn that you have lost two."[21] Marmont's worst fears were to be realized.

Throughout Napoleon's rise to greatness he had consistently refrained from decentralizing command authority, and now could count on none of his immediate subordinates to act with enterprise unless he personally directed their movements. His most capable independent commander, Davout, was tied to the fortress of Hamburg and had been given the mission of conducting an active feint. The only other marshals who had shown any talent for high command were Massena and Soult. The former was now too old for field duty, while the latter was on his way to Spain to pick up the pieces left in the wake of Joseph's disastrous loss at Vitoria. MacDonald had shown some promising capabilities in 1809, but was disliked by the other corps commanders. Oudinot was personally brave, but possessed little talent for commanding anything besides infantry forces and had no ability for independent command at all. As the campaign would reveal, Napoleon could not go north to supervise Oudinot's advance because he was needed to supervise his subordinates' responses to movements of the Allied armies in Silesia and Bohemia. Moreover, because he refused to abandon Dresden—to which he had committed part of his central reserve—and therefore could not fight actively on all fronts, he had made it impossible to derive the

maximum benefit from the advantage of interior lines. "What is important to me," he wrote to St. Cyr, "is not to be cut off from Dresden and the Elbe; it matters little to me to be cut off from France. . . . It is clear that 400,000 men, supported by a system of prepared strongholds, on a river like the Elbe . . . cannot be outflanked."[22] At the same time he was apparently thinking, "and besides, I alone am worth another 100,000 men."[23]

The Coalition Tests Napoleon's Mobile Defense

There was no military genius worth 100,000 men in the Allied camp. The supreme commander, however, had compensating talents, one of which was the ability to promote harmony. To this end, he arranged a great review of the Army of Bohemia before the three monarchs on August 19. The high point of the ceremony was the dedication of a flag to the Cuirassier Regiment of Emperor Francis, during which the Tsar's sister presented a streamer for the standard. "A great day is coming," Schwarzenberg announced to his troops, and he carefully delineated their purpose: "not against France, only against French supremacy outside the French borders is this great Alliance risen."[24]

Almost at once, the forces of disunity began to work on the high command. Every conceivable enemy course of action

Karl Philip Schwarzenberg, Prince of Austria

had been foreseen except that which Napoleon now appeared to have chosen—an inert defensive. It therefore became necessary to call a council of war* to decide what should be done. After much debate and discussion, Schwarzenberg persuaded the monarchs and their advisers to approve an advance on Leipzig. The necessary directives were issued, and the Bohemian army lumbered forward, over trails through the Erz Mountains, heading for Saxony.

Within two days, Schwarzenberg and Alexander were at cross-purposes. Napoleon had been personally sighted on reconnaissance in the Zittau gap on August 19, and Alexander was concerned that the Emperor of the French might advance on Prague "in order to throw himself between the Main Army and the Silesian Army." Schwarzenberg was adamant in his belief that Napoleon's main force could be found opposite Blücher or Bernadotte. Besides, supplies had already been stocked and routes assigned for a march into Saxony, not Silesia. Asserting his monarchial right, Alexander called another council of war which strongly urged that the main army (the Army of Bohemia) shift its direction of advance to the east, toward Dresden. *(See Atlas Map No. 56.)*

Schwarzenberg had already contemplated a similar maneuver, but he had planned to make the eastward wheel after the army cleared the mountain defiles. The difference of views was so great that Schwarzenberg complained to Metternich that Alexander was unnecessarily complicating his already difficult task. Metternich replied that Schwarzenberg should rely more on the services of the diplomats attached to Supreme Headquarters. For the moment, he advised, "the most sincere understanding between us and our Allies is so important that we cannot offer too great a sacrifice . . . "[25]

The sacrifice was to change the army's direction of march just as the columns were astride the mountains; without regard for supply problems or availability of routes. Difficult lateral trails had to be used, which slowed the march. Columns crossed. Since the positioning of pre-planned magazines and depots could not be adapted to unexpected changes of direction, supply problems became acute. To add to the troops' discomfort, it rained for two days. As a consequence of these frictions of war, which were multiplied by the friction of command, the attack on Dresden was delayed.

Meanwhile, Napoleon had been very active personally in responding to the multiple Allied threats to his troop dispositions in Saxony and Silesia. After a final inspection of the Dresden area, he moved to Bautzen on August 16, where he learned from his spies' reports that large numbers of Russians were marching from Reichenbach (near Schaednitz) toward the Austrian border. *(See Atlas Map No. 56.)* Viewing this as

an indication that the Allies meant to concentrate in Bohemia in preparation for an advance either toward Dresden or westward into Bavaria, Napoleon decided to concentrate his reserve forces near Zittau. From that location he could attack southward into Bohemia and strike the reinforcing Russians in the flank, or at least get behind the forces of Schwarzenberg. His reconnaissance on August 19, already mentioned, convinced him that the Russians—and Schwarzenberg's army—were moving slowly. At the same time, reports from the Silesian front indicated that Blücher was still advancing to the west, apparently aiming for Zittau. (That Prussian general had ordered his Silesian army forward on August 14, deliberately violating the terms of the armistice, and was pushing back the French troops opposing him.) Napoleon now decided to take reinforcements to the east and to force Blücher to withdraw. Accordingly, on August 21 he arrived at the Bober River with the Guard, gathered up the corps that had been withdrawing, and launched a strong attack against Blücher. Abiding by the Trachenberg Concept, the Prussian withdrew promptly. Napoleon halted the advance at the Katzbach River, partly because Blücher would not stand and fight, and partly because by the twenty-second he was receiving urgent calls for help from St. Cyr, who was then facing Schwarzenberg's army on the approaches to Dresden. Then, on August 23, the Emperor created the Army of the Bober under MacDonald, ordering that commander to drive Blücher east of the Katzbach and then to take up a defensive position on the Bober, with his corps well concentrated.

At this time, Napoleon was envisioning mounting a strong attack on Schwarzenberg. He planned to move with the Guard and Marmont's corps back toward Dresden while the corps of Victor and Vandamme were preparing for action in the Dresden area. Then, with his forces concentrated, he would launch a strong attack against Schwarzenberg's right flank by crossing the Elbe southeast of Dresden with at least two corps. St. Cyr's ability to maintain his position in Dresden would be critical to this plan. (As it turned out, St. Cyr had to be reinforced, thus depriving Napoleon of the forces needed to make the counterstroke decisive. Vandamme, who was forced to mount the attack alone, achieved little success.)

The Battle of Dresden

While Napoleon was moving troops to oppose Blücher and then sending them on a forced march back toward Dresden, Schwarzenberg's army was closing ever so slowly on that city. As it adjusted to the change dictated by Alexander's insistence on shifting the direction of march eastward while still in the mountains, the Allied command's many-sided brain

*It was the first of 17 councils of war held during the campaign.

conceived of another distracting proposal. Toll felt that a movement on Dresden would not produce a decisive battle, as Napoleon had advanced so far to the east that he could not return to the Elbe in time to contest the crossing. He therefore proposed that the army assemble to the southwest of Dresden, and there await the Emperor's inevitable attack. After some discussion, the orders were issued, and the army wearily responded. At this time, Schwarzenberg received news confirming that Napoleon had left only one corps to defend Dresden, and had moved with the mass of his army against Blücher. Schwarzenberg now decided to renew the advance on Dresden, and managed to persuade the various Allied factions of the merit in this plan. Revised instructions galvanized the regiments into motion, the Allied main army finally appearing before Dresden on August 25. Napoleon had not yet arrived.

Even as Barclay's lead elements took the thinly-stretched French defenders under fire in the suburbs, another council of war convened, and serious divisions again developed within the staff. At first, Alexander urged Schwarzenberg to lose no time in pressing the attack. Jomini concurred, but Toll had returned to his original idea of luring Napoleon to battle in the open. Moreau felt that the city's defenses were too strong.* "Sire, you will sacrifice 20,000 men . . . it is inadvisable to demoralize our troops in such a way."[26] After the remaining hours of daylight had been wasted in deliberation, Alexander at last announced that there would be no attack. Since the Austrian troops could not carry the town alone, Schwarzenberg capitulated. Disgusted, he returned to his headquarters, where another consultation reversed the decision again, providing for a limited attack on August 26. Early that morning, partly concealed by a driving rain, Napoleon splashed into Dresden with the Guard and two corps at his heels. The Allies launched the attack that afternoon, half beaten psychologically before the signal cannon boomed the order to advance.

After a hard-fought struggle at the city wall on August 27, Napoleon drove the Allies out of Dresden. During the confused retreat through the muddy countryside, Austrians, Russians, and Prussians became intermingled, each commander having to fight his way out as best he could. Although Napoleon remained in Dresden, he urged his subordinates to press their troops forward, hoping to cut off parts of Schwarzenberg's army in the defiles short of the mountains. In the confusion, Vandamme's corps became isolated and was trapped at Kulm between the Austrian rearguard and a Prussian corps. Vandamme was captured, enabling the Allies to claim a victory.

To Schwarzenberg, the advance to Dresden had been anything but victorious. The main breakdown in the coalition was clearly in Supreme Headquarters. "It is unbelievable how I suffer," he wrote to his wife, "they did not attack at Dresden when I directed and on the day I wanted, but on the following day."[27] To Francis, he complained:

> His Majesty the Tsar of Russia . . . leaves me alone neither in my headquarters nor even at the moment of battle . . . he allows almost every general to give advice and suggestions. . . . General Barclay has absolutely neither sense of obedience nor understanding for operations, and, besides is jealous in the worst way. . . . I find it absolutely necessary, therefore, to request . . . that either the Tsar of Russia be advised to leave the army alone, General Barclay be removed, and the corps of Kleist, Wittgenstein, and Miloradovich be each advised that they are under my immediate orders, or someone else be entrusted with the command.[28]

There were several obvious reasons for this state of vast confusion. First, the Austrian staff was inefficiently organized, not having been reorganized along the simple, functional lines of the Prussian General Staff. Second, Schwarzenberg's overworked headquarters was simultaneously responsible for three different echelons of command. It not only supervised the operations of the three Allied armies, but also functioned as the controlling headquarters for the Army of Bohemia, as well as serving as the command organ for the Austrian forces in that army. Only a staff of the most sophisticated kind could have performed smoothly under this arrangement. While trifling details concerning the Bohemian army flooded the operations section, little information was available on the location, strength, and situation of the Russian and Prussian forces.

Presumably, some of these difficulties might have been overcome if the whole atmosphere of supreme headquarters had not suffered from the disruptive comings and goings of numerous advisers, diplomats, and generals, each of whom had singular ideas and advice. Neither Schwarzenberg nor Radetzky could establish a procedure for dealing with these visitors, whose responsibilities were as ill-defined as their presence was unpredictable. The faulty organization and functioning of supreme headquarters must, however, be traced ultimately to the mistakes of the Allied sovereigns themselves. They were unsure of themselves, but, at the same time, they were afraid to entrust control of military operations to the supreme commander. Considering this ill-coordinated command system, the Allies were fortunate to have escaped from Dresden without suffering a major defeat.

While these events were taking place at Dresden, the outcome of the action on other fronts suggested that the overall

---

*Ironically, one of Napoleon's aides was assuring the Emperor at the same time that Dresden's defenses could not withstand a determined assault for 24 hours.

Allied strategy might be succeeding. Not only was Napoleon's army diminished by the fights at Dresden and Kulm, but he had been compelled to divide his reserve, which was further weakened by forced marches to and from Silesia. This, in turn, allowed the other Allied armies to take the offensive against his isolated forces.

On the northern front, Oudinot had initially made good progress in carrying out Napoleon's original instructions to advance toward Berlin. Moving through broken country, he drove Bernadotte's outposts before him, but in so doing allowed his corps to draw so far apart that they moved beyond supporting distance. This advance, coupled with Davout's movement from Hamburg and the movement of General Girard's division from Magdeberg, proved unsettling to Bernadotte, who might have evacuated Berlin had not Friedrich von Bülow, commanding a Prussian corps, stiffened the Crown Prince's resolve. On August 23, one of Oudinot's corps captured Gross Beeren, but without support from other French units it could not stop Bülow's counterattack, and was forced to withdraw. This small action apparently unnerved Oudinot, who ordered a withdrawal to Wittenberg, thus uncovering Napoleon's northern flank. Bernadotte's caution irritated Prussian generals, who began to feel that they were fighting on their own. Thus, suspicion and antagonism marked the Northern army's operations. The Prussians were simply unable to accept the Crown Prince's announced strategy:

> to avoid every unequal battle, under all circumstances to keep open the line of retreat to Straslund . . . , in the event of a personal attack by the Emperor to stay always one march ahead of him . . . , never to be exposed to Napoleon's crushing blow, but to tire him by an exhaustive, slow, methodical war.[29]

Blücher's March Across the Elbe

An exhaustive, slow, methodical war was no more acceptable to Blücher than it was to Bülow and the Prussians serving under Bernadotte. Blücher's personality and outlook on life carried over into his philosophy of war. In his opinion, it was far better to die at the head of a roaring cavalry charge than to sit at headquarters and contemplate the proper time for commencing the offensive. He had waited seven long years to give the French a taste of the Prussian brand of war, and would not be satisfied until Prussian hussars clattered down the Champs Elysées. One of the King's senior diplomats reproached Blücher for violating the armistice by ordering the Silesian army forward two full days before the expiration of the truce. Blücher responded that he was responsible for his actions to no one but the King, and "least of all to the

French."[30] And, it might be added, hardly at all to Schwarzenberg, unless it suited him.

Schwarzenberg himself was partly responsible for the apparent indifference toward Allied strategy displayed by his fiery Prussian subordinate. Instead of explaining Blücher's orders personally, the supreme commander delegated that responsibility to Barclay de Tolly. On August 9, Barclay met with Blücher and assigned him his task—to do as much damage to the French as possible, once the enemy turned against either of the other two armies. On the other hand, Barclay continued, Blücher must avoid battle against a superior force. Blücher testily observed that the Fabian way of war was unknown to him; he would rather have some other post than command an army that was hobbled by such rules. Under closer questioning, Barclay agreed that if favorable conditions arose, Blücher should indeed seek to strike the enemy, but he declined to formalize the agreement by placing it in writing. Before departing, Blücher stated that he wished the monarchs to be advised of his views. If they did not concur with his intentions, they should find another post for him. Receiving no further comment concerning this conversation, Blücher assumed that the three monarchs had sanctioned his proposal to act according to his own judgment.[31]

Blücher had problems enough within his own army. During a clash with what was thought to be the enemy rearguard, he discovered that his troops had partly enveloped the corps of Marshal Ney, which was drawn up for battle east of the Bober River. *(Action not depicted on map.)* Blücher responded quickly, ordering Yorck's Prussian corps to fix the enemy while one Russian corps blocked the enemy's northern escape route. The other Russian corps, commanded by Langeron, was to march toward the French south flank to block a key crossing site. At this critical moment, Langeron refused, protesting that his troops were already exhausted and that an additional night's march would be impossible. As a consequence of his disobedience, Ney's corps escaped into the night.

Blücher dismissed the matter as a misinterpretation of his orders. However, he knew that Langeron was a general of the old school who considered himself superior to "le bon sabreur," as he sarcastically referred to the commander of the Army of Silesia. What Blücher did not know was that Barclay—as a personal favor—had privately discussed Schwarzenberg's strategy with Langeron. Both of the Russian generals interpreted the Trachenberg Plan in a cautious, defensive way. However, Barclay apparently did not advise Langeron of his conversation with Blücher, in which the latter's aggressive concept had been tacitly approved. The seeds of discord had been firmly planted—by an indiscretion and by differing interpretations of the overall military strategy.

Another misunderstanding with Langeron occurred several

days later during the French advance into Silesia discussed earlier. When Napoleon arrived in Silesia on August 21, Blücher ordered a withdrawal, in keeping with Barclay's instructions. However, he specified that the retreat should continue only if the French followed closely in pursuit—and only with his personal permission. As soon as the French cavalry made contact with Langeron's outposts, that general ordered the retreat, forcing Blücher to abandon prematurely an excellent defensive position.

In spite of the fact that its commanders seemed not to understand each other, the Silesian army won a victory less than a week later. *(See Atlas Map No. 56.)* Napoleon had marched posthaste to Dresden to fight off Schwarzenberg's assault, turning over the contest with Blücher to MacDonald. In direct contradiction to his instructions (calling for a defensive on the Bober) MacDonald pursued the Allies across the Katzbach River, where he was caught astride the swollen stream and fiercely counterattacked. At first, Blücher had intended to cross the river and strike at his enemy without delay. But Gneisenau's cool suggestion—to wait until the French were across the river—prevailed. Even so, the victory was not won without another fierce altercation—this one between Yorck and Gneisenau.

Throughout the preceding week, which had included much marching, little fighting, and incessant rain, Yorck had complained that the problem "lay in the indecisiveness of the general staff who do not know whether to go backwards or forwards . . . ."[32] Several times he requested permission to rest his troops rather than undertake another arduous night march, which he knew would only end with his corps retracing their steps on the following morning. Blaming the general staff officers really meant blaming Gneisenau, who directed the staff and clashed with Yorck over that corps commander's criticism. In contrast to Langeron, however, Yorck proved to be a reliable subordinate. "Yorck is a poisonous fellow," Blücher later noted, "he does nothing without complaining, but when the attack is on, he bites like no one else."[33] The friction caused by Yorck might have been avoided, however, if either Blücher or Gneisenau had explained to Yorck that the army's vacillating movements were necessary because of its mission—to stay in close touch with the enemy, but nonetheless to avoid a major battle. The pressures and dangers of combat always cause a certain amount of strife. Blücher was perfectly willing to accept them as long as his subordinates obeyed his orders. *(See Atlas Map No. 57.)*

Assessing the situation early in September, Schwarzenberg

The Battle on the Katzbach River, August 1813

Prussian Soldiers in Action

and Radetzky had some cause for satisfaction. News of French problems in supply and morale indicated that the separate engagements fought in August had materially weakened Napoleon's army. Time was clearly working against the Emperor. Only a great battle could solve his strategic problem and the coalition had already demonstrated that it was capable of preventing any such fatal confrontation. To insure that no mistakes were made, Radetzky drafted two defensive plans, in both of which Blücher's army was to play little part, merely "adjusting its movements according to circumstances."[34] Napoleon would be destroyed, not by a great battle, but by attrition.

Napoleon's actions played into the Allies' hands. Throughout September, the Emperor's attention remained divided as he sought to simultaneously defend Dresden against a renewed attack from Bohemia, strike at Blücher whenever his army advanced from Silesia, and launch a coordinated drive on Berlin. On September 3, he replaced the ineffective Oudinot with Ney, who promptly lost a battle with Bernadotte's troops at Dennewitz. Napoleon should have supervised this action himself, but Blücher had materialized again, and the Emperor could not trust MacDonald to drive him back. The Prussians recoiled from Napoleon's furious attack, enabling the Emperor to return to Dresden in time to oversee an indecisive skirmish with Barclay's troops south of the city. After two weeks of inactivity on both sides, Napoleon reluctantly decided to abandon his attempts to force Blücher to fight, and ordered a withdrawal behind the Elbe. It began on September 24.

The Allies now had to analyze a new situation. Although some members of the multi-national staff believed that Napoleon was commencing a retreat from the Elbe, Radetzky correctly interpeted the Emperor's intentions. He realized that Napoleon's forces were no longer strong enough for an active defense forward of the Elbe. He also knew that if Napoleon abandoned the Elbe, he would be surrendering Saxony and all of Germany. It was now time for the Army of Bohemia to launch its offensive, he insisted, but this time the advance should aim farther west, toward Leipzig. To provide for the security of Bohemia, a directive was dispatched to Blücher, requesting him to march his troops south and join Schwarzenberg's army.

Schwarzenberg's general scheme had been to weaken French reserves by causing them to dash back and forth, snapping at his encircling forces, and to exhaust the French army by a steady constriction of its operational area. The Allies would converge for the kill only when Napoleon slowed his movements or retreated, thus allowing the decisive blow to be struck with certainty. Certainty and unity were the trademarks of Schwarzenberg's strategy, and patience was his prime virtue. The fiery Blücher, however, sought to destroy Napoleon in battle. His energetic chief of staff urged audacious maneuver and the resolve to accept battle wherever the enemy could be found. Patience was not a virtue in the Silesian army, as was indicated by the prophecy of one of the young writers who frequented the headquarters: "Gentlemen, you shall soon eat grapes on the Rhine."[35]

It is therefore not surprising that Blücher declined Schwarzenberg's invitation to march for Bohemia. "For the overall welfare and good," he pleaded, "keep me from having to join the Main Army; what could such an enormous mass accomplish in such a wasted area?"[36] At the same time, Gneisenau wrote to the Tsar, formally proposing that the Silesian army join the Northern army in a daring march across the Elbe. This movement, he advised, "should not be difficult, since the defeated army has withdrawn across the Elbe and, according to the latest information, has taken the road to Leipzig."[37]

Responding to Blücher's plea with extraordinary flexibility, Schwarzenberg, pressured by the Tsar, approved his flank march to the north and diverted Bennigsen's army to Bohemia. *(See Atlas Map No. 58.)* At the end of September, therefore, the situation was as follows: Schwarzenberg's command was shifting west for an offensive toward Leipzig; Bennigsen's reserve army had crossed from Silesia into Bohemia; Blücher's troops had departed Silesia under cover of an active cavalry screen; Bernadotte's forces had closed up against the Elbe, which Ney defended at Wittenberg; and Napoleon was in the process of deciding to fall back from the Elbe toward a more central location at Leipzig.

On October 1, Blücher's lead elements crossed the Elbe near Wittenberg. Encouraged by this feat, the Northern army crossed two days later. Both Bernadotte and Blücher based their plans on two important assumptions: that the Army of Bohemia was energetically advancing on Leipzig, and that Napoleon was still in Dresden. Both assumptions were dangerously incorrect. Schwarzenberg did not even issue the final order for the Army of Bohemia's advance until October 3. When Blücher and Bernadotte met to coordinate their plans several days later, Napoleon's reserves were already in motion for Leipzig (Napoleon left two corps in Dresden, just in case the French might need the town again). Then, early on October 8, Napoleon altered the direction of march of his striking force in order to meet the Silesian army head-on as it advanced toward Leipzig. *(See Atlas Map No. 59.).*

The news of Napoleon's approach with a force at least twice the size of the Army of Silesia shattered the uneasy harmony between Blücher and Bernadotte. Neither Blücher nor Gneisenau now felt that an advance on Leipzig was possible. However, neither wanted to avoid a battle if the Crown Prince could be persuaded to join in the fight. Gneisenau dispatched a member of the staff to Swedish headquarters to determine Bernadotte's intentions. The Crown Prince at once announced his plan to withdraw behind the Elbe and avoid the coming fight. Blücher's representative stated that in such an event the Silesian army would march to the west, cross the Saale, and, leaving the Army of the North behind, attempt to join the Army of Bohemia. The Crown Prince was astounded, remarking that such a movement was against all the rules of war. It would mean abandoning the army's communications and supplies. Finally he asked, "and what will become of Berlin?" "If Moscow could be burned, then Berlin can also be sacrificed,"[38] was the liaison officer's prompt retort, neutralizing the last of Bernadotte's objections.*

Immediately after learning the outcome of this meeting, Gneisenau issued orders for the march to the west. His prompt reaction undoubtedly saved the Army of Silesia from destruction. The French onslaught barely missed the main body, catching a part of Blücher's rearguard and trains to the east of the Mulde River. The confused melee of stragglers and supply columns plus a heavy mist made it impossible for Napoleon to determine the direction of Blücher's movement. Had he crossed the Mulde to the west, or retreated to his base behind the Elbe? Skillful staff work in Prussian headquarters and Blücher's decisiveness had combined to throw the French off the scent. The Allies were granted one more day to put their house in order.

*The liaison officer was Major Ruhle von Lilienstern, who had been one of Scharnhorst's select group of pupils.

Schwarzenberg's Advance to Leipzig

While Blücher was striving to draw Bernadotte's forces into action on the north, the Army of Bohemia finally overcame its chronic inertia and began to move toward Leipzig. Metternich himself encouraged the transition from inactivity to the offensive. "God has given me enough cold-bloodedness to operate politically thus far," he declared, "now I will conduct business militarily. . . . Tsar Alexander, who even at the beginning wanted to press on somewhat quickly, believing that Napoleon must be devoured in a week, is now entirely in agreement with Schwarzenberg and myself. As soon as the hour of battle shall have arrived, I will be the first who will counsel battle."[39]

Uncertainty as to the whereabouts of Napoleon delayed the decision to advance into Saxony. Once the order was issued, uncertainty remained regarding the purpose of the maneuver. Schwarzenberg was now in favor of concentrating the Allied forces to the west of Leipzig in order to surround Napoleon and force him to battle against overwhelming odds. Since any rash moves might upset the timing of his scheme, he preferred a careful, methodical deployment. Thus, the governing idea was to threaten Leipzig in order to develop the situation while the three Allied armies maneuvered for position and attempted to unite.

Napoleon had already shifted the mass of his mobile strength toward Leipzig, but had left Murat (with 45,000 men) to face Schwarzenberg's 170,000-man army. In spite of the fact that his men were suffering from inadequate supplies and cold, wet weather, Napoleon wrote optimistically on October 7 to Murat:

> The entire Army of Silesia has debouched by Wartenburg, and has nothing from Dresden to Berlin. Marshal St. Cyr remains at Dresden. Delay the Austrians as long as you can, in order that I can strike Blücher and the Swedes before their assembly with Schwarzenberg's army.[40]

The situation was all too familiar—he must maneuver from a central position against uncoordinated Allied forces. For the first time in Napoleon's career, however, he was unable to capitalize on the advantages of interior lines. As he would soon discover, his central position at Leipzig was a deadly trap.

The Battle of Leipzig

During the first two weeks in October, the Allies steadily tightened the ring around Napoleon's weakening army. (All told, the Allies numbered some 370,000 men, whereas Napoleon barely had 220,000.) It was apparent to all participants that a major confrontation was coming. Napoleon's vigorous counterattack had separated Bernadotte from Blücher, but the latter had courageously carried out his promise to march west of the Elbe in hopes of joining Schwarzenberg's main army. Napoleon now ordered his tired troops back to Leipzig, writing to Marmont on October 12, "My entire army is in motion; they will all arrive on the 14th and I will then deliver battle to the enemy with 200,000 men."[41] *(See Atlas Map No. 60.)*

The position at Leipzig was made for disaster. Five rivers and streams came together there, and the ground to the west of the town was marshy. The town itself was a substantial obstacle. Napoleon knew that it was imperative to maintain the initiative and not be driven back into the town, where he would have insufficient room for maneuver. This was all the more important since there was only one bridge across the Elster, and any withdrawing troops would have to traverse a mile-and-a-half-long causeway across the marshes to the west.

The Hydra-headed Allied staff issued a directive on October 13, setting forth Schwarzenberg's intentions. Apparently, he had no immediate plans for forcing the issue; the operation was characterized as a reconnaissance in force, which "must avoid any serious action, because any large army corps which becomes prematurely engaged could force us to come to its support."[42] General Toll, the Tsar's chief adviser, felt that the moment had come for decisive action, and prevailed on Alexander to order Schwarzenberg to alter his plan from a cautious advance to a more aggressive attack. Schwarzenberg's second plan was even worse, requiring the Allies to attack from four different directions. Again Toll intervened, protesting the "unholy absurdity" of Schwarzenberg's concept. The second confrontation between supreme commander and Tsar was violent. Alexander finally lost his temper, exclaiming, "All right, Sir Field Marshal . . . you can do what you wish with the Austrian Army; however, concerning the Russian troops . . . these will go over to the right bank of the Pleisse, where they should be, and nowhere else."[43] Thus did the Tsar produce the final shift in a kaleidoscopic series of changes that exasperated the supreme commander, exhausted his staff, and left the troops in virtual bewilderment about what they were expected to do.

On the French side, Napoleon appeared serenely unconcerned with the overwhelming array of troops closing in around him. On October 14 he wrote to Marmont, "I send

The Battle of Leipzig, October 1813

you an account of Gustavus Adolphus' battle, showing the positions you are occupying."[44]

On October 16, Napoleon attacked the straggling advance forces of the Bohemian army, while fighting a successful defensive action against Blücher on the north. Although Schwarzenberg was halted, Blücher finally broke into the outskirts of Leipzig. Napoleon was forced to admit that he had failed to gain the decisive victory he needed. Late that night, he sent word to the Austrian Emperor asking for an armistice. This was virtually an admission of defeat. On October 17, with ammunition running low, he decided to withdraw his troops from the tempests swirling around them.

The retreat began on October 18 and lasted into the night. MacDonald, Poniatowski, and Reynier formed the rearguard. During the evening, French columns became intermingled and disordered in the narrow streets. The one bridge across the Elster was prepared for destruction, but in the confusion, the officer in charge had no way of knowing when the last French unit had crossed. Leaving a non commissioned officer in charge, he left to ascertain the situation. The frightened soldier promptly blew up the bridge while three corps were still on the far side. Some Frenchmen managed to escape; many were captured. Poniatowski drowned attempting to swim the river.

The Battle of Leipzig, also known as "The Battle of the Nations," was a tactical defeat unparalleled in Napoleon's military career. It was caused as much by his own stubborn refusal to surrender Saxony as by any brilliant feat of arms on the part of the Allies. The coalition had refused to fight except on its own terms, and that strategy had paid off. Allied victory, in turn, both stimulated the rising tide of popular feeling in Germany and confirmed the maturing professionalism of the Prussian officer corps. Most important, the battle conclusively put an end to Napoleon's empire.

The Campaign of 1814

The bitterness of defeat was written on Napoleon's face as he rode west from Leipzig along a road littered with the debris of his shattered army. Less than 100,000 men marched with him. Over 80,000 more were locked up in garrisons along the Elbe River, while many more wasted away in Poland and Eastern Germany. Meanwhile, Saxony and Bavaria had changed sides; Switzerland allowed free passage to advancing Allied formations; and, in January, Murat turned against his brother-in-law. In November, Metternich attempted to take advantage of the Empire's disorder by offering peace if Napoleon would agree to confine his ambitions within France's natural boundaries. However, the lure of a great win

The Emperor at Bay

that would restore the Empire prevented Napoleon from accepting the treaty until it was too late. In December, the Allies offered stiffer terms, although Schwarzenberg still refrained from crossing the weakly defended Rhine. While the Allies squabbled among themselves over final territorial settlements, Napoleon roused the war-weary French for a desperate all-out defense of the homeland. (*See Atlas Map No. 61a.*)

The Emperor's scheme was to fortify Paris for protracted resistance, while he maneuvered his reserves against the converging Allied armies and attempted to defeat them in detail. "Come, we must repeat the campaign of Italy," he said to Berthier.[45] However, the odds were infinitely worse than in 1796. According to Radetzky's calculations, the Allies could count on 610,000 men; Napoleon was hard-pressed to scrape up 120,000.[46]

Once again, the Allied plan was a combination of Schwarzenberg's concept of methodical attrition and Blücher's audacity. While the Army of Bohemia wriggled through the Swiss passes, the Army of Silesia struck directly across the Rhine.

Bernadotte marched through the Low Countries, which were already in a state of rebellion. Another army pressed Eugène back through the Po Valley, and Wellington's veterans had already entered the south of France in November. If Napoleon sensed that the end was coming, he failed to show it. Resorting to instinct, he resolved to profit by his adversaries' dispersion. On January 29 he struck at Blücher. *(See Atlas Map No. 61b.)*

Napoleon's piecemeal attack was successful, but Schwarzenberg marched to Blücher's support and the French were forced to withdraw. Believing that Napoleon's resources had been exhausted, the Allies began to march on Paris. At the same time they offered new peace terms, now based on France's original pre-Revolutionary territory. Steeling his nerves against the anguish of misfortune, Napoleon drew the weary French forces back to a position northeast of Paris and watched for an opening. On February 9 he learned that Schwarzenberg and Blücher had separated again. In rapid-fire succession, he struck Blücher's scattered corps and defeated them in three battles fought just south of the Marne River. On February 18, he won a battle over Schwarzenberg, but now time ran out.

The French people had supported Napoleon's wars for nearly a quarter of a century. They could no longer stand for the bloodshed, especially now that it was taking place on French soil. Throughout March, Napoleon seemed unaware that he had lost the support of France. Twisting and turning, fighting off one enemy while bluffing another, recapturing

Napoleon at Fontainebleau, 1814

key provincial towns while holding firmly onto Paris, he waged a masterful campaign of maneuver. At last, his former foreign minister, Talleyrand, wrote to the Allied monarchs and advised them of Napoleon's lack of public support in Paris. Reacting to this news, Alexander persuaded Schwarzenberg to march for Paris.

On March 31, the Allies entered the French capital. That night, the Allied sovereigns met at Talleyrand's house, and agreed that the Allies would not negotiate with Napoleon. They required the French Senate to establish a provisional government, of which, not surprisingly, Talleyrand became the head. The senators then debated Napoleon's status and declared him deposed on April 3. Three days later, the Senate called Louis XVIII to the French throne. It was the same day on which Napoleon, after a vain effort to abdicate in favor of his son, abdicated unconditionally.[47]

The Abdication of the Emperor

To the very end, Napoleon believed that if only the Army had followed him, he could have driven the haggling Allies out of Paris. Marmont, his comrade in arms for 18 years, had de-

ceived him, signing a secret agreement with Schwarzenberg that immobilized one-third of the French troops. Even the indestructible Ney and the stouthearted Lefebvre refused to fight. At last, on the morning of April 6, Napoleon summoned his marshals to Fontainebleau and scornfully announced his willingness to abdicate:

> Neither you nor the army need shed any more blood. Resign yourselves to living under the Bourbons and to serving them faithfully. You wanted peace, now you can have it. But the peace that you long for will destroy more of you as you lie in your feather-beds than war would have done in our bivouacs . . . [48]

The Treaty of Fontainebleau, signed on April 11, 1814 by the Allies and France, decreed Napoleon's fate. He was granted the Mediterranean island of Elba as a sovereign principality and an annual income of 2,000,000 francs, to be paid by the French Government. The Allies also allowed him to retain the title of Emperor and a small guard. His wife, Marie Louise, received the duchies of Parma, Piacenza, and Guastalla, in trust for her son. Napoleon had last seen Marie Louise and his son in January, prior to leaving Paris for the field. He was destined never to see them again.

Napoleon's imperial rule over France had ended.

Notes

[1] There are many accounts of this famous meeting. The best are: Felix Markham, *Napoleon* (New York, 1963), p. 188; Metternich's version in *Memoirs of Prince Metternich, 1773–1835*, ed. by Prince Richard Metternich, trans. by Mrs. Alexander Napier (5 vols.; New York, 1880–1882), I, 182–198; Harold Nicolson, *The Congress of Vienna* (London, 1946), pp. 43–45. The most accurate is probably that in Metternich's *Memoirs*, II, 538–540.

[2] Heinrich von Treitschke, *History of Germany in the 19th Century*, trans. by Eden and Cedar Paul (7 vols.; London, 1915–1919), I, 508.

[3] *Urkundliche Beiträge und Forschungen zur Geschichte des preussischen Heeres*, ed. by German General Staff (Berlin, 1914), II, Appendix I.

[4] *Correspondance de Napoleon I* (32 vols.; Paris, 1858–1870), XXV, No. 20070, p. 346.

[5] A.W. Ward and G.P. Gooch (eds.), *The Cambridge History of British Foreign Policy, 1783–1919* (3 vols.; Westport, Conn., 1971). I, 396–399, 410–411.

[6] Mary Loyd (ed.), *New Letters of Napoleon I* (New York, 1897), p. 306.

[7] A. von Holleben, *Geschichte des Pruhjahrsfeldzüges 1813 und sein Vorgeschichte* (Berlin, 1909), p. 332.

[8] Heinrich Ommen, *Die Kriegführung Erzherzogs-Karl* (Berlin, 1900), pp. 39–40.

[9] Hugo Kerchnawe, *Feldmarschall Karl Fürst zu Schwarzenberg* (Vienna, 1913), p. 139.

[10] U. von Prokesch-Ostens, *Denkwürdigkeiten aus dem Leben des Feldmarschalls Fürst Karl zu Schwarzenberg* (Vienna, 1861), pp. 179–180.

[11] Felix Theodor von Berhardi, *Denkwürdigkeiten aus dem Leben des kaiserl. russ. Generals von der Infanterie Carl Friedrich Grafen von Toll* (4 vols.; Leipzig, 1856–1858), III, 21–23.

[12] Wilhelm Oncken, *Oestereich und Preussen im Befreiungskriege, Urkundliche Aufschlüsse über die politische Geschichte des Jahres 1813* (2 vols.; Berlin, 1876–1879), II, 423–426.

[13] J.A.C. Pflugk-Hartung, *Das Befreiungsjahr, 1813* (Berlin, 1913), pp. 229–231.

[14] *Ibid.*

[15] Johann Joseph Radetzky von Radetz, *Dei k. k. österreichische Feldmarschall Graf Radetzky. Eine biographische Skizze* (Stuttgart, 1858), pp. 159–160.

[16] Oskar Regele, *Radetzky* (Vienna, 1957), p. 124.

[17] Ernest F. Henderson, *Blücher and the Uprising of Prussia Against Napoleon, 1806–1815* (New York, 1911), p. 115.

[18] G.H. Pertz, and Hans Delbrück, *Das Leben des Feldmarschalls Grafen Neithardt von Gneisenau* (5 vols.; Berlin, 1864–1880), I, 301–302.

[19] Bronsart von Schellendorf, *The Duties of the General Staff* (London, 1905), p. 21.

[20] Gordon Craig, *The Politics of the Prussian Army* (New York, 1964), pp. 62–63.

[21] J.F.C. Fuller, *A Military History of the Western World* (3 vols.; New York 1954–1956), II, 467.

[22] *Correspondance*, XXVI, No. 20398, pp. 78–79.

[23] Wolfgang von Groote and Klaus-Jürgen Muller (eds.), *Napoleon I und das Militärwesen seiner Zeit* (Freiburg, 1968), p. 39.

[24] Regele, *Radetzky*, p. 118.

[25] E. von Glaise Horstenau, *Feldzug von Dresden*, Vol. III of *Befreiungskriege, 1813–1814*, ed. by Austrian Kriegsarchiv (Vienna, 1913), p. 27.

[26] Bernhardi, *Denkwürdigkeiten von Toll*, III, 144.

[27] F.K. zu Schwarzenberg, *Briefe des Feldmarschals Fursten Schwarzenberg an seine Frau, 1799–1816*, ed. by J.F. Novak (Vienna, 1913), p. 333.

[28] Kerchnawe, *Feldmarschall Karl Fürst zu Schwarzenberg*, pp. 166–167.

[29] *Die Befreiungskriege*, ed. by the German Association for Military Policy and Science (Berlin, 1938), pp. 62–63.

[30] *Kreigsgeschichtliche Einzelschriften*, ed. by the Military History Section of the Great General Staff (9 vols.; Berlin, 1885–1914), I, No. 5, p. 53.

[31] Rudolf Friederich, *Geschichte des Herbstfeldzuges, 1813*, in *Geschichte der Befreiungskriege, 1813–1815* (9 vols.; Berlin, 1903–1909), I, 235–237.

[32] Johann Gustav Droysen, *Das Leben des Feldmarschalls Grafen York von Wartenburg* (3 vols.; Berlin, 1851–1852), II, 262.

[33] Wolfgang von Unger, *Blücher* (2 vols.; Berlin, 1907–1908), II, 80.

[34] Hugo Kerchnawe, *Radetzky: Eine Militarische Biographische Studie* (Prague, 1944), pp. 184–185.

[35] Pertz and Delbrück, *Das Leben Gneisenau*, III, 311.

[36] Unger, *Blücher*, II, 91.

[37] Pertz and Delbrück, *Das Leben Gneisenau*, III, 318.

[38] Friederich, *Geschichte des Herbstfeldzuges, 1813*, II, 321.

[39] M.R. von Hoen, *Feldzug von Leipzig*, vol. V of *Befreiungskriege, 1813–1814*, ed. by Austrian Kriegsarchiv (Vienna, 1913), p. 34.

[40] *Correspondance*, XXVI, No. 20718, pp. 303–304.

[41] *Ibid.*, No. 20775, p. 339.

[42] Friederich, *Geschichte des Herbstfeldzuges, 1813*, II, 432.

[43] Bernhardi, *Denkwürdigkeiten von Toll*, III, 424.

[44] *Correspondance*, XXVI, No. 20805, p. 360.

[45] Markham, *Napoleon*, p. 198.

[46] Johann Joseph Radetzky von Radetz, *Denkschriften Militärisch-politischen Inhalts, aus dem handschriftlichen Nachlass des . . . Grafen Radetzky* (Stuttgart, 1858), pp. 253–255.

[47] Georges Lefebvre, *Napoleon* (2 vols.; London, 1969), II, 351–352.

[48] Octave Aubry, *Napoleon*, trans. by M. Crosland and S. Road (New York, 1964), p. 312.

The Downfall of Napoleon at Waterloo

8

Accompanied by a small band of troops, Napoleon escaped from the island of Elba on February 26, 1815, landed in the Gulf of Juan four days later, and marched for Paris. Within a week he encountered opposition—a battalion of regulars deployed across the road near Grenoble. Would they join him or remain loyal to the King? The major in command of the battalion let it be known that he was determined to follow orders. A shiver of anticipation ran through the ranks. In the distance they could clearly make out the familiar figure of their erstwhile chief walking at the head of the column. As the distance closed, commands rang out. Napoleon stepped forward, and finally the major shouted: "Fire!" Not one musket was raised. "Soldiers," Napoleon called, "if there is one among you who wants to kill his Emperor, he can do so. Here I am." In reply, they roared, "Vive l'Empereur" and ran forward to embrace him.[1]

The Congress of Vienna

It is almost axiomatic that only great dangers stir coalitions to concerted action. The events that followed Napoleon's abdication proved no exception. The Peace of Paris, signed on May 30, 1814, had referred the settlement of Europe's wartime differences to a congress, which was to meet at Vienna in October. The victors would negotiate the peacetime balance of power in the cultured atmosphere of the Austrian capital. From all over Europe, emperors and kings, princes and dukes, barons and counts converged on Vienna to press their claims for territory and influence. Their mood was expectant, almost carefree; the city was like a carnival. However, the unity that the Allies had briefly displayed on the battlefield promptly vanished in the drawing rooms of the diplomats. With Napoleon safely caged on Elba, every nation could now pursue its own interests without fear of interference from the "God of War."

Vive l'Empereur!

Castlereagh arrived in Vienna hoping to win acceptance of his formula of a "just equilibrium," in which Prussia and Austria were to form a strong counterweight against French or Russian imperialism. Alexander claimed the right to settle the future of Poland and demanded the restoration of that Polish territory previously ceded to Prussia and Austria. Metternich, ever playing the double game, objected strongly to Russian expansion into Poland, and at the same time opposed Prussia's acquisition of Saxony. Prussian interests lay somewhere between Frederick William's almost childlike dependence on the Tsar and the independent threats of the Prussian General Staff that denial of Prussian claims on Saxony would be tantamount to war. The resulting deadlock posed a problem that only the most skillful of negotiators could resolve. The situation was made to order for Talleyrand.

The French Minister's bold solution to the impasse was to propose a secret military alliance to Metternich and Castlereagh. In January 1815, the three ministers agreed to a treaty in which they promised one another mutual support if any of their countries were attacked. Because France was no longer diplomatically isolated, Talleyrand wrote to the French King, "The coalition is dissolved."[2] This would not be true for long.

The news of Napoleon's escape from Elba reached Vienna early in the morning of the same day that Napoleon confronted loyalist troops at Grenoble. A servant awakened Metternich, who later wrote in his memoirs: "I was dressed in a few minutes, and before eight o'clock I was with the Emperor [of Austria]."[3] Within an hour, Metternich had secured an agreement between Francis, Alexander, and Frederick William. War was subsequently declared.

In his memoirs, Metternich recorded the conversation with Talleyrand that took place that day:

> *Talleyrand:* Do you know where Napoleon is going?
>
> *Metternich:* The dispatch does not say anything about it.
>
> *Talleyrand:* He will embark somewhere on the coast of Italy, and throw himself into Switzerland.
>
> *Metternich:* He will go straight to Paris.[4]

If Metternich had the clearer view of Napoleon's intentions, Talleyrand had the correct solution to the problem. Remembering his humiliation in 1809, and weighing every word for precise effect, he personally drafted the declaration of war:

> The Powers declare that by breaking the agreement which had established him on the island of Elba, Napoleon has destroyed the sole legal title to which his existence was bound; that by reappearing in France, he has placed himself beyond civic and social relations, and that, as an enemy and disturber of the peace of the world, he has delivered himself up to public vengeance.[5]

For the first time, the coalition had acted decisively and firmly.

Meanwhile, true to Metternich's prediction, the "disturber of the peace" was marching on Paris. Louis XVIII, who had found the nation largely indifferent to his return a year earlier, now discovered that the middle class, the Army, and the Marshallate were all unwilling to stand by him. Michel Ney rode out of Paris swearing his hatred of the "adventurer" and promising to "bring him back in an iron cage."[6] Napoleon knew Ney better, and wrote to his former marshal that he was counting on his support: " . . . come join me at Chalon. I will receive you as I did on the day after the Battle on the Moskva."[7] The old magic was too much for Ney, a man whose supreme loyalties had been forged in the heat of Europe's most spectacular battles. The memories of Ulm, Jena, Eylau, and Borodino overrode his better judgment, and he promptly joined Napoleon, proclaiming that "the cause of the Bourbons is lost forever."[8]

The news of Ney's defection convinced the King that his cause was indeed lost, and he fled to Belgium, leaving Paris once more to Napoleon. Carnot, Fouché, and Caulaincourt rejoined the Emperor as ministers; Davout, Soult, and Suchet returned to the army. However, many famous names were missing: Berthier and Augereau were inactive; Marmont, Victor, St. Cyr, Oudinot, and MacDonald could not be trusted because of their support of the Bourbons; Murat promised his loyalty, but was spurned by his brother-in-law after launching a premature attack into Italy that served only to announce the militance of Napoleon's new regime; and Massena, the oldest of the marshals, remained inactive. Although times had changed since the *Grande Armée* had roamed the northern plains of Europe, Napoleon's habits remained unchanged. Well aware that the Allies would soon move against him, he immediately set in motion plans to improvise a new army.

The Opposing Strategies

Allied Agreement

Though wary of Napoleon's potential strength, the Allies were alert to his weaknesses. Berthier, who helped escort King Louis XVIII out of France, was quoted in April as saying that Napoleon had only a small army, and that he was short of both money and guns. However, Berthier predicted that "If you give him time, he will be able to appear with large masses."[9] Meanwhile, Wellington rode for Brussels to assume command of the Anglo-Dutch army,* and Blücher received command of the Prussian Army. Russian formations bound for home received orders to turn back; Schwarzenberg assumed command on the Rhine. Altogether, the four great powers had promised 450,000 men backed by British gold; the smaller states were to contribute a quarter of a million more. At the end of May, reliable sources in France estimated that Napoleon's army was composed of 280,000 men, many of whom were immobilized for want of clothing and arms.

Under these circumstances, Wellington judged that an immediate offensive with all available forces was the best course of action. Blücher concurred. In Vienna, however, more conservative counsels prevailed. The Austrians preferred to insure an overwhelming superiority of combat power before invading France; Alexander wanted Russian soldiers to be in on the kill. Moreover, until June, it was uncertain whether Napoleon would attack or keep peace with his neighbors.

---

*This formation was actually a mixture of British, Dutch, and German forces that were of uneven experience and were variously trained and organized.

At length, a plan was formulated, apparently heavily influenced by Gneisenau. The three forward armies, commanded by Wellington, Blücher, and Schwarzenberg, would enter France and drive for Paris, heedless of each other's progress. The reserve army (Russian) would prepare to reinforce success, cut off French communications, or rescue one of the forward armies if it suffered a reverse. "This plan," Gneisenau observed, "is founded on the numerical superiority of the Allied armies."[10] Considering this substantial superiority, it is all the more evident that Napoleon's hope hung on a slender thread.

French Deficiencies and Napoleon's Plan

While the armies of Europe converged on France, Napoleon threw himself into the task of mobilization. Barely 200,000 men strong in March, the French Army counted less than 60,000 in the ranks; 33,000 were on furlough, and 85,000 had deserted.[11] It was not a question merely of filling out an existing army; it was necessary to create a new one. In spite of this shortage of men, Napoleon shrank from ordering conscription, correctly inferring that Frenchmen would prefer to volunteer rather than be drafted to defend the homeland.

In addition to being reduced in numbers, the Army was virtually unequipped with arms. There were thousands of artillery pieces in the armories, but at least half a million projectiles were needed, not to mention horses and harness. Muskets were available for less than half the men who entered the depots. Peasants were offered rewards for renovating fowling pieces; locksmiths and cabinet-makers worked with gunsmiths to turn out additional pieces. In spite of herculean efforts to restore weapons, outfit cavalry, and renovate fortresses, there was still a glaring shortage of men and arms when the army took the field in June. For the entire army, less than 1,000 shoes remained in reserve. *Cuirassier* squadrons remained idle in the depots waiting for *cuirasses,** until Napoleon ordered them to the field, asserting that "a man can fight without a cuirass."[12]

Napoleon's most pressing task was to find experienced men to fill the key positions in both the Army and the Ministry of War. Davout was ideally suited for the administrative requirements of Minister of War. His selection for that post, however, created a gap in the field commands. None of the original corps commanders remained, except Soult, and Napoleon chose this veteran campaigner to fill Berthier's vacant position as chief of staff.† At the end of May, Ney was still unfit for field duty, and there was no adequate re-

placement for Murat. Napoleon worked desperately to place the right men in the proper positions. He assigned Grouchy, who had served valiantly at Eylau, Friedland, and Borodino, to command the cavalry. To the crude and insubordinate Vandamme, who had performed well as a division commander under Soult at Austerlitz and under Lefebvre at Abensberg-Eggmühl, as well as having distinguished himself as a corps commander in the Leipzig Campaign, went the command of one corps. Generals Jean B. D'Erlon, Henri C. Reille, M.E. Gérard, and the Count of Lobau—all competent division commanders but untested at corps level—were assigned to command the others. For the first time in over a decade, the French Army would march into battle with untried leaders in key positions. As in the Marengo Campaign, Napoleon would have to depend on his own judgment and stamina to make up the difference.

In the area of experience among the soldiers of the ranks, France still held primacy. Most of the soldiers were veterans. They, like their junior leaders, had learned the art of warfare on battlegrounds in nearly every corner of the Continent. There was no need to instruct a man like Coignet, who had survived the retreat from Moscow, on the arts of soldiering. Men like Coignet, however, were quick to note that the spirit of earlier times was missing. When Napoleon called on his men to swear their defense of their regimental eagles, "the vows were made without warmth; there was but little enthusiasm: the shouts were not like those of Austerlitz and Wagram, and the Emperor perceived it."[13] Although there was great talent in the Army, it was an army that lacked confidence in its leaders and itself. It was capable, wrote one French authority, "of heroic efforts and furious impulses. . . . Never before had Napoleon an instrument of war, which was at once so formidable, and so fragile."[14]

The greatest deficiency of Napoleon's Army of the North, as he titled it, was not in weaponry, organization, or experience, but in size. It was common knowledge in Paris that the Allies could have over 700,000 men on a wartime footing within two months after declaring against the "Corsican Usurper." After deducting minimum essential requirements to guard the Rhine, the Alps, and the Italian frontier, Napoleon would have barely 160,000 men in reserve. *(See Atlas Map No. 62.)* At the same time, the Vendée erupted in revolt and a corps was diverted to quell it. To secure Paris, 20,000 more were required. Napoleon's mobile striking force was too small to stand up to the Allied formations. Speed would have to multiply its numbers.

Few commanders have faced more overwhelming odds. Not only did France encounter opponents who held a 4 to 1 superiority, but her opponents were also united as never before in their resolve to banish from Europe the man who in their minds was the "heir to the Revolution." Unable to wait

---

*A *cuirass* is a metal breastplate worn by heavy cavalrymen.

†This was an unfortunate choice. Soult proved to be neither diligent nor competent in this position.

PROCLAMATION

DU

MINISTRE DE LA GUERRE

Aux Sous-officiers et Soldats en congé ou en retraite dans l'intérieur de la France.

Vous avez voulu votre Empereur; il est arrivé vous l'avez secondé de tous vos efforts. Venez afin d'être tout prêts à défendre la patrie contre des ennemis qui voudraient se mêler de régler les couleurs que nous devons porter, de nous imposer des Souverains et de nous dicter des constitutions. Dans ces circonstances, c'est un devoir pour tous les Français déjà accoutumés au métier de la guerre, d'accourir sous les drapeaux. Présentez une frontière d'airain à nos ennemis, et apprenez-leur que nous sommes toujours les mêmes.

Soldats, soit que vous ayez obtenu des congés absolus ou limités, soit que vous ayez obtenu votre retraite (que vous conserveriez toujours), si vos blessures sont cicatrisées, si vous êtes en état de servir, venez; l'honneur, l'Empereur, la patrie, vous appellent. Quels reproches n'auriez-vous pas à vous faire, si cette belle patrie était encore ravagée par ces soldats que vous avez vaincus tant de fois, et si l'étranger venait effacer la France de la carte de l'Europe!

Paris, le 10 avril 1815.

Le Maréchal Prince D'ECKMUHL.

A PARIS, DE L'IMPRIMERIE IMPÉRIALE. Avril 1815.

Proclamation by the French Minister of War, Asking for Volunteers, April 10, 1815

for his armies to reach full strength, Napoleon was forced to choose between two unpromising courses of action.* His first option was to adopt a defensive posture and, using the strategy of maneuver so brilliantly employed in 1814, delay the outcome until his armies were larger. By so doing, he would force upon his enemies the responsibility for the war by causing them to invade France. In that regard, however, Napoleon was painfully aware that the campaign of 1814 had failed, not on the battlefield, but in Paris. Therefore, it was necessary to consider the alternative.

The offensive had much to offer. By carrying the war to his enemies, Napoleon could dictate the place and time of battle, and thus seek out the weakest links in the encircling formations. By striking first at the nearest of the Allied armies, he might defeat his opponents in detail, postpone the invasion of France, and perhaps even cause a key member of the coalition (such as Austria) to lose stomach for the war. It was a desperate gamble, but Napoleon preferred to accept the risks and capitalize on the hesitations of his slower moving and slower thinking enemies. The decision to attack was entirely in keeping with the strengths and weaknesses of Napoleon's temperament. A trademark of his character was his conviction that to achieve great ends one must hazard great dangers. He did not agonize over the decision.

Napoleon was painfully certain, however, that a military victory would be barren without support from Paris. Even before finalizing his strategy, he addressed the Senate:

> A formidable coalition of kings threatens our independence; their armies are on our frontiers. . . . It is possible that my first duty as prince will soon call me to lead the nation's children into battle for our country. The army and I will do our duty. You, Peers and Representatives, must set for the nation the example of confidence, energy, and patriotism . . . you must be resolved to die rather than survive the dishonor and degradation of France.[15]

Once again, the Napoleon of Arcola, Austerlitz, and Wagram, in defiance of fate, was stirring French emotion and calling for national unity by the appeal to arms.

Napoleon's plan was amazingly simple. *(See Atlas Map No. 63.)* Using the strategy he had employed in Italy almost 20 years before, his army would drive between the Prussian and British forces. Wellington's communications lay to the north through Brussels to Antwerp; Blücher's ran east through Liège. Once separated, the Allies would be forced to fall back in opposite directions. Correctly judging that Schwarzenberg could not move before the end of June, Napoleon planned to defeat the British and Prussians in detail, and

*Napoleon estimated that he might have 800,000 men under arms by October.

then turn east to fight off the Austrians. Although his plan was perilous, it offered the hope of a substantial political byproduct: a decisive win in Belgium would surely unite the French behind him. A success on the battlefield might also bring Austria to the negotiating table.

At no other time in his life did Napoleon show such extraordinary energy. While still managing the mobilization of his military resources and fighting an insurrection in the Vendée, he was compelled simultaneously to commence the deployment of his most ready forces. Furthermore, he had to carry out this deployment in such a way as to avoid unnecessarily alarming his enemies. Security was vital. It could only be achieved by arranging elaborate demonstrations to mislead his opponents, and by hermetically sealing the coasts and frontiers against any communication with the enemy. On June 1, the French Army of the North was cantoned over a frontage of 150 miles. Within two weeks, it had concentrated behind the Sambre River, ready to strike at Wellington and Blücher. The proclamation that Napoleon delivered to his troops as they prepared to cross the Belgian border was stirring, as well as prophetic: "Soldiers, today is the anniversary of Marengo and Friedland, which decided for all time the destiny of Europe. . . . the moment has arrived to conquer or perish."[16]

English and Prussian Preparations

Whereas Napoleon displayed absolute confidence in the condition of his extemporized army, his opponent showed some dissatisfaction with the forces entrusted to their commands. Wellington, in particular, was displeased with his "allied" formation, admitting that "the army is not a very good one," and complaining that "I am overloaded with people I have never seen before."[17] Furthermore, he was concerned about the inability of the Allied supreme command to establish an orderly procedure for procuring supplies, the lack of which encouraged his Dutch troops to "pillage and steal wherever they go."[18] At first, he was also unenthusiastic about the Prussians, apparently believing that "the Republican spirit" tended to undermine their discipline. However, he had considerable respect for Blücher, and, after meeting the Prussian marshal, he seemed to recover his confidence, exclaiming in May, "I am inclined to believe that Blücher and I are so well united, and so strong, that the enemy cannot do us much mischief."[19]

Blücher held a similarly high opinion of his British colleague. He was seriously concerned, however, about the discipline of the Saxons attached to his command. They had a disturbing tendency to mutiny whenever combat appeared to be imminent, and on one occasion broke into his headquarters to protest their integration into the Prussian Army. Moreover, Blücher's view of logistics differed from that of Wellington: Prussians would take their rations where they could find them. Let the French pay to feed the Allies! In spite of these differences and difficulties, Blücher radiated confidence and, according to an aide, "thought of nothing, spoke of nothing, except the great events which would soon occur."[20]

During the first two weeks of June, a steady stream of reports flowed to British and Prussian headquarters concerning French troop movements. These dispatches confirmed the strengthening of French forces in the Givet-Maubeuge area, but gave no clear indication of Napoleon's intentions to attack. On June 12, Gneisenau wrote: "the danger of an attack has almost disappeared."[21] On the following day, Wellington issued a terse report couched in assuring terms:

We have reports of Buonaparte's joining the army and attacking us; but I have accounts from Paris of the 10th, on which day he was still there; and I judge from his

The Duke of Wellington

speech to the legislature that his departure was not likely to be immediate. I think we are now too strong for him here.[22]

Wellington's staff was briefly alert to the possibility of an attack on the fourteenth (the anniversary of Marengo and Friedland). When this date passed without any major change in the situation, however, headquarters in Brussels concluded that the Allies were far too strong in Belgium for Napoleon to tempt fate in that area.

Throughout that day (June 14), however, sufficient evidence had accumulated to suggest a reappraisal. Blücher's forward units picked up a French drum major who had deserted with the news that the French were rapidly concentrating. At noon on the same day, warning orders were sent to Generals Bülow and Johann A. Thielmann: "enemy information indicates that Napoleon concentrates at Maubeuge, and it appears he intends to begin his offensive against the Netherlands."[23] Thus, in the Prussian headquarters there was a full awareness of Napoleon's swift concentration, but even Gneisenau was doubtful of the imminence of attack until late that night, when two more deserters stated positively that Napoleon would attack the Prussians on the morning of June 16. Blücher had already retired for the evening. *(See Atlas Map No. 63.)* Rather than awaken him, Gneisenau, on his own initiative, issued the necessary orders for concentration. Generals George D. Pirch and Thielmann promptly set their commands in motion to close on Zieten's corps. Bülow, 45 miles from the scene of action, read Gneisenau's nonimperative orders ("I have the honour humbly to request your Excellency to be kind enough to concentrate the 4th Army Corps . . . .") and decided not to tire his troops with a night march.[24] Napoleon was far away; the movement could wait until the sixteenth.

If there was lack of urgency in Blücher's army, there was downright indolence in Wellington's headquarters. No small part of it was due to the British commander himself. Having made the assumption that Napoleon would not attack, he spent most of June 14 and 15 squiring a succession of women to various social events in Brussels. When a message arrived on the evening of the fifteenth reporting Blücher's concentration around Ligny, Wellington merely ordered a southeastward shift of his forces located west of Brussels, but gave no indication of the purpose of this movement.[25] Having dashed off these orders, he then left for the ball being given by the Duchess of Richmond, where he remained until 2:00 a.m. on the following morning.

At midnight, Wellington received a report that Napoleon had indeed commenced the offensive and was marching not through Maubeuge but through Charleroi. "Napoleon has humbugged me, by God!" he exclaimed, and proceeded to order the Anglo-Dutch army to concentrate at Quatre Bras.[26]

The Battles of
Ligny and Quatre Bras

The French advance caught the Allies with their units badly dispersed, but Napoleon had problems of his own that slowed the French deployment. On June 15, some of his divisions still had not crossed the Sambre River; the army was strung out over 25 miles of road. To add to his worries, a corps chief of staff and a division commander had deserted to the Allies. On the right wing, Emmanuel Grouchy's unhurried move against Blücher's covering force south of Sombreffe aroused Napoleon's displeasure. A quick visit to that sector put new life into the advance, but disclosed the danger that the Prussians might easily slip away if the offensive were not pressed vigorously forward. Meanwhile, Napoleon had appointed Marshal Ney to command the left wing and ordered him to march on Quatre Bras. The plan was to strike for Brussels, severing the Nivelles-Namur highway, the only lateral route by which the Allies could unite.

At midnight, Ney rode into headquarters at Charleroi to confer with Napoleon. Their exact conversation remains unknown. After Ney's departure, Napoleon took a short nap; then, at about 6:00 a.m. on June 16, he sent an important message to his famous marshal, outlining the basis of his plan:

> I have adopted as a general principle, during this campaign, to divide my army into two wings and a reserve. Your wing will be composed of . . . not much less than 45 to 50,000 men. Marshal Grouchy will have about the same force and will command on the right wing. The Guard will form the reserve, and I will employ it on either wing, depending on the situation. . . . Depending on the situation, I may draw forces from one or the other wing, in order to augment the reserve.[27]

From this directive, it appears that Napoleon planned to strike the main blow against Wellington's scattered forces. Ney was to be ready to march on Brussels, which he could easily reach by 7:00 a.m. on June 17. However, sometime during the morning of June 16, Grouchy's cavalry reported that large Prussian columns (the corps of Pirch and Thielmann) were moving west from Namur. Abruptly, Napoleon made up his mind: he would attack Blücher first, and then turn against Wellington.[28]

Gneisenau was not optimistic about the situation. Only two of the four Prussian corps had closed in their assigned positions. The right flank was wide open to envelopment, and even if all the Prussian corps arrived before Napoleon's attack, there were six miles of rolling ground to be occupied. A message from Bülow reported that the IV Corps' arrival could not be expected before June 17. The decision to stand and fight, therefore, depended on the extent of the support provided by the British.

During the evening of June 15, the Prussian liaison officer had forwarded a report on Wellington's intentions. This report arrived on the morning of June 16, and stated that Wellington had decided to concentrate for a rendezvous with the Prussians:

> As soon as the moon rises, the Reserve will begin its march, and if the enemy does not attack at the same time at Nivelles, then tomorrow [June 16] the Duke will be in the Nivelles area with his entire force in order to support Your Excellency . . .[29]

Blücher and Gneisenau could not know that Wellington's reserve was at least ten miles away from Nivelles; it was another six and a half miles to Quatre Bras, and seven more to Ligny. Nor could they know that Wellington was still ignorant of the exact dispositions of his own troops. Placing faith in the promise of their ally, however, they resolved to stand at Ligny and to deliver battle.

Shortly after noon on June 16, the Prussian army (minus Bülow's corps) was formed for action. At about this time, Wellington arrived to confer. He apparently expressed some distaste for the Prussian tactic of taking position in plain view of the French. "What would you like for me to do?" he then asked Gneisenau. The Prussian chief of staff thought briefly of asking the British to strike against Napoleon's rear, but he knew that time was short, and could see the French already mustering for the assault. He therefore requested Wellington to reinforce the Prussian right flank by a direct march via Quatre Bras. According to some sources, Wellington replied, "Well, I'll come, provided I am not attacked myself." The British commander then rode back to his army, just as the first cannon shots announced the French attack at Ligny.[30] (*See Atlas Map No. 64.*)

Sustained by Napoleon's belief that Blücher's forces were half the strength of his own, the French advanced with two full corps in line. Vandamme's assault promptly cleared Zieten's troops from the southernmost villages, but could make no further progress. Gérard's corps advanced against the town of Ligny and stalled. As the fight swayed back and forth, Blücher steadily committed his reserves into the fight around his open right flank. Watching the battle from a windmill south of Ligny, Napoleon sensed that the moment had come to break through the weakened Prussian center at Ligny. Listening for the noise of Ney's action to the northwest, he had heard no sound of artillery, and therefore concluded that Ney had taken Quatre Bras without a fight. To complete the destruction of Blücher's hard-pressed force, he now ordered Ney to maneuver to the east and envelop the

Napoleon at the Battle of Ligny, June 1815

Prussian right flank. "The fate of France is in your hands," Soult wrote to Ney.[31]

If so, the fate of France was in very bad hands. In spite of Napoleon's specific orders for a vigorous advance, Ney had spent most of the day in puzzled inactivity. At the most, he had only to contend with some 8,000 troops under the command of the Prince of Orange, but he had failed to collect his own force in time, and thus had to send his units into action piecemeal. After a brief clash, the Prince of Orange retired to Quatre Bras. There, the arrival of Wellington spurred a renewed defense, which held Ney in check for the rest of the day. Ney's rearward corps, commanded by D'Erlon, merely waited for orders.

D'Erlon's corps finally got under way about noon, but shortly became detoured by a misunderstanding that materially influenced the outcome of the day's fighting. The corps had halted once and resumed the march, whereupon it was diverted by fresh orders from an unidentified staff officer to reinforce Napoleon's attack on Ligny. Unknown to Ney or Napoleon, D'Erlon's troops swung to the east and, at about 5:30 p.m., bore down on the smoke-shrouded action at

Ligny—not against Blücher's rear, but on Vandamme's left flank!

Just as he was preparing to launch the Guard to smash through the Prussian center, Napoleon's plans were foiled by the unexpected appearance of D'Erlon's formation. Was it Ney or Wellington? The attack was suspended while an aide galloped west to determine the identity of the intruders. Just as the messenger reached D'Erlon's corps, the lead columns turned back again to the west. Ney had finally discovered where his misplaced corps was and had recalled it. The enforced delay caused by this combination of error and mischance allowed Blücher time to prepare a counterattack, which he decided to lead personally. Meanwhile, swallowing his disgust at Ney's amateur generalship, Napoleon grimly resolved to attack at Ligny, regardless of the consequences.

French artillery exploded into action against the town of Ligny, followed by an assault made by the entire Guard infantry. The French movement was shrouded in near darkness because of a thunderstorm that had begun simultaneously with the attack. The Prussian infantry was already badly depleted; Wellington clearly would not come. Blücher now

Blücher's Fall, June 1815

drew his sword and led his remaining cavalry in a dauntless charge. "Stand fast, brave lads," he shouted to the faltering battalions in the burning town.[32] Led by their chief, the Prussian squadrons swept down the slopes, plunged into the melee, and dispersed in the confusion. (Later it was reported that Blücher's horse had fallen and that the old warrior had been trampled underfoot.) The Prussian lines collapsed and the scattered units fell back into the protection of the night.

While Napoleon smashed the Prussian defenses, Ney and Wellington engaged in a mutual exercise of piecemeal attacks at Quatre Bras. The result was a standoff until Ney worked himself into such a temper that his men feared him more than they feared the British guns. A final headlong cavalry attack actually penetrated to the outskirts of Quatre Bras, but because they were unsupported by infantry, the horsemen had to fight their way back out again. Wellington's counterattack, which ended at nightfall, restored the status quo. On balance, both sides had lost equally at Quatre Bras.

At Ligny, Blücher had suffered a serious and bloody defeat. Not only were their losses twice Napoleon's, but the Prussians had also lost their revered commander, leaving the fragments of the splintered army without direction. In the absence of Blücher, however, Gneisenau proved capable of assuming the mantle of leadership. In spite of the severe losses suffered, he resolutely ordered the corps commanders to direct the retreat to the north toward Tilly—not to the east to Liège. It was a courageous decision that would earn Gneisenau

undying fame, as well as one that the pursuing French would rue forever.*

The Pursuit That Failed

"Fortune is like a woman," Napoleon wistfully observed some years later from his island prison in the Atlantic, "if you let her slip one day, you must not expect to find her again the next."[33] Unaccountably, the Emperor who had once boasted that he would "never lose a minute" had let both the Prussian and British armies slip from his grasp on June 17. His own lethargy contributed to their escape.

On the morning after the fight at Ligny, Napoleon was troubled by incomplete information. *(See Atlas Map No. 65.)* He knew that he had won a resounding victory over the Prussians, but he had no way of knowing the extent of his win or the status of Blücher's crippled army. One corps commander (Pajol) sent an early morning report that the Prussians were in full retreat toward Namur and Liège. Ney reported that only eight regiments of enemy infantry and 2,000 horsemen remained at Quatre Bras. After walking among the wounded on the battlefield at Ligny and engaging in a spirited discussion of French politics with Grouchy, Napoleon at length resolved

*Wellington termed Gneisenau's action "the decisive moment of the century."

to turn his main force against Wellington. Grouchy, he decided, would be assigned the task of pursuing the Prussian army.

At about 11:00 a.m., Napoleon informed Grouchy of his mission and placed under his direction two infantry and two cavalry corps—the largest command that the recently promoted marshal had yet handled.* According to Grouchy, Napoleon then added, "all the probabilities lead me to believe that it is upon the Meuse that Blücher is making his retreat."[34] It was upon the Dyle, however, that the Prussians were making their way. This was the kind of error often caused by uncertain knowledge of the situation. Grouchy proceeded to compound the initial mistake by conducting a fumbling, dilatory march that reached Gembloux—six miles from the battlefield—only that night (June 17).

After Grouchy's departure, Napoleon apparently had misgivings about his subordinate's mission. He later wrote a clarification of the marshal's task, directing him to "reconnoiter in the direction of Namur and Maastricht" and to "pursue the enemy . . . and inform me of his movements. It is important to discover what Blücher and Wellington are trying to do; whether they propose to unite their armies in order to cover Brussels and Liège, in trying the fate of another battle."[35] His mind numbed by the unaccustomed responsibilities of his sizable command, Grouchy failed to grasp the urgency of the mission. He was also baffled as to the Prussians' exact line of retreat. Two hours before darkness, his troops came to a halt. A heavy rain poured throughout the night, encouraging the marshal to postpone any further pursuit until the following morning, when the situation would be clearer. However, Grouchy was evidently alert to the danger that Blücher's army might yet join Wellington's. At 10:00 p.m., he wrote to Napoleon:

> It appears according to all the reports that . . . the Prussians have divided themselves into two columns; one has taken the route to Wavre. . . . One may perhaps infer from this that a portion are going to join Wellington, and that the center, which is Blücher's army, is retiring on Liège. . . [36]

Whatever he may have thought, Grouchy failed to act. Instead of ordering his troops to march directly on Wavre, he waited out the night. On the following morning, when he did move, he pursued not toward Wavre, but toward Liège.

Meanwhile, at the outskirts of Quatre Bras, Wellington stamped impatiently back and forth while awaiting the first reports of Blücher's fate. When the bad news arrived at about 7:30 a.m. on June 17, he could hardly conceal his chagrin. "Old Blücher has received a damned good mauling," he dryly observed. "As he has fallen back, we must fall back also."[37] Shortly afterwards, however, a messenger arrived from Gneisenau informing Wellington of the Prussian retreat on Wavre and asking for clarification of the British commander's intentions.† Wellington immediately responded with a decision that must rank with Gneisenau's earlier retreat order in its dire import for the French:

> I am going back into position at Mont St. Jean, and I shall await Napoleon there in order to deliver battle to him, if I am supported even by a single Prussian corps.[38]

While Ney's men ate their morning soup, Wellington's forces defiled to the rear, covered by the cavalry of Lord Uxbridge.

At mid-afternoon, Napoleon arrived on the scene. Seeing at a glance that Ney had utterly failed to carry out his task, he gathered together a few squadrons of cavalry and artillery in a vain attempt to halt Wellington's withdrawal. At that moment, the rains began, impeding Napoleon's futile pursuit. He was too late. The battle with Wellington would have to be fought somewhere near Waterloo.

The Battle of Waterloo

Sunday, June 18, dawned sunny and clear, to the immense relief of at least 200,000 rain-drenched men. While soldiers from all three armies stretched their stiffened muscles and dried steaming clothes before hundreds of smoking campfires, their officers were hard at work reconnoitering and planning. *(See Atlas Map No. 66.)* The terrain in this area south of Brussels is open and rolling; occasional masks, hollows, and ravines are almost invisible from a distance. Small patches of woods break the otherwise smooth appearance of the land. The low ground is invariably wet, especially after hard rains. The major features to which both attacker and defender had to pay careful notice were the series of undulating plateaus, which crisscrossed the high road between Charleroi and Brussels, and the sturdy walled hamlets that dotted the countryside.

Wellington's defenses took full account of every terrain detail. His main line of resistance lay along the crest of the plateau described by the country road running from Wavre to

---

*Emmanuel Grouchy was a superb cavalryman who lacked confidence in his own abilities for high command. In 25 years of service he received nearly two dozen wounds, but he was a "man of a single hour, a single maneuver, a single effort." Clearly, he was not the man to whom Napoleon should have entrusted the pursuit of the Prussians.

† During the night, Blücher had been carried to a farmhouse north of Ligny, where by pure chance he met Gneisenau. According to some sources, the old marshal revived after a brisk rubdown of gin and rhubarb, and confirmed Gneisenau's decisions with the words, "Well, we've taken a hard blow but tomorrow we'll straighten out the dent."

Château de Goumont in 1970 (View From the West)

Braine L'Alleud. However, the Duke was careful to hold part of his main force and his reserves on the reverse slope of the plateau, where they were concealed from enemy observation and protected from direct fire.* To further strengthen his defenses, he had posted strong points in advance of the main defense line. The most important of these was located forward of the British western wing at the Château de Goumont (also called Hougomont), an enclosed brick and stone redoubt, made nearly impervious by ditches, thick hedges, an orchard, and garden walls. Directly in front of Wellington's center, and only several hundred yards from it, was a second fortified outpost, La Haye Sainte. Of brick construction, La Haye Sainte was no less stout an obstacle than the larger outpost at Goumont. Farther to the east were several smaller strongholds covering Wellington's east flank. Because of Blücher's proximity on this side, Wellington was less concerned about its protection. His chief preoccupation was with the preparation of his main defenses for a fight to the finish. He neither considered nor planned for a retreat.

The French positions lay along the next low plateau to the south, no more than 1,500 yards from the British. Napoleon had expressed some anxiety during the evening that Wellington might decamp, but a morning reconnaissance disclosed adequate evidence—cavalry pickets, campfires, and occasional flashes of red coats—to convince him that his enemy intended to stand and offer battle. The French-held plateau was slightly higher than that of the British, but not high enough to reveal the extent of Wellington's reverse-slope defenses. Napoleon's main concern was with the soft

* Wellington had perfected this technique in Spain.

ground at the bottom of the valley that separated the two armies. Cavalry and artillery would be slowed; therefore, Napoleon decided to forego his preferred envelopment, choosing instead to attack Wellington's center in an attempt to rupture the British position.

Meanwhile, still aching from his mishap at Ligny, Blücher was riding up and down along his Prussian columns, urging his tired men on. *(See Atlas Map No. 67.)* The miry route from Wavre to Mont St. Jean greatly retarded the march. However, Blücher had the satisfaction of learning from his patrols that the French had no large formations stationed between the Dyle River and Lasne Creek. Early in the previous evening he had sent a message to Wellington, informing him of his resolve to "arrive at the head of my troops to attack the right flank of the enemy, if Napoleon attempts to move against the Duke." Having pledged his support, the old soldier now put the spurs to his troops: "Forward, lads! I have promised my brother Wellington. You don't want to cause me to break my promise, do you?"[39]

While the three armies prepared to come to grips with each other on the morning of June 18, Grouchy delayed the departure of his 33,000 troops from Gembloux. At 7:30 a.m., he finally ordered a march toward Wavre. By 11:00 a.m., two Prussian corps had already passed through that town, and Grouchy's advance guard was still two miles south of it. Shortly, the noise of gunfire could be plainly heard to the northwest, and his subordinates urged Grouchy to "march to the sound of the guns." Irritated, the marshal refused, standing on the principle of seniority and the letter of his orders.

Observing Wellington's positions from La Belle Alliance, Napoleon had made the decision to postpone the main assault from 9:00 a.m. until around noon. *(See Atlas Map No. 66.)* He wanted to allow more time for the ground to dry. He ordered Reille to launch a limited supporting attack toward Goumont at 11:30 a.m., and told Ney to stand by to support or lead D'Erlon's attack on Mont St. Jean. Although possession of the plateau of Mont St. Jean was the primary French objective, the contest for Château de Goumont actually claimed the larger share of the initial French effort.

Reille's attack commenced as ordered, and within an hour the woods south of the château were in French hands. The leading division commander had been told merely to keep the château under fire. Now, he decided to assault it. Wellington poured artillery fire into the attacker's ranks, then committed part of his reserve to reinforce the strongpoint. Reille, in turn, reinforced from his reserve, and the battle blazed out of control. As a result, nearly half of Reille's corps became snarled at the château, fighting for an outpost of dubious value to the French.

At this point, Napoleon noticed the appearance of a large formation of troops on the forward slopes of the hill to the east of Lasne. *(Not shown on Map.)* A cavalry patrol was dispatched and returned with prisoners from Bülow's corps who confirmed that Blücher had given Grouchy the slip and was marching to Wellington's assistance. The most critical decision of Napoleon's career now lay plainly before him. As yet, the two main forces (72,000 French and 68,000 Anglo-Dutch) were only partially committed. There was still plenty of time to disengage, fall back toward Charleroi, and seek battle again under more favorable circumstances. In a strategic sense, however, Napoleon could not delay a battle with Wellington very long—his time was running short. Every day wasted on indecisive maneuver merely allowed Schwarzenberg's army of 250,000 men to move that much closer to Paris. Most important, he sensed that public opinion in France would not wait either. Instinctively, he knew that the battle had to be fought out then and there, on the slopes of Mont St. Jean and La Haye Sainte. "This morning we still had ninety chances out of a hundred in our favor," Napoleon calculated. "Bülow's arrival cost us thirty, but we still have sixty against forty."[40] Disguising even the slightest trace of anxiety, he ordered the main attack to begin.

Eighty cannon thundered out over the plains for half an hour, but most of Wellington's men were hidden behind the crest of the plateau. D'Erlon's cheering and shouting men then advanced through the wet cornfields in immense columns that soon became crowded together. The first wave of the attack sloshed around the strongpoint of La Haye Sainte, putting one Belgian brigade to flight, while the British troops stationed farther back jeered at allies and enemies alike. The assault slowed when it reached the hedge-lined road where the British were waiting. A well-timed volley staggered the French as they crested the hill. A savage counterattack by Uxbridge's cavalry drove the attackers back. While D'Erlon gathered his corps together, Wellington sent more troops forward to stiffen the defense of La Haye Sainte. At about 4:00 p.m., the attack began again, accompanied by heavy artillery barrages fired by both sides. Wellington's center gradually disintegrated under the shellfire and began to withdraw. *(See Atlas Map No. 68.)*

At this point, Ney intervened in the battle. Believing that Wellington's line was faltering, he yielded to instinct and sent forward the cavalry of Milhaud's corps, unsupported by infantry or artillery, in a vain charge against Wellington's right center, which was yet undamaged. Milhaud's horsemen moved past the still-contested La Haye Sainte, picked up speed as they dipped into a small hollow, and crested the hill to discover the British drawn up in squares, bristling with muskets and cannon. A British officer described the French cavalry charge: "The very earth seemed to vibrate beneath their thundering tramp. . . . Every man in the front ranks knelt, and a wall bristling with steel, held together by steady

hands, presented itself to the infuriated *cuirassiers*."[41] Another vicious counterattack by Uxbridge's splendid horsemen stymied the French cavalry. One member of the Scot's Grey's later recalled his fight with half a dozen Frenchmen:

> One made a thrust at my groin. I parried it off and cut him down through the head. A lancer came at me—I threw the lance off by my right side and cut him through the chin and upwards through the teeth . . . [42]

An artillery captain described the confrontation between French *cuirassiers* and British 9-pounders:

> Their pace was a slow but steady trot. None of your furious galloping charges was this, but a deliberate advance, at a deliberate pace, as of men resolved to carry their point. . . . the only sound that could be heard from them amidst the incessant roar of battle was the low thunder-like reverberation of the ground beneath the simultaneous tread of so many horses. On our part was equal deliberation. Every man stood steadily at his post, the guns ready, loaded with a round—shot first and a case over it; the tubes were in the vents; the port fires glared and sputtered behind the wheels; and my word alone was wanting to hurl destruction on that goodly show of gallant men and noble horses.[43]

Even a Murat could not have broken those tenacious rectangles of men and guns that laced the ground with interlocking bands of fire. Even a Ney could not prevent the pellmell retreat that occurred after four fruitless charges. The piecemeal attack failed dismally against Wellington's carefully prepared and doggedly manned defenses.

By 6:00 p.m., Napoleon was faced with a critical situation. Although Ney had finally taken La Haye Sainte, Wellington's main positions were holding and Blücher's lead corps was across the Lasne River and climbing the slopes of Plancenoit. Reille's corps was wrapped around the château at Goumont. D'Erlon's men were fully committed against La Haye Sainte and along the slopes of Mont St. Jean. Grouchy was apparently out of the action somewhere near Wavre. Only the Guard remained—11 battalions of the most deadly fighters in the world.

If Napoleon had ridden forward and personally committed his Guard, he might well have shattered Wellington's badly weakened center. (It was during this crisis that Wellington was heard to mutter, "Night or Blücher.") Now Napoleon had a more pressing task—to fight off the assault on Plancenoit which, led by Blücher, was already threatening the French rear. Using Lobau's corps and two battalions of the Guard, he managed gradually to force the Prussians back down the hill into the creek bed. This success insured him at least two hours of respite on that side. *(See Atlas Map No. 69.)*

Marshal Ney at the Head of the Guard–Waterloo, June 1815

While Napoleon's attention was diverted by Blücher's threat to the French east flank, the Guard—Napoleon's last resort—passed by default to the command of Ney. That hothead had long since lost any ability to reason. Without thinking, he now sent the Guard infantry into action, battalion by battalion, as they became available. When Napoleon returned from reinforcing the flank against a renewed attack from one of Blücher's corps, the Guard was already gone, having been led by the screaming, cursing, sword-brandishing Ney. Defiance was the best part of Ney, but it was also his greatest flaw. He had totally lost the ability to think under fire.

Again, the fiery marshal became disoriented. Again, he led his men against the strongest part of the British line. Again, British artillery and infantry fire pounded the attacker in front and flank. One eyewitness, a member of the 1st Foot Guards, painted a dramatic picture of the close combat:

> . . . suddenly the firing ceased, and as the smoke cleared away a superb sight opened on us. A close column of Grenadiers (about seventy in front) . . . were

seen ascending the rise. . . . They continued to advance till within fifty or sixty paces of our front, when the Brigade was ordered to stand up. Whether it was from the sudden and unexpected appearance of a Corps so near them, which must have seemed as starting out of the ground, or the tremendous heavy fire we threw into them, *La Garde*, who had never before failed in an attack, *suddenly* stopped.[44]

The repulse of the Guard's last charge marked the end of Napoleon's hopes for victory at Waterloo. The cave-in of the French right flank, which occurred moments later, ended Napoleon's chances of escaping a defeat. "I wish one of these bullets would strike me dead," Ney cried as he led one more futile assault against the unyielding British lines.* Napoleon's thoughts during those fatal minutes when defeat became apparent were not preserved for posterity.

In defeat, Napoleon displayed the calm judgment of the superb commander that he was. Wasting no time on remonstrances or criticism, he ordered the remainder of his Guard to form squares across the road south of La Haye Sainte. Lobau continued to hold Blücher off the French line of retreat while the corps of D'Erlon and Reille withdrew behind the Guard. Even when all their ammunition was gone, the Guard held firm, silent and motionless. The French Empire was no more, but the soul of the *Grande Armée* lived on.

Waterloo may well have been the most fateful and most decisive battle of the nineteenth century. It has also become a synonym for defeat. "What would have happened if . . ." has ever since been one of the favorite games of historians and military buffs.† No one can say "what if," because the alteration of one event would not necessarily have affected the outcome of the battle. The correction of one of Ney's errors might at the same time have rectified an error by Wellington. However, it is possible to trace Napoleon's defeat to its proximate causes. Therein lies an exercise of value for the inquiring mind seeking to understand the great events of our times.

Why did Napoleon lose the battle at Waterloo? Because Grouchy failed to occupy the Prussians! So stated Napoleon at St. Helena. "The conduct of Marshal Grouchy . . . was as unforeseeable as if his army had been surprised by an earthquake and swallowed up."[45]

Neither historian nor military critic can be satisfied with this apologetic excuse. There are only two possible explanations for the failure of Grouchy to carry out his mission. Neither reflects credit on Napoleon. Either the Emperor

---

*In *1815, Waterloo*, Henry Houssaye claims that Ney said something more glorious: "Come and see how a marshal of France can die." In either event, Ney's assaults were futile, and he must have known it.

†The two most rehashed battles in history have surely been Waterloo and Gettysburg. In both, the preponderance of sympathy is for the loser.

British Counterattack Captures French Guns at Waterloo, June 1815

failed to give his cavalry commander the resources and guidance he needed to carry out his semi-independent task, or Grouchy was unfit for the task. Even if one overlooks Napoleon's ill-advised directive ordering Grouchy to advance toward Namur and Liège, the fact remains that Napoleon was responsible for selecting the inexperienced marshal for so critical a mission. The selection of Ney was similarly unwise. Although "the bravest of the brave," Ney was nonetheless a maniac, devoid of judgment on the fields of Mont St. Jean. Inevitably, the critic returns to the same starting point—the mind of Napoleon. Just as his genius carried France to its most glorious victories, his unbridled determination to attempt the impossible plunged the nation into bitter defeat.

Napoleon's unfortunate choice of subordinates, which relegated the dependable Davout to the Ministry of War in Paris, was only one of the many causes of the French defeat in 1815. One must also number among them the overwhelming superiority of Allied forces (at least 800,000 to 280,000 overall, without counting unmobilized reserves). Both Napoleon's inactivity on June 17 and his inability to begin the attack early on June 18 may be cited as critical instances that called for a more dynamic performance on the part of the Emperor. Moreover, during the battle he failed to exercise sufficient control over his subordinates, particularly Ney, Grouchy, and D'Erlon. Although one can offer as an excuse his preoccupation with the right flank, Napoleon also failed to react promptly at the critical time—when Wellington's center was collapsing and the commitment of the Guard could have been decisive. Nor can the critic overlook the performance of the Allied commanders, who Napoleon tended to underestimate. Wellington's choice of position and cool, tenacious defense of it were praiseworthy; and Blücher's indomitable spirit and determination to reinforce Wellington

were crucial to the outcome of the battle. Even if all these cumulative human obstacles to Napoleon's will had been overcome, fortune would still have played its wild card and brought down the storm that turned the ground to mud, impeding the movements of the Emperor's forces. Confronted by these handicaps—numerical inferiority, a shortage of experienced senior officers, and the prospect of facing the indomitable Blücher and the resolute Wellington—and dogged by the weather, the salvation of the French lay in a superior display of generalship by Napoleon. He was good, but on that eighteenth day of June in 1815, he was not good enough.

The Legend of Napoleon

Napoleon's greatest victories were not won on the battlefield. They were won in the annals of history. After the loss at Waterloo, he returned to Paris to find that the mood of France had turned against him. For the second time, he abdicated, this time considering an escape to America. Contrary winds frustrated that plan, and he finally threw himself on the mercy of the British for safe transportation out of France. The British promptly took him aboard one of His Majesty's ships and carried him to the island of St. Helena. *(See Atlas Map No. 70.)*

From this remote exile, the departed Emperor prepared his revenge against the monarchies that had finally overwhelmed him. While three dedicated companions took turns scribbling frantically, Napoleon dictated his memoirs. "I have unscrambled Chaos," he said, "I have cleansed the Revolution, ennobled the common people, and restored the authority of kings." There was just enough truth in these assertions to appeal to those historians of a later generation who would help

THEATRE ROYAL, DRURY-LANE.
THIS EVENING, RULE A WIFE AND HAVE A WIFE.
Leon, Mr. Kean.
To which will be added, CHARLES THE BOLD.

THEATRE ROYAL, COVENT-GARDEN.
THIS EVENING, ISABELLA.
Isabella Miss O'Neill
To which will be added. COMUS.

For the Benefit of Mr BRANDON, Box-Book and House-keeper.
THEATRE-ROYAL, COVENT-GARDEN.
On FRIDAY, June 30, THE DUENNA.
Carlos, Mr. Sinclair, who will Introduce ' Just like Love;'
Clara, Miss Stephens.
In the course of the evening, Black Ey'd Susan', and ' The
Storm,' by Mr. Incledon
With a FARCE and other ENTERTAINMENTS.
Tickets and places to be taken of Mr. Brandon, at the Box-office

ROYAL AMPHITHEATRE, (ASTLEY'S).
THIS EVENING, at half past six precisely, HORSEMAN-
SHIP by Mr. Avery, and a comic Act, by the Clown, Mr. Brown,
A New splendid Serio-Comic Equestrian Pantomime with ex-
traordinary preparations, called The LIFE, DEATH, and RE-
STORATION of the HIGH-METTLED RACER; or, Harle-
quin on Horseback. In the course of twenty one interesting
scenes will be introduced a REAL HORSE RACE, and a
REAL FOX CHACE. A favourite comic Song by Mr. Herring
Equestrian Exercises, by Mr. W. Davis. After which, a Comic
Musical Piece, called KING HENRY VIII AND THE COB-
LER. To conclude with (16th time) THE SAILOR'S LOVE, or
Constancy Rewarded. Second Price at half past eight.

The last Week of the present Arrangements.—The Public are re-
spectfully informed, that in consequence of the extraordinary
expensive Preparations making for a Ship Launch on real Water,
no Aquatic Scene can be exhibited this week.

SADLER'S WELLS.
THIS and 3 following EVENINGS only, a new Dance, called
THE PLOUGH BOY; a Comic Song, by Mr. Sloman; a fa-
vourite pantomime, called THE MERMAID, Clown Mr. Grimaldi.
The Entertainments to conclude with a new Melo-Drama, called
THE RED HANDS; or, Welch Chieftains. Box 4s.; Pit 2s.;
Gal. 1s.; Doors opened at half past 5, and begin at half past 6;
places kept till half past 7. On Monday, June 26, will be pro-
duced a new Pantomime, which has been a long time preparing,
called Harlequin Brilliant; or Clown's Capers; to conclude with a
Ship Launch on real Water.

VAUXHALL.
Under the Patronage of his Royal Highness the PRINCE REGENT.
TO MORROW Friday, June 23, will be a GRAND GALA,
and brilliant EXHIBITION of FIRE-WORKS by Signor Bologna.
Admission 4s.—Doors open at half past seven, and the Concert
begins at half past 8.

LONDON, THURSDAY, JUNE 22, 1815.

OFFICIAL BULLETIN.

" DOWNING-STREET, JUNE 22, 1815.

" The Duke of WELLINGTON's Dispatch, dated
Waterloo, the 19th of June, states, that on the preceding day BUONAPARTE attacked, with his whole
force, the British line, supported by a corps of
Prussians; which attack, after a long and sanguinary
conflict, terminated in the complete Overthrow of
the Enemy's Army, with the loss of ONE HUN-
DRED and FIFTY PIECES of CANNON and TWO
EAGLES. During the night, the Prussians under
Marshal BLUCHER, who joined in the pursuit of the
enemy, captured SIXTY GUNS, and a large part

alone, as marks for the indignation of Europe, and just
sacrifices to insulted French honour.

Those who attended minutely to the operations of
the Stock Exchange yesterday, were persuaded that the
news of the day before would be followed up by something still more brilliant and decisive. Omnium rose
in the course of the day to 6 per cent. premium, and
some houses generally supposed to possess the best
information were among the purchasers. For our
own parts, though looking forward with that confidence which we yesterday expressed, we frankly
own this full tide of success was more than we
had anticipated. We were very well satisfied
that Mr. SUTTON's account, so far as it went,
was correct,—that BUONAPARTE's grand plan had
been frustrated, and that he had not only been
prevented from penetrating between the English
and Prussian armies, but forced to fall back
again behind the Sambre. How far the Duke of
WELLINGTON and Prince BLUCHER might have
thought it prudent to pursue him, was a point on which
we did not conceive ourselves warranted to form any
decisive opinion from the evidence before us. We had no
doubt that he would be harassed in his retreat, and perhaps ultimately be driven into his entrenched camp, or
under the guns of his fortresses; but without some distinct official information, we repeat, that we could not
have ventured to anticipate such a triumphant result as
that on which we have now to congratulate our country
and the world.

Among the rumours which obtained some credit in
the city yesterday, was one of an insurrection in Paris.
We are not much inclined to give credit to this, con-
ceiving that the Parisians will not move until the
tyrant's force in the field is broken. We know, however, that a spirit of hostility to his usurpation is very generally and very boldly expressed in the French capital.
We have received from thence a paper which has obtained
extensive circulation there, and which will be found in
another of our columns. It contains an address to the inhabitants of the Fauxbourgs St. Antoine and St. Mar-
ceau, and a Declaration in the name of the Duke of
ORLEANS. Both these documents are plainly and
ably drawn up. The one successfully opposes the
ferocious doctrines of the Jacobins, the other the
more insidious views of those who seek to cover their criminality with the respect justly due
to a brave and honourable Member of the House
of Bourbon. Whether his Serene Highness has
authorised this avowal of his sentiments, we know
not; but it is one, which appears perfectly con-
genial with that fair and manly conduct which he has
always observed. The Duke of ORLEANS has never at
any time given the least countenance to those criminal pro
jects, which, under the specious pretence of attachment
to himself, would as completely break down the principle of legal succession, as if a BUONAPARTE or a Ro-
BESPIERRE were the object of election. That principle

restore the romantic image of imperial France. "I have pushed back the boundaries of greatness."[46] In these lines, the Romantic Age would find great material with which to ennoble a hero. At the same time, conservatives could claim that Napoleon's greatest achievements were in his classic reforms of law, education, and society.

The most powerful influence of the Napoleonic legend was not on law, government, or education. It was on the art of war. "Many faults, no doubt, will be found in my career," he exclaimed, "but Arcola, Rivoli, the Pyramids, Marengo, Austerlitz, Jena, Friedland—these are granite: the tooth of envy is powerless here."[47] Enthused by the writings of theorists such as Jomini, Clausewitz, and Schlieffen, military men in the Western World accepted the history of these famous battles as an inheritance to be preserved and, when possible, emulated. "The Ghost of Napoleon," to quote Sir Basil Liddell Hart, came to play a greater role in the wars of the twentieth century than did the real general on his authentic European battlegrounds in the previous century.

Almost a century passed between Waterloo and the first of the great wars to end all wars.* Unfortunately, for those who had accepted Napoleon's strategic brilliance as an unfailing pattern for victory, time and circumstance had so changed conditions that the strategic patterns no longer held true. But Napoleon's inspiring generalship would never be obsolete. How did that incredible genius seem always to have a solution to the unexpected problems that confronted him? When cornered by two Austrian armies near Verona, he turned lightning-quick and fell unexpectedly on the rear of one of them at Arcola; after Nelson sank his fleet in Aboukir Bay, he marched boldly into Syria; when he failed to gain the naval superiority required to make a crossing of the English Channel, he about-faced and hurled the *Grande Armée* across the Rhine and across the rear of Mack's unready forces. Even after a sharp repulse at the hands of the Archduke Charles, he

crossed the Danube again and won the next round at Wagram. The losses in 1812 and 1813 were caused more by the Emperor than by the general.

Napoleon may have lost very few battles, but he committed the unpardonable sin of losing the last one. During the later years of his career, he began to discount the fact that even a triumph on the battlefield could not compensate for the harmful effects of his campaigns on the people he claimed to represent. Napoleon destroyed the Prussian Army at Jena, but he lost Prussia by his mistreatment of the royal family. He overran Italy in two short months, but he outraged the Italians by intimidating the Pope. This extraordinarily heroic figure who "spoke to the soul" of the soldier and acted "on the imagination of the nation" never struck the proper balance in his dealings with people. He could inspire battalions to charge bravely across a bridge swept by cannonfire, but he could never convince the London banker or the Austrian Cabinet of his sincerity when he spoke of peace. He wanted to restore order, but agitation and revolt trailed his every giant step across the European Continent.

Perhaps it is understandable that Marengo, Austerlitz, and Jena have faded from memory, while Waterloo will be remembered forever. The gambler tempted fate once too often and was punished. Failure, however, does not discourage men from attempting to tread anew along the paths of conquest. In fact, gigantic failure sometimes sharpens the appetite all the more. Georges Lefebvre, the noted French historian, explains why this is so: " . . . men will always be haunted by romantic dreams of power, even if only in the passing fires and disturbances of youth . . . ." Napoleon had already said as much in 1802: "It would be better never to have lived at all than to leave behind no trace of one's existence."[48]

---

*A century governed to no small extent by the *Pax Britannica*.

Notes

[1] J. Holland Rose, *The Life of Napoleon I* (2 vols.; London, 1901–1902), II, 433.

[2] Harold G. Nicolson, *The Congress of Vienna* (London, 1946), p. 177.

[3] Clemens L.W. Metternich-Winneburg, *Memoirs of Prince Metternich, 1773–1835*, ed. by Prince Richard Metternich; trans. by Mrs. Alexander Napier (5 vols.; New York, 1880-1882), I, 254.

[4] *Ibid.*, p. 255.

[5] Claude Manceron, *Napoleon Recaptures Paris*, trans. by G. Unwin (New York, 1969), p. 42.

[6] Louis Madelin, *The Consulate and the Empire, 1809–1815*, trans. by E.F. Buckley (2 vols.; New York, 1934–1936), II, 383.

[7] *Correspondance de Napoleon I* (32 vols.; Paris, 1858–1870), XXVIII, No. 21689, p. 9.

[8] Felix Markham, *Napoleon* (New York, 1963), p. 213.

[9] Oscar von Lettow-Vorbeck, *Napoleons Untergang 1815* (2 vols.; Berlin, 1904–1906), I, 141.

[10] G.H. Perz and Hans Delbrück, *Das Leben des Feldmarschalls Grafen Neithardt von Gneisenau* (5 vols.; Berlin, 1864–1880), IV, 346–347.

[11] Henry Houssaye, *1815, Waterloo* (Paris, 1901), pp. 1–2.

[12] *Correspondance*, XXVIII, No. 21991, p. 243.

[13] Loredan Larchey (ed.), *The Narrative of Captain Coignet*, trans. by M. Carey (New York, 1890), p. 278.

[14] Houssaye, *1815, Waterloo*, p. 83.

[15] *Correspondance*, XXVIII, No. 22023, p. 261.

[16] *Correspondance*, XXVIII, No. 22052, p. 281.

[17] Antony Brett-James, *Wellington at War, 1794–1815* (London, 1961), p. 306.

[18] Arthur Wellesby, Duke of Wellington, *The Dispatches of Field Marshal the Duke of Wellington . . . From 1799 to 1815*, comp. by Lieutenant Colonel Gurwood (12 vols. plus index; London, 1834–1839), XII, 513.

[19] *Ibid.*, p. 360.

[20] Wolfgang von Unger, *Blücher* (2 vols.; Berlin, 1907–1908), II, 252.

[21] Lettow-Vorbeck, *Napoleons Untergang 1815*, I, 192.

[22] *Wellington's Dispatches*, XII, 462.

[23] Lettow-Vorbeck, *Napoleons Untergang 1815*, I, 196.

[24] *Ibid.*, p. 198.

[25] *Wellington's Dispatches*, XII, 472–473.

[26] J.F.C. Fuller, *A Military History of the Western World* (3 vols.; New York, 1954–1956), II, 503.

[27] *Correspondance*, XXVIII, No. 22058, pp. 290–291.

[28] Unger, *Blücher*, II, 281.

[29] *Ibid.*, pp. 283–284.

[30] Perz and Delbrück, *Das Leben Gneisenau*, IV, 373–374; Lettow-Vorbeck, *Napoleons Untergang 1815*, I, 310.

[31] Houssay, *1815, Waterloo*, p. 206.

[32] Perz and Delbrück, *Das Leben Gneisenau*, IV, 383.

[33] *Correspondance*, XXXI, 418.

[34] Houssay, *1815, Waterloo*, p. 228.

[35] *Ibid.*, p. 229.

[36] *Ibid.*, p. 248.

[37] *Ibid.*, p. 253.

[38] Lettow-Vorbeck, *Napoleons Untergang 1815*, I, 360.

[39] Unger, *Blücher*, II, 296, 298.

[40] *Correspondance*, XXXI, 190.

[41] J.C. Herold, *The Battle of Waterloo* (New York, 1967), pp. 114–115.

[42] G.W. Picton, *The Battle of Waterloo* (London, no date), pp. 242–243.

[43] Cavalie Mercer, *Journal of the Waterloo Campaign* (New York, 1969), p. 174.

[44] Fuller, *A Military History of the Western World*, II, 536.

[45] *Correspondance*, XXXI, 211–213.

[46] J.C. Herold, *The Mind of Napoleon* (New York, 1955), pp. 272–273.

[47] *Ibid.*, p. 274.

[48] Count Yorck von Wartenburg, *Napoleon as a General* (2 vols.; London, 1902), I, 122; Georges Lefebvre, *Napoleon: From Tilsit to Waterloo, 1807–1815*, trans.by J.E. Anderson (New York, 1969), p. 370.

Arc de Triomphe

EPILOGUE

Yes, Agincourt may be forgot,
And Cressy be an unknown spot,
*   And Blenheim's name be new;*
But still in story, and in song,
For many an age remembered long,
Shall live the towers of Hougomont,
*   And the field of Waterloo.*
                        Sir Walter Scott

Selected Bibliography

Andolenko, Serge. *Histoire de l'Armée Russe*. Paris, 1967. The most recent and authoritative study on the Russian Army.

Angeli, M. von. *Erzherzog Karl als Feldherr und Herres Organisator*. 6 vols. Vienna, 1895–1897. A detailed study of the military life of Archduke Charles as a field commander and reformer.

Aubry, Octave. *Napoleon*. Trans. M. Crosland and S. Road. New York, 1964. Superbly illustrated, this biography contains a wealth of detail on Napoleon's personal life.

Barnett, Corelli. *Britain and Her Army, 1509–1970*. New York, 1970. Contains an excellent chapter on the army that fought against Napoleon.

Bruun, Geoffrey, *Europe and the French Imperium, 1799–1814*. New York, 1938. An excellent survey of Napoleon's conquests and the uprising of Europe against him.

Camon, H. *La Bataille Napoleoniene*. Paris, 1899. An interesting analysis of Napoleon's method of battle.

Caulaincourt, Armand de. *With Napoleon in Russia*. Trans. J. Hanoteau. New York, 1935. A reliable eyewitness account of the disastrous campaign of 1812.

Chandler, David G. *The Campaigns of Napoleon*. New York, 1966. A comprehensive and easy-to-ready study of Napoleon's military campaigns.

Clausewitz, Carl von. *On War*. Ed. and Trans. Michael Howard and Peter Paret. Princeton, 1976. Clausewitz's enduring classic contains numerous comparisons between the wars of Napoleon and Frederick II.

Coignet, Jean. *The Narrative of Captain Coignet*. Trans. M. Carey. New York, 1890. One of the more reliable of the soldier-memoirs.

Cooper, Duff. *Talleyrand*. Stanford, 1932. A colorful biography of Napoleon's foreign minister.

Crawley, C.W. *The New Cambridge Modern History*. Vol. IX. Cambridge, 1957. An excellent authoritative source for background information on the period.

Davout, Louis N. *Operations du 3 Corps, 1806–1807: Rapport du Marechal Davout, Duc d'Auerstadt*. An excellent after-action report on the high point of Davout's sparkling career.

Delbrück, Hans. *Geschichte der Kriegskunst im Rahmen der politischen Geschichte*. Vol. IV. Berlin, 1920. This monumental work has never been surpassed in its comprehensive approach to the problems of military tactics, strategy, and policy.

Delderfield, R.F. *Napoleon's Marshals*. Philadelphia, 1966. A colorful treatment of the key personalities in the *Grande Armée*.

Dumolin, Maurice. *Precis d'Histoire Militaire*. 3 vols. Paris, 1906. A thorough, factual, well-documented study of Napoleon's wars through 1809.

Earle, Edward M. (ed.). *Makers of Modern Strategy*. Princeton, 1943. An excellent interpretation of the evolution of military thought, with emphasis on eighteenth and nineteenth century military history.

Esposito, Vincent J. and John R. Elting. *A Military History and Atlas of the Napoleonic Wars*. New York, 1963. An unmatched source for operational details of Napoleon's campaigns.

Fuller, J.F.C. *The Conduct of War, 1789–1961*. New Brunswick, 1961. A superb analysis of the evolution of modern war, beginning with the French Revolution.

Godeschot, Jacques, et. al. *The Napoleonic Era in Europe*. Trans. B. Hyslop. New York, 1971. The most recent of several new interpretations of Napoleon's political, economic, and military achievements.

Goodspeed, Donald. *The British Campaigns in the Peninsula, 1808–1814*. Ottawa, 1958. A succinct and authoritative account of the war in Spain and Portugal, largely from the British viewpoint.

Guedalla, Philip. *Wellington*. New York, 1931. This remains the best of the many biographies on a popular subject.

Henderson, Ernest F. *Blücher and the Uprising of Prussia, 1806–1815*. London, 1911. A straightforward but largely uncritical account of Blücher's role in leading Prussian soldiers against Napoleon.

Herold, J. Christopher. *The Mind of Napoleon*. New York, 1955. A valuable compendium of Napoleon's thoughts on a variety of subjects.

Jany, Curt. *Geschichte der preussischen Armee vom 15 Jahrhundert bis 1914*. Vols. I–III. Osnabruck, 1967. Jany's massive, well-organized work contains a gold mine of information about all aspects of the Prussian Army.

Kissinger, Henry. *A World Restored*. New York, 1957. A classic account of conflicting state interests at the close of the Napoleonic era.

Lachouque, H. and Anne Brown. *The Anatomy of Glory*. London, 1961. The story of Napoleon's Guard.

Lefebvre, Georges. *Napoleon*. 2 vols. New York, 1969. A detailed portrait of the man operating against the forces of nationalism, religion, and legitimate authority.

Liddell Hart, Basil H. *The Ghost of Napoleon*. London, 1933. A unique analysis of the influence of thought on action.

Lovett, Gabriel H. *Napoleon and the Birth of Modern Spain*. New York, 1965. The best account of the Spanish war against Napoleon.

Mahan, Alfred Thayer. *The Influence of Sea Power Upon the French Revolution and Empire*. 2 vols. London, 1892. Although outdated, this classic remains a source of many interesting ideas and interpretations of naval policy and strategy.

Marbot, Baron de. *The Memoirs of Baron de Marbot*. Trans. A.J.

Butler. 2 vols. London, 1892. Colorful and authentic.

Markham, Felix. *Napoleon*. New York, 1963. A concise, authoritative biography.

Marshall-Cornwall, James. *Napoleon as Military Commander*. New York, 1968. A concise synthesis of Napoleon's military campaigns.

Morvan, Jean. *Le Soldat Imperial, 1800–1814*. 2 vols. Paris, 1904. An excellent study on the various aspects of the imperial army.

Napoleon. *Correspondance de Napoleon I*. 32 vols. Paris, 1858–1870. The prime repository of Napoleon's collected correspondence.

Nicolson, Harold. *The Congress of Vienna*. New York, 1961. A thoroughly readable study of personalities and diplomacy.

Palmer, R.R. and Joel Colton. *A History of the Modern World*. New York, 1971. A superb survey of the history of the Western World, which gives ample treatment to the Napoleonic era.

Paret, Peter. *Yorck and the Era of Prussian Reform*. Princeton, 1966. A scholarly treatment of the impact of revolution on Prussian reform.

Parker, Harold T. *Three Napoleonic Battles*. Durham, 1944. Excellent description of Friedland, Aspern-Essling, and Waterloo.

Parquin, Denis Charles. *Napoleon's Army*. Ed. and Trans. B.J. Jones. London, 1969. The best of the soldier memoirists.

Quimby, Robert S. *The Background of Napoleonic Warfare*. New York, 1957. A detailed description of Bonaparte's doctrinal inheritance.

Ritter, Gerhard. *The Sword and the Scepter*. Trans. H. Norden. Vol. I. Coral Gables, 1969. An eminent historian's interpretation of the problem of German militarism.

Rose, J. Holland. *Life of Napoleon I*. 2 vols. London, 1902. An appealing, if dated, biography.

Glossary

This glossary includes those commonly used military and historical terms that appear in the text. In general, the intent was to use phraseology and concepts applicable to the Napoleonic era; however, in the interest of clarity, some translation into twentieth century terminology was necessary. Precise definitions of doctrinal terms have been deliberately avoided, and general concepts such as professionalism, strategy, logistics—the elements of war in general—have also been excluded. The purpose of this glossary, therefore, is identification and explanation, rather than definition.

aides-de-camp. In the *Grande Armée*, these officers—frequently, experienced generals—were responsible for the delivery and interpretation of orders and, often, the supervision of their execution as well.

Amalgamé. The amalgamation of regular and volunteer units that took place in 1793–1796. Two volunteer battalions and one regular battalion formed the new composite demi-brigade (regiment).

ancien régime. A French phrase that means literally "former government." In generally accepted usage among scholars, the term has come to refer to the entire social and governmental system existing in Europe, particularly France, prior to 1789. It is often used to imply that a way of life, comfortable for some, had passed forever from the scene in 1789.

artillery ammunition. The following types of ammunition were used during the Napoleonic era.

solid shot. A round iron ball.

case shot or canister. A can filled with musket balls, giving a buckshot-like effect.

grapeshot. The same as canister except that it used a larger pellet (not to be confused with the heavier naval variety) and the pellets were held together with rods or wire.

explosive shell. Hollow shot, filled with explosives, which was still largely in the experimental stage during the Napoleonic era.

shrapnel. An experimental device produced by the British in which the bursting charge could be ignited with a precalculated fuse.

hot shot. Ordinary shot heated to incandescence in ovens prior to loading; useful for igniting buildings behind castle walls or destroying vessels lying off the coast.

rockets. An inaccurate device developed by the British from their experience in India; useful primarily as an area-type weapon or for stampeding an enemy's horses.

artillery weapons. The following artillery weapons were used during the Napoleonic era.

12-pounder gun. Range with shot: 920-1,050 yards; range with cannister: 600-700 yards; weight: 4,400 pounds; crew: 15.

6-pounder gun. Range with shot: 820-920 yards; range with cannister: 500-600 yards; weight: 3,000 pounds; crew: 12.

4-pounder gun. Range with shot: 820-920 yards; range with cannister: 400-500 yards; weight: 2,100 pounds; crew: 8.

6-inch howitzer. Range with shot: 750-1,300 yards; range with shell: 450-600 yards; weight: 2,600 pounds; crew: 13.

assignat. Paper money, badly depreciated, issued by the French Government during the first years of the Revolution.

Aufklarüng. The German word for the Enlightenment. Predominantly South German, this term is frequently used in historical texts.

balance of power. A theory of international relations, supported by the philosophy of the eighteenth century, stating that no one power should be allowed to gain undue influence in Europe at the expense of the others. This theory was subscribed to by Metternich and Talleyrand.

batallion square *(bataillon carré)*. The term used by Napoleon to describe the army corps formation in the approach march that facilitated a rapid concentration of the bulk of the army. The corps were positioned in the form of a square (or diamond) so that they could turn in any direction to repulse an enemy attack, and so they could reinforce each other rapidly.

battleships. Referred to as ships of the line, these vessels composed the main fighting force capable of sustained action on the high seas. Usually these ships were armed with 50 guns or more.

Berlin Decree. Napoleon's proclamation issued from Berlin in November 1806 in which he proclaimed a blockade of the British Isles. In actuality, Napoleon's decree was an embargo, because of his inability to physically blockade the United Kingdom.

blockade. The interception of seaborne commerce by troops or ships. In Great Britain's case, the obstruction of shipping to and from French ports or ports controlled by France. See also: Continental System; embargo.

Bourbon. The ruling family of France from 1589 to 1792 and 1814 to 1830.

bourgeoisie. The professional and commercial middle class.

cavalry. The following types of cavalry were in use during the Napoleonic era.

> **carabinier.** Heavy cavalry, similar to *cuirassiers*.

> **chasseurs-à-cheval.** Light cavalry with a capability of mounted fire.

> **chevaux légers.** Light cavalry used for screening missions; similar to hussars.

> **cuirassier.** Heavy cavalry, used primarily for defeating enemy horsemen.

> **dragoons.** In Napoleon's opinion, a distinct type of cavalry capable of fighting on horse or on foot.

> **hussars.** Light cavalry, used for scouting, screening, and limited fighting; very flamboyantly uniformed.

> **lancers.** Light cavalry armed with the lance.

cavalry reserve. Consisting of dragoons, *cuirassiers*, and *carabiniers*—the heavy cavalry—these troops were usually committed to exploit tactical success. The light cavalry, also, was under control of the cavalry reserve commander (Murat or Bessières) for use in screening and pursuit missions.

cavalry screen. The cavalry screen was intended more as a means of preventing the enemy from detecting the French army's size, location, and direction of movement than as a means of gaining intelligence. That role was assigned to spies, agents, and large formations with reconnaissance-in-force-type missions.

class. The term given to that portion of each year's male population available for conscription (also may refer to social class).

Committee of Public Safety. The executive governmental organ formed in April 1793. This was a dictatorship of nine members, including Danton, Robespierre, and Carnot. It ended on July 27, 1794 (9 Thermidor) when Robespierre's colleagues in the National Convention courageously "outlawed" him, having tired of "virtue" induced by terror. The group that triumphed in this phase of the Revolution was the bourgeoisie.

Confederation of the Rhine. A political structure created by Napoleon in July 1806. It included Bavaria, Württemberg, Baden, Hesse, Darmstadt, Berg, Nassau, and other territories previously controlled by or allied to Prussia and Austria.

Congress of Vienna. The meeting of all European powers to settle the territorial affairs of Europe, after the downfall of Napoleon's empire in 1814. (The chief participants were Austria, Prussia, Great Britain, Russia, France, and the Papacy.) In principle, it was an admission of equality between major states. In actuality, it was a period of conflict between states attempting to contain the power of revolution and intriguing to gather the spoils of Napoleon's defeat. The Congress, which met at Vienna, lasted from 1814 to 1815. Its actions resulted in a series of treaties that were designed to allow France to remain a great power, but to prevent a resurgence of French imperial aggression; e.g., the Kingdom of the Netherlands was a buffer state.

conscript. A soldier compulsorily enrolled in military service. See also: recruit; volunteer; regular.

Consulate. The system of government under which Napoleon was elected to the highest position of political power in France. The First Consul received assistance from two other consuls, who had consultative powers only. This system, in the hands of the powerful Bonaparte, quickly established the ascendancy of the executive power (the Consulate) over the legislative bodies—the Tribunate, which discussed measures but could not vote, and the Legislative Chamber, which voted but could not debate. The Consulate was ready-made for exploitation by a powerful First Consul, and Bonaparte was able to use the consular system as a steppingstone to a form of personal rule closely akin to enlightened despotism. For

French Republicans, Bonaparte's Consulate was a regressive form of government.

Continental System. A larger political conception than the *Grande Empire*, this system, which came into being in 1807, embraced the entire European Continent. At first intended as an economic weapon to combat British commercial strength, Napoleon intended it to ultimately result in a politically and economically united Europe.

corps. The French *Corps d'Armée* was a self-contained tactical team that had its own infantry, light cavalry, artillery, engineers, and logistic support, thus allowing it to operate semi-independently. The *Corps d'Armée* was not a standard organization, but varied in size and numbers of divisions depending on the mission assigned to the corps and the talent of its commander. The French corps came into being on an experimental basis in 1800, and was adopted as an institution in 1805, when the *Grande Armée* was formed. The Austrian corps was modeled on the French corps and made its first appearance in 1809. Prussia retained the linear, unitary type of army until her defeat in 1806, after which Prussia began to convert to the corps system. Russia never adopted the corps system during the wars against Napoleon.

demi-brigade. A formation organized during the Revolution consisting of one battalion of regulars and two of volunteers. The demi-brigades became regiments after Napoleon secured control of the French Government.

depot. A facility from which a field army resupplies its stocks of clothing, food, and other materials. Napoleon's armies maneuvered relatively independently of depots except in Spain, East Prussia, and Russia. See also: magazine.

Directory. The form of government invested by the French Constitution of 1795, which decreed that the executive function should be shared by five directors. The Directory proved ineffective in controlling the war effort (in 1796-1797) and had great difficulty in retaining popular support, primarily because of self-imposed restrictions on the franchise. A government of the upper middle class, it was beset by republican and monarchist enemies and became dependent at the very beginning upon military support, thus providing one of the conditions necessary for Napoleon to become a powerful political as well as military figure. From the famous "whiff of grape" of October 5, 1795, used by Bonaparte to crush the early opposition to the Directory, to its dissolution after the coup d'état of 18 Brumaire (November 9, 1799), the fate of the Directory became increasingly intertwined with the career of Napoleon.

division. In Napoleon's France, a term designating a military organization consisting of a variable number of brigades, each normally composed of three regiments (or demi-brigades). The Prussian division was a combined-arms force—hastily organized prior to the Jena Campaign. Austrian and Russian divisions were *ad hoc* organizations formed on the eve of a campaign and entrusted at the last minute to commanders, normally members of the royal family. Also used to designate two companies abreast in a battalion column formation, i.e., battalion in column of divisions.

embargo. A governmental order prohibiting the movement of ships to and from certain ports. In the case of France, the decree that prohibited (though it did not prevent) British trade with the European Continent. See also: blockade; Continental System.

émigrés. The nobles who fled from France during the Revolution.

emperor. Of higher rank than a king, an emperor is the ruler of an empire. The terms tsar (Russian) and kaiser (German) are synonymous with l'empereur (French).

enlightened despot. A ruler, such as Joseph II and Frederick II, who, while retaining the supreme authority of the monarchy, instituted certain social reforms and was strongly influenced by the progressive views of the Enlightenment.

Enlightenment. The age, roughly coincident with the eighteenth century, during which European thought adopted more progressive views based on the influence of science, logic, and philosophy. As a consequence of this general movement of thought and attitude, the social, religious, and political foundations of the old order were called into question. Europeans viewed themselves as having emerged from a "long twilight" into a new time of light. From this age emerged the modern philosophy of optimism, which asserts man's ability to make measurable and, to some, inevitable progress toward bettering life on earth. See also: *Aufklarüng*.

French Empire. Existing from 1804 to 1815, it consisted of metropolitan France, plus Piedmont, Holland, and the Illyrian Provinces on the east side of the Adriatic Sea. In 1810 and 1811, the French Empire reached its greatest area—130 departments (administrative districts). In 1812, the French Empire comprised about 750,000 square kilometers and approximately 44 million people.

French Republic. Technically, the First French Republic lasted from May 1789 until May 1804, when the First Empire was proclaimed.

Revolution. The overthrow of the Bourbon dynasty *France* resulting from the influence of various social and economic pressures on the middle class; the inefficient, inequitable system of government that had developed under the Bourbon kings; and the near bankruptcy of the French Government.

fusilier. A standard French infantryman.

Gendarmerie. Originally, French *gendarmes* were members of heavy cavalry units. In Napoleon's time, the term referred to personnel responsible for the administration of the rear areas of the army. Today, it is a paramilitary organization with both civil and army duties.

Gendarmerie d'élite. An element in Napoleon's Guard concerned with security and the duties now associated with military police.

Germany. During the Napoleonic era, that part of Europe distinguished by a common language and culture, in which German nationalism began to coalesce. Not yet a political entity, Germany became a powerful national force in the resistance to Napoleon's empire.

Grande Armée. The *Grande Armée* was Napoleon's personal creation, consisting initially of seven combined-arms *Corps d'Armée*, the cavalry reserve, the Imperial Guard, the general headquarters, and a variety of logistical agencies for support. In 1805–1806, the *Grande Armée* was composed almost entirely of French troops; from 1807 on it incorporated growing numbers of foreign soldiers and assumed additional non-battle tasks, such as occupation of conquered areas, coastal guard, pacification of rebellious regions, and police duties. The *Grande Armée* was activated in 1805, served in Germany, Spain, and Russia, and was destroyed in 1812.

Grande Empire. Imperial France was only the core of a larger political conception, which included the vassal states governed by Napoleon's relatives and foreign princes. These states were: The Kingdom of Italy, ruled by Eugène de Beauharnais as Viceroy for Napoleon, who reserved for himself the title of King of Italy; the Kingdom of Holland, ruled by Napoleon's brother Louis until 1810, when Holland was annexed to Imperial France; the Kingdom of Spain, ruled by brother Joseph; the Kingdom of Naples, under brother-in-law Murat; and the Kingdom of Westphalia, under brother Jerome. The Confederation of the Rhine, Switzerland, and the Grand Duchy of Warsaw maintained their semi-autonomous status, but were prepared to furnish troops and money at their "protector's" call. Napoleon conceived this entire structure as a federation.

Grande-Quartiers Général. General headquarters, which consisted of both the field headquarters for the *Grande Armée* and the Imperial Headquarters for Napoleon's governmental suite.

grenadier. An elite infantryman.

Grognard. Napoleon's nickname for the Guard Infantry; meaning "Grumbler."

Guard. Napoleon's guard originated as a form of personal escort (guides) in Italy, and grew into a sizable formation that became ideally suited for use as a tactical reserve. The Guard evolved from the Consular, to the Imperial Guard, which was divided into the Young, Middle, and Old Guard. Composed of select, highly motivated soldiers, the Guard included infantry and cavalry. By 1809, it had become a combined-arms team of 7,500 men, and began the campaign in Russia (1812) with an overall strength of over 50,000.

Hapsburg. The ruling family of Austria from 1486 to 1918. The House of Hapsburg was founded in 1218.

Hofkriegsrat. Loosely translated as the Defense Ministry, or Supreme War Council, this advisory council in the Austrian Government (first established in 1560) became a powerful department, with authority in political, economic, and judicial spheres. All the military forces of the Hapsburg Crown were administered by the *Hofkriegsrat*.

Hohenzollerns. The ruling family in Brandenburg-Prussia from 1417 to 1918.

Holy Roman Empire. Consisting chiefly of German-speaking peoples, this ancient empire was established in 962 and dismantled in 1806. The Pope was considered to be its spiritual lead. In the eighteenth century, the Hapsburg Emperor normally was elected as its political head.

The Hundred Days. The period between Napoleon's return from Elba and his defeat at Waterloo.

Illuminati. The members of an intellectual sect that propagated the ideas of the Enlightenment.

infantry square. A defensive tactic, usually formed by battalion, to fend off cavalry assaults.

intendant. The army supply officer (also called the commissary).

legitimacy. A term useful both to the political scientist and to the historian. In the conceptual sense, legitimacy is that necessary approval and/or tolerance that a sovereign or government obtains from the political groups that "matter" in a society. In the historical sense, this term describes the political principle used as philosophical justification for the actions taken by the Congress of Vienna to restore as much as they could of the *ancien régime* (q.v.). An example of this was the restoration of the German princes deposed during the Napoleonic era.

levée en masse. The term refers to France's early efforts to conscript all available able-bodied men. In August 1793, the French government first decreed the *levée en masse*, which later became known as the nation at arms.

lines of communication. That system of routes (roads and rivers) connecting an army operating in the field with its base. Normally, armies in the eighteenth and nineteenth centuries operated out of advance bases—that is, provincial capitals or commercial centers such as Leipzig, Vienna, Königsberg, and Thorn—rather than relying on the homelands for the provision of repair parts, food, and expendables. The only traffic that routinely used the extended line of communication with the homeland consisted of personnel reinforcements and messengers.

line of operation. A term devised by military theorists and used frequently by Napoleon to describe the major direction of advance of the army.

Lines of Torres Vedras. A series of three defensive lines ordered by Wellington in October 1809 for the protection of the English base at Lisbon. The success of this system in 1810–1811 made these famous lines a model of efficient field engineering.

magazine. A facility from which a field army normally resupplied its operating level of munitions and weapons. (Magazines and depots were often combined in the same facility.) An army replenished its stocks by convoy. See also: depot.

Maison. The center of Napoleon's headquarters.

La Marseillaise. The battle song of the revolutionaries—and now the national anthem of France—it is a call to war against tyrants.

Marshal. The grade established for corps commanders in the imperial army. The term "Marshal of France" thus implied that an officer so designated served as an officer of the French Empire. Only one of Napoleon's 18 marshals (Murat) became a king in the French Empire; several became princes; almost all achieved the rank of duke.

monarchy. A government headed by a king or emperor. It may or may not have viable constitutional bodies that participate in the governing process.

natural frontiers. The Rhine, Alps, and Pyrenees—sought by Frenchmen for centuries and by Louis XIV especially—for the protection of France against invasion by land. (Also referred to as France's natural boundaries.)

noblesse. French aristocracy; nobility; the privileged order.

Order in Council. Issued in January 1807, this established British retaliation against the Berlin Decree by forbidding neutrals to trade with France and with French allies.

ordre mince. Essentially, a linear formation of the type used by most armies in the eighteenth century.

ordre mixte. A highly flexible tactical formation incorporating elements of line, column, and skirmishers, and capable of adapting to various enemy situations and terrain.

ordre profound. In contrast to the line, a columnar formation relying on shock rather than firepower for success on the battlefield.

Papal States. Established as a protectorate under Charlemagne, these lands were ruled by the Pope until 1870. The award of these lands to the Pope represented a tacit agreement that the popes were the rightful rulers of the Holy Roman Empire in Italy.

philosophes. Generally refers to those French intellectuals such as Voltaire, Rousseau, and Diderot, who questioned the traditional basis of social life, governmental authority, and religious dogmatism.

Prussian General Staff. An innovation in command and staff practice that delegated a major share of the authority in the decision-making process to the staff. The Prussian staff system, elaborated by Scharnhorst between 1806 and 1813, encouraged independent consultation within the staff network in order to assure unity of effort throughout a theater of operations.

recruit. A newly enlisted soldier.

regular. A member of a standing military formation, enrolled on a long-term basis (more applicable to British than French troops).

reverse slope defense. A concept of defense developed and practiced by Wellington in the Iberian Peninsula. Wellington's tactics placed his main forces on high ground behind the topographical crest, and thus allowed him to commit these unused reserves at an unexpected time and location.

Romanovs. The ruling family of Russia from 1613 to 1917.

skirmishers. Soldiers whose task was to loosen up an opposing formation by individual action, aimed fire, and open order tactics. Usually, men with an independent spirit and unusual bravery were chosen for this task. See also: *tirailleur.*

streltsi. Russian household troops of the sixteenth and seventeenth centuries. Destroyed by Peter the Great in 1699, the tradition of a palatial guard nonetheless persisted in the Russian Army.

tirailleur. A skirmisher or individual fighter.

Tory. The political part in England that acquired the reputation of conservatism. See also: Whig.

trains. Napoleon's strategy normally allocated secure routes and positions for the supply and service agencies of the army. These elements, consisting of bakeries, ambulances, remounts, and other administrative units, composed the trains. Each corps was also entitled to a smaller, more responsive, and also more vulnerable aggregation of trains units which followed closely behind the combat units.

Vendée. A western department of France swept intermittently by civil war during the Revolution and the Consulate. Religious beliefs, royalist allegiances, and a hatred of conscription stirred the Vendeans against the Government. Later, the Vendée was an area of renewed royalist agitation during the Hundred Days.

voltigeur. An elite soldier of extraordinary physical endowments who could keep up with the cavalry on the march.

volunteer. An individual who enrolls in military service of his own free will. See also: conscript; regular; recruit.

weaponry–infantry and cavalry. The following weapons were used during the Napoleonic era.

bayonet. About 15 inches long, this weapon apparently caused few casualties. However, cold steel could quickly clear a battlefield once the enemy lost heart for the fight.

carbine. A short, light shoulder weapon used by cavalry and supply units.

dragoon musket. A shorter, lighter, and less accurate gun for mounted use.

lance. A long thrusting device, difficult to use without extensive training.

musket. A smoothbore, muzzle-loading, flintlock shoulder arm used principally by the infantry. The French weapon varied in caliber from .69 to .71. Its maximum range was about 1,000 yards, but its effective range was only 200-250 yards against enemy formations, and 100 yards against individuals.

musketoon. A sawed-off infantry musket used by some cavalry units.

pistols. Many versions were used, each of caliber, weight, and design to suit the owner's taste. The effective range was pointblank.

swords. The heavy cavalry normally used a long, straight, thrusting sword; the light cavalry (hussars) preferred a light, curved, cutting saber.

Whig. The liberal party in England, although traditionally the party based on property interests. The new Whigs, allied to industrial growth, championed various governmental reforms. See also: Tory.

Index

THE CHRONOLOGY OF NAPOLEON BONAPARTE'S CARE R

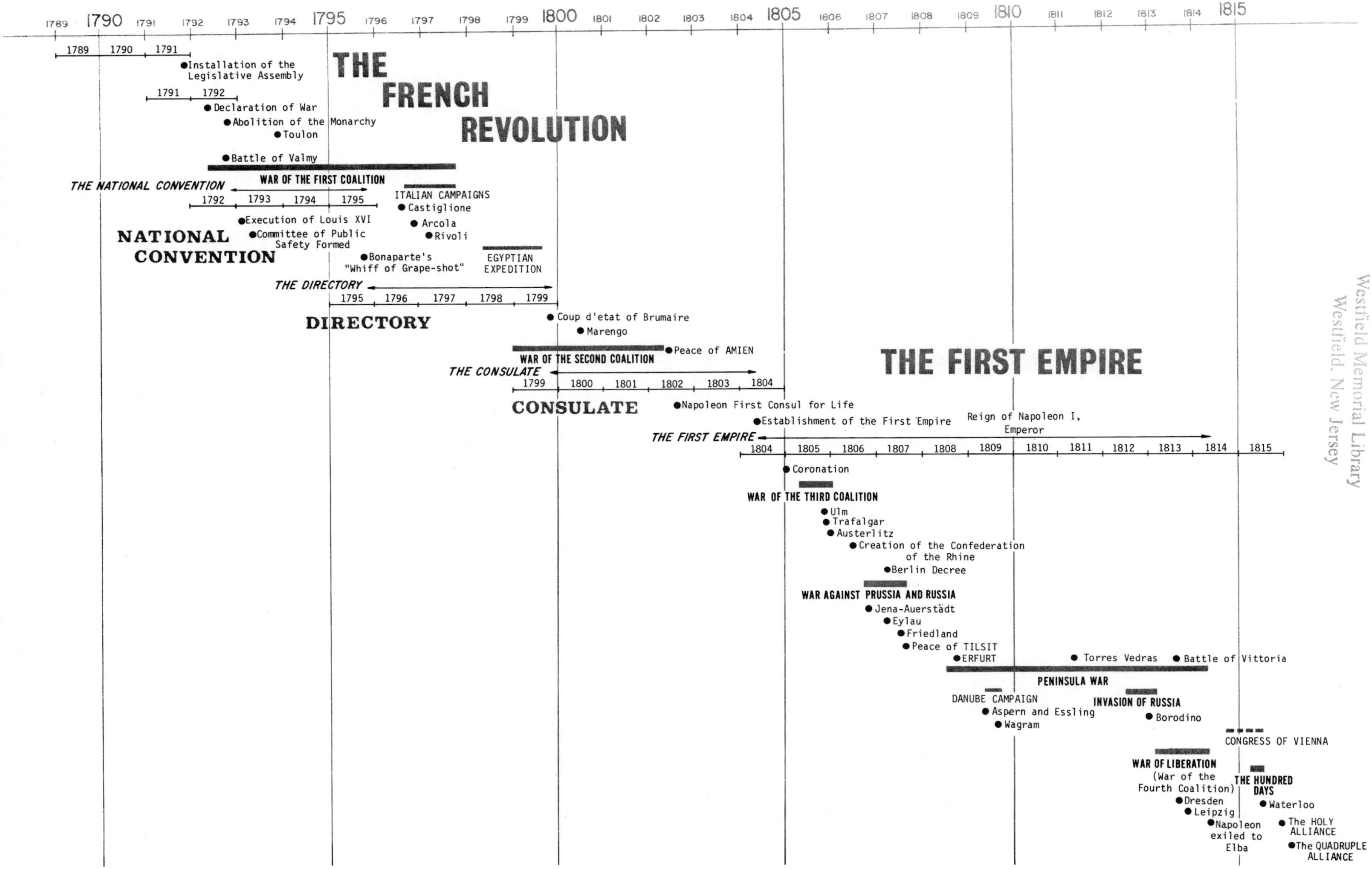

1789 1790 1791 1792 1793 1794 1795 1796 1797 1798 1799 1800 1801 1802 1803 1804 1805 1806 1807 1808 1809 1810 1811 1812 1813 1814 1815
THE FRENCH REVOLUTION
1789 1790 1791
Installation of the Legislative Assembly
1791 1792
Declaration of War
Abolition of the Monarchy
Toulon
Battle of Valmy
WAR OF THE FIRST COALITION
THE NATIONAL CONVENTION
1792 1793 1794 1795
ITALIAN CAMPAIGNS
Castiglione
Arcola
Rivoli
Execution of Louis XVI
Committee of Public Safety Formed
NATIONAL CONVENTION
Bonaparte's "Whiff of Grape-shot"
EGYPTIAN EXPEDITION
THE DIRECTORY
1795 1796 1797 1798 1799
DIRECTORY
Coup d'etat of Brumaire
Marengo
Peace of AMIEN
WAR OF THE SECOND COALITION
THE CONSULATE
1799 1800 1801 1802 1803 1804
CONSULATE
THE FIRST EMPIRE
Napoleon First Consul for Life
Establishment of the First Empire
Reign of Napoleon I, Emperor
THE FIRST EMPIRE
1804 1805 1806 1807 1808 1809 1810 1811 1812 1813 1814 1815
Coronation
WAR OF THE THIRD COALITION
Ulm
Trafalgar
Austerlitz
Creation of the Confederation of the Rhine
Berlin Decree
WAR AGAINST PRUSSIA AND RUSSIA
Jena-Auerstädt
Eylau
Friedland
Peace of TILSIT
ERFURT
Torres Vedras
Battle of Vittoria
PENINSULA WAR
DANUBE CAMPAIGN
Aspern and Essling
Wagram
INVASION OF RUSSIA
Borodino
CONGRESS OF VIENNA
WAR OF LIBERATION (War of the Fourth Coalition)
Dresden
Leipzig
Napoleon exiled to Elba
THE HUNDRED DAYS
Waterloo
The HOLY ALLIANCE
The QUADRUPLE ALLIANCE